# CLAUDIUS

# ʹCLAUDIUSʹ

## Barbara Levick

YALE UNIVERSITY PRESS
NEW HAVEN AND LONDON

First published in 1990 in the United Kingdom
by B. T. Batsford Limited

Published 1990 in the United States by Yale University Press

Copyright © 1990 by Barbara Levick.

Printed in Great Britain.

Library of Congress catalog card number: 89.51800

International standard book number: 0-300-04734-7 (cloth)
0-300-05831-4 (pbk.)

10  9  8  7  6  5  4  3  2

# CONTENTS

# MAPS

# ILLUSTRATIONS (between pages 144 and 145)

# ACKNOWLEDGEMENTS

Colleagues and friends must come first, having lived with my Claudius for three years. They and many others have given ready and active help, immeasurably enhancing with their generosity the pleasure I have had in writing the book. In medical and scientific matters I am indebted to Dr Pamela MacKinnon and Dr Jane Mellanby and particularly to Professor Gilbert Glaser, as well as to my cousin K.A. Kearsey. In connexion with Messallina's 'marriage' to Gaius Silius Professor Susan Treggiari has most generously allowed me to read the chapter on Roman divorce from her forthcoming book, as well as discussing the topic with me by letter; while personal conversation with Professor Herbert Devijver and Dr Lawrence Keppie has clarified my mind on the military. It has been an inestimable advantage to be able to consult Professor Geoffrey Rickman on Claudian policy and dealings with the people. Above all I should like to thank Dr Sybil Wolfram and Mrs Barbara Mitchell, who have read the book in draft – in Oxford term-time, too! – and made many improvements.

For the illustrations I am greatly indebted to Professor Kenan Erim, who has most kindly permitted me to reproduce photographs of the reliefs from the Sebasteion at Aphrodisias taken by Mr M.Ali Döğenci; the advice of Professor Walter Schmitthenner and of Dr R.R.R. Smith, who drew my attention to the Claudian cameos, has also been most helpful. The Ny Carlsberg Glyptothek, and Bibliothèque Nationale, and the Department of Coins and Medals, the British Museum, have all most kindly supplied photographs. Dr M. Metcalf, Keeper of Coins in the Ashmolean Museum, Oxford, encouraged me to seek expert aid in the Heberden Coin Room. The advice and practical help that I have had from Dr C.J. Howgego in choosing and obtaining illustrations, many of them specially taken by Ms Ann Holly from coins in the Ashmolean Collection, would alone have put me very greatly in his debt; there is more help to be acknowledged, with profound gratitude, in the notes. Map 3 is taken from *Atlas of Classical History* edited by R.J.A. Talbert (Croom Helm, 1985) and Map 5 from Britannia: History of Roman Britain by Sheppard Frere (Routledge, 1987).

It is a particular pleasure, also, to thank Mr Peter Kemmis Betty, Managing Director of B.T. Batsford, Ltd, who has both given me the opportunity of writing on a topic that I have long wanted to tackle and has encouraged me throughout.

B.M.Levick
St Hilda's College,
Oxford

BRITANNIA

Camulodunum

FRISII CHAUCI

Novaesium
Gesoriacum

Langobardi
Cologne CHERUSCI
Bonn CHATTI
Moguntiacum

Ems Wesser Elbe Oder

HERMUNDURI

LUGII

BELGICA

LUGDUNENSIS

Rhine

Günzburg
Ulm
Risstissen

Danube

MARCOMANNI
QUADI

Carnuntum
Iuvavum Arrabona
NORICUM
Teurnia Virunum
Poetovio
PANNONIA
Siscia
Sirmium

Burdigala Lyon
AQUITANIA

RAETIA

Tridentum Aquileia
Po

ALPES

Asturica
Bracara

NARBONENSIS
Narbo
Massilia

Ravenna
Ariminum
Pisae
Etruria

DALMATIA
Salonae

TARRACONENSIS
Tarraco

CORSICA

LUSITANIA

Rome
Campania
Neapolis
Tarentum

Turris
SARDINIA

Corduba
Hispalis
Gades BAETICA

Eryx
SICILIA

Caralis
Actiun
ACH

Tingis
Lixus Tamuda
Sala TINGITANA
Volubilis MAURETANIA

Tipasa Rusuccuru
Iol-Caesarea Cirta Carthage
CAESARIENSIS

NUMIDIA

ATLAS

AFRICA

Kasr T
Ptole

0
0

- - - - Provincial boundary

# THE ROMAN WORLD

ALANI

Don

Aorsi

AZOV
Bosporan
Kingdom
Panticapaeum

SIRACI

CAUCASUS

Heraclea
Chersonesus

pe

ESIA

Phasis

HIBERI

Artaxata ● Gorneae?

Sinope

PONTUS et
BITHYNIA

ARMENIA

A

Sophene

ADIABENE

GALATIA

Melitene

CAPPADOCIA

ASIA

Samosata
● Edessa

P A R T H I A

Smyrna
●Ephesus

LYCIA

CILICIA

Zeugma

Euphrates

Tigris

Antioch

Clesiphon

Rhodes

SYRIA

Seleucia

us

CYPRUS

● Damascus

Tyre

Galilee

Ptolemais

JUDAEA

ARABIA

Jerusalem

Alexandria

NABATAEANS

AEGYPTUS

Myos Hormus

Nile

● M. Claudianus

iles

n

# ABBREVIATIONS

Dates are of the Christian era, except where indicated. Works cited in the notes in easily recognized form are not included in this list.

| | |
|---|---|
| *cos.* | consul |
| *HS* | sesterce (coin; for purchasing power see B.Levick, *The Government of the Roman Empire* (London and Sydney, 1985) xvif.) |
| *SC* (plural *SCC*) | *Senatus consultum* (decree of the senate) |
| suff. | suffect consul (substitute consul holding office for the later months of the year) |

| | |
|---|---|
| *AP* | *Anthologia Palatina* |
| DC | Dio Cassius, *History of Rome* |
| G*I* | Gaius, *Institutes* |
| J*A* | Josephus, *Antiquitates Judaeorum* |
| J*B* | Josephus, *Bellum Judaicum* |
| P*Ep* | Pliny the Younger, *Epistulae* |
| P*NH* | Pliny the Elder, *Natural Histories* |
| S*C* | Suetonius, *Divus Claudius* (other biographies with fuller title) |
| S*A* | Seneca, *Apocolocyntosis* (other works with fuller title) |
| T*A* | Tacitus, *Annals* |
| T*Agr* | Tacitus, *Agricola* |
| T*H* | Tacitus, *Histories* |
| VP | Velleius Paterculus, *Histories* |

| | |
|---|---|
| *AA* | *Deutsches Archäologisches Institut, Archäologischer Anzeiger* |
| *AC* | *L'Antiquité classique* |
| AJ | F.F. Abbott and A.C. Johnson, *Municipal Administration in the Roman Empire* (Princeton, 1926) |
| *ABSA* | *Annual of the British School at Athens* |
| *AÉ* | *L'Anneé épigraphique* |
| *AJA* | *American Journal of Archaeology* |
| *AJP* | *American Journal of Philology* |
| *ANRW* | *Aufstieg und Niedergang der römischen Welt*, ed. H. Temporini (Berlin, 1972- ) |
| *Ath.* | *Athenaeum* |

| | |
|---|---|
| *Ath. Mitt.* | *Mitteilungen des deutsches archäologischen Instituts (in Athen)* |
| *BCH* | *Bulletin de correspondence hellénique* |
| *BGU* | *Ägyptische Urkunden aus den Staatlichen Museen zu Berlin, Griechische Urkunden* |
| *BJ* | *Bonner Jahrbücher* |
| Brit. | *Britannia* |
| Bruns | K. Bruns, *Fontes iuris romani anteiustiniani*, ed. 7 by O. Gradenwitz (Tübingen, 1909) |
| *CAH* | *Cambridge Ancient History* |
| *CIG* | *Corpus Inscriptionum Graecarum*, ed. A. Boeckh (4 vols., Berlin, 1828-77) |
| *CIL* | *Corpus Inscriptionum Latinarum*, ed. F. Ritschel *et al.* (Berlin, 1862-) |
| *CP* | *Classical Philology* |
| *CPJ* | V. Tcherikover, A. Fuks, and M. Stern, *Corpus Papyrorum judaicarum*, 3 vols. (Cambridge, Mass., 1957-64) |
| *CQ* | *Classical Quarterly* |
| *CR* | *Classical Review* |
| *CRAI* | *Comptes rendus à l'Académie des Inscriptions* |
| *CREBM* | H. Mattingly, *Coins of the Roman Empire in the British Museum* 1 (London, 1923) |
| *CW* | *Classical Weekly/World* |
| Docs. | E.M. Smallwood, *Documents illustrating the Principates of Gaius, Claudius, and Nero* (Cambridge, 1967). [See Concordance] |
| EJ² | V. Ehrenberg and A.H.M. Jones, *Documents illustrating the Reigns of Augustus and Tiberius* (ed. 2, by D.L. Stockton, Oxford, 1976) |
| *G and R* | *Greece and Rome* |
| *FGH* | F. Jacoby, *Die Fragmente der griechischen Historiker*, 14 vols. (Berlin, Leiden, 1923-58) |
| *GRBS* | *Greek, Roman and Byzantine Studies* |
| Hist. | *Historia* |
| *HSCP* | *Harvard Studies in Classical Philology* |
| *HTR* | *Harvard Theological Review* |
| *IG* | *Inscriptiones Graecae* (Berlin, 1873- ) |
| *IGRR* | *Inscriptiones Graecae ad res Romanas pertinentes*, ed. R. Cagnat (1, 3, 4, Paris, 1901-1927) |
| *ILS* | *Inscriptiones Latinae Selectae* ed. H. Dessau (3 vols., Berlin, 1892-1916, repr. 1954-5) |
| *JHS* | *Journal of Hellenic Studies* |
| *JNG* | *Jahreshefte für Numismatik und Geldgeschichte* |
| *JRS* | *Journal of Roman Studies* |
| *JS* | *Journal des Savants* |

| | |
|---|---|
| *Lat.* | *Latomus* |
| *LCM* | *Liverpool Classical Monthly* |
| *MAAR* | *Memoirs of the American Academy in Rome* |
| *MB* | *Musée Belge* |
| *MÉFRA* | *Mémoires des Écoles françaises de Rome et d'Athènes* |
| *MH* | *Museum Helveticum* |
| Mommsen, *St.* | Th. Mommsen, *Römische Staatsrecht* – (3 vols. Berlin, 1³, 1887, 2³, 1886, 3³, 1887, repr. Basel, 1952) |
| *NC* | *Numismatic Chronicle* |
| *NNM* | *Numismatic Notes and Monographs* |
| *OCD²* | *Oxford Classical Dictionary,*, ed. N.G.L. Hammond and H.H. Scullard (ed. 2, Oxford, 1970) |
| *PBA* | *Proceedings of the British Academy* |
| *PBSR* | *Papers of the British School at Rome* |
| *PCPS* | *Papers of the Cambridge Philological Society* |
| Pflaum, *Carrières* | H.-.G. Pflaum, *Les Carrières procuratoriennes équestres sous le Haut-Empire romain. Inst. fr. d'Arch. de Beyrouth, Bibl. arch. et hist.* 57 (3 vols Paris, 1960–61) |
| *Phil.* | *Philologus* |
| *PIR* | *Prosopographia Imperii Romani* ed. H. Klebs *et al.* (3 vols., Berlin, 1897-8); ed. 2 by E. Groag *et al.* (Berlin, 1933- ) |
| *PP* | *La Parola del Passato* |
| *RE* | *Paulys Real-Enzyclopädie der classischen Altertumswissenschaft*, ed. K. Wissowa *et al.* (Berlin, 1894-1980) |
| *RÉA* | *Revue des Études anciennes* |
| *RÉL* | *Revue des Études latines* |
| *RG* | *Res Gestae Divi Augusti* (in EJ²) |
| *RHDFÉ* | *Revue historique du Droit français et étranger* |
| *RIC* | *The Roman Imperial Coinage* I *(31 BC–AD 69)* ed. 2 by C.H.V. Sutherland (London, 1984) |
| *RM* | *Rheinisches Museum für Philologie* |
| *Röm. Mitt.* | *Mitteilungen des deutschen archäologischen Instituts, Römische Abteilung* |
| *SEG* | *Supplementum Epigraphicum Graecum*, ed. J. Hondius *et al.* (Leyden, 1926– ) |
| *TAPA* | *Transactions and Proceedings of the American Philological Association* |
| *TvG* | *Tijdschrift voór Geschiedenis* |
| *WS* | *Wiener Studien* |
| *YCS* | *Yale Classical Studies* |
| *ZPE* | *Zeitschrift für Papyrologie und Epigrafik* |
| *ZSS* | *Zeitschrift der Savigny-Stiftung (Rom. Abteilung)* |

# KEY DATES

| | |
|---|---|
| **31** BC | Octavian and Agrippa defeat Antony and Cleopatra at Actium. |
| **30** | Capture of Alexandria; death of Antony and Cleopatra; Octavian in sole power. |
| **27** | Constitutional settlement and conventional beginning of Principate; Octavian takes name Augustus. |
| **19** | Final constitutional settlement. |
| **12** | Attack on Germany begins. |
| **10** | Claudius born at Lugdunum. |
| **9** | Claudius' father Nero Drusus killed in Germany. |
| **2** | Augustus takes title Pater Patriae (Father of his Country); disgrace of his daughter Julia. |
| **4** AD | Augustus adopts Tiberius and Agrippa Postumus; Tiberius adopts Germanicus and is given Tribunician Power. |
| **5–8** | Agrippa Postumus and his sister the younger Julia disgraced. |
| **9** | Loss of three legions in Germany. |
| **12** | Tiberius co-ruler. |
| **14** | Death of Augustus; Tiberius assumes sole power. |
| **14–16** | Germanicus continues campaigning in Germany. |
| **17–19** | Germanicus' command in the east ends with his death. |
| **22** | Tiberius' son Drusus Caesar given Tribunician Power. |
| **23** | Death of Drusus |
| **23–31** | Ascendancy of L. Aelius Sejanus, ended by his execution. |
| **37** | Death of Tiberius and accession of Gaius (Caligula); death of Claudius' mother Antonia. |
| **38** | Death of Gaius' sister Drusilla. |
| **39–40** | Gaius suppresses alleged conspiracy of Gaetulicus on the Rhine; his surviving sisters Julia Livilla and Agrippina the younger disgraced; excursions east of Rhine; conquest of Britain mooted. |
| **41** | Gaius assassinated; Claudius takes power with the help of the Praetorian Guard; exiles return; birth of his son (Britannicus). Gaius' sister Julia Livilla and Seneca exiled; Agrippa I given kingdom of Herod the Great, his brother Herod given Chalcis. |
| **42** | Claudius Pater Patriae; execution of Appius Silanus; unsuccessful revolt of Camillus Scribonianus in Dalmatia. |
| **43** | Death of Drusus Caesar's daughter Julia; Lycia annexed; Claudius invades Britain. |

# I

# THE PRINCIPATE

Claudius came to power in AD 41. The Augustan Principate had been established nearly seventy years, but it was still developing. It owed its existence to the struggles of Republican dynasts: Marius, Sulla, Pompey, Caesar, Mark Antony, and Octavian (the later Augustus), against each other and against the collective interests of the Senate. Rivalry was inherent in the Republic, exposed by a constitution that gave the supreme magistrate, the consul, power for a year with an equal colleague who could make him ineffective. After the expulsion of the last king at the end of the sixth century BC the Senate itself became an assembly of 'kings', the heads of the clans to which they owed primary loyalty, and it kept its power as an oligarchy by restricting the power of magistrates.

The tension between the authority of the senate and the power of individuals did not end when Augustus established his own supremacy after the death of Antony and Cleopatra in 30 BC. First, his claims to primacy rested in part on his relationship to Julius Caesar (his mother's mother was Caesar's sister!), reinforced by a spurious 'testamentary adoption', and in the last analysis on military force. Second, Augustus had to keep himself in power at first by holding existing offices, later by assuming the powers they conferred, as vehicles for his position: a consul's *imperium*, that of a governor of provinces (*imperium proconsulare*), the power of a tribune in protecting the people (*tribunicia potestas*). Even when separated from the offices, granted for life, and enhanced as they were for Augustus, they still carried connotations of magistracy and could not be inherited by an heir.

Augustus overcame this problem by having powers like his own conferred on partners such as his contemporary Marcus Agrippa and on his stepson Tiberius, so that they would be able to maintain the dynasty's position after his own death. As a result of assuming powers without taking offices limited to a tenure of one year, Augustus was able to transmit the formal and constitutional position that he held virtually unchanged to his eventual successor Tiberius and beyond. But the use that they made of these powers varied according to circumstance and temperament, and there was much that they could do outside their legal powers if they chose, for example securing the election to office of candidates they favoured. The way a ruler used this power to get things done without legal authorization (*auctoritas*) gave his principate much of its style. *Auctoritas* had always been characteristic of leading men, *principes*.

In the course of a long supremacy — 'principate' was an acceptable informal term for it — the adaptable Augustus moved between the modest executive and defender of the constitution, anxious not to infringe the prerogatives of colleagues in office, the man who remitted decision-making to the senate and people, as he expressly claimed to have done in 28–7 BC, and the autocrat, making extreme use of his powers and *auctoritas*, as he did in a period of political crisis, 24–3 BC, when for the first time he took powers in the Empire that were officially defined as superior to those of provincial governors (his *imperium maius*). One might term these two extremes 'minimum' and 'maximum' principate respectively.

But individual rivalry was only one factor in the making of a new form of government under Augustus. The rivals would have been helpless without the support of groups in Rome, Italy, the provinces and dependent states, whose needs were not catered for by senatorial government, either for lack of funds or because the body as a whole feared the power that would accrue to the individuals who would gain if they could pass measures satisfying these groups.

The dispossessed Roman peasantry were the first such group to emerge, attracting the attention of the tribunes Tiberius and Gaius Gracchus, who in 133 and 123 BC passed measures to provide them with plots from state land. The numbers of dispossessed increased after this in some areas of Italy at least, as big landholders took over.

Some of them went to swell the population of Rome (*plebs urbana*): the total population of Rome at the end of the first century BC has been estimated at between three quarters of a million and a million, with up to three hundred thousand men eligible for the distributions of free grain that had been introduced in 58 BC. The population now was made up partly of the descendants of enfranchised slaves, partly of country people who had not been allocated plots. On the spot in Rome, whether recent arrivals or at home there for several generations, they had their own officials, the tribunes created centuries before to look after the interests of ordinary citizens; they could take part in assemblies of the entire Roman people (*Comitia Centuriata* and *Tributa*) and at worst could demonstrate in the theatre or riot in the streets. Their demands for plots of land or, as they became more urbanized, adequate and cheap or free supplies of grain, and sometimes for a greater share in the running of the state, gave politicians disgruntled with the senate the chance to advance themselves as *populares*, supporters of measures put forward in the people's interest despite opposition from the senate.

The political importance of the plebs, even before the century of revolution ushered in by the Gracchi, has recently been given greater recognition. It could not stand up against an army that marched against Rome (as happened for the first time in 88 BC), but it was still a formidable political force during the Second Triumvirate (43–33 BC). When his opponents cut Rome off from its grain supplies Octavian (the later Augustus) was held responsible and nearly lost his life in a bread riot in the Forum.

Table 1: *The family of Augustus*

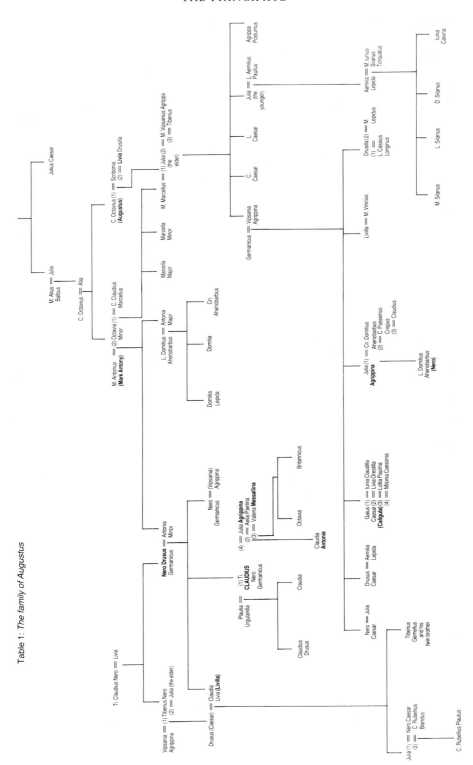

As Princeps he demonstrated solidarity with  the plebs: after offending the senate by misusing his powers as consul between 27 and 24 BC, he took the powers of a tribune for life in 23 BC, thus outclassing any annual holder of that office. In the four years that followed  the people showed during Augustus' absence that they were ready to insist on his holding one of the consulships every year, and rioted on his and their own behalf, coming almost to the point of burning down the senate house. Faced with chaos, the senate had to call for his help, giving him in 19 BC the final and decisive political success of his Principate. Augustus continued to look to the interests of the plebs by taking measures against flood and water-shortage, fire and famine and by laying on  entertainments in the theatre, circus and arena that he was careful to attend himself. In his last decade, when his position was entrenched and difficulties such as lack of money, inconclusive warfare in Germany, political controversy  over the succession, and a persistent shortage of grain were giving rise to discontent amongst all classes, he established the non-senatorial offices of Praefectus Vigilum (Chief of the Watch) and Praefectus Annonae (Officer in charge of the Grain Supply), while unruly members of the plebs were drafted into the army.[1]

Overlapping with the interests of the peasantry were those of the Roman citizen army, the legions, 25 since three were lost  in Germany in AD 9, and so totalling about 137,500 men. Legionaries sprang from the peasantry; both wanted land as a secure livelihood that conferred status as well.  Armed and organized as they were, they were far more formidable than the urban plebs, if less well placed to bring instant pressure to bear. They had become a political force at the end of the second century BC, and in commands extorted from the senate, or offered over their heads by the people, provided rival politicians with forceful backing and the means of acquiring enormous wealth, usually by extending the Empire, sometimes from victims of civil war. Military success, booty, and welfare in service were also of concern to men who might serve for decades in the overseas wars of the first century BC;  so was an early or at least predictable discharge.

Augustus, like Caesar and other commanders before him, had trouble with his troops, who mutinied in support of their demand for discharge. He recognized their importance by establishing a fixed period of service, eventually twenty years, but found it hard to stand even by that. It was only after he had been in sole power for three decades and by taking drastic measures that he reached a permanent arrangement for discharge bounties: a special Military Treasury (Aerarium Militare), was set up in 6-7; but it had to be fed by new taxes,  including a five per cent inheritance tax payable by Roman citizens on legacies to persons other than close relatives. This remained a bitter grievance with the well-to-do, who had paid no tax on their Italian land for a more than a century and a half and regarded themselves as entitled to benefit from Rome's empire.

Augustus's superior *imperium* gave him the auspices — the right to ascertain the will of the gods: all victories were due in part to his mediation.

4

He also tried to ensure the army's loyalty by downgrading most of its commanders to the status of his subordinates (*legati Augusti, pro praetore* if they governed entire provinces); he could overrule even independent commanders (proconsuls). The Triumph, a formal celebration of military success in which the commander paraded through Rome with his troops, captives, and booty, came to an end for outsiders. Augustus was the supreme commander (*imperator*, whence our 'Emperor' and the alternative name for the Principate, the 'Empire', both opposed to the Republic it had replaced); he was determined to bind the troops to himself and his family, and the men who became Augustus' partners in power, Agrippa and Tiberius, each won three triumphs and became the most successful general of his generation; their intended heirs, Gaius and Lucius Caesar, were likewise destined for early military advancement through commands in the East and Spain. Gaius, like Tiberius' younger brother Nero Drusus in 9 BC, actually died in AD 4 of injuries received on active service. Tiberius' son Drusus Caesar won an ovation (a lesser form of triumph) in AD 20 for success in a Balkan command; but it was his adoptive brother Germanicus Caesar whose aggressive expeditions in his father's old territory in the years 13-16 and annexations in the East made him a military hero and conferred charisma on all his kinsmen, especially his only surviving son Gaius, who as 'Bootsie' (Caligula) had lived as an infant with the Rhine legions.

Apart from the legions and the numerically equivalent auxiliary troops who were normally recruited in the provinces and were not Roman citizens, there was the élite force of the Praetorian Guard that had not existed in permanent form before Augustus came to power, although there had always been men on duty at a commander's headquarters (*praetorium*). By 2 BC Augustus had nine cohorts of 500 men (so the equivalent of nearly a legion) stationed in Italy under two equestrian prefects. A single commander, Tiberius' trusted minister L.Aelius Sejanus, held office from about 17 onwards; by 23 he had gathered the cohorts into one barracks adjoining the city walls: the nearest legionary troops were in Pannonia, ten days' march away. Recruited from traditional sources of manpower, Etruria, Umbria, and the old Latin towns, the Praetorian Guard had preferential pay and terms of service, as well as an easier life; hence strong *esprit de corps.*

Another factor in the development of one-man rule at Rome, by no means so significant as army and people, were foreign protégés, who might offer a politician or commander support in money, influence, or manpower in return for favours to themselves and (strengthening their own position in it) their community. Legal privileges, exemptions from tax, even admission to the Roman citizenship, had played their part in securing loyalty, first to the Roman state, later to one individual or another, since Rome's expansion had begun.

The leaders of native levies in the early Principate could expect to be given Roman citizenship, if they had not received it already, in return for *virtus* (bravery) on the battlefield; on occasion entire troops were enfranchised. Julius Caesar was particularly generous during the Gallic and Civil wars of the fifties and forties, notably in his enfranchisement of a whole legion recruited as non-citizens, the Fifth Alaudae ('Larks'). The principle that men who had served Rome had earned her citizenship was turned to the advantage of the individuals who were responsible for seeing that it was conferred: the last law known to have given the right to enfranchise was the Lex Titia passed in favour of the members of the Second Triumvirate in 43 BC. Augustus and his successors continued to use this method of securing useful members of the citizen body, establishing centres of loyalty in the provinces, and showing that that they knew how to acknowledge debts of gratitude.[2]

With the turmoil that marked the ending of the Republic the pace of social mobility increased, and the Princeps' opportunities for patronage were an important part of his power, sometimes openly exercised, as at elections, sometimes silently. It was no open revolution: outward forms were preserved, but gaps left in the senate's ranks by death, exile, impoverishment, or boycott were rapidly filled, partly by the Princeps' men. The senate that the Dictator Sulla had re-established in power in 81 BC with a membership of 600, topped 900 at Caesar's death and 1000 by the end of the Second Triumvirate; Augustus reduced it to the Sullan level in 18 BC by forcing men to retire, after which it was replenished as it had been before, by the entry of men who had held junior magistracies; as prosperity returned Augustus was able to establish the property qualification for senators at one million HS.

The second order in the state, that of the Equites or Knights, consisted in the main of landowners on a large or small scale (the property qualification was only 400,000 HS). Some were the close kin of senators, even men entitled by birth to enter the senate but preferring not to embark on a political career, although they might be ready to serve on the prestigious jury panels at Rome. More of them were squires from the country towns of Italy (*domi nobiles*). Whether they were primarily landowners or were multiplying their fortunes out of tax farming or banking in the provinces, they were vulnerable to confiscation and could be politically suspect. New fortunes were made, first from Italy, then from the provinces, and won places in both orders, senatorial and equestrian. The first non-Italian consul (40 BC) was Cornelius Balbus of Gades, the protégé of Caesar and Pompey.

The advance of new men continued after the civil wars came to an end in 30 BC. The approved ladder was army service, where loyalty and ability were at a premium, but it was still looked at askance when a new man rose unduly fast or far, as it had been when Marius of Arpinum, aged nearly fifty, clawed his way to his first consulship of 107 BC and claimed the war in Africa. Tacitus' obituary notice of the new man P.Sulpicius Quirinius of Lanuvium, *cos.* 12 BC, shows the suspicion and resentment that such meteoric success could arouse.[3]

The Principate gave further cause for resentment to the senate because of the advancement of men of substance outside the senate, the knights, to official posts. They were required to deal with the tasks that the Princeps made his responsibility, such as the defence of Rome against fire and famine. These were long-term positions, unsuitable for senators on the ladder of promotion. The Prefecture of the Watch, involving the command of ex-slaves, was arguably beneath the dignity of a senator. The governorship of Egypt was not, and its equestrian prefect was formally made the equal in power of a senatorial governor who was an ex-consul. Nor were many senators equal in power to the Prefect of the Praetorian Guard, a position that realised its full possibilities in the hands of Tiberius' minister Aelius Sejanus.

Even below this level the reduction in power of senatorial posts made lesser equestrian positions in the gift of the Princeps, the procuratorships which dealt with the emperor's private estates and, in imperial provinces, with state revenues, more attractive to some ambitious men who (perversely, a senator would think) preferred to confine themselves to equestrian procuratorships instead of making a career in the senate, where their newness might prove a disadvantage.[4]

These procurators, and, more particularly and obviously since theirs was a military title, the prefects, who administered difficult districts in the Alps or small provinces such as Judaea, were advanced from army posts proper; but the patronage of the Princeps or of someone close to him was important. It was not just their tenure of governorships or the prefectures at Rome that caused resentment but, as with Sejanus, the influence that the most important of them enjoyed. The influence of *equites* had caused resentment since the Dictatorship of Caesar: men such as C.Matius, Oppius, the Cornelii Balbi, were hated then, as were C. Maecenas and Sallustius Crispus under Augustus and Tiberius. It was a source of satisfaction to senators that their influence so rarely proved to last. The service of the Princeps, then, military and civil, and his private friendships, which also acquired significance from his position and made his friends and servants courtiers, was a source of status dissonance and social discord.[5]

Augustus' swings between maximum and minimum Principate were repeated by his successors. Tiberius maintained from the start of his principate in 14 that the senate should discuss all matters of state, the Princeps should be its servant, indeed the servant of the whole state. He failed partly because he was mistrusted by politicians who had opposed him, partly because he came to power so old that the succession was a live issue right from the start and became a burning one with the deaths of his direct heirs (19 and 23): the reign ended in 37 amid deadly struggles for influence over the next incumbent, Gaius, punctuated by equally deadly interventions from Tiberius, now isolated on Capri. Gaius acceded at the age of twenty-four having held no other office than that of quaestor (Tiberius would not allow young members of the imperial family advancement quicker than his own had been, and was intent on forwarding both Gaius and his younger cousin Tiberius Gemellus as joint heirs). The Principate shook Gaius into experimenting to discover its limits for himself. As he told his grandmother Antonia, for him any act, against no matter whom, was lawful.[6]

Gaius' view was partial, that of the Princeps himself. But the Princeps is also like Tolstoy's Napoleon, a stick on the stream of history, carried along as helplessly as any peasant. His interests were at the mercy of the wishes of his subjects — senate, knights, plebs, army, even of provincials. 'Power' depended on maintaining a balance between all these constituencies, and Tiberius saw himself as holding a 'wolf by the ears'.[7] While Rome and Italy pressed for guaranteed material benefits and privileges, the provinces, if exploited without recompense, might react violently. It would be a policy fully or half conscious, to respond to these pressures and function as a mechanism for the distribution of goods. Equally, the Principate might be interpreted as a new device for shoring up old structures; the Princeps was the greatest property-owner of all, and by mediating between landless and landholders, offering the minimum acceptable to the former, he preserved the existing social system for another three centuries. In virtue of his official position, too, the Princeps can be seen as a catalyst of social mobility and the summit of a new hierarchy in which status was regulated by salary, and which was required to deal with the relations of central government and empire. As the fount of patronage he moderated social advancement, from peregrine to citizen status and up the ladder within the citizenship, giving a place to merit as well as to birth and wealth.

No single-level interpretation of the Princeps' role will suffice. But there can be no doubt of his role in speeding up a fundamental process, the shift from a vertical distinction between Italy and the provinces towards a homogeneous cluster of societies, horizontally divided by class. The robber's nest of Rome had lived off the victims of conquest, who were financing their own suppression and Rome's further advance to the mature status of a brutally imperialistic world power. At certain points this entailed admitting the earlier conquests to equal rights, otherwise the process could not continue, for want of manpower and finances. After the reign of Augustus, expansion slowed down, and effort was concentrated on assimilating and exploiting what had been won. By preserving the social structure of Rome on the one hand and facilitating the admission of the wealthy and powerful in provincial communities to office on the other, and by redistributing property and power, the Emperors stabilized the entire structure, secured their own position as redistributors, and levelled their subjects down as they achieved their own supremacy. Panegyrists of Rome, such as Aelius Aristides, made this necessity into virtue (he was not honest in claiming that the Roman regime pleased rich and poor alike).[8] The distinction between Romans and non-citizens disappeared when Caracalla enfranchised all free inhabitants of the Empire in 212; by the first third of the second century a distinction was being drawn throughout the Empire between *honestiores*

8

and *humiliores* and their legal rights.

However little the Princeps controlled the overall evolution of his empire, he was perceived as powerful and it was clear what qualities were required of him. Military ability or at least charisma was prime, given the strategic importance and political power of the armed forces. But descent, implying inherited qualities of character and intellect, was also important. At political crises, 'sons' of Tiberius Gracchus and of Gaius Marius had been produced as trump cards to win over the people. Antony told Octavian that he owed everything to his name of Caesar, and Tiberius owed his final painless accession to his adoption, ten years previously, by his stepfather and former father–in–law. Gaius enjoyed advantages far greater than those of Tiberius: his mother the elder Agrippina may have been the daughter of the new man Marcus Agrippa, but her mother was Augustus' own daughter, so that Gaius was Augustus' great-grandson in the female line and legally a Julius himself through the adoptions of Tiberius and Germanicus in AD 4. He also embodied the line of Mark Antony, through Antony's younger daughter, who was Germanicus' mother. Heredity carried him to the Principate with the support of plebs, army (with the Praetorian Guard and its commander Macro taking the initiative in saluting his accession) and provincials, and with the acquiescence of the senate. The troops remembered Nero Drusus and Germanicus and saw Gaius inheriting their skill and enthusiasm for military life, while the senate recalled their civility and dwelt on a fantasy: the belief that they intended in some sense to restore the senatorial government of Republican times.

# 2

# THE EDUCATION OF A PRINCE

Claudius — or Tiberius Claudius Nero, to give him the full name of his infancy — was born on 1 August, 10 BC. It was twenty years to the day since Octavian had captured Alexandria and brought his rival Mark Antony and Queen Cleopatra VII of Egypt to suicide, and Claudius' branch of the ruling family was coming to the fore. Two factors that blighted Claudius' own prospects will be examined in this chapter: the political vicissitudes of that branch in the second half of Augustus' Principate; and his ill health, which forced him back on a scholar's life.

Claudius' father was Nero Claudius Drusus, born in 38 BC as the younger son of the woman who had already parted from her husband to become Augustus' wife, Livia Drusilla. With his elder but less dashing brother Tiberius, the future Princeps, Nero Drusus had conquered the Alps and now, as governor of Gaul, was overrunning Germany beyond the Rhine. When Augustus' coeval Marcus Agrippa, the leading general of their generation, died in 12 BC, he left the two stepsons clear, glorious — and dangerous — fields of action in Illyricum and Germany. Agrippa's own oldest two sons Gaius and Lucius had been adopted into the clan of the Julii Caesares by Augustus, their maternal grandfather, but at eight and five they were too young to be his immediate heirs. Tiberius and Nero Drusus must come first (as Tiberius' speedy marriage to Agrippa's widow Julia showed), and their own sons could not fail, it seemed in the three years that followed, to share some of their glory or to have exceptional opportunities of winning their own.[1]

Nero Drusus' wife Antonia accompanied him to Gaul and Claudius was born at the leading city of Comata, the Roman colony of Lugdunum (Lyons). Later he could refer to himself as a native Gaul — and be mocked as one. Antonia was not the daughter of the Princeps, like Tiberius' new wife Julia, but of his defeated rival Antony, by Augustus' sister Octavia. Born in 36 BC, Antonia had already had one son about five or six years before she gave birth to Claudius, as well as a daughter, Livilla, and at least one other child who had not survived. The eldest child acquired the name Germanicus, by which he has always been known, not at birth, but after his father's death, the result of a fall from his horse on campaign in Germany in 9 BC, when it was conferred by the senate on the dead hero and as an hereditary title for the head of the family in memory of his achievements.[2]

Nero Drusus' death at twenty-nine was a tragic personal blow to his mother Livia, to Augustus the loss of a brilliantly successful general, to the ordinary people of Rome that of an affable hero. For his immediate family, his wife and sons, whatever else it meant, it was a severe political setback, precisely because of the advance it entailed for his brother Tiberius. At the first opportunity he was elected to a second consulship, which he held in 7 BC, and in the following year he was awarded proconsular power in the eastern provinces, with the charge of securing the Roman hold on Armenia Major against the Parthians; and this power was to be held in conjunction with the authority of a tribune which only Augustus himself and his friend Marcus Agrippa had held since it was devised to mark the Princeps' supremacy in 23 BC. Tiberius became Augustus' partner in power. Agrippa's sons Gaius and Lucius, who had been adopted by Augustus, were next in line, and the interests of Nero Drusus' offspring fell into the shade. Any additional lustre would fall now on Tiberius' closest relation, his son Drusus, born in 13 or 14 BC.

Antonia insisted on widowhood, in spite of Augustus' urging. Physically she may not have been strong (a number of doctors and ailments are known), but she was strong-minded. Her advice was sought and was thought influential. From her father Mark Antony she inherited wide connexions, especially in the East, which were to be significant for Claudius, and like her mother-in-law Livia she played an important role as educator and patron. Her friends included Herod the Great's niece and daughter-in-law Berenice, whose husband Aristobulus was executed in 7 BC. Their son Agrippa was brought up in Antonia's household alongside Claudius.[3]

Ironically, Tiberius' own action blighted his prospects and those of his family scarcely three years after Nero Drusus died; he threw up his assignment in Armenia and retired to Rhodes. His extraordinary renunciation may have been due purely to pique and anger at the mistrust shown him by Gaius and Lucius, or rather by their mother Julia, Tiberius' estranged wife, and their other backers. But some part in it may have been played by regret for his brother and grief that it was due to Nero Drusus' death that he had risen so high. Tiberius' self-imposed exile certainly meant no improvement in the prospects of Nero Drusus' sons Germanicus and Claudius. Between 5 BC and AD 2 Augustus pinned his hopes of securing power for his dynasty on the survival to distinguished manhood of Marcus Agrippa's sons Gaius and Lucius.[4]

That phase came to an end when Gaius and Lucius died on service abroad, in AD 2 and 4. A few months after the death of Gaius, Augustus in June AD 4 adopted Tiberius along with Gaius and Lucius' younger brother Agrippa Postumus, then aged sixteen. As a preliminary to his own adoption, Tiberius had himself adopted his nephew, the twenty-year old Germanicus, which made him too, like Tiberius' son Drusus, into an adoptive descendant of Augustus. This produced an incongruous cluster of five dynasts, present and future, consisting of Augustus, two adopted sons, Tiberius and Agrippa Postumus, and the two grandsons by adoption, Germanicus and Drusus Caesars. Tiberius dominated this scheme, and that revived the old mistrust of Tiberius in the minds of Gaius and Lucius' supporters. After an unsuccessful intrigue intended to speed his advance, Agrippa Postumus fell from Augustus' favour in 5 and was sent into final exile in 7, bringing down his sister the younger Julia, her husband Paullus Lepidus, and other supporters in a crushing political defeat. Germanicus went in Agrippa's place to the Balkans, where revolt had broken out among Pannonians and Dalmatians, adding to the problems that Augustus had to face in his last years. Talent as well as age put Germanicus ahead of Tiberius' natural son Drusus Caesar, but their place in the family made them future partners in power — a prospect that came even closer on Augustus' death on 19 August 14, and unchallenged acknowledgement of Tiberius as Princeps.[5]

Claudius had just celebrated his twenty-third birthday. It was ten years since he had taken the surname Germanicus as youthful *paterfamilias* of the Claudii Nerones when his brother Germanicus had passed into the clan of the Julii Caesares. The orphan would remain in tutelage, presumably that of Augustus, until his twenty-fifth birthday, but as the only brother of the future Princeps Germanicus he could look forward to a career second only to his. That career did not materialize. Something more fundamental than the political vicissitudes of the descendants of Livia and her first husband had brought it to nothing before it had even begun; the adoptions of Tiberius and Germanicus and the posts conferred on them only showed Claudius how far behind he was to fall.

The first known public acknowledgment that something was wrong came when Claudius took the *toga virilis*, the garb of manhood, probably at the age of 14, in 5–6. Normally a ceremonious occasion for rejoicing in which the youth was conducted into the crowded Forum by his father, in Claudius' case it was a furtive nocturnal event. In the same year, 6, when Germanicus and Claudius presented games in honour of their dead father, Claudius appeared swathed in a pallium, the enveloping and concealing dress of the invalid. Circus games were also given by Augustus in 8 in the names of Germanicus and Claudius; the former was in the field; was Claudius allowed to appear? The phraseology of the historian Dio suggests not. And even after Claudius passed from *tutela* he still went about accompanied by a tutor *cum* attendant.[6]

There is comparatively rich information on Claudius' condition, but historians cannot examine the patient and their opinions seem to have reflected current medical preoccupations. Just before and after the Second World War it was commonly accepted that Claudius had poliomyelitis ('infantile paralysis'). The view that Claudius suffered from cerebral palsy, involving some degree of spasticity, is more satisfactory.[7]

Seneca's scathing comment on Claudius after his death was that 'nobody thought he had even been born'. In connection with this a remark of his mother Antonia recorded by Suetonius may be relevant. He claims that Antonia used to speak of her son (she need only have said it once for it to be presented as a *leitmotiv*!) as 'a monstrosity of a human being, one that

Nature began and never finished'. Antonia's hostility to her 'unfinished' youngest child was probably intensified when she almost immediately lost her husband, and, a quarter of a century later, her even more brilliant elder son: now primacy was lost to her family. But the start may have been a difficult birth. Claudius may have been premature and perhaps suffered an injury that might have caused the palsy. On the other hand, the possibility of a pre- or post-natal infection cannot be ruled out.[8]

Suetonius insists that when standing still or seated Claudius was a figure of dignity, and Seneca admits that he was well built: there was no question of deformity, nor any of the gross twisting movements of arms and hands that are sometimes found with cerebral palsy and are due to lesions in the basal ganglia and related brain structures. All the same, Dio remarks that 'his head and hands shook slightly', and Seneca portrays him sending the goddess Fever off to execution with a wave of his limp hand — which was strong enough only for that gesture. Claudius dragged his right leg. There was weakness on that side, spasticity or stiffness, which may also have affected the hand. If Claudius was right-handed, being a keen student who devoted himself to literature from a very early age, he may have found his left hand stronger for writing and have trained himself to use it instead of the right. His paternal uncle Tiberius was left-handed and very strong in that hand; Claudius may have inherited some potential ability. If he developed it, that would help to account for his speech difficulty: children who are forced to use the hand that is not naturally their stronger or dominant one are said sometimes to develop a stammer; King George VI is a famous example.[9]

Physical handicap alone is not enough to account for all Claudius' oral and vocal peculiarities. He had a cracked and hardly intelligible voice; it belonged to no land-animal (wrote Seneca) but was the kind of voice a sea-creature has, raucous and throaty: you couldn't even tell what language he was speaking. Dio claims that Claudius used to give his speeches in the senate to his quaestor to read; but those would be routine announcements. According to Suetonius, Claudius, when emotionally involved, had disagreeable traits such as an uncontrollable laugh; when he was angry it was even more unpleasant: he snarled and slobbered and his nose ran. All this sounds as if he had real physical difficulties in speaking which may have been due to lesions of the cerebral cortex associated with the palsy but which were aggravated at times of emotional strain. The only marked change over time in his health is recorded by Suetonius; after he became Emperor it was much better than before, and he was troubled only by painful stomach disorders; this suggests that there was a psychological component in his condition, which was mitigated after he had something to live for.[10]

For historians perhaps the most important aspect of the disability caused by cerebral palsy is its effect on Claudius' mental and emotional state. It may be accompanied by epilepsy and mental retardation. There is no sign of either in Claudius. He was often referred to as stupid, but he was not mentally backward. It takes intellect to write history, however bad. Claudius wrote history, and his research was used as a source by Tacitus.[11] He did however display personality defects, combining apparent apathy with well-attested outbursts of anger. As Emperor he earned a reputation for hastiness in court; the people of Ostia took a sharp rebuke for their failure to send ships to meet him when he was sailing the Tiber — but suddenly he forgave them, almost as if it was his fault. Indeed, Claudius was aware of his failing, and issued an edict in which he excused both irascibility and ire. He distinguished the two, and undertook that while the first would be shortlived and not dangerous, the second would be well justified. The apathy itself was perhaps in part a political device but might sometimes be a sign of depression: victims of cerebral palsy tend to become both emotional and depressed. Claudius probably suffered from the psychological effects of physical frustration, of not having his body at his command. This he openly intimated in the senate in 48, when he (quite irrelevantly) attacked the memory of a man forced to suicide for treachery as 'a prodigy of the wrestling ring'.[12]

As a secondary outcome and at a superficial level Claudius' disabilities must have affected his public persona and behaviour, because he was aware that he was an object of curiosity and derision. The speech defect may also have been aggravated by this awareness, and by the strain of performing in public, especially without a prepared text or when he was involved in controversy: according to Augustus, echoed by Tacitus, he could read a script perfectly satisfactorily. For his family, what was most important about his disabilities was the unfavourable impression they made. We do not have a clinician's picture of the symptoms, which may have been relatively mild, rather those of hostile witnesses who had reason for reporting them at their worst. It was the sensitivity of Romans to matters of decorum (appearance, bearing, dress, and speech, areas in which Claudius was plainly deficient) that made his family hesitate to let him appear in public.[13]

Claudius' ill health is the reason offered by ancient writers for his unspectacular taking of the *toga virilis* in 5–6, and there can be no other explanation for the way his later public appearances were handled and for the stifling of any political career for him after the supremacy of Tiberius was finally assured in 8. But in March of 5 Agrippa Postumus also took the toga. He was two years older than Claudius and the ceremony had been delayed, probably because of the uncertain political situation in March, 4: Gaius had died in Lycia the previous month after a long illness, and although the news arrived in Rome only early in April it must have been expected. Until the compromise of June, 4, was reached, by which both he and Tiberius were adopted by Augustus, Agrippa and his supporters may have hoped for the same treatment as his older brothers: they had been conducted into the Forum by Augustus, who had taken the consulship for the purpose, been given the title Princeps Iuventutis (Leader of the Youth), and promised the consulship five years hence, at the age of nineteen. Postumus got none of those things, and as far as is known, eventually enjoyed only the conventional honours of the occasion.[14]

Consideration for Agrippa Postumus cannot have operated beyond the year 8, when his sister Julia, brother-in-law Paullus Lepidus, and other supporters had been disgraced, or even beyond Agrippa's first exile, to Surrentum in 5. Their disappearance from the scene cleared the way for Tiberius' son Drusus Caesar, and in 9 Claudius reached the age of eighteen, when the young members even of run-of-the-mill senatorial families were holding minor magistracies as a preliminary to their military service. But Claudius took no known part in civil life, let alone military. On the arch erected at Pavia in 7–8 in honour of the dead Gaius and Lucius Caesar the disgraced Agrippa Postumus and his sister Julia the Younger are omitted; Claudius is on the end of one of the wings of the group – and to Augustus' left: he is beyond Livia, the two dead princes, and Germanicus' younger son. To the right stand Tiberius, his sons Germanicus and Drusus, and Germanicus' elder son. Claudius was insignificant in the dynasty, and the only public distinctions he won in this period were social: the prestigious priesthood due to any male member of a family of this standing, the augurate, and membership of a much less distinguished college, the Sodales Titiales. Claudius' first marriage was celebrated in about 9-10. He had first been betrothed to Aemilia Lepida, daughter of Julia and Paullus, but that match had been broken off when the parents were disgraced. Not surprisingly Lepida was replaced by the daughter of a protégé of Tiberius, Furius Camillus (cos. 8), but she died on the wedding day. The girl he finally married belonged to another family favoured by Tiberius: Plautia Urgulanilla's father M. Plautius Silvanus (cos. 2 BC) had won triumphal decorations for his services with Tiberius in the Balkans.[15]

In 12 a final decision on Claudius' future in public life was sought by Augustus and Tiberius, in response to a query from Livia, and in consultation with Claudius' mother Antonia. The occasion that prompted Livia, with her semi-public position, and her double authority as Claudius' grandmother and senior and most influential member of all the Claudii (her father had been born a Claudius Pulcher), to raise the question was the Games of Mars, held in May of that year of Germanicus' consulship, and the part to be played in them by Claudius. A more acute difficulty would arise a few weeks later. When the consul left Rome to celebrate the Latin Festival he customarily appointed some young relative to act as Prefect of the City, and Claudius would have been the obvious choice, unless he were accompanying his brother to the Alban Mount, where the Festival was held, a possibility that his family had already ruled out. On both occasions Claudius would be full in the public eye, and that was what tormented his relatives. So far they had taken agonized decisions on each separate occasion — and evidently had at least once found Claudius and themselves the butt of popular and aristocratic sneers and jokes; this time (Augustus and Tiberius resolved) the decision was to be one of principle, leading either to a full career, through the same steps and stages as Germanicus', as Augustus put it, or to complete exclusion. Either on this occasion or still in a series of smaller decisions the rulers took the cautious view: Claudius was to be excluded from taking any part in public life, except when his peculiarities could be masked or controlled by friendly advisers; at the Games of Mars he was allowed to preside over the Salian Priests' banqueting hall — under the supervision of his wife's brother, Plautius Silvanus, who was also a member of the college. Cruel irony had allowed Claudius to become a member of the Salii Palatini ('Palatine Leapers'), a priesthood confined to patricians, sometimes those of little ability and destined to win nothing better. (It was open only to boys with both parents still living, so Claudius must have been enrolled in his first fourteen months of life: if disabilities showed it must have been hoped that they would diminish.) The outcome of these anxious deliberations on the part of Claudius' closest relatives was negative, and Augustus had no positive idea for helping Claudius to improve beyond recommending him to find a good model whose gestures, dress, and gait he could imitate. Later Claudius wrote bitterly in a memoir of the 'barbarian' ex-commander of a mule train who had been his tutor *cum* attendant (*paedagogus*) to knock sense into him. He also remembered rare acts of kindness. There was a man who gave him a glass of cold water when he was ill; years later he gave that as a reason for supporting the man's son as a candidate for office.[16]

Augustus showed in his will of 2 April, AD 14, that he still adhered to the plan agreed two years earlier. Claudius was named, but only among heirs of the third degree — that is, he would inherit only if two intervening heirs declined their inheritance. Unlike the disgraced Agrippa Postumus, Claudius was a member of the family as such; what he was to be excluded from was the potent offices and prerogatives that membership brought. But by using dynastic marriages, adoptions, and wills to secure the accession of the men he favoured, Augustus had been conniving at the development of the Principate into what Tacitus called 'virtually the inheritance of a single family'; in time relationship would outweigh every other claim. Claudius could not foresee that. In his early twenties what was forced on his attention was the fact that he had no serious part to play in public life. It would have been natural to feel frustration, sharpened by the brilliance and popularity of Germanicus, perhaps too by the reflection that in the preceding generation his own outgoing, venturesome father Nero Drusus, the younger brother, had almost eclipsed Tiberius, gifted general and orator though he was.[17]

Claudius' family had not neglected his education and he remained assiduously devoted to the cultivated pursuits (*disciplinae liberales*, as Suetonius calls them, consisted of literature, rhetoric, music, mathematics, and jurisprudence). A speech impediment was an unfortunate failing in a would-be orator, but it had been overcome by the consummate Demosthenes. Delivery remained difficult: and knowing that he was hard to follow may have infuriated him. Claudius did not lack address and even personal dignity as a speaker, as long as he remained seated, and Tacitus followed Augustus in allowing that he could perform well, as long as he kept to his prepared text. Nervousness when he was not engaged in a neutral exercise would make him depart from it, and make his mind seem to wander in the way that Augustus had deplored, importing deprecatory references to himself, intended to be ingratiating, irrelevant and feeble jokes, and instances that Claudius was aware were likely to help his opponents' case. The speech made to a hostile senate in 48, controversially advocating that Gallic nobles be permitted to stand for senatorial magistracies, and taken down verbatim, is the longest specimen we have of his oratory. Besides showing the influence of Cicero and Livy, it has these faults, notably towards the end of the surviving part, where Claudius at last and with ostentatious hesitation comes to the point after a long historical introduction designed to disarm his hearers by proving that novelty was no novelty at Rome. In written or edited texts his style shows (in Bardon's words) more exact study than elegance of form. Cicero, whose style Claudius defended against Asinius Pollio in a monograph, had shown that firm knowledge was necessary for the orator; this was something that Claudius misinterpreted. Scholars have taken Claudius' regard for Cicero very seriously, as an indication of his political views; but his use of Cicero could well be opportunistic and emollient; before he died for the Republic Cicero had presented a varying political face. The speech that Claudius drew on when he advocated the admission of Gauls to the senate was the *Pro Balbo,* delivered for the benefit of Pompey and Caesar's Spanish protégé, just as he echoed the speech of the tribune Canuleius in favour of allowing intermarriage between patricians and plebeians from Livy's fourth book.[18]

Claudius' interest in history led him to produce several major or at least long works during his enforced leisure. In Greek, the language of scholarship, he wrote twenty books of Etruscan history and eight of Carthaginian while he was still a private individual, taking foreign, unsympathetic, even hostile powers as his subject. History is an honourable activity for men who have left politics, as Sallust pointed out, with his mind on Thucydides. The exclusion of Thucydides and Sallust from public life must have been an additional stimulus to the aspiring young historian. If one was being prevented from taking part in the making of Roman history, it was natural to look elsewhere for historical subjects: Rome was not everything. Claudius' marriage to the child of a house with Etruscan connexions and his betrothal of their son to the daughter of an Etruscan notable of Volsinii, Aelius Sejanus, must have had something to do with his choice of both subjects, for Etruscans in the early Empire were taking an interest in the exploits of the Carthaginians. If there is anything in the story that the Claudii, boasting as Claudius himself did a Sabine origin, were really of Etruscan descent, there was even better reason for his interest.[19]

But with the encouragement of Livy (who died probably in 12) and with the help of his secretary or tutor Sulpicius Flavus, evidently a man well-known in his day, Claudius had the courage as a youth, and so before his political future was determined in 12, to embark on a topic much nearer to home, indeed dangerously domestic: the history of Rome from the assassination of Julius Caesar, this naturally written in Latin. Claudius must have asked himself as he worked on his Roman history what the outcome would have been if not Augustus but Mark Antony had been the victor at Actium. Sympathy for the cause of Antony, unsurprising in his grandson, would be offensive to Augustus. Suetonius, writing in the early second century, says that the forty-three books survived in his time. The first two probably covered the years 44–3 BC. Then there was a gap: the years of the Second Triumvirate, at the urging of Livia and Antonia, were omitted, and the work continued until the end of Augustus' principate: forty-three years in all. Claudius went on working on this history indefinitely, so that it must have been interrupted by the Etruscan and Carthaginian projects, which may have been put in his way to divert him. He gave recitals of his own work and remained a keen auditor — at least if the leading historian Servilius Nonianus (*suff.* 35) was performing. It is noteworthy too that two, possibly three men who reached high office in his reign had forbears who were distinguished scholars of the late Republic: Cicero's friend A.Caecina and Tarquitius Priscus, Etruscans; and Veranius, who may be identical with Catullus' friend.[20]

Along with an interest in history went one in language, and an understandable concern for speakers. Before he came to power Claudius wrote a monograph advocating the introduction of new letters into the Latin alphabet. He put theory into practice as censor in 47. Tacitus follows his notice of this measure with a history of the alphabet, which may have formed part of a senatorial speech or edict by Claudius, or an extract from his treatise. Claudius' letters did not survive him, but Tacitus says they could be seen on official inscriptions, and Suetonius mentions books, records, and monumental inscriptions. Claudius favoured -ai- for -ae-, as in Caisar, an antiquarian spelling of the diphthong, and his new letters rationalized spelling. The inverted digamma usefully stands for the w sound of v/u between vowels, and is frequently found; what may have been a western Greek *psi* for b+s and p+s, less useful because it merely abbreviated a combination, is not epigraphically attested; and a rough breathing half-H, or more plausibly a fifth century BC Boeotian vowel character, for y̆, the Greek *upsilon*, as in the name Nymphius, in Latin a sound between e and i, has given rise to modern controversy.[21]

Claudius was well versed in Greek and may have travelled in Greece, Thessaly and Attica, in 10–11. He listened to poetry and was ready with a quotation or misquotation from Homer. But we hear nothing of a more active interest in philosophy or in poetry and drama, except for acts of piety towards his dead brother Germanicus, the production of a Greek comedy of his at Naples, which won a crown, and the publication of his translation of Aratus' *Phaenomena*; there are no compositions of his own. As Princeps he had few philosophers at court: if there were others beside Tiberius Claudius Balbillus, son of a Tiberian courtier, they were not prominent. Claudius, preoccupied with action and politics, concentrated his attention on oratory and history. He was however well supplied with philosophical precepts for the consolation of his freedman Polybius, who was mourning a brother. They were eloquently uttered, too, in his usual style, according to Seneca, who was in exile at the time (about 43) and in no position to essay sarcasm if he hoped to return. Twelve years later Seneca, in power at Nero's court, was freer to refer to a dead Emperor's idiosyncratic speech with the distaste he felt.[22]

There was another discipline that was particularly familiar to Claudius, more so than to most members of the political élite at Rome: medicine, of which he had personal experience since his earliest childhood, both from his mother's attendants and as a result of his own physical weakness. His uncle Tiberius considered himself versed in medical matters, but with the object of avoiding doctors. A robust man in an age of high mortality, he mistrusted them: after a man is thirty he should be able to know what is best for his health. Claudius was not afraid of doctors, and took an interest in their skills and lore. He took medical men on his journey to Britain in 43, C.Stertinius Xenophon of Cos, who had a brother Quintus also in the imperial service as a doctor, and the freedman Callistus' protégé Scribonius Largus. This interest took a generous form, the wish to share the benefits of his physicians' and his own knowledge: during his censorship of 47–8 he issued an edict on the value of yew in the treatment of snake-bite, and some wag had him meditating another edict on the salutary effect of breaking wind. A late tradition seems to put him in correspondence with a sheikh of the Scenite Arabs and receiving advice on bird therapy, in particular on the use of vulture's liver, boiled in its own blood with honey and taken over a period of three weeks as a cure for epilepsy, or of the heart of the same, dried and given in water.[23]

# 3

# THE FRUSTRATION
# OF A POLITICIAN

When Augustus died on 19 August, AD 14, the annual elections to the consulate had been held, but those for the lower magistracies, including the lowest of all, the quaestorship that gave membership of the senate, were still to come. Claudius asked Tiberius for a post. Perhaps it was for the quaestorship itself, for which any young man of senatorial rank might stand at his age, perhaps for something higher but unspecified. Tiberius refused, remaining faithful to decisions taken jointly by him and his predecessor; or used the fact that they were joint to discourage attempts to reverse them. Certainly here a decision of principle or a series of precedents made refusal easy, if not obligatory. He offered him consular decorations (*ornamenta consularia*), an honour accorded to foreign potentates and (under the Principate) to knights whose distinction would have ensured them the office of consul — if they had not been out of the running.

It was a definitive exclusion. Claudius' only achievement was to be appointed a member of the new priesthood that was to devote itself to the cult of the deified Augustus, the Sodales Augustales. His conversation and manners might vex the man he sat next to at sodality banquets; but if he blundered at the sacrifices there would be kinsmen to check him. In any case, the priesthood lacked prestige: the first colleagues, except for the obligatory members of the imperial family who gave it what cachet it had, were chosen by lot. It was not enough: Claudius did not accept Tiberius' refusal. He applied again, perhaps just before the elections of the following summer. This time the response was rude: Claudius had had his present of forty gold pieces at the last Saturnalia and Sigillaria festival (December 14): what more did he want? Tiberius remained adamant to the end of his reign of nearly twenty-three years, and his will put Claudius where Augustus' had: among the tertiary heirs and with no chance of inheriting. This time however he had an interest in one third of the estate.[1]

The disgrace or death of kinsmen gave the only hope of advancement for a man who lacked merits of his own. The death of his older brother Germanicus in Syria on 10 October, 19, gave a glimmer of hope, however much of a personal blow it was. It put ideas into the heads of some of Germanicus' ardent admirers, who were now left without a leader or a patron; especially of those of them who disliked or had cause to fear his adoptive brother Drusus Caesar, now Tiberius' only natural heir. (That could be any who had transferred their allegiance to Germanicus at the death of Gaius Caesar in 4.) The question was what Tiberius would do to meet the blow to his own and Augustus' dynastic plans. There could be a substitute for Germanicus, to take his place alongside Drusus Caesar. Or Tiberius could do what Augustus had done when Nero Drusus died: advance the surviving brother and raise him to near equality with himself by granting him the token of supremacy, tribunician power, with the consulship to herald the new disposition: in 23 BC Augustus himself passed from consulship to tribunician power, and Tiberius made the same step in 7-6.

From the death of Germanicus until the end of Tiberius' reign in 37 there was political turmoil as politicians shifted their ground to put themselves behind now one, now another prospective successor. Consider the choices open to the adherents of Germanicus immediately after his death. They could continue loyal to his widow Agrippina and her young sons — but what patronage could women and children exercise, and would the boys ever come to power? They could transfer their loyalty to his brother by adoption, the Princeps' own son Drusus Caesar — that was the practical course. Or if they found him unacceptable they could try to promote Germanicus' younger brother Claudius, who was usefully committed to a marriage tie with the Prefect of the Praetorian Guard, Aelius Sejanus.

When the ashes of Germanicus reached Italy in the early spring of 20 Claudius made one of his rare public appearances in a semi-official capacity: he went to Tarracina to greet his grieving sister-in-law and took part in the interment ceremonies at Rome. There followed the trial and suicide of Gnaeus Piso, charged with poisoning Germanicus. When it was over, the senate voted thanks to the friends of the dead leader for their successful prosecution of vengeance. L.Nonius Asprenas rose to ask if it were by accident or design that the name of Claudius had been omitted from the motion. It was a probing question. Certainly, Claudius had played no public part in the conduct of the prosecution; any action of his had been behind the scenes. It is also possible to explain the fact that the text of the senatorial decree that had provided for Germanicus' closest relatives — his adoptive father and brother, Livia, Antonia, and his wife the elder Agrippina — to approve the proposed funerary honours had nothing to say of Claudius by referring to Germanicus' adoption away out of the Claudian *gens* into that of the Julii. However, the arch to be set up in Germanicus' honour in the Circus Flaminius at Rome was to have statues of the imperial family round the hero's image in his chariot: those of Germanicus' father Nero Drusus, of Tiberius Caesar, Antonia, Agrippina, his sister Livilla, of his brother Claudius and of all his sons and daughters; so Claudius finds a position here as a member of the family — a humiliating one between Germanicus' sister and children. Asprenas did not venture actually to propose the alteration of the vote of thanks, because he could not be sure how much support such a change would get, but his question showed a flag.[2]

There is no doubt as to Tiberius' plans in 20: Drusus Caesar was consul for the second time in 21, elected in the year after Germanicus' death, and took tribunician power in 22. As to the misgivings that this caused —

Drusus Caesar had a reputation for roughness — there are faint indications, coming between Germanicus' death and Drusus' appointment. They must have been felt by Germanicus' widow for her fatherless children: Tiberius, now in his sixties, might not live to give them the advancement that would ensure future dominance, for all his commending of them to the Senate. But there is no sign of anxiety from her. It came from other friends of Germanicus, and perhaps from Sejanus. It shows itself in the timid attempts to put Claudius on the political board, more clearly in a spiteful fantasy about the death of Drusus Caesar, entertained by known friends of Germanicus and Claudius.

In 21, after Drusus Caesar had vacated his portentous second consulship, there was another trial in the Senate, followed this time by execution. The victim was a silly poet, Clutorius Priscus, who had been paid by Tiberius for an elegy on the death of Germanicus and who now produced another, on the death of Drusus Caesar, who had been ill. Drusus survived, but Clutorius recited his poem all the same. He was an equestrian nobody and was made to pay for an offence that happened not to stand on the statute book by being hurried off to execution with such speed that Tiberius wrote from Campania to remonstrate. The salon in which Priscus had read his piece was in the house of P.Petronius, the suffect consul of 19 who was a long-standing boon companion of Claudius. The guests included Petronius' mother-in-law Vitellia, a member of a family that with the support of Tiberius and Germanicus had risen high in the last decade of Augustus and which was to rise even higher in the reign of Claudius and beyond. Vitellia claimed to have heard nothing, and the poet alone took the consequences. The two clans of the Vitellii and Petronii were allied to a third, that of the Plautii, and Claudius' first wife was Plautia Urgulanilla. The marriage produced offspring, a son asphyxiated in adolescence as he played at throwing up a pear and catching it in his mouth (physical agility might well preoccupy a son of Claudius). This boy was engaged at the time of his death to a daughter of the Prefect of the Guard, Sejanus of Etruscan Volsinii.[3]

These connexions reveal a little more about Claudius' position: unpromising as he was, his membership of the imperial family in itself made him a desirable match (as a woman of the family might be), and the two prospective brides he had already lost, Aemilia Lepida and Livia Medullina Camilla, were women from the most aristocratic and politically prominent families. Claudius' son likewise was a desirable match, at any rate for the equestrian Sejanus' daughter. This connexion with Sejanus is particularly significant, not because of his Etruscan origin, but because he too had reason to fear the accession of Drusus Caesar to sole power, if the quarrel between the two of them had already broken out. One grievance certainly could go back well before 20: both assisted at a fire, and quarrelled about how to deal with it. There was a fire in 15, and both Sejanus, as Prefect of the Guard, and Drusus, as consul, would have had a part to play in quelling it.[4]

The language of Suetonius suggests that it was probably this fire of 15, rather than one of the later ones of 22, 27 or 36 that gave occasion for members of the senate to demonstrate their affection for Claudius, the obscure ruler in waiting — or their discontent with one of the designated heirs: they proposed that his house, which had been destroyed, should be restored at public expense (a nice touch if Drusus' negligence could be held responsible for the damage). Another proposal seems to be coupled with this, and it too favours the year 15: it was that Claudius should speak in the House amongst senators of consular rank. This would have been an improvement on the *ornamenta consularia* and so perhaps a criticism of it; the proposal, without Claudius having had to pass through the same steps and stages as Germanicus, would have put him into some relation with Drusus, consul that year. Tiberius declined both proposals, for the second invoking Claudius' infirmities and making the first redundant by paying for the restoration himself. There was probably more to his exclusion of Claudius, then, than devotion to the injunctions of Augustus; having accorded a prime position in the succession to Germanicus, who left Tiberius' natural son Drusus Caesar much to do in the way of acquiring distinction and popularity, Tiberius was disinclined to make concessions to Germanicus' incapable younger brother.[5]

It seems, then, that signs of the senate's regard given in 15 were followed up between 19 and 21 with efforts to bring forward Claudius as a claimant to the succession, at least alongside Drusus Caesar. It is at latest to the period before Drusus' second consulship in 21 that the comment ascribed to Claudius' sister Livilla must belong: hearing it foretold that Claudius would come to power, she pitied the Roman people if they were ever to have him as an emperor. The unsisterly remark is easily understood: Livilla was married to Drusus, and her children's prospects depended on his.[6]

These tentative efforts on Claudius' behalf came to nothing, and even when Drusus Caesar died in 23 it brought no advantage. Tiberius was looking to the next generation, to Germanicus' sons Nero and Drusus Caesars, who were not yet out of their teens. But that allowed scope for ambitious intruders of the generation between, and Sejanus, now presenting himself to Drusus Caesar's widow as the champion of the rights of her surviving twin son Tiberius Gemellus, born in 19, himself came to aim for supremacy in one form or another. By about 27, when Sejanus' power made it necessary for the friends of Germanicus' family to show discretion, Claudius had divorced Urgulanilla on the grounds of adultery and, more sensationally, suspicion of murder. Whom could she have killed? Perhaps a slave, but other deaths are known: apart from that of her son, for which the general term '*homicidium*' would hardly have been used, there was the sensational defenestration or fatal tumble downstairs of her brother's wife during his praetorship in 24. Tiberius himself investigated at the scene of the crime, the accused husband pleading that he had been bewitched by a former wife. If Urgulanilla was jealous of her new sister-in-law she would have had a motive for helping to push her out of the window, and if she was suspected of complicity if would have been good grounds for divorce; provisionally then I would put the divorce in 24.[7]

Claudius' next wife, Aelia Paetina, acquired at least by 28, since their daughter Antonia was married in 41, was a distant kinswoman of Sejanus. Family loyalty would have counted for more than these marriage connexions with the upstart Sejanus, however, and Claudius's loyalty to the memory of his brother and to Germanicus' family has never been questioned. His only recourse during the period between Drusus Caesar's death and the fall of Sejanus in October of 31 was to lie low. That fall was probably brought about by Gaius Caesar, the future emperor, and a small group of courtiers who benefited from it, one by promotion to Sejanus' post, others by enhanced influence with Tiberius, now a recluse on Capri. Tiberius learnt through them of Sejanus' machinations against Germanicus' widow Agrippina and their elder sons, Nero and Drusus Caesars. Of any part played in this coup by Claudius, not a trace. He is found only in a formal role, carrying to the consuls the congratulations of the equestrian order on the suppression of the traitor.[8]

Enforced seclusion and this series of small reverses kept Claudius at his other occupations. Work on the Roman History would have continued, but there were less intellectual activities: the arena (only to watch), womanizing, gourmandizing, heavy drinking and obsessive gambling. He was not the only discontented politician to indulge in them, but addiction to gambling suggests counsels of despair: Claudius believed that with everything else against him he might be favoured by luck or that he was clever enough to beat a system — in fact he wrote a book on the subject. Drinking gave release from the tensions of court life, best indulged in trustworthy company. Tiberius too had been a drinker, notorious for it in his younger days, but Claudius continued to be carried out helpless from banquets until the last night of his life.[9]

When Gaius Caesar (Caligula) came to power on Tiberius' death on 16 March, 37, Claudius' political position apparently improved. Gaius initially needed Claudius in a way Tiberius had not. He was an inexperienced young man of 24; he had held only one magistracy and had had no dealings with the army, and his position rested, legally on the provision made for him in Tiberius' will, effectively on the popularity of his father Germanicus and his mother the elder Agrippina, who had died in exile in 33, and through whom Gaius was the great-grandson of Augustus. He buttressed his claim to the Principate by repudiating everything that had made Tiberius so much disliked. The ashes of Agrippina and of Gaius' oldest brother Nero Caesar, who had also died in exile, were brought home by Gaius personally for solemn interment as one of his first acts, and his elder brothers' portraits featured on coins. The survivor, Claudius, was rescued from the political limbo to which Tiberius had consigned him (Augustus' part could have been forgotten). He became Gaius' colleague in the consulship held from

1 July until 31 August, 37, and Suetonius claims that he was promised a second term in four years' time.[10]

Taking office at last, at the age of nearly forty-six, Claudius left the equestrian order, of which he had been the most socially illustrious member all his adult life. Three times, beginning in 14, when he conveyed their plea to carry the body of Augustus into Rome, had Claudius represented the views or requests of the order to Princeps or consuls, the congratulations they offered to Gaius on his accession being the last message he conveyed for them. But the consulship would not have ended the relationship created by his activity as representative of the order. Claudius was not a new man of equestrian stock, like Marius or Cicero, but like them he was a politician who more than others needed support wherever he could find it. A trace of the respect he had earned may be seen from a document from Alexandria Troas in Asia. An equestrian officer from the colony, active in the decade before Claudius' accession, ordered in his will that a monument be erected in Claudius' honour.[11]

Previously the nephew of an Emperor, Claudius was now the uncle. That made him a man of the past, with rank now, but little more power. He was popular with the people, who would greet him affectionately as the Emperor's uncle and Germanicus' brother when he appeared at shows in the imperial box, representing the absent Gaius; but great courtiers or senators would not see him as someone to cultivate. Claudius was known as a decent man of culture and learning, but those qualities, essential though they were for a Roman in office, were nothing without decorum.[12]

The new Princeps was soon taking Claudius for a joke, an embarrassment, or a subject for bullying, threatening him with loss of his consulship for slowness in putting up statues of Nero and Drusus Caesars and as he grew more confident in the exercise of sole power he showed his opinions ever more clearly. Once again, in the autumn of 39, Claudius was sent on a happy mission, this time of senators, delegated to congratulate Gaius on his suppression of an alleged conspiracy. Cn. Lentulus Gaetulicus (cos. 26), commander of the upper Rhine army for ten years, was the man whose name appears in the records of the Arval Brethren, but members of the imperial family were implicated: Gaius' sisters Julia Livilla and Agrippina went into exile, and the husband of his dead sister Drusilla, M.Lepidus, who had had prospects of becoming his heir, was killed.[13]

There has been scepticism about the conspiracy of 39, but Gaius' fear and anger seemed real. He was as unlucky as Henry VIII in his marriages: his first wife died in childbirth and he went on to two other ladies, both soon divorced. Before he committed himself to the fourth, Milonia Caesonia, she was eight months pregnant by him, and the marriage was announced on the day of his daughter Julia Drusilla's birth, in the last months of 39 or the opening of 40. Caesonia is said to have had three daughters by a previous husband, but Gaius might now hope for an heir of his own body. Since the death of his sister Drusilla in mid-38 M.Lepidus' prospects of being brought into the succession had grown dimmer and the imminent birth of a child put even Gaius' sisters in the shade. Efforts to reassert their power may have determined him to clear them out of the way.[14]

Gaius was suspicious of the senate in any case and after the conspiracy of Gaetulicus forbade it to offer further honours to his relatives; nor were all the members of the delegation received when they arrived on the Rhine to congratulate him on checking the plot. It may have been to placate Gaius, or out of malice, to embroil the imperial family still further, that Claudius was appointed to the delegation, and one story (not credible, and Suetonius did not credit it) had him actually thrown into the river when he arrived. This was a fantasy on Gallic themes: unsuccessful performers at the literary contests for Gauls held annually at Lugdunum were thrown into the Rhone; it would be amusing for Gaius to have made a similar 'sacrifice' of his Lugdunensian uncle.[15]

Suetonius notices that after 39 Claudius was asked his opinion last of all the consulars. We cannot exclude a desire to humiliate Claudius as the motive, but it is not the only interpretation. In the first years of his principate Tiberius had found himself in difficulties over his place in the voting order: senators wished to know that the Princeps' view was, so that they could follow it. Concern for senatorial independence made him too slow in letting his views be known and in 15 a friend warned him to disclose salutary views early in the proceedings; in 20 Drusus Caesar, who as consul designate should have given his vote first, was relieved of this duty at Cn. Piso's trial. Gaius by remaining silent and preventing his uncle from disclosing the palace's view of senatorial motions came to know the minds of senators.[16]

Gaius' verbal reaction to Claudius' appearance on the Rhine in 39, that he was not a child to have his uncle sent to him, has been invoked to support the view that Claudius was taken seriously at Gaius' court as a man to give advice, by the Emperor himself and by courtiers. That would be wide of the mark. Gaius' own attitude may have wavered or developed; a court is subject to faction; and even personal likes and dislikes must be taken into account, as well as the points of view of participants, contemporary reporters, and later historians. They may have reported Claudius' discomforts with glee, but they were real, included physical violence, and increased after the Gaetulicus affair and the disgrace of his nieces. He was the Princeps' closest relative, but received no more than his original consulship and remained without experience. A sober estimate of his position would not have held his prospects bright, whether Gaius lived or died.[17]

One reason for the contempt in which Claudius was held was that he had never been well-off; Augustus noticed that he had only a few cronies for company at dinner. What he possessed, which included some gardens, an establishment in Rome, a house outside the city, and a Campanian villa, must have come from his share of Nero Drusus' property: he gained only modest legacies from imperial wills (eight hundred thousand HS from Augustus, two from Tiberius), while that of his grandmother Livia (she had died in 29) was not put into effect until he came to power. What became of his mother Antonia's property when she died in 37 remains unclear; her slaves are found in Claudius' ownership when he was Emperor; their fate before 41 is uncertain. He probably received a substantial share of her fortune. But enforced entry into yet another priesthood, that of Gaius himself in 40, mulcted Claudius of eight or even ten million HS, the sum that a man must possess to be a senator. This he had to borrow and, being unable to meet his obligations, had to sell property. It may have been in connexion with this case that a Treasury clerk made an unreasonable attack on him which Claudius requited when he became Princeps by relegating the man; but it may have been part of a scandal in which Claudius was also involved — apparently quite innocently — as a witness to a forged will.[18]

Gaius' 'cult' was partly a means of making money while having fun: some of the wealthiest men in Rome were made priests besides Claudius. More dangerous was Claudius' prosecution on a capital charge by his own slave Pollux, allegedly at Gaius' instigation. That is likely to have been a political matter. But the story that Gaius followed this failure with a series of attempts to get his own freedman, C. Julius Callistus, to poison Claudius, while Callistus kept on putting off the murder with one excuse after another, is rightly rejected by Josephus: Gaius would not have tolerated repeated failure. Josephus' view was that Callistus invented the story to ingratiate himself with Claudius. There is no reason to suppose that Claudius was any more credulous than Josephus. The accusations against Gaius may only have come later to provide both Claudius and Callistus with a plea of self-defence if they were connected with the assassination. But the financial and legal attacks on Claudius do show that he was coming to be seen as a man who could be harassed with impunity. If there was a threat to him, it was not because he was a man to take account of in his own right: a relative, even an incompetent, might seem a distasteful rival to Gaius.[19]

When he came to power in 41 Claudius stressed the weakness of his position under Tiberius and Gaius in a way that conveniently also made away alike with his own observed failings and with the court's discourtesy: he claimed in a series of short speeches to have pretended to be a fool to save himself. As J. Mottershead has suggested, Claudius probably compared himself with Junius Brutus who expelled the Tarquins. The comparison was doubly apt, because it should also have given the Senate much-needed reassurance about its new Princeps.[20]

Increasingly since 9 BC the court had been becoming a dangerous place. A lesson was forced on Claudius, consciously or unconsciously absorbed: his own weakness, being out of things and knowing nothing, was a protection; servants and others even more vulnerable than himself were willing to act for him in return for what protection he could offer. The defence, originally learned in precisely the years (AD 4–9) in which he realised that he was to be kept out of public life, had to be practised for eighteen years before his accession. But defences learned in adolescence do not always prove adequate for maturity.

# 4

# ACCESSION

Gaius Caligula spent nearly four years exploring what it meant to be Princeps and the limits of what he could do as Princeps. He became hated and feared. Italy and Rome suffered most from his autocratic ways, but in the provinces he mulcted wealthy Gauls of cash and outraged Jewish monotheists with claims to divine honours. He achieved no success in the field: the Parthians were checked by L.Vitellius before Tiberius died in 37, the submission of the British chieftains in 39 was nominal, and the training campaigns he ordered east of the Rhine after the fall of Lentulus Gaetulicus perhaps restored morale, but brought no booty. The political classes, after the brief respite of the honeymoon period, found his régime no improvement on that of Tiberius during his long absence from Rome, and property owners were having to finance his experiments in government (there were demonstrations against his tax demands during the circus games of January, 41). Gaius even antagonized the officers of the Praetorian Guard, by inflicting cruel duties and personal humiliation on them. Finally, his attacks on members of his own family, his two sisters Agrippina and Livilla, and his brother-in-law M. Lepidus, whom he had treated as a prospective successor, discredited the imperial family, damaged his relations with the people, and made him vulnerable to assassins, especially since, like Julius Caesar, he lacked a son of mature years. Gaius' assassination was on the cards from the autumn of 39 onwards, became a subject of speculation, and was achieved on 24 January, 41. The conspirators let slip opportunities for the murder, perhaps because they could not agree about what was to follow it, but finally agreed on the last day of the games in honour of Augustus that Livia had established on the Palatine. Gaius had not forgotten that he was Mark Antony's great-grandson, and was planning a visit to Egypt, where he could expect an enthusiastic reception from the Greek population. This would have caused alarm to senate and commons, who were equally interested in the primacy of Rome and Italy.[1]

With a dilatoriness maddening to the conspirators Gaius left the Palatine theatre for lunchtime refreshment, passing by way of a narrow passage where he was cut down by officers of the Praetorian Guard under the tribune Cassius Chaerea. His personal bodyguard of Germans began to run amok at the scene and killed three senators, including an Asprenas, probably P.Nonius Asprenas (*cos.* 38), and a Norbanus even more distinguished and senior, if he was L.Norbanus Balbus (*cos.* 19).[2] Praetorian guardsmen under the tribune Julius Lupus invaded the Palace, found Gaius' wife Caesonia

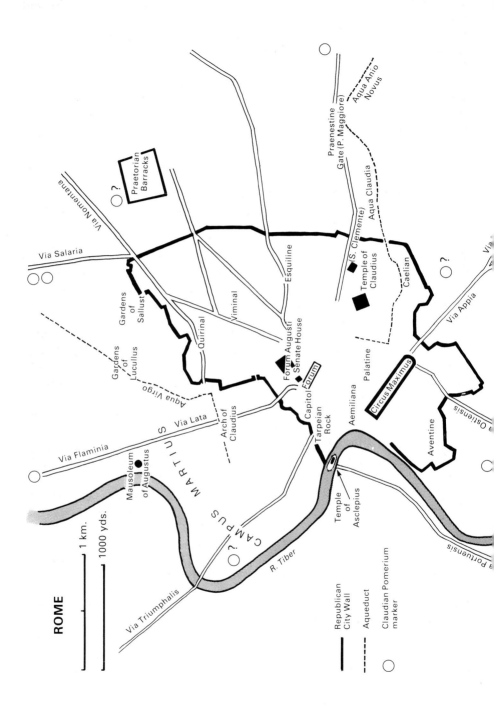

ROME

1 km.

1000 yds.

Via Triumphalis

Via Flaminia

Mausoleum of Augustus

Via Lata

Arch of Claudius

Aqua Virgo

CAMPUS MARTIUS

?

R. Tiber

Temple of Asclepius

Via Ostiensis

Via Portuensis

Gardens of Lucullus

Gardens of Sallust

Via Salaria

Via Nomentana

?

Praetorian Barracks

Quirinal

Viminal

Esquiline

Forum Augusti

Senate House

Forum

Capitol

Tarpeian Rock

Aemiliana

Palatine

Circus Maximus

Aventine

Caelian

Temple of Claudius

(S. Clemente)

Aqua Claudia

Praenestine Gate (P. Maggiore)

Aqua Anio Novus

?

Via Appia

Via

Republican City Wall

Aqueduct

Claudian Pomerium marker

?

and her child and killed them. Claudius, who had also left the theatre and reached the Palace, took refuge in a room called the Hermaeum, and then on a balcony, where he was found by a guardsman with the appropriate name of Gratus ('grateful'), saluted *imperator*, and taken in a litter to the barracks abutting the city wall at the Viminal gate.

The senate meanwhile was meeting, not in the Curia Julia of hated name, but on the defensible Capitol under the presidency of the consuls Cn. Sentius Saturninus and Q.Pomponius Secundus. No male Julii Caesares survived, and some senators were resolved, after the bitter disappointments of 37-41, on bringing the Principate to an end, even by exterminating the remaining members of the family. Others, having already accepted the Principate as an inevitable necessity, were content, according to Josephus' earlier account, to be able to elect Gaius' successor. Saturninus, though his speech has been worked up by Josephus' source, spoke for 'liberty' and the rule of law. That might mean either alternative. He knew that Claudius had reached the praetorian barracks and that the nine Praetorian Cohorts were not backing the senate. They did have the three Urban Cohorts, 1500 men, at their disposal under the Prefect of the City, the excellent L.Volusius Saturninus (suff. 3). They also controlled the funds of the State and Military Treasuries, which had been conveyed to the Capitol and put under guard. In the Forum the people, a mob angry and frightened at the loss of their ruler, were being harangued, even browbeaten, by Valerius Asiaticus (*suff. 35*), who boldly claimed to wish he had been involved in the assassination himself, thus proclaiming his innocence. Twenty-seven years had passed since the people had played a real part in electing even magistrates; there was no reason to expect unified action from that quarter.[3]

Two tribunes, Q. Veranius and a man called (probably Sertorius) Brocchus, were sent to warn Claudius against attempting a violent coup, to lecture him on obedience to the senate, and according to Suetonius to request his presence so that he could put his point of view. It was a miserable deputation, but the senior magistrates were probably fully engaged and not to be risked as potential hostages, and tribunes' persons were sacrosanct. The invitation seems to imply that belonging to the family of the Claudii Nerones gave him no claim on the Principate. Whether that would save his life once he had entered the House was another matter. Claudius sent back a diplomatic answer: he was forcibly detained in the barracks and not free to attend. The tribunes, already well disposed or intimidated by the forces behind him, seem to have made a vital concession on their own account — and on their knees — that he should at least accept the Principate from the hands of his peers.[4]

Before dawn on the 25th another meeting of the senate was summoned, but not more than 100 members were present, the most strong-minded of a putative 600. In the face of Claudius' intransigence and the wavering loyalty of the Urban Cohorts, discussion veered from any possibility of a return of the Republic to the sole question of which senator to elect to the vacant Principate. If the Urban Cohorts were to be pitted against the Praetorians they would expected tangible gratitude, and individuals were thought more reliable in that respect; even the Praetorians might be won over if a suitable candidate were presented.[5]

There were several candidates. M.Vinicius, (cos. 30), brother-in-law of Gaius, put himself forward, but was blocked by the consuls, who are said to have realized that their game was over. The rich upstart from Vienna (Vienne) in Narbonese Gaul, Valerius Asiaticus, put forward a claim that must have seemed out of place to senators of older lineage, though his wife was the sister of a former wife of Gaius, the wealthy Lollia Paullina. It was naturally resisted by M.Vinicius' kinsman, perhaps a nephew, L. Annius Vinicianus. According to Dio, Vinicianus too was one of those who had been proposed.[6]

These were in Rome. But another candidate said to have been mooted was Gaetulicus' successor in command of the Upper Rhine legions, the blue-blooded Ser. Sulpicius Galba (cos. 33). If Galba's friends did urge him to seize power it was a week after Claudius had already taken control, because of the ten days it must have taken for the news of Gaius' assassination — and requests for support from consuls and senate — to reach him. Dispatches from the new Emperor containing his promises of a donative would have arrived the following day, and the troops would have wanted to know the contents. It would have been surprising if all the officers on Galba's staff could have been trusted to cooperate in suppressing news of the promises. It has been suggested that A.Plautius (suff. 29), governor of Pannonia, also received messages as well as Galba. They will have reached him several days earlier, and his initiative in accepting the settlement between Claudius and the senate reached on 25 January, though not surprising, given the longstanding connexion between Claudius and his family, will have been particularly welcome to the new Princeps: in a moment of despair during the Pannonian Revolt of 6-9, Augustus had broadcast the fact that rebels from that province could be at Rome in ten days. More: Plautius' army (two legions) and that of the legate of Dalmatia (another two) must unite or clash if the distinguished L.Arruntius Camillus Scribonianus (cos. 32) made the move that Dio thinks was even then expected of him. The same was true of P.Memmius Regulus (suff. 31), who had controlled the vast regions of Moesia, Macedonia, and Achaea, with two legions, since 35; but he was further distant, and was a new man with a compliant temperament.[7]

None of these men could have intervened before the first round of the game had been played out in Rome. According to Josephus it was when the senate's envoys left that Claudius paraded the Praetorian Guard, was saluted *imperator*, secured their oath of loyalty, and so their pledge of armed support, and promised them a donative of 15,000 or 20,000 sesterces each, with *pro rata* gratuities to officers and legionaries, an enormous sum also intended to shake the loyalty of the Urban Cohorts to the senate by arousing their jealousy. Certainly at their next meeting, before dawn on the 25th, the senators found themselves surrounded by a crowd of soldiers demanding the elevation of a single man as Princeps — Claudius. Suetonius puts the parade of the Praetorian Guard on the the 25th, which could also be before the second meeting of the senate, but he implies that its growing weakness was a factor in Claudius' acceptance of power from the Guard. Whatever the timing of the parade, Claudius in any case can hardly have passed the night in the barracks without giving some intimation of a reward to his supporters; the parade was only the formal culmination of a developing understanding between Claudius and the troops.[8]

The Praetorians did not have only donatives in mind: they were concerned for the very survival of their corps if the Principate as they knew it came to an end. Claudius must know as well as his predecessors what was due to a loyal Praetorian Guard. And whatever his weaknesses as a candidate, this was the son of Nero Drusus, the brother of Germanicus, the uncle of their late Emperor, and so linked, though in ways that might be difficult for the man in the street to specify, with the founder of the dynasty, Augustus. True, Claudius was not a natural heir of Gaius, but he was a kinsman, and a kinsman of Gaius' predecessor.[9]

The messages conveyed by the tribunes between the senate and Claudius may not have been the only ones that passed, whatever the role played by the Jewish King Agrippa of Judaea. Claudius' tone remained unyielding but conciliatory. The gist of his case was that he had not sought power, but would not go back on an offer he had accepted; that the senate had nothing to fear from a man who had witnessed the fatal results of tyrannical behaviour; and that his administration would have a place for all. He promised just rule if he were accepted, vengeance if he were not. Faced with this firm stance, and with their own inability to agree on a rival candidate to command the support of the deserting Urban Cohorts, they gave way. Claudius returned, escorted by his Praetorians, from the barracks to the Palatine and summoned the senate there. The next significant decrees passed by the House were those putting in motion the conferment on Claudius of all the vital powers and privileges of Augustus, Tiberius and Gaius.[10]

Such were the complex events of 24–5 January, as far as they can be established. There are three main problems that make it hard to interpret them. First, the main authorities, Josephus, Suetonius and Dio, who ultimately depend on sources oral or written that were put together close to the events — and so more or less partisan — and later reworked, diverge on details and have their own interpretations to offer. Suetonius is intent on the paradoxical rise of a fool, Josephus, writing in the *Antiquities* to enhance the role of Agrippa I, presents Claudius as panic-stricken and incapable. There must have been an official version, put out during the reign of Claudius, but few traces remain. Its main features will have been Claudius' withdrawal to the Palace after the assassination, the unexpected arrival of the Praetorians, their spontaneous salutation of the reluctant

Claudius, and their demand that he should go with them to the barracks where, still reluctant, he was formally acclaimed and committed to his unsought position.[11]

Second, the assassination and what was intended to follow were planned in secret, and, quite apart from the intervention of the German bodyguard immediately after Gaius' death, did not go according to plan, or at least not according to the plans of all the conspirators.

Third, the aims of the plotters themselves diverged; like the Catilinarian conspiracy of 63 BC, the plot was a confederation, and members had in common only the wish to be rid of Gaius. Once that had been achieved, each group intended to pursue its own aims independently or in collaboration with those whose interests coincided most closely with its own. Josephus distinguishes three actual plots: one led by an Aemilius Regulus of Corduba, another by Cassius Chaerea, and a third by L. Annius Vinicianus. Regulus is otherwise unknown, although his city of origin links him with Seneca and so with Gaius' disgraced sisters Livilla and Agrippina. A group of leading senators involved in the plot was led by Vinicianus, who had also been a friend of the disgraced Lepidus. Josephus implicates Asprenas, the senator who urged Gaius to leave the theatre and who was one of the three killed in encounters with the Germans, who were attacking guilty and innocent alike. The story that Asprenas' clothing had been spattered with blood from the morning's sacrifice to Augustus may have been devised to suggest his innocence: it was a bad omen, and explains why the Germans believed him guilty. Norbanus appears as an innocent victim, while Anteius was caught gloating over the body of Gaius, who had first exiled and then executed his father. Josephus does not accuse him of being involved, and he does not name any other guilty senators. The reason for the shortage may be the amnesty for senators that followed the assassination. Claudius did all he could to put the events of 24-5 January out of people's minds. Vinicianus, who joined the conspiracy against Claudius in 42, could be named openly.[12]

It was officers of the Praetorian Guard, led by Cassius Chaerea, who were the active wing of the conspiracy and who paid for it. Chaerea brought in other officers: Cornelius Sabinus and Julius Lupus, Papinius, the man called Aquila who gave Gaius the *coup de grâce*, and one or both of the Prefects. Lupus was a kinsman of one of the Prefects, M.Arrecinus Clemens.[13]

Powerful freedmen of Gaius were said to be implicated in these plots, although the only one specified is Callistus. Fear for his wealth is the reason given; a better explanation is that he saw Gaius as a danger to himself and likely to fall victim to a conspiracy, and prepared for the future. For him that must be by preparing for a new master in the family: Claudius. Whether the physician Alcyon, an expert in treating wounds (and so perhaps employed by the Guard) who was in the Palatine theatre and got some of the spectators away to safety, was implicated is uncertain; he was relegated to Gaul by Claudius (charge unknown), then recalled to make another fortune.[14]

The hypothesis to be adopted here is that the initiative came from Chaerea and his fellow-officers; was accepted by Vinicianus and other senators who meant to turn the outcome to the advantage of their order (or of some individual member); and was exploited while the senate hesitated under consuls who had divided loyalties by a third group acting in the interests of Claudius; these last included Callistus and, unless they were very lucky when Gratus and his fellow Guardsmen allegedly stumbled on Claudius, someone who could control at least a substantial sector of the Praetorian Guard and get Claudius to the barracks. Whether Gratus was actively looking for Claudius depends on whether the troops had conferred amongst themselves, or had received instructions before the Palace was ransacked, and on that the sources are divided. But Gratus would have been taking much on himself by offering the salutation of his own accord.

Circumstantial evidence suggests Claudius' complicity. First, according to Josephus, Claudius was afraid of the guardsmen because of Gaius' murder — which amused Gratus; if Claudius were involved he had to fear not only the Germans and extremist republicans but Guardsmen loyal to Gaius' memory. So Claudius' apparent panic at the time, if genuine, does not preclude knowledge of what had been planned. The German bodyguard alone were enough to terrify an accomplice who had seen the heads of Asprenas and other victims in the hands of their killers. Second, three men apart from Chaerea and Vinicianus are said to have left the theatre just before Gaius' assassination, that is, before Gaius himself rose for lunch. This would be an act of surprising discourtesy, but it should have enabled them to get clean away and be free to act in the aftermath. The three were M. Vinicius, Valerius Asiaticus, and Claudius himself.[15]

Claudius was in grave danger on 24 January, from extremists in the senate and the officers of the Praetorian Guard who had killed Caesonia and her child. Claudius was not responsible for their deaths. He gained only very marginally from them, and if he had been responsible, he would hardly have raised Caesonia's half-brother Domitius Corbulo to command of the Rhine legions. When Claudius had the Praetorian officers executed, he claimed that it was because they had intended to kill him as well as Gaius; this could have been a pretext intended to satisfy the need for vengeance while more exalted conspirators were let off, but it may have been true: extremist officers were committed to wiping out the entire family.[16]

Senators who aimed at a return to republican government could not afford Claudius' survival; nor could any rival candidate. Even after he was safely in the barracks, if Josephus is to be trusted, the senate 'declared war' on Claudius, which must mean that they declared him a *hostis* or public enemy. That put him into the same category as Catiline after he had left Rome in 63 BC, or Mark Antony after the battle of Actium in 31 BC (only a man outside the city walls made a plausible *hostis*). In the *Apocolocyntosis* Seneca jibes that Claudius did what a Gaul must be expected to do: he captured Rome.[17]

The murder of Caesonia and the 'declaration of war' show that Claudius like Callistus had been in danger ever since Gaius' assassination had become a likelihood. But Claudius was not safe in Gaius' court either, so that it is reasonable to ask if he did not seek, again like Callistus, to anticipate an uncontrolled assassination that would lead to his own death by one that he could control and which would put him in the power that he had long sought to share. Claudius executed Cassius Chaerea, Julius Lupus and a few other officers not named (Cornelius Sabinus, who perhaps had not been involved in the attempt to commit the Prefect of the Guard to the destruction of the entire dynasty, was spared life and post, but loyally killed himself). That does not prove Claudius' innocence. They were probably paying for having acted as the unwitting agents of the men who had taken over. It would not be the last time that an officer instrumental in conferring power on an Emperor died in disgrace: Casperius Aelianus, Prefect in 97, allowed his men to riot against Nerva and force him to adopt the commander of the Upper Rhine army, Trajan, as his successor and partner in power. On Nerva's death Aelianus was summoned to the new Emperor and executed; even the fact that he had once served under Trajan's father won him no mercy.[18]

It is time to look for Claudius' supporters. Josephus' claim that only Callistus foresaw the outcome of the assassination is designed to put the role of Claudius' friend Agrippa into a more brilliant light as Claudius' sole ally. Agrippa is even credited with deterring the panicky Claudius from a massacre of the senate. But even in the senate there must have been many who like the two tribunes Veranius and Brocchus were realistic enough to understand that once Claudius had been received into the barracks he would become Princeps. Some senators may even have been sympathetic towards Claudius beforehand. The Asprenas murdered by the German bodyguard is likely to have been an active participant in the conspiracy, and in Claudius' interest. If Asprenas was the consul of 38, he was the son of the L. Nonius Asprenas who had enquired in 20 whether Claudius was to be included in the vote of thanks offered to the vindicators of Germanicus. Claudius tried to avenge the victims of the Germans by allowing the Thracian officer Sabinus who had been in command of them to be killed in a gladiatorial show. Later he raised the Nonii to high social distinction, the patriciate.[19]

The ranks of Claudius' partisans may have attracted men who had been protégés of Germanicus, or whose parents had. Continued loyalty to the family would give them the best prospects of future advancement. Anteius, another victim of the Germans, may be taken to represent this group. He is otherwise unknown, but an 'Antius' was on the staff of Germanicus in 16 and P. Anteius Rufus, clearly a relative, is found ten years after the assassination in charge of a key province, Dalmatia, as consular legate of the Emperor. Appointed in the year after Claudius' death to the prime command in the east, that of Syria, he was prevented from taking it up and fell foul of Nero because of his ties with the Emperor's hated mother Agrippina; he was forced to suicide in 66. Evidently the cruelty of Gaius was not sufficient to damage his loyalty to Germanicus' brother and daughter.[20]

Not all senators friendly to Claudius need have been in the conspiracy: the plebeian tribune Veranius, for example. Both the junior posts he held under Gaius gave proof of high social standing and political favour. Veranius must have owed them to his father's connexion with Germanicus: the elder Q.Veranius had annexed Cappadocia as Germanicus' legate and two years later in 20 had taken part in the prosecution of Cn. Piso; early in life he may even have been on the staff of Nero Drusus in Germany. By chance or design, the senate in 41 sent Claudius a man he would find acceptable as a negotiator. Perhaps it was Veranius who as praetor in the very next year was one of those who loyally celebrated the anniversary of Claudius' accession, and the first birthday of Claudius' son. In 43 Veranius was sent to make Lycia provincial territory and to act as its first governor, a responsible, even dangerous job in a disturbed area, comparable with what his father had done as Germanicus' legate. Elevation to the patriciate followed, and the consulship of 49; Veranius was ultimately sent to continue the conquest of Britain, where he died, still in high favour, in 57.[21]

Still other senators must have inclined to be loyal to the dynasty in 41, either genuinely so or out of political realism: all the men who had benefited under Gaius and who must lose by the 'return to a republic' that would end in another usurping supreme power must look to Claudius as their hope of uninterrupted advancement, as Claudius proved King Agrippa's best hope for the enlargement of his kingdom. Other members of these three overlapping groups — personal sympathizers, connexions of Germanicus, and those who had done well under Gaius — played no known part in the events of 41, but their good will as Claudius perceived it may be gauged from the success they went on to win; obvious names, besides that of the Plautii, are those of the Petronii and Vitellii and their dependents the Flavii.

In 41 muscle and fire-power were required to bring Claudius to the Principate; one influential freedman and some sympathetic senators were not enough. A split between the two Prefects of the Praetorian Guard has been detected from the way that the Prefects are handled by the sources: one, Arrecinus Clemens, glorified, the other anonymous. Gaius had already tried to set them at loggerheads, and there were differences in the outcome in 41. One prefect was evidently unacceptable to Claudius: he was cashiered and replaced by Rufrius Pollio even before the senate had accepted Claudius as Princeps. It must have been the other who ordered Claudius to be conveyed to the barracks. The choice of H.Jung for this role was the prefect whose name we do not know; M.Arrecinus Clemens he regards as attached to the group of L.Vinicianus and the junior officers Cassius Chaerea, Cornelius Sabinus, and Julius Lupus, who killed Milonia Caesonia and her child, implicating his relative Clemens (which according to Josephus was

37

precisely why he was assigned to the task). But the brilliant picture of Clemens may be a tribute to his son's success as a senator under Vespasian and Domitian, when he held two suffect consulships. Chaerea did not trust Clemens to keep his mouth shut, and it is Clemens who is best seen as acting in Claudius' interests, the other prefect with Chaerea and the senators. The opportunist Flavius Vespasian betrothed his son Titus, who was born in 39, to one of Arrecinus Clemens' daughters (the marriage took place in the sixties), and perhaps his elder brother Flavius Sabinus did likewise. If Clemens disappears from the record soon after Claudius' accession it must be remembered that he was already advanced in years and may simply have died.[22]

There is a spectrum of possibilities for the degree of Claudius' involvement in the attack on Gaius. They range from leading a group of his own into a coalition with other plotters, to acquiescence in a plan already devised by one group or another or by a coalition (practically the entire court and senate seem to have known that there was a plot). As we have seen, Claudius most probably led or was carried to power by a section of the conspiracy that gained control of events by exploiting the Praetorian Guard; the question is how active a part he took. At first sight all the evidence suggests a very passive role. At no other crisis either does Claudius show decision or courage in action. The picture is consistent, but so might a fiction be, hostile writers preferring to present him as a fool than as an assassin (which would have damaged the claims of his heir and successor Nero). But Claudius' outsider's position at court forced him to rely on inferiors for knowledge of what was going on, and on the other hand conspicuous rank made it difficult for him to enter direct negotiations. His precise role cannot be determined. Very likely it was kept indeterminate, his agents having to interpret or anticipate his wishes.[23]

The technique, disreputable, essentially infantile, but useful and adopted by others — by Henry II and Elizabeth I in England against internal threats (1170 and 1587) and by Reagan in the U.S.A. against Iran and Nicaragua — is that of allowing others to act or engineering them into it, while the principal continues 'ignorant' of what is going on. Thus servants or subordinates have to take responsibility, eschewing the defence of superior orders. A faint echo of the technique can be heard even in Claudius' letter to the Alexandrians: he had been declining the statue of the Claudian Augustan Peace that they offered him, because it seemed too arrogant to accept — but on the insistent urging of his most honoured friend Barbillus it would be set up at Rome. Seneca makes Augustus denounce it roundly in connexion with the death of Messallina: not knowing one has killed is worse than killing.[24]

One may guess, then, that friends whose interests were threatened by Gaius' behaviour or by his impending assassination put the facts to Claudius, pointing out that the alternatives were the Principate if he allowed them to act on his behalf, death if the Republic were restored or a rival were successful. Callistus was at the centre of this group, M.Arrecinus Clemens was vital to it, and its senatorial members probably included P.Nonius Asprenas and Anteius. Claudius let it be understood that they should act in the best interests of all.

The fact that all senatorial conspirators were let off gave Claudius the chance to proclaim his own forebearance with the coin legend commemorating the lives of Roman citizens saved: OB CIVES SERVATOS. It also muffled whispers about Claudius' own involvement — and left him with a free hand to deal with future offences: implication in the murder compounded with ungratefulness for clemency.[25]

It was a month after the assassination before Claudius entered the senate and then it was with a bodyguard (in 63 and 62 BC Julius Caesar had similarly refrained from attending when he was in bad odour with the *patres*). There was an even clearer point of resemblance. The historian Claudius must have compared his own coup and Caesar's: both owed ascendancy to sudden and naked use of the army. These two accessions to power were very different from Octavian's: he could claim to be defending the west against an aggressive oriental monarch and her minion. Tiberius' too was more reputable: investment with recognized power by senate and people, over a period lasting more than a decade. Claudius did not have even Gaius' single-minded acclamation from Guard, senate, and people. He owed his accession to the Praetorians and — reluctant as he had been to accept! — he did not have to hide it. Claudius' debt to the Praetorian Guard was advertised on gold and silver coinage dated 41-2. One design, with IMPERATOR RECEPT(us), has a view of the barrack gate and a figure holding a military standard in front of it. Another, with PRAETOR(iani) RECEPT(i), shows a guardsman shaking hands with the Emperor. Both are thought to commemorate the mutual trust of Emperor and Guard. Probably these issues were used to pay the actual donative; but the designs were struck again and again.[26]

# 5

# FROM PRINCEPS TO EMPEROR

'Claudius was the first Roman Emperor'. That was the unpublished and convincing doctrine of C.E. Stevens, innocently anticipated by the Gauls who dedicated a fountain at Lugdunum to Jupiter 'because Claudius is *imperator*'. Augustus had made a position, a bundle of powers collected at different times, cemented by the authority of success, and reinforced by the ultimate sanction of force, and he had changed it more than once. Tiberius, receiving the powers likewise at widely separated intervals, and with his minimalist interpretation of his position, had begun by acting as if he were still a private individual who happened to have had distinct powers conferred on him. Even the legitimacy of speaking of his 'accession' has been questioned. Addressed by an insensitive senator as *dominus* (lord), Tiberius clarified his position: he was master of his slaves, *imperator* (commander) of his troops, and Princeps in relation to everyone else. Official language bears this out: the conspiracy of Libo Drusus in 16 was aimed against Tiberius, his sons and 'other *principes*' (leading citizens). Some of the honours he either failed unequivocally to accept, like the name Augustus, which his predecessor had asked him to take in his will, or persisted in refusing, like the title Pater Patriae (Father of the Fatherland). Gaius by contrast had received virtually all the powers of his predecessors at one blow. In 37 he had held only the quaestorship, and as soon as the news of Tiberius' death and the Praetorian's salutation of Gaius reached Rome the senate put the necessary machinery into action. In Josephus' phrase, Gaius 'informed' the senate of his accession. It is to this occasion that scholars trace the ancestry of the enactment surviving only in part and known as the 'Lex de imperio Vespasiani'. One law, they believe, conferred all the customary powers on Gaius and his successors.[1]

The fusion of public and private functions is neatly shown for Claudius by his operating on official business at his 'headquarters' at the holiday resort of Baiae. Like Gaius, Claudius received the title Augustus and all significant powers at a stroke — against the wishes of the majority of the senate. He refused the title Father of his Country (Pater Patriae), never held by Tiberius, but took it in January, 42, conceivably when news broke of Appius Silanus' 'conspiracy'. The Principate was now a single office and Claudius was Emperor for a day before the senate confirmed him; at Vespasian's accession to power nearly twenty-nine years later this interval extended to a period of five months, from 1 July, 69, when he was proclaimed by his troops, until 20 December, when they captured Rome and forced senatorial recognition. The day that Vespasian celebrated as the anniversary of his accession (his *dies imperii*) was July, and he renewed his tribunician power on that date. The proclamation by the troops was given overriding legitimacy. This both emphasized Vespasian's blatant dependence on them and paradoxically had a primeval legitimacy, since Rome's supreme assembly, the Comitia Centuriata, or Roman people divided into their centuries, was also in origin the Roman people under arms. Designation to the consulship was desirable. Gaius had taken the suffect post available three and a half months after Tiberius' death; Claudius accepted the next regular consulship (42). The supreme pontificate, which made the Princeps head of the state religion, must be assumed: it had been held by Julius Caesar from 63 BC, by Augustus from 12 BC, and by Tiberius from March, 15; but neither Augustus nor Tiberius had been in a hurry for election.[2]

Given the real basis of imperial power — the army — and the manner of Claudius' and Vespasian's accession, it is doubly appropriate that the word commonly used to designate Rome's rulers is derived from their military title of Imperator. Claudius, like Tiberius and Gaius, refrained from using the title as forename (*praenomen*), as Octavian in his early years had done in a brazen attempt to enhance his military reputation, becoming, in 27 BC, Imperator Caesar Augustus. The practice of taking the *praenomen imperatoris* (not instead of but preceding the normal forename) was resumed by Otho and Vespasian in 69 and never abandoned.[3]

Over the charismatic surname (*cognomen*) 'Caesar', which, as the surname of the Julian clan, had acquired special status only with the Dictatorship and supremacy of its most famous holder to date, Claudius was clear and determined. Although blood relationship with Gaius justified his assuming it instantly and so keeping the name alive, he probably had it formally voted to him. 'Caesar' was legitimately transmitted to Octavian as a condition of his taking over Caesar's bequest, and it passed to Tiberius, Germanicus, Drusus, and Gaius by legitimate adoption and inheritance. It had never been part of Claudius' name. Seneca in the *Apocolocyntosis* dismisses Claudius' claim; but when a Roman family died out it was common for a kindred branch to revive its prestigious *cognomen*. For Claudius the name 'Caesar' probably had a particular significance, as that of the dynast whom he most revered. But already its hereditary character in a family in which only Germanicus was a prolific father was making 'Caesar' virtually a title. Later, again under Vespasian, it was to join the forename Imperator before every emperor's name and to precede the name of his sons. Its use for the successors, without 'Augustus', made it specially characteristic of the Emperor's heirs, the Caesars. Hence the two Augusti and two Caesars of the Tetrarchy: Diocletian and Maximian, Augusti together 286-305; Galerius and Constantius, Caesars together 293-30.[4]

Claudius had powers identical with those of his predecessors. Neither of the two pieces of evidence that might support a different view is cogent. At the celebration of his British victory in 44, the senate decreed that any agreements that he and his legates struck should be binding. At the Durbar of Camulodunum Claudius had already accepted the submission of a number of tribes. The first surviving clause of the 'Lex de imperio Vespasiani' confers the right to make treaties, apparently making any special grant to Claudius in 43 redundant. But if the 'Lex' does not represent powers normally conferred by law on each Princeps from Gaius onwards, but a grant to Vespasian of powers that his predecessors had exercised in virtue of their personal influence (*auctoritas*), Claudius in securing the legal recognition of his activities in Britain was simply dotting his i's in putting in his request, as well as savouring his achievements. Alternatively the motion was promoted by senators with tongue in cheek: the senate gave its sanction for Claudius to do — what he had just been doing.[5]

Dio also says that Claudius 'took' a kind of consular power to celebrate the triumph. The reason was that if he had not done so etiquette would have demanded that the consuls absent themselves from the celebrations, for the consuls' *imperium* in the city put a proconsul who had crossed the Pomerium, shedding his main *imperium*, under their authority, and they would have had to preside at the banquet. Courtesy demanded that they kept out of the way. Claudius did not want the consuls to be absent, either because he was too good-natured to let them miss a party or because it would look like a boycott. Taking consular *imperium* made Claudius their equal, he could preside, and they could stay. 'Taking' seems to imply that Claudius did not possess consular *imperium* and so was deficient in a basic power of the Principate that Augustus had painstakingly recovered in 19 BC. But if Claudius did not 'take' power but only deployed it after issuing one of his explanatory edicts, the difficulty disappears. It is not credible that Claudius in 41 tried to dispense with consular power.[6]

In spite of these stipulations of 44, Claudius' accession, like Gaius' entire principate, made steps on a road leading towards the coalescence of the powers, so that it was no longer worth enquiring in virtue of what authority any action was taken, *imperium* or *auctoritas*; the *privatus cum imperio* became an emperor, waking and sleeping. This would seem like the apotheosis of *auctoritas*, or, in its detested form, *potentia*, a virtual tyranny. But the powers of the Princeps had always been vast. The timidity of the senate contributed much to this: they could not ask questions in the deepening autocracy of Augustus' last grim decade; then Tiberius' forbidding character and later his absence had encouraged acquiescence. The significance of the events of 41 was that it was acknowledged that there was a single post, which must be filled.

This coalescence exposed and enhanced the military and the popular aspects of the Roman body politic. Claudius and Gaius were swept to power on the hopes of soldiers and people. (A similar dynastic populism made Napoleon III President and then Emperor.) For these elements ancient constitutional niceties dear to the senate were less important than the legitimacy of the recently established dynasty. Since neither Gaius nor

Claudius had anything besides blood to commend them, their accessions mark a further strengthening of the hereditary element in the Principate.

There could be different types of inherited claim to the Principate, not equally strong: the 'inheritance' should pass to children in the power of the incumbent, according to the rules of succession (only to sons in this case); it could pass to adopted sons just as well. But charisma did not follow the routes prescribed by the rules of succession. Once the direct male (blood) line was left, as it was with Tiberius, all blood connexions counted, even through women, and collateral descent was also worth appealing to (Claudius referred to Augustus, who was his mother's mother's brother, as his 'avunculus' and to Tiberius as his 'patruus'). 'There never was any such thing as the Julio-Claudian dynasty', writes T.P.Wiseman; '...It was the Julian dynasty, and Claudius did not belong to it.' But once the simple criterion of direct blood descent in the male line was given up for lack of candidates, no single criterion applied, and candidates held cards that were of indeterminate value: did blood descent in the female line or adoption count for more? That depended on other qualities of the claimant and his rivals, and on how they were perceived.[7]

When Nero came to power in 54, his supporters found justification in his ancestry (where else to find it?), partly because of the contrast with the alien Claudius: it was a victory for 'the Iuli of his mother', a reference to the fact that his mother Agrippina was not only a great-grandchild of Augustus in the female line but an actual member of the *gens Iulia*, her father Germanicus having been adopted into it. (We are to forget that it was only because that paradigmatic usurper Tiberius had adopted him and in turn was adopted by Augustus that Germanicus was a member of the clan!); correspondingly Claudius' claims to blood relationship with Augustus (his grandmother's brother) are dismissed by Seneca in the *Apocolocyntosis*, although Claudius possessed only marginally less of Augustus' genetic material than Nero.[8]

Gaius had met the problem of remoteness of his blood relationship to his great-grandfather Augustus in two ways. He had stressed the honourable position of his great-grandfather Mark Antony in Triumviral history, and he toyed with the idea that his mother the elder Agrippina had not been the child of the elder Julia by Marcus Agrippa, but by Augustus himself, even though the union would have been incestuous. Another such fantasy benefited Claudius. Augustus was particularly fond of his father Nero Drusus — and was rumoured to be his father. In one contemporary literary product Claudius is Caesar and grandson of Augustus.[9]

Besides the blood of the founder, the wishes of the current incumbent were relevant. Gaius had enjoyed the partial support of Tiberius' will, which he had invalidated only to destroy the claims of his young cousin Tiberius Gemellus. He himself made at least one will, allegedly naming Drusilla his heir; nothing is heard of another, drawn up after her death. If there was no will, Gaius' surviving sisters were the legitimate heirs, not Claudius, who was not of the same *gens*. Although they were divorcees (part of the penalty for adultery was compulsory divorce), they were not debarred from inheriting by the Lex Papia Poppaea because the statutory eighteen months within which divorcees had to remarry, if they were to qualify for inheritance, had not elapsed before Gaius died; and in any case they were close kin to the dead man and so exempt. Indeed, Claudius, quashing the convictions, recognized the continuing validity of Livilla's marriage to Rubellius Blandus. But an Emperor is unlikely to have died intestate. Nor would the will simply have been declared invalid, producing the same awkward intestacy. A plea of undutifulness (*querela inofficiosi testamenti*) must have been lodged on political grounds, as with Tiberius' will, and accepted, giving Claudius the chief share. Then he could have been generous to his nieces, besides restoring their property when they returned from exile.[10]

Other members of the family besides Augustus commanded love and respect, Germanicus above all. The legitimacy of his claims to power has always been overstressed, showing that relationship with the founder, personality and achievement, and the searching by subjects of all classes for men suitable to carry their affections are interrelated; it was not the dynastic claim alone that determined a position in a struggle for power. Claudius benefited from Germanicus' achievements, and the crowd hailed him not only as the uncle of the Princeps Gaius but as the brother of Germanicus, who perhaps was missed the more as his son was proving a disappointment.[11]

However, Claudius deployed every relative he could, using statuary, buildings, coins and festivals to display connexions: in particular his parents Nero Drusus and Antonia — with a glance at his grandfather Antony — and his grandmother Livia. Claudius at once instituted memorial services and annual birthday celebrations in the form of circus games for his parents (31 January for Antonia, and either 14 January or mid-March to mid-April for Nero Drusus); and the title Augusta that Gaius offered Antonia just before her death in 37 was once again conferred. The war hero Nero Drusus was important. His reputation had helped to build up Germanicus'; now both were to help the survivor. When he had his own success in Britain, a match for anything that Nero Drusus or Germanicus had done, Claudius' need lapsed and Nero Drusus fades from view. In the Volubilis inscription of 44 Claudius is 'Divi filius', son of the Deified, rather than 'Drusi filius'.[12]

Livia received the supreme honour of a state cult. The deification, which took place in 42 on the day she had married Augustus, 17 January, was long overdue according to Claudius' friend Persicus. It did not cause much expense: Livia's statue was placed in the existing temple of Augustus. Circus games were held for her too according to Dio and a carriage drawn by elephants was to carry her image (Augustus was given the same honour). More has been postulated by modern scholars. In 43 a dedication to *Pietas Augusta* (Augustan Devotion), voted by the senate in 22, was finally given material shape. Its nature is unknown. It was long considered to be an 'Ara

Pietatis Augustae' (Altar of Augustan Devotion), reminiscent of Augustus' Ara Pacis (Altar of Peace). But that was a modern construction using the dedication to Pietas, the Claudian Valle-Medici reliefs, and fragments from S. Maria on the Via Lata; it has been mercilessly demolished by G.Koeppel.[13]

Another interpretation of the *Pietas* dedication is needed. *Pietas* appears on obverses of 23 with Drusus Caesar, holder of tribunician power for the second year, on the reverse, and on obverses of Gaius, starting in his first year, with the temple to the Deified Augustus on the reverse. It is connected with the devotion of members of the family to a senior, and the dedication of 22 is most plausibly related to the grant of power to Drusus, requested by Tiberius with explicit references to the precedent set by the deified Augustus. In 43 Claudius' dedication gave notice that he would follow the same principles in advancing possible successors: regard for family and respect for precedent in the choice of a mature man capable of holding office (unlike Gaius).[14]

In spite of his admiration for Cicero's skill, Claudius favoured the memory of his grandfather Mark Antony, the victim of Cicero's *Philippics* of 44-3 and in orthodox history chiefly responsible for Cicero's death. As Octavian's rival, Antony was a worthy ancestor, the most distinguished that Claudius could muster. Claudius' elder daughter, born in the twenties, received her grandmother Antonia's resonant name; and, introducing his father's birthday games in 41, he proclaimed that their celebration was all the more important to him because the birthday was also Antony's.[15]

The prominence of women in the principates of Gaius and Claudius shows how much progress had been made towards making the supreme position virtually the hereditary possession of a single family. In the *Annals* the younger Agrippina presides alongside her husband Claudius at a tattoo in 51 and conducts herself as joint possessor of power bequeathed them by their ancestors. If Gaius and Claudius could take over, an untried young man of twenty-five and an inexperienced savant of fifty, who might be next? A child — Nero was sixteen when he came to power; an incompetent (as witness Seneca's joke about Crassus Frugi: 'stupid enough to be an emperor'); even a woman. That was particularly difficult, however. She might stand on a tribunal and attend councils of state. She could not be granted military *imperium* or even tribunician power; the magistracies of Rome and their derivatives were beyond her. She could wear military garments, Agrippina's *paludamentum*, to which C.E.Stevens drew attention, but at Rome that did not make her, as the British sovereign is, colonel of the regiment. Suetonius' claim that Gaius had intended to name his sister Drusilla as his successor cannot be accepted at face value. His private fortune and the title Augusta were within her grasp, but her husband would have had to take official powers. The status of consort ('*sociam imperii*') claimed by the younger Agrippina in 51 was not new; it had been applied to Agrippa and, in variant form, to Sejanus. Phrases of that non-committal type were invaluable at the court of a monarch where immense power was wielded by persons disqualified from office.[16]

The Emperor's servants — knights, freedmen and slaves — were also affected by the changes that were coming in with Gaius and especially with Claudius. Some of them were already performing duties that might occupy a magistrate: an equestrian fiscal procurator responsible for the collection of taxes in an imperial province was doing what a quaestor did elsewhere. In emergencies even freedmen were entrusted with official posts: in 32 the freedman Hiberus held the Prefecture of Egypt for some months; in 48 Narcissus was made Prefect of the Guard for one day. Others were dealing with public business at a high level but not in capacities appropriate for a magistrate: the freedmen of the secretariat. Some were acting in a purely personal capacity: the managerial procurators of the Emperor's private domains. Each of these categories had freedman subordinates. All servants of the Emperor enjoyed standing, those who had the Princeps' ear in particular.

The enhanced status of Claudius' servants was shown in separate but overlapping ways. First, fiscal procurators and the servants of his household were awarded honours without effective content that showed their services to be comparable with those performed by senators of a particular rank. Under the Republic favoured kings were allowed to wear the insignia of the highest senatorial office, the *consularia ornamenta*. That continued, but began to be extended to distinguished equestrian officers, Prefects of the Guard and the like; eventually it was a man with few friends who, while holding that prefecture, obtained only the *ornamenta praetoria*, the honorary rank of the second magistracy. Claudius was particularly generous, according to Suetonius offering consular decorations even to procurators in the provinces who were holding posts of the second rank, bringing in 200,000 HS a year rather than 300,000 HS. This claim may be a generalization based on a single instance. Consular decorations were given to one such man, Junius Chilo, procurator of Bithynia. He had performed unusual services (escorting the Bosporan Mithridates to Rome) in a province in which senatorial governors were proving inadequate. Chilo's colleague Aquila, who had seen active service in the Bosporan kingdom, won the *praetoria*.[17]

More untoward was the award of the honour to freedmen, usually at lower points on the scale. Narcissus obtained the *ornamenta quaestoria*, those of the lowest magistracy, but Pallas had his proposal for the enslavement of free women who entered into liaisons with slaves recognized by the grant of the *praetoria*. There would be additional gall in this for knights, since it was an honour that men of their rank had obtained. A related form of recognition was the admission to the senate house of freedmen in attendance on the Emperor. Polybius, it was noted, was 'often' seen about Rome walking between the two consuls. Claudius' reign saw these grants of honorary senatorial rank at their height. Under Nero the *ornamenta* were given in recognition of literary merit, and they became altogether less common after the Julio-Claudian period.[18]

47

Military decorations were also being awarded to men who were not soldiers: Greek-speaking courtiers of equestrian rank who accompanied Claudius to Britain held honorary military positions to justify their decorations; but what of the eunuch Posides, awarded the *hasta pura*? It was a joke, as W.M.Calder III pointed out.[19]

The second change concerns the titulature of equestrian governors. Equites sent to govern small provinces or districts such as Judaea or Raetia had been styled by the military title of Prefect. Prefects vanished from all provinces except Egypt, where the title was buttressed by law, and 'praesidial' procurators (a modern term for *procuratores Augusti ius gladii*, those who govern a province and enjoy capital jurisdiction over soldiers and civilians) replaced them. Given the high prestige of a military title, the change is remarkable: it looks like a downgrading, likely to cause resentment.[20]

The change from prefects to procurators did not take place simultaneously all over the Roman world. The first known instance of the title procurator (*pro legato*, 'acting legate') in a formal epigraphic reference to an equestrian governor occurs in 44, in the newly provincialized area of Mauretania. In Sardinia L. Aurelius Patroclus set up a milestone in 46 as Praefectus, although in a document of 69 that refers to the last equestrian governor M. Iuventius Rixa (67), he is styled Procurator. The hesitancy or vacillation is puzzling, and the explanation cannot be that the change was made when one governor succeeded another. In Judaea Pontius Pilate styled himself Praefectus in the inscription he set up at Caesarea during Tiberius' reign, but literary sources, not only Josephus but Philo, referring to the pre-Claudian period, use both titles. Claudius himself in 41 calls the Prefect of Egypt Vitrasius Pollio 'my procurator' in his letter to the Alexandrians, and in Judaea he seems to refer to Cuspius Fadus in 44/5 in the same terms. This can be explained by invoking the fact remarked on by Jones, that prefects also performed the financial functions of procurators and bore that title in addition. It seems that the title 'Procurator' prevailed only gradually, encouraged by the Emperor's preferred usage; P.Garnsey and R.Saller believe that it was designed to reflect the success of pacification, insecure though that was in Judaea.[21]

What determined the Emperor's preference may be detected from the cases of Judaea and Mauretania. M.Ghiretti has demonstrated that precisely when Judaea was annexed on the orders of Augustus it was attached to Syria and that the prefect was subordinated to the senatorial legate of Syria. In Mauretania the senatorial generals who subdued it were probably accompanied by procurators to organize taxation and take over the former ruler's property; when the senatorial commander was withdrawn, the province was divided and left in charge of two procurators, who continued their responsibilities while working as 'acting legates' (*pro legato*). Mauretania was not particularly peaceful; on the contrary, it continued to give trouble into the mid-second century. The use of the title 'procurator' emphasizes *Claudius'* personal control of the province; prefects might have been taken to be the appointees of the preceding senatorial commander, and that was not to be tolerated. There was a legal point as well: after the first procurators there was no senatorial commander to act as their superior: the title prefect would have been out of place.

Claudius' insistence on the procuratorial element in the title of the governor of Judaea was not a quirky preference for one that bound subordinates to him by personal rather than by official ties, significant though even that would have been, but an insistence on his own role in the province as opposed to that of a senatorial governor who delegated the Prefect's *imperium* to him in what was essentially a joint appointment (nicely illustrated by Pontius Pilate, who referred to himself as Prefect and yet was sensitive to the charge that he was not 'Caesar's friend', the characteristic of the procurator).[22]

It may be that other prefectures are to be interpreted in the same way: certainly — to leave aside Republican examples — the prefects of small sections of Roman territory newly conquered or rebellious received their commissions from senatorial commanders or governors: the Alpine territories, cantons in Moesia, Asturia and Galicia in Spain, come to mind. Thrace bordered on Moesia and the governor of Moesia had been involved in military activity there before it was annexed, no doubt by him, in 46; there, as in Mauretania and Noricum, which survived as a client state until his time, Claudius insisted on the title Procurator from the start. Exceptions to the change in title seem to happen only in provinces for which no original dependence on a senatorial official can be demonstrated: Sardinia and its obscure appanage Corsica; there the original proconsuls were superseded in 6 by a series of prefects, an emergency measure in face of brigandage; any change in titulature there should be due to a falling into line with other provinces. Jones noticed that in one or two provinces traces of the previous title survive: precisely in Sardinia a governor is 'Praefectus et Procurator' under Domitian. Jones convincingly accounts for this and for the use of the title 'acting legate' in Mauretania by invoking the importance of their military duties.[23]

It was not all gain for knights working for the Princeps, because the officialization of the post of procurator eroded the informality, the 'friendship' with the Princeps that was supposed to underlie them and which makes talk of an procuratorial 'career' misleading, of a 'civil service' out of place. In squabbles that sometimes broke out in a province between the senatorial governor and the imperial procurator, the procurator might no longer enjoy much advantage. After the revolt of Boudicca in Britain in 60-1, the repressive measures of her conqueror Suetonius Paullinus alerted the new procurator, Classicianus. His alarming report was read at Rome — but not directly acted upon: Nero, who had probably never set eyes on Classicianus, decided to find out the truth, and sent his own inspector, the freedman Polyclitus.[24]

The development of the procuratorship under Claudius was marked in a more substantial way. Tacitus reports that in 53 the Emperor, after repeated comments on the subject, brought a motion to the senate granting them power 'on a fuller and more generous scale than before': their decisions were to have the same force as if they had been delivered by Claudius himself. Precisely which procurators were included in the grant, 'praesidial', fiscal, or the managers of imperial estates; whether they were all knights or (as the end of the chapter might lead one to believe) freedmen as well, perhaps the subordinates of the main procurator in a province; and precisely what privileges they were now to enjoy, are questions that have been under continuous discussion.[25]

Tacitus probably means that Claudius was making an extension of the juridical powers already enjoyed by 'praesidial' procurators to the managers of the Emperor's private property, whose powers he mentions at the end of the chapter. In the second century Vipasca mining documents they have rights similar to those of city magistrates. In short, he was making them judges in their own cases. Tacitus' account of the background, which in part came from Claudius' speech (so that it might not be altogether relevant) recalls the struggle for control of the jury courts that raged between senate and knights from 124 to 70 BC. This suggests that the losers in the present case too were senatorial officials, because they lost jurisdiction over territory and persons within the domains, even when they were involved in disputes with outsiders. This view seems to fit previous developments: Tiberius in 23 found one of his procurators in Asia exceeding his brief (the Princeps' property, slaves and cash) and taking over the troops that were under the proconsul's command to enforce his own decisions. This case is less apposite than it looks. Even by the early third century the procurator had acquired no title to give judgment in non-fiscal cases, only to assess the property to be confiscated (what happened in practice is another matter). More illuminating is the credit given Tiberius for having recourse to the due processes of law when he was in dispute with private individuals. If Claudius granted jurisdiction to managerial procurators in disputes over imperial property, boundaries, rent, and so on, Tiberius' conduct would indeed be worth comment. After his accession speech which dealt in part with senatorial jurisdiction, Nero may have withdrawn jurisdiction from the managerial procurator.[26]

Claudius' repeated utterances of 53, that his procurators ought to have powers equivalent to his own, must have been vented during judicial hearings which he believed should never have come to him. This was the year before Claudius' death, and he was under pressure. Was he being empowered to delegate cases that had come to him in the first instance or denying appeal against his procurators' decisions? The latter interpretation is more likely. It fits what Tacitus says about the grant being 'on a fuller and more generous scale', but requires an antecedent grant of jurisdiction in the first instance. Evidence can, however, be detected for a change earlier in the reign. Although the relevant chapters of Tacitus are lost, Suetonius seems to mention a grant, putting it third of four instances of Claudius' civility to senate and consuls. First, he did not recall any exile without their sanction. Then there is a pair of requests, one for officers of the Guard to accompany Claudius into the senate, one that 'the judicial decisions of his procurators should be deemed valid'. Finally he requests the right to hold markets on his private property. All these requests may belong to the beginning of the reign: the recall of Seneca did not come until 49, but the first exiles to return were Gaius' sisters in 41; and a Prefect is found in the House with Claudius in 42. It may be then that Suetonius' grant represents the first of two made by Claudius, while that of 53 was an augmentation, giving the decisions of the administrators as much force as if he had made them himself. In the eyes of hostile critics he was making these men, some of them, in relatively small estates, of servile origin, equal to himself and the laws. These conditions would be fulfilled if Claudius was making the decisions of his fiscal and domain procurators inappellable.[27]

Such a decision would rightly be unpopular. The procurators would become little monarchs, protected against appeal to the Emperor, let alone to the governor of the province. Yet the measure could not always be enforced. (That may have been one of the reasons why a senatorial decree-Senatus Consultium, SC — was considered necessary, the other being Claudius' wish to commit the senate to his schemes.) There were men in the provinces too powerful to submit to a procurator when they knew that the Emperor would listen to them. The position stabilized eventually so that the jurisdiction of procurators outside the imperial domains covered fiscal matters and customs dues (portoria). In these the proconsul was also competent but it was better for him not to interfere. The fiscal jurisdiction of the procurator was subject to appeal, but not to the governor.[28]

If the powers of Claudius' servants were enhanced during his reign, it is natural to ask what advance was made, through fear or a sense of his own importance, towards the formality of a court. There is little sign of it. He was interested in practicalities, and in speech and demeanour made no effort to distance himself, as Gaius did (Tiberius had simply wanted to be alone). Touches of humour were designed to ingratiate him with his hearers, in court he bandied words with litigants, not always emerging with dignity; he joked with the crowd at popular festivals — and on one occasion was pelted with stale crusts in the Forum. Any distancing came for practical reasons. After the accession soldiers accompanied him to banquets (where some acted as waiters) and throughout his principate callers without exception were rigorously searched. Augustus had ordered the same precaution on occasion, and it once saved Claudius from assassination. Praetorians were still escorting the then Emperor, Galba, out to dinner in 69, and there is no reason to suppose that the practice stopped with him. At home freedmen ushers gave access to Claudius, and the right was formalized to some extent: the pass was a ring with a gold portrait of the Emperor. Vespasian, to Pliny's approval, abolished the rings in the seventies, as he did the searches: he himself had suffered from one member of what may already have come to be called the Admissions Office. His son Domitian (81–96) was more ceremonious, and the younger Pliny in 100 lauds the accessibility of Trajan. Byzantine obeisances belonged to the distant future; there had been Republican politicians known for unapproachability. Seneca, reproaching Gaius Gracchus, the tribune of 124–3 BC, with it, makes no complaint on this score against Claudius.[29]

# 6

# POLITICS AND THE COURT I: 41–48

Republican dynasts like Sulla and Pompey had 'courts', especially when they were abroad. During Caesar's Dictatorship, 49–44 BC, quotation marks came off: the court was where he and his entourage were. Tiberius and Gaius both contributed to its development: Tiberius isolated himself with a retinue of intimate friends, servants and guests; Gaius insisted on his uniqueness and his special position.[1]

The court flowered under Claudius and Nero. It may be seen as a series of concentric circles of diminishing power, with their centre at the Emperor's bed and his bedroom; next his board and his dining room; then private offices and reception rooms. All who had access to them were sustained directly by their ties with the Emperor, indirectly by deploying the influence that the ties gave him. If a courtier made his influence felt widely enough, he would win more value in the Emperor's eyes — or be more difficult to discard. Contention on behalf of protégés is presented at its clearest in the competition for Claudius' hand in 48, when allegedly each of three of Claudius' freedmen had his own candidate, but the chain of patronage ran to the outside world, senators, Roman people at large, and provincials: in a dispute between Jews and Samaritans in 52, leading freedmen supported the latter, while his wife Agrippina was enlisted on the side of the former. The word for this kind of power was *potentia*, with connotations of outrage and illegitimacy: Tacitus uses it, or related words, of the Emperor and of members of the court, wives, freedmen, the senators C.Silius and L.Vitellius, who had his own circle of protégés, such as the Veranii and Flavii, and *equites*. Money changed hands, as when positions or citizenship were procured, but the purchaser's obligation was never wiped out: what he bought was clearly more valuable than what he paid, because theoretically it was not for sale.[2]

A courtier was preoccupied with maintaining his own position. This guaranteed loyalty to the Emperor, as long as he was secure in his supremacy, and fostered both the development of a counterweight to the inherently hostile senate and cut-throat enmities within the court. He also had to guard against his patron's mortality, as Gaius' freedman Callistus did. The monarch's successor was a focus of intrigue. Even when a monarchy is an hereditary one with established prerogatives, problems arise if the ruler leaves behind only women or minors. In the Roman Empire, failure to establish precise rules of succession has rightly been identified as a source of political weakness. But if we bear in mind the origin of the institution, and

Table 2: *Messallina's Connexions*

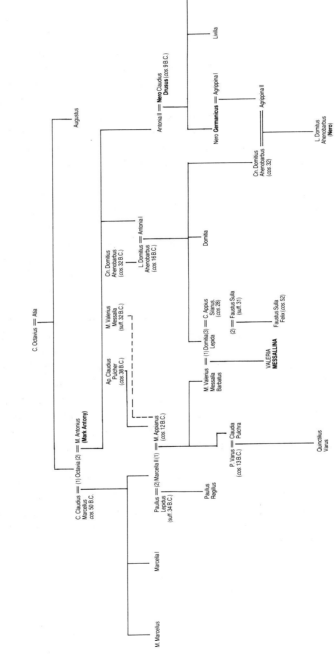

See Syme 1986, Tables VI, VII, and X.

the fact that the Romans could never bring themselves quite to recognize it as a monarchy, the failure is understandable. Hence the turmoil of the last quarter of Augustus' principate and of Tiberius' entire reign. Claudius took over at the age of fifty and his health was bad. Speculation on the succession, and misconduct, were to be expected.[3]

The exacting role of the monarch is first to keep his own power, allowing courtiers to deploy it externally only on what he sanctions. Convention or written protocol cannot guarantee that, and in the developing Julio-Claudian court there was little of either. Secondly he has to cope with disruptive internal struggles. Straightforward management takes a firm and confident personality. Claudius, with years of a weak position at court behind him, might be expected to exploit dissidence rather than check it. A central figure in Claudius' court was his third wife Valeria Messallina, and it will be worth looking at her position and how she defended it before going on to other influential courtiers, the freedmen, with whom she co-operated at first and then alienated.

Claudius married Messallina by 38 or at latest early 39: their daughter Octavia was born in 39 or early 40. Claudius' improved status at Gaius' court was probably why he divorced Aelia Paetina 'for no good reason'; it was the superior merits of Messallina that brought about the marriage to Claudius. Her political associations can have done her only good with Gaius and his kinsmen: her aunt and cousin, Claudia Pulchra and Quinctilius Varus, had suffered prosecution and condemnation in the twenties — allegedly for loyalty to Germanicus' widow. Then there was her descent. Not only was she a connexion of the other patrician Claudian clan, the Pulchri, as her aunt's name shows; she was, even more importantly, doubly the great-granddaughter of Augustus' sister Octavia, both through her father Messalla Barbatus, the son of the younger Marcella, and through her mother Domitia Lepida, who was a daughter of the elder Antonia. As Claudius' mother was the younger Antonia, Messallina was Claudius' cousin (once removed); through the two daughters of Octavia, the woman whose name was bestowed on their first child, they were both descended from Mark Antony.[4]

Claudius has been taken to be Messallina's first husband. That would mean that she married, at the normal age of about fourteen or fifteen, a man approaching fifty; the disparity, indeed, the fact that she was adolescent, has helped explain and excuse a desperate profligacy. R.Syme long since showed that Messallina would have been marriageable four years before she was given to Claudius. Her mother must have borne her half-brother Faustus Sulla in 20: he was consul in 52.[5]

The birth of his son Ti. Claudius Caesar Germanicus, later Britannicus, followed Claudius' accession by less than three weeks, on 12 February, 41. No formal honours were granted her yet, but the birth gave Messallina immense influence: Britannicus was the hope of the dynasty, 'Spes Augusta', as coins of the year had it, to be held up for people and soldiers to see at games and reviews.[6]

The birth of Britannicus also made her a target for the ambitious, as the mother of an heir apparent who would be likely to succeed before he acquired either official powers or the *auctoritas* to rule alone. Her position was like that of the elder Julia when Tiberius left for Rhodes in 6 BC, leaving her as the mother of two young prospective heirs and the daughter of a Princeps surely near the end of his life. If Claudius died and there was a coup, how could she ensure her son's survival? Subtle contenders would plan beforehand and engage themselves to protect Britannicus' interests. If the approach was sexual, with the idea of controlling her, that was a move that Messallina could turn to her own advantage: her partner would certainly be made away with if suspected, while her relationship with the heir would protect her. Adultery was an offence that could not safely be imputed to her for some years after his birth. When the elder Julia fell in 2 BC her sons had both taken the *toga virilis*; and the charge of adultery that was brought against the elder Agrippina in 29 accompanied the disgrace of her children. In short, Messallina should not be seen as an adolescent nymphomaniac; in the main she used sex as means of compromising and controlling politicians.

In spite of Britannicus, Messallina's position was not entirely secure. There were attractive women closer to the core of the imperial family; marriage to one of them would strengthen Claudius' position. It was an obvious move to secure their disgrace. Messallina's first victim had only recently returned from exile at the beginning of Claudius' reign. She was Julia Livilla, Gaius' sister, born in 18, exiled in the autumn of 39. As the restored wife of M. Vinicius, who had been proposed for the Principate, Livilla gave credibility to his claim and so was a threat to Claudius as well as to Messallina. Before the end of 41 she was on another island, Pandateria, and her alleged paramour Seneca in relegation on Corsica; it was not long before a soldier came to kill her. Messallina's responsibility is confirmed by the fact that Seneca was allowed to return only after her fall.[7]

Another Julia went in 43, daughter of Tiberius' son Drusus Caesar and of Germanicus' sister Claudia Livilla. Ten years before she had been safely consigned to a man of no family or pretentions, Rubellius Blandus. Innocent and virtuous, Julia was nonetheless attacked for immorality by Messallina, who may have had the idea of putting her son Rubellius Plautus right out of the running as a contender for power. The work was done by one of her allies in the senate, P. Suillius Rufus, who had been an adherent of Germanicus. At the time this was taken to be the cause of his exile for extortion under Tiberius, but he proved to have a genuine interest in money. Gaius recalled him and he attained immense and terrifying power under Claudius. But what Suillius achieved in 43 did not seem adequate to Nero; he forced Plautus first into retirement, then to suicide.[8]

Julia may not have been quite the innocent victim that she appears. Juxtaposed with her fall in Dio's account comes that of a Prefect of the Guard, Catonius Justus, who was destroyed (it was said) before he could inform Claudius of Messallina's intrigues. This man's first appearance in history was during the mutiny in Pannonia in 14, when as a leading centurion he was sent along with two members of Drusus Caesar's entourage to carry the requests of the legions to Tiberius. Like Chaerea in the Lower Rhine army, he won promotion for his role in the mutinies. His association with Drusus in 14 (he was not said to belong to the entourage) may have made him suspect as a partisan of Drusus' daughter. Justus' removal made it possible for a replacement to be brought in, Lusius Geta or Rufrius Crispinus, both committed supporters of Messallina and her children.[9]

About three years after Julia's condemnation there was another 'conspiracy', which nobody seems to have taken seriously, not even its intended victim: the guilty party, Asinius Gallus, and his probable accomplice, T.Statilius Taurus Corvinus (*cos.* 45), grandsons of great orators, were perhaps just marginal windbags. Gallus was an undersized, ill-favoured person; his father was the ambitious politician who had died in prison in 33. But that made him half-brother of Drusus Caesar and so Julia's uncle. He was merely sent into exile, his brother Ser. Celer, suff. 38, may have died as a result of Gallus' scheming, and the fate of Corvinus is unknown. Many freedmen and slaves were involved; it looks like a tidying–up operation after the death of Julia in which internal feuds were also settled.[10]

Second in intimacy with the Emperor were his 'secretariat', the freedmen whose political interests lay primarily in loyalty to their master: senatorial government had no more to offer them than it had for women, and this tended to create solidarity among them, for all their natural rivalry. If freedmen were safe to have as confidants, because excluded from formal politics, eunuchs were safer still. Not surprisingly Claudius had several at court, at least one of them highly regarded. For the first time they come into prominence in Roman court history; they are more conspicuous in Nero's reign, but their great period came only in the Byzantine age. But however dependant on Claudius he was, each freedman had to consider his future, back his candidate for power, and help him win. They varied too, in their connexions: Claudius complained that there were members of his household who did not realize that he was their patron. Narcissus and Polybius seem closer to Claudius than Pallas was, while Callistus like Pallas was a big man before Claudius came to power. Even if it is not true that Pallas acted in 31 as a go-between for Antonia in her alleged revelation to Tiberius of what his minister Sejanus was doing, the story is significant.[11]

Claudius shared a problem with Messallina: there were those who had a better title to power; the posterity of Augustus, led by the Junii Silani, one of whom had married the younger Julia's daughter by Paullus Lepidus and produced a large family. Then came descendants of the Republican dynasts, Sulla, Pompey and Crassus, offering a fresh start, untainted with Caesarian associations. Claudius' policy, hopeless for a usurper, was to conciliate both groups, to connect them with himself, offering high positions and prospects. Republican dynastic families had been kept at a distance, as Syme has pointed out; but the Silani and their close connexions the Lepidi had already suffered from nearness to power: the younger Julia's alleged adultery had been with a D. Silanus.[12]

The earliest moves were made in the first year of the reign. Crassus Frugi (consul in 27) found himself as Claudius' legate in the newly annexed province of Mauretania, with triumphal decorations (*ornamenta triumphalia*) to follow; his son Cn. Pompeius Magnus was married to Claudius' elder daughter Antonia, though without pomp, while L.Silanus was betrothed to the infant Octavia. The new actual and prospective sons-in-law were not let off the minor magistracies, known collectively as the Vigintivirate, that were a preliminary to a post in the army and to the quaestorship that gave access to the senate; but they were given prominent ceremonial duties, standing in as Prefects of the City when the consul, Claudius in 42, was absent holding the Latin Festival; when Silanus' elder brother Marcus held the consulship in 46 he was allowed to remain in office throughout the year. Perhaps in the euphoria of the British triumph of 44, Magnus and Silanus were given permission to hold office five years before the normal age. Their expectations would take time to fulfil and so to pall. Magnus and Silanus were also being kept on a more or less equal basis, although Octavia's infancy put Silanus at a disadvantage.[13]

Clearly, if anything happened to Britannicus, they would stand a chance of coming to power; but it is unlikely that Claudius or Messallina was unrealistic enough to think of them in any sense as temporary successors who would stand aside when Britannicus came of age, or as deterrents to the Emperor's own assassination. Prudential measures were also taken. C.Appius Silanus, who like Messallina was connected with the Claudii Pulchri (through his maternal grandmother), and whose cousin Junia Claudilla had been Gaius' first wife, was quickly removed from the governorship of Tarraconensis, where there may still have been the three legions that Augustus had posted there, to return to Rome and marry Messalina's mother Domitia Lepida. He was relegated to the generation before Claudius' own and became an implausible successor in a move that was the mirror image of Gaius' when he adopted as his son his cousin and rival Ti. Gemellus. Crassus Frugi, Magnus and L. Silanus were all among those who accompanied Claudius on his expedition to Britain.[14]

All were destroyed, Appius Silanus in 42, Frugi and his son four or five years later, L. Silanus not until 49; members of their families fell with them. The same explanation need not be applicable to each, nor were the same agents responsible. Their deaths may mean that Claudius found his fears of them unallayed by his attempts at conciliation; or that he was satisfied, but that his wife feared for her own power and the future of her son; most probably both were afraid (as may have been the case with Julia Livilla) and acted in collusion, explicit or tacit.[15]

The story of Appius Silanus is paradigmatic. Claudius one day informed the senate that Silanus had determined to assassinate him; this had been revealed in dreams experienced the previous night by Narcissus and Messallina: first Narcissus had burst into the Emperor's bedroom before dawn to tell his dream (showing how far the freedmen could get in an emergency), then Messallina had revealed hers. And early in the morning Silanus had duly appeared, confirming them. He had of course been summarily executed. That was what Claudius said, but the sources tell more: that it was Messallina and Narcissus who had been responsible for summoning Silanus and making him fulfil their prognostication, and that Messallina's motive was pique at Silanus' unwillingness to become her lover. This looks like mechanically applied embroidery at first, but if a sexual relationship was advantageous to Messallina the story may be true. Responsibility may be assigned in this case by considering what Claudius publicly told the senate: that he had been guided by a pair of dreams which had almost been fulfilled. The senate had two options: of going along with Claudius in believing in the dreams or of deeming him a coward duped by wife and servant. Either way he escaped full responsibility for the execution of a nobleman without trial, and, if the story were not believed, it would be Messallina or Narcissus (as Tacitus holds) who bore the odium of it. But it was Claudius who benefited: the very fact that he had married Silanus to his mother-in-law suggests apprehension. Now he was free from the menace without Silanus having had the chance to defend himself in public, with no questions asked, and two scapegoats available if necessary; there is something blatantly ironical in Claudius' congratulating Narcissus on his vigilance for the Emperor even during sleep. Either Claudius arranged the entire charade or he tacitly allowed Messallina and Narcissus to arrange it; they 'thought it was what the President wanted'. On this view Claudius was refining Gaius' method of evading responsibility: Gaius is said to have had men executed — but to continue summoning them before the court. When their deaths became public, he claimed that they had committed suicide. We have already noticed Claudius probably employing a similar technique of putting responsibility on to others at the time of Gaius' assassination.[16]

Such actions had unwelcome repercussions: in the following year the death of Silanus led directly, or provided incentives and a pretext, to a full-blown revolt — Tacitus calls it a civil war — on the part of L. Arruntius Camillus Scribonianus (*cos.* 32), the governor of Dalmatia, who instructed Claudius to resign his powers. Ironically, he was brother of the Livia Medullina who would long ago have married Claudius if she had not died on the wedding day: their father M. Furius Camillus (*cos.* 8) had been high in favour with Tiberius. But beyond this, and his illustrious name, Scribonianus had another claim to consideration: he was the son by adoption of the distinguished L. Arruntius who had been cast in anecdote at the time of his suicide in 37 as the man most capable of empire in Augustus' eyes — and one who would not shrink from the responsibility. The soldiers in Scribonianus' legions were loyal to Claudius, the revolt lasted less than five days, and Scribonianus, who fled to the island of Issa, was killed.[17]

Scribonianus' accomplices were brought to Rome or rounded up there. They included Q.Pomponius Secundus (suff. 41), who had been charged with *maiestas* (diminishing the majesty of the Roman People) and so 'driven to armed revolt' by his half-brother P.Suillius, presumably for his actions during the accession crisis; after his condemnation his name was erased from public monuments and the list of consuls. Another man, a praetor, had to resign his office, like the Catilinarian conspirator Cornelius Lentulus in 63 BC, before he could be put on trial and executed. The most famous victim was Arria. Her husband A.Caecina Paetus (suff. 37) had been in Dalmatia and joined the rebels. Arria's friendship with Messallina, which must have gone back to days when they were both in private life, did not help her husband. She showed him the way to die ('it doesn't hurt, Paetus'), confirming her family in intransigence towards the Julio-Claudian dynasty and the Flavians. Less gloriously Scribonianus' widow Vinicia gave information, earning relegation and a stinging rebuke from Arria. Other survivors, senators and knights, were prosecuted in the senate, including a Cloatilla who had buried her guilty husband and was defended by the notorious accuser Domitius Afer. But the most significant culprit was Annius Vinicianus, leader of the plot at Rome, an object of fear, and so fearful himself, ever since he had engineered the death of Gaius.[18]

The traumatic effect of the revolt on Claudius is clear from the prejudicial watchword he issued to the Guard, 'revenge on those who struck first'. Torture was used not only on slaves, which was normal, but on free men of the upper classes, a thing that Claudius had forsworn. The trial properly took place in the senate, with the consuls presiding, but in the presence of the Prefects of the Guard and the freedmen. The latter did not remain silent but conducted some of the interrogations. The condemned were executed in prison and the bodies dragged on hooks to the Gemonian stairs, exactly as had happened to the great traitor of Tiberius' principate, Sejanus, and his associates.[19]

The aims of the conspirators cannot finally be determined because they were probably various, presented differently to different constituencies. In Suetonius Scribonianus is a candidate for the purple. Dio claims that the troops would not support a bid for restoration of the Republic. Any claim to be 'restoring the republic' was challenged in the House. Narcissus asked the freedman Galaesus 'what he would have done if Scribonianus had become Emperor', and the reply, tart though it was, to be savoured by senators and endured by Narcissus, allowed the point: Galaesus 'would have stood behind him and kept his mouth shut'.[20]

Even after this trial Claudius did not give up his policy of conciliation, his only hope in a situation which essentially had not changed since January 41: the sons of conspirators, including the younger Scribonianus, whom Claudius apparently nominated for his father's place in the Arval Brotherhood, were given immunity and even money from the property confiscated, so that they could live and carry on a public career. However, nine years after the revolt he was brought down by Tarquitius Priscus, not an agent of Agrippina, on a charge of consulting astrologers on the life-span of the Emperor; his exiled mother was also implicated. Scribonianus did not long survive his exile.[21]

Vinicianus' distinguished kinsman, the unimpeachable — Syme's word for him — M.Vinicius (cos. 30), had no part in this plot and survived it, as he had survived candidacy for the Principate and the exile of Julia Livilla the year before. When he had been betrothed to her by Tiberius in 33 the intention was clear: Vinicius' origins were not great enough to present problems: he could not be a rival to Gaius. The loss of Livilla made him tolerable to Claudius. He too was taken to Britain in the entourage and when he died in 46 the year after his second consulship he was given a state funeral. It was only to be expected that Messallina be reported as having had him poisoned (he had repulsed her advances, and she was afraid that he wanted revenge for the fate of Livilla).[22]

The marriage of Cn. Pompeius Magnus to Claudius' daughter Antonia raised hopes in a family of distinction but little ability. Claudius may have thought of providing the dynasty with supports in the form of young men in the generation between his own and his son's, just as Augustus had done when he advanced Tiberius and Drusus in the infancy of his adoptive sons Gaius and Lucius Caesars during the years 17-12 BC, but the measure was clearly another expedient designed to placate the nobility. But it was a more delicate matter than the betrothal of L.Silanus to the infant Octavia; that union could not be consummated until she reached marriageable age in about 53. Early in 47 Magnus was killed *in flagrante delicto* with a male lover. Whatever Claudius felt about Magnus, Messallina can have had no use for him, a rival to her six-year-old son and, unlike Silanus, her own daughter's fiancé, no support. There was a clean sweep: Frugi and his wife Scribonia (the resonant name recalls Furius Camillus Scribonianus, her uncle Libo Drusus, and Augustus' wife, the mother of the elder Julia) were also killed. Antonia was assigned to another famous name, a Faustus Sulla, Messallina's half-brother. Ironically, her fears may have been self-justifying; in January 69 it was another son of Frugi and Scribonia that Galba chose for his heir.[23]

The most striking achievement credited to Messallina, almost the last before her fall, was the destruction of a larger-than-life figure, Valerius Asiaticus of Vienna (Vienne). The prominence that Tacitus and Dio accord it shows how significant it was held to be. Yet the occasion was apparently trivial: Messallina was hankering for the gardens of Lucullus, which had passed into Asiaticus' hands, and she believed that he had had an affair with Poppaea Sabina, her rival for the actor Mnester: by destroying Asiaticus, Messallina could rid herself of Poppaea without involving Mnester.[24]

Asiaticus was brought to the Palace in chains by the Praetorian Prefect Crispinus from a holiday at Baiae, and faced Claudius and his advisory council, which included L.Vitellius, Claudius' colleague as consul (*ordinarius* for the third time) at the beginning of the year, and as censor during its later months. Along with the freedman Sosibius, Suillius brought the first charges: failure to maintain discipline amongst his troops and homosexual acts, which Asiaticus rebutted neatly by referring Suillius to his sons, if he wanted to know.

We are to understand that the Emperor was about to acquit Asiaticus and consulted his advisers. Vitellius, instructed by Messallina, discoursed on Asiaticus' services to the state, their common devotion to the Emperor's mother Antonia — and recommended accordingly that the accused be permitted to choose his own manner of death. Poppaea Sabina, who had not been brought to trial, also committed suicide.

Not all scholars have accepted the ancient accounts of Asiaticus' downfall, although it is hard to believe that a man from Vienna could have presented a threat to Claudius or Messallina. As Claudius pointed out the following year, Asiaticus had reached the consulship before his native city had even achieved full citizen rights as a colony, and it was nineteen years before another provincial, Seneca, could be thought of as a prospective Princeps. But Asiaticus' rise, like his second consulship, shows his unusual importance, and his behaviour in 41 suggests that he did not accept a low estimate of his chances. His family had probably obtained Roman citizenship as Allobrogian magnates from a Valerius Flaccus as early as the eighties BC. It was sustained by immense wealth won in the first instance in his native province, where the capital city of his tribe, the Allobroges, itself developed sensationally during the first century of the Principate. Clientships amongst the tribe must be assumed, but Asiaticus also had the highest connexions. The attentions paid to Antonia, perhaps originally by Asiaticus' father, may have begun during her stay in Gaul with her husband (13-9 BC) and continued when Asiaticus came to Rome. Asiaticus' wife was Lollia Saturnina, sister of the fabulously rich owner of emeralds Lollia Paullina, who had briefly been married to Gaius; on their mother's side these women had a grandfather who was cousin to Tiberius. Moving in this circle he had enjoyed the friendship of Gaius himself, while Gaius had made it clear that he enjoyed that of Asiaticus' wife.[25]

Tacitus includes political material in Sosibius' revelations. Claudius is reported as taking the affair much more seriously than the plotting of Asinius Gallus; and the unguarded utterances of the Emperor after the event show that he thought of Asiaticus as something more than a person whose handling of his troops could be faulted: he was a 'brigand' (*latro*), a word used by Cicero of the Catilinarian conspirators of 63 BC. The word implies robbery with violence or murder: Claudius believed that Asiaticus' wealth was being increased by aggravated extortion — from subjects in a province or his fellows in Gaul. It was an easy step to believing that ill-gotten gains were being deployed to win undue influence, perhaps for treason. Asiaticus' fall was a political matter that destroyed the career of his brother. Further, the Prefect Crispinus was well rewarded for his achievement in arresting an active and athletic culprit: one and a half million HS and the insignia of a praetor.[26]

What threat could Asiaticus plausibly have posed? The connexion between Narbonensis and the Rhine armies was becoming yearly stronger. By 68 nearly forty per cent of Rhine legionaries had been recruited in Narbonensis, and the troops depended on Gaul for the financial support derived from taxation, as well as the maintenance of supplies. In this the goodwill of a few magnates, of whom Asiaticus was the greatest, probably played a helpful part. Vienna in particular was a rich source of legionaries, outnumbering all other Narbonensian towns.[27]

Claudius had been cock-o'-the-walk in Gaul, and Asiaticus could be presented as cutting him out there. In the speech on the admission of Gauls to the senate, the Allobroges and their capital are prominent. First he mentions the senators they had long provided (but Claudius shies away to his friend the knight L.Iulius Vestinus, and to the prospects of Vestinus' children, before the thought of the 'brigand' bursts through). Then Claudius is fatally but irresistibly drawn to reminding his audience of how formidable the Allobroges had been in the past by speaking of the title Allobrogicus that their conqueror had won. He was right: in the year of Catiline's conspiracy their unrest had been a source of fear; and dissensions as late as 11 or 12 called for Roman intervention. Gaius too had executed Gauls, perhaps in connexion with the conspiracy of 39. Asiaticus' son seems to have remained in private life until he played a leading part in the revolt of Vindex against Nero, demonstrating how formidable his local power base was. Galba made him governor of the province of Belgica and promised him the consulship of 70.[28]

Asiaticus then, even if he was not a threat in his own right, was in a position to deploy decisive wealth and manpower in a crisis. Members of the court believed that it would not be deployed in their interest, and they persuaded Claudius that it would not be in his. Fear of Asiaticus must never be allowed to emerge as the motive, and the right occasion to strike must be chosen. Trouble had been working up for some time. There had been Asiaticus' harangue to the people in 41, and his own nod at the Principate; then there was the second, *ordinarius* consulship that he was to have held for the whole of 46, but which he had to give up 'to avoid jealousy'. Dio sets the resignation against others: those of magistrates who were unable to afford the expenses of office. Senators were even giving up their seats during this period, just before Claudius took up his censorship. The contrast between the plutocrat from Vienna, whose circus games are significantly labelled as too costly, holding an office unprecedented for men of his origin, and what Tacitus presents as poverty-stricken senators from Latium may have roused intense ill-feeling. Further, one of Asiaticus' descendants was called Taurus, inviting the conjecture that there was a connexion between Asiaticus and the Statilii Tauri, consuls in 44 and 45, the latter sent into exile for conspiracy precisely in 46.[29]

Vulnerable though Asiaticus was, his destruction proved a mistake, and the turning point for Messallina. This was the most notorious *intra cubiculum* hearing of the reign, and the senate was summoned only afterwards to hear what had happened and to try two equestrian brothers called Petra who had allegedly lent Poppaea and the actor Mnester their house for lovers' meetings, and one of whom had a dream that portended grain shortage or the death of the Princeps. The condemnation of an ex-consul without a hearing from his peers hardened opinion against Messallina and her collaborators, notably the freedmen and Suillius. L.Vitellius' role makes little sense in Tacitus' account and may have been based on his predictable (consular?) proposal that Sosibius should receive a reward of a million HS. If Vitellius had played an active part in the destruction of Asiaticus it would be astounding in the civil wars twenty-two years later for Asiaticus' son to have emerged as a supporter of the censor's son Aulus Vitellius, who gave the younger Asiaticus his daughter in marriage — that is, intimated that he would make him his successor; admittedly the alliance seems not to have lasted for long.[30]

The Emperor lost ground too, whether as Messallina's dupe or, as in the killing of Appius Silanus, a beneficiary who willed the end and let others devise the means. In 47 a Roman knight, Cn. Nonius, was discovered armed with a sword amongst the morning callers; put to the torture, he gave no accomplices away. Perhaps he had none but was intent on a family feud: Asiaticus' wife came on her mother's side from the Nonii.[31]

Muffled rumblings now came from the senate. Following up his success, which had encouraged other accusers, Suillius made the mistake of taking 40,000 HS from a Roman knight, Samius, to act as his advocate and of letting him discover that he was in collusion with his opponents: Samius committed suicide in Suillius' house. The ex-praetor C.Silius took the opportunity of proposing that advocates should be bound by the Cincian Law of 204 BC to act without fee. In response to a storm of protest from advocates, Claudius kept the fee, limiting it to ten thousand, but a point had been made.[32]

It was only the beginning. Tacitus presents the fall of Messallina as another product of her passions. Madness (*furor*) brought Messallina down, we are to believe. This time love for the handsome consul designate undermined Claudius' position so far that at least one of his three leading freedmen decided that the risk of warning him was worth taking, provided that they used two of his mistresses as intermediaries. Tacitus singles out Narcissus in the overthrow of Messallina, but Dio makes the freedmen act in concert as he does for the ensuing marriage to Germanicus' daughter Agrippina. Dio's account differs in another way: he claims that the freedmen had been afraid for their own positions ever since Messallina had made away with the freedman Polybius, the *a studiis*. The occasion was the 'marriage' between Messallina and Silius that was solemnized during the celebration of the vintage in 48. Curiously, although Silius is presented by Tacitus and Juvenal as passive and fatalistic, the 'marriage' was his idea. It was an attempt at self-protection, committing Messallina further than she might have been willing to go: her consent had been witnessed; she had by implication repudiated her husband.[33]

Claudius, convinced of the threat to his prestige, and so to his position and his life, came up from Ostia at speed. There were few he could trust, because few were sure what the outcome would be. Vitellius and Turranius, Prefect of the Grain Supply, were aware of the liaison between Messalina and Silius, and both Praetorian Prefects were unreliable (we have seen Rufrius Crispinus in action against Asiaticus, but Lusius Geta was the man immediately involved, as he was with Claudius at Ostia). Narcissus persuaded Claudius to transfer the command to him for the day. Vitellius and Caecina Largus, who had held office all through the year with Claudius in 42, both of them men with a family history of devotion to the house of Germanicus, were in the carriage with the Emperor, but thought more about how the affair would turn out than about Claudius' interests; Narcissus sat with them trying to get them to commit themselves. When Messallina intercepted the carriage, playing her ace, the children, he trumped it with a list of previous amours. Next came a high-minded woman intent on justice for a member of her sex. The senior Vestal Vibidia demanded a hearing for the Emperor's consort, and Narcissus had to promise it before he could push the lady away and get her to go and mind her own rites.

After a brief stop at Silius' house to inspect in his hall the bust of the father who had been condemned for extortion and treason in 24 (though presumably rehabilitated when Germanicus' son Gaius came to power thirteen years later) and, further inside, heirlooms of the Nerones and Drusi, which Messallina had lavished on her paramour, the party passed on to the Barracks and a drumhead court martial, with Silius as the first to be brought in. He offered no defence, simply asked for a speedy death.

Tacitus begins with a love affair, but again provides evidence for political factors at work. Some scholars have accepted the view that there was a deadly plot against the Emperor, its author Silius. Another view is that Messallina felt she had reason to fear Germanicus' daughter and Gaius' only surviving sister Agrippina and her son L. Domitius Ahenobarbus, better known by his future name of Nero, who in the Trojan Games held as part of the Secular celebrations of 47 (already the young showman!) had attracted warmer applause than her own son Britannicus. Finding no help against them from Claudius, Messallina determined to replace him with Silius, who in Tacitus' version does indeed offer to adopt her son as his heir. The suggestion that Agrippina's son, now in his tenth year, emerged at this point is not to be ruled out. He had only to grow to manhood to become a plausible rival to an emperor whose accession and later dealings with senators and others, including members of the Julian clan, had made him resented. But the construction as a whole is as risky as the plan it envisages; Messallina might lose as much as she gained, and as the mother of his children she was vital to Claudius; the longer he lived the better chance Britannicus had of taking over. Only if Messallina thought that Claudius' death was imminent should she have brought in a substitute. And if she was doing that it was she who should have been keen to celebrate a marriage with the incoming Princeps.[34]

A more modest scheme than that of assassinating the Emperor, and one in which the consul designate exercised more initiative than Tacitus allows, may have been afoot. The prevarication of Vitellius and Largus then appears in a less discreditable light, if Claudius himself was in no real danger. Why should they let their own position be undermined?

Messallina underestimated the odium that Asiaticus' downfall would bring on the imperial household and was opposed in it by the majority of the freedmen, led by the most influential, Polybius. A preliminary attack of 46 disposed of Statilius Taurus, Asinius Gallus, and Polybius and his henchmen, perhaps the four freedmen victims named in the *Apocolocyntosis*, clearing the way for the disposal of Asiaticus. Narcissus is significantly absent from the final proceedings against him. Narcissus and others were beginning to see Messallina as a danger, to themselves and the régime. This cannot have escaped Messallina, who probably looked for support from elsewhere, notably from men who could be counted upon for hostility to the freedmen. Her search for additional security was the more urgent when she saw the potential threat posed by Agrippina and her son, for Agrippina had lost her husband C.Passienus Crispus (consul II 44) in 46 or 47 and was free to remarry.[35]

Paradoxically, then, Messallina's attack on Valerius Asiaticus led to her seeking allies in the senatorial and equestrian orders, both of which had lost influence to the court. Her lover was a young man of family and of impeccable antecedents — his father a victim of Sejanus — looks, and courage; and he was about to hold the consulship, presumably as *ordinarius* of 49. Silius had himself begun an attack on his personal enemy P.Suillius in the aftermath of the Asiaticus affair which was based precisely on the conduct of accusers. From his point of view, if Messallina's affections could be won and her political support put to use, the Emperor could be turned against the men who had engineered so many deaths, provided with a new set of advisers, and brought round to support the interests of established political circles. With Messallina on their side and Silius as consul to take the initiative, determined senators might be able to bring their influence to bear on the Emperor. Not only senators: leading knights were among the men executed after the plot was discovered. Seneca ascribes the death of six Roman knights to Narcissus, as well as those of Silius and an ex-praetor, Juncus; knights even more than senators were losing ground to the freedmen as confidants of the Princeps, a prerogative of wealthy non-senators since the time of Julius Caesar, as Tacitus testifies. Accordingly, Silius had committed himself to Messallina by divorcing his wife in 47. Messallina was won and induced to commit herself to the 'marriage' ceremony as proof of good faith.[36]

Tacitus himself holds the 'marriage' hard to credit. Even with so few witnesses, it was bound to come out, as Juvenal remarks. Suetonius resists the tale that Claudius was tricked into sanctioning it himself by a tale of danger to Messallina's husband. An alluring modern fantasy interprets it away as Bacchic ritual. E.Meise rightly defends the Tacitean account, and exploits the 'marriage' for his theory of a deadly plot against Claudius. Not only marriage, but the adoption of Britannicus by Silius was another precondition of Messallina's involvement. There are difficulties. The adoption of a child not *sui iuris* was a form of sale, and Claudius could not be expected to take part in that. Moreover, he did not know that he had been divorced, and that was necessary for a recognized fresh marriage. The ceremony must be seen then as a precursor of other such charades, also conducted in due form, but equally invalid, the 'marriages' of Nero to Pythagoras and Sporus.[37]

The freedmen, once driven to move, did so too quickly for their adversaries. Using the Emperor's mistresses, the freedwomen Calpurnia and Cleopatra, as their first informants, they deployed the 'marriage' ceremony itself and its implications to bring home to Claudius that he was as vulnerable as ever to rivals, and that he could not now afford to let Messallina's actions and her new alignment go unnoticed.[38]

Narcissus takes chief credit for the action both in Tacitus and in the *Apocolocyntosis*, in the sense that he is there the murderer of numerous senators and knights. His role in Tacitus is surprising when he is later portrayed as the champion of Messallina's son Britannicus, who if he had become Emperor would have avenged his mother. Pallas by contrast is portrayed by Tacitus as cowardly and irresolute, taking action only when it came to proposing Claudius a new wife — Agrippina; in Seneca's skit he fails to put in an appearance at all. But that too is explicable: by the end of 54, with young Nero on the throne the executions of Silius and his associates had become another atrocity of the old régime, the dead Narcissus the villain responsible; it was only when Vespasian came to power in 70 that Claudius' leading freedman could be assigned his role as the protector of the legitimate heir, perhaps by the elder Pliny. Pallas in 54-5 was sharing and anticipating the eclipse that Agrippina herself was to undergo: he was forced to resign from his charge of the imperial finances very soon after Nero's accession. Agrippina was still strong enough for him not to be shown as a villain; he had already become someone to be ignored.

# 7

# POLITICS AND THE COURT II: 48–54

Making a break with the death of Messallina, as Tacitus does, should not tempt writer or reader into exaggerating the differences between the beginning of Claudius' reign and its end. Politicians and historians had their reasons for portraying the two imperial wives in contrasting styles, during the Emperor's lifetime and after; so did Tacitus, for his literary purpose. Messallina's career lacked the dramatic ups and downs that Agrippina's had already had when she married for the last time; it must not take from that drama.[1]

Yet something corresponded to this scheme: Messallina had been carried to power by her husband's destiny; Agrippina made her own way by marrying him. Agrippina's behaviour was more overtly 'political', even if we acknowledge that the deaths that took place between 41 and 48 were not due to Messallina's frustrated lust but were part of the imperial couple's precautions against rival claimants. Messallina's father had not reached the consulship; Agrippina's was a commander posthumously compared with Alexander the Great. Her mother's character and public role were even more impressive: she had been a personality in the Rhine camp, making a dramatic exit felt by the mutineers in 14 and standing guard over the Rhine bridge when hope for the survival of the expeditionary force of 15 was beginning to fade. Agrippina's expectations of acknowledged power, which she first tasted in Gaius' reign, were greater than Messallina's, even if she too still had to wield it vicariously in part, through her husband and later her son Nero.[2]

Narcissus' role in Messallina's downfall damaged his position, immediately and irrevocably for the future. His loss of influence, reflected in the modest award of the *ornamenta quaestoria*, was in part due to the damage he had done to the Emperor himself by destroying his wife. She was now held responsible for the death or exile of a number of distinguished persons, the survivors soon to return. These punishments, inflicted or condoned by Claudius, now looked different; and there were fresh wounds to the body politic inflicted by the executions of 48 themselves.

Claudius needed support. Hence his new marriage and his choice of a wife. In the barracks he had shamefacedly told the Guard to kill him if he ever remarried; political considerations soon prevailed and the marriage to Agrippina was celebrated within three months, perhaps on 1 January, 49. The Emperor's sexual needs are not relevant, as women in plenty were available, although the thirty-three year old Agrippina's seductive behaviour is graphically presented by Tacitus. The determination of leading freedmen to provide Claudius with a spouse who would acknowledge her debts is also conspicuous. Lobbying, even the round-table discussion of candidates' merits, may be admitted; but the choice was not in doubt. Aelia Paetina, presented as Narcissus' candidate, had only the negative merit of inoffensiveness: Claudius had been married to her before and she would introduce no new element into the imperial house; but something new was what the house needed. Her supporters may have hoped to bring the husband of Paetina's daughter Antonia to the throne along with Britannicus; but Faustus Sulla was the half-brother of Messallina and in 48 that told against him, however lacking in energy he was. Callistus is said to have favoured Lollia Paullina, a woman of enormous wealth who was also worth consideration because she had once briefly been married to Gaius. But Agrippina was the last surviving daughter of the beloved Germanicus and his martyred wife, descended from Augustus, and the victim (it might be claimed) of several political vicissitudes already. By marrying her, Claudius could both right old wrongs and immeasurably reinforce his political position.[3]

The legal snag that Agrippina was Claudius' brother's daughter was quite outweighed by the redoubled political support that the union would bring. Vitellius prepared the ground in the senate, the prohibition was removed, and the marriage was urged on the Emperor by senate and people.[4]

Agrippina's son, whose prominence was highlighted by the timely disclosure of Messallina's attempts to murder him, was three years older than Britannicus, and could ensure the security and continuation of the dynasty. There were admirable precedents for a paired succession: Augustus' grandsons Gaius and Lucius, born 20 and 17; Tiberius Nero and Nero Drusus, four years apart and destined, between the death of M.Agrippa in 12 BC and that of Nero Drusus three years later, for joint supremacy; Germanicus brought into the house of Tiberius in 4, a brother for the younger Drusus Caesar. As Princeps Tiberius continued the pattern, even in his last years obstinately retarding the career of one grandson, Gaius, so that the other, Gemellus, should stand his chance. No such unhappy example would have been in Claudius' mind, nor in the advice of Vitellius and the freedmen; rather the harmonious, if short, partnership of Germanicus and Drusus Caesars, 4–19.[5]

The alternative was for Claudius to promote Britannicus by himself. In 43 the exiled Seneca expressed the wish that Britannicus would be Claudius' consort long before he became his successor, attributing to Claudius the plan devised by Augustus for Tiberius in 9 BC and exploited by Tiberius for Drusus in 21–3. When there was only one suitable heir in the next generation the dynasty was to be continued by advancing the younger man towards parity with the older. But in autumn 48 Britannicus was only seven, and Claudius' own power had just been shaken to its roots. The idea that in his last years Claudius began to fail has displaced assessment of the actual weakness of Claudius' position from 48 onwards.[6]

Agrippina found an immediate obstacle to the accession of her own son in place of or, as Claudius envisaged it, alongside Britannicus: L.Junius Silanus who was promised to Britannicus' sister Octavia. Within four years Octavia would be of marriageable age and capable of providing her husband with heirs and high position. Vitellius accordingly accused Silanus in the senate of incest with his sister, the attractive Junia Calvina. He resigned his praetorship and killed himself — on the day of the Emperor's marriage; Junia Calvina, embarrassingly a former daughter-in-law of Vitellius, was neatly exiled.[7]

Octavia was now free for Agrippina's son. Intermarriage between branches of the imperial family had been common, strengthening dynastic claims and promoting unity, but the marriage of a Princeps' political heir to his daughter was the relevant precedent: marriage to Augustus' daughter Julia would have carried his nephew Marcellus to the Principate, if he had not died in 23 BC; her last husband, Tiberius, did gain the prize.[8]

The speedy return of Seneca from exile, and other changes, were to be expected with the elevation of Agrippina. He was not only elected to a praetorship for 50 but given a high place at court as the instructor of Agrippina's son. There were still persons whose existence threatened the new dispensation. Lollia Paullina's wealth, her connexions with the Volusii, kinsmen of the Neros, above all her previous marriage to Gaius, had made her a possible wife for the Emperor. Consulting astrologers and an oracle on the subject of Claudius' marriage was the charge brought against her. Claudius stressed their relationship in his speech in the senate on her case, omitting all reference to her marriage to Gaius. She was removed, first of all into exile, then, on the arrival of an officer (presumably of the Praetorian Guard, which was devoted to Agrippina), by suicide.[9]

Agrippina's son was adopted on 25 February, 50. L.Domitius Ahenobarbus became Nero Claudius Drusus Germanicus Caesar at the same time as she was granted the title Augusta, the first living female member of the dynasty to accept it since Livia herself — and she had had it only as a widow, when it could not enhance her majesty to a level too close to her husband's. Such events did not pass unnoticed in the provinces, if it was at the request of the Ubii in lower Germany that the foundation of a colony named after the Empress was now put through. Agrippina's power was approaching its height. Daughter of Germanicus, sister and wife of Emperors, and soon to be mother of another holder of *imperium*, she held a position unique until Tacitus' own day. Certainly from 51 onwards she appeared at ceremonial occasions in a gold-threaded military cloak, and on a tribunal (distinct from that of her husband, however), greeting ambassadors; her greetings were officially gazetted. A fire brought her to the scene with Claudius, as a concerned member of the imperial family. When the Arval Brothers offered vows for the recovery of Nero from illness some time between 50 and 54 he was anomalously given the style 'offspring of Agrippina' before his official filiation; mint officials were equally sensitive, as her prominence on coin types shows.[10]

Tacitus presents the adoption as the work of Pallas, and claims to know the precedents he cited: Claudius parroted them in the senate. But it would be surprising if Claudius had not had the advancement of Tiberius and Nero Drusus, and Tiberius' adoption of Germanicus in mind even when he decided to marry Agrippina. The unfortunate point that it was the first time that patrician Claudii had made use of adoption smacks of Claudius himself, and Suetonius attributes it to him, Tacitus preferring learned observers. It is typical of Claudius' way of meeting objections head-on and of his argument that everything has to have a first time. Pallas cannot be excluded from the episode, but he is not essential to it. Nero's adoption meant that if he were to marry Octavia she would have to be emancipated or adopted into another family; an easy step.[11]

It is to 50 that Tacitus ascribes the celebration of British successes since 47. The resistance leader Caratacus was brought to Rome in chains, paraded before the imperial couple, and made the subject of an oration in the senate. But Tacitus also puts his capture in the ninth year of the war in Britain, and the dedication of the commemorative arch over the Via Flaminia also belongs to 51. Tacitus has allowed British affairs to carry him beyond 50, as he reached back for the beginning of his account. This quasi-triumphal occasion most probably yielded a further honour to Agrippina: the right granted in 51 to be borne during festivals in the ceremonial *carpentum* that Messallina had used at Claudius' triumph of 44.[12]

Tacitus counterpoints the theme of Agrippina's successes with that of the neglected condition of Britannicus, the dismissal of servants and officers loyal to ·him. These juxtapositions, they have at least a dramatic truth: Britannicus and 'Nero' (as Britannicus conspicuously failed to call him) were now brothers, but Nero as the older by three years would take the toga of manhood correspondingly earlier than Britannicus, become eligible for office that much earlier, could hardly fail to acquire the corresponding advantage in *auctoritas* (prestige and influence), and, if Claudius died before Britannicus attained the same privileges, would be left in a commanding position. The parallel advancement of two brothers with three years between them had never come to fruition; there had been seven years between Gaius Caesar and Tiberius Gemellus, too great a gap for the aged Tiberius to help his grandson to power. That was a sinister precedent in the eyes of Britannicus' friends.[13]

In 51 Nero took the toga of manhood, with Claudius leading consul of the year to enhance the dignity of the ceremony, as Augustus had been in 5 and 2 BC, when he conducted his adopted sons Gaius and Lucius Caesars into the Forum. It looks as if the decision was taken only in the course of 50, when Claudius was designated to this consulship. His holding it all the year was hardly due to uncertainty as to when Nero should take the toga; more probably Claudius was using the consulship to highlight ten years in power, and his sixtieth birthday on 1 August. Tacitus observes that the ceremony was brought forward in Nero's case: fourteen was the normal age for taking the toga, but he had been born on 15 December, 37, so at the beginning of 51 he was just into his fourteenth year. The regular season for the ceremony was March 17th, at the festival of the Liberalia; even then Nero was nine months in advance; but his appointments to consulship and pontificate belong to 4 and 5 March.[14]

More interesting are the reasons for the advancement of 51: different for Claudius from what they were for Agrippina and her supporters. For Claudius at sixty, there was a smooth succession to work for. The sooner both boys were capable of high command the better. For Agrippina, the premature advancement of Nero was itself an advertisement of her power, and if in the sequel that of Britannicus could be kept at a normal pace or retarded, so much the better. From now on, the Roman mint, so sensitive to the realities of power, looked to Agrippina and Nero, as did Balkan and other provincial mints; ignored at Rome, Britannicus still kept a place alongside Nero in provincial issues, and at Sinope even took an obverse, Nero appearing on the reverse. Time proved this a misreading of the situation.[15]

Formally, Claudius was following the precedent of Augustus in advancing Gaius and Lucius Caesars. There was also an echo of the early career of Octavian himself. He had not been twenty when he took up his first consulship. Now not only was Nero made supernumerary member of the major priesthoods, as well as becoming a Sodalis Augustalis in virtue of his membership of the family; Claudius yielded to the senate's request for Nero to hold the consulship at nineteen, with the title Princeps Iuventutis (Leader of the Youth) meanwhile. There were less extravagant possibilities: the ten years' remission that had been granted to Augustus' nephew Marcellus, the five to his stepsons Tiberius and Nero Drusus (which Tiberius thought proper for his own grandsons). But Nero was also granted proconsular power outside the city limits, an unheard-of novelty for a boy of his age. It was comparable with the power that Augustus had possessed between 23 and 19 BC, though in that case it was declared superior to that of provincial governors and did not operate within Italy; or with Agrippa's powers before 13 (when they too were declared superior). More important than the precedents were the purpose and effect of the grant, which were of course to provide Nero with interim power from which he could not be dislodged in the event of Claudius' death. To Claudius, given the low stock of his Principate after 48, ensuring the succession even of his adoptive son must seem preferable to leaving the matter open.[16]

The new arrangements were celebrated with tips to soldiers and citizens, just as they had been on comparable occasions by Augustus and Tiberius, and Nero gave thanks in the senate. The people had an opportunity to show appreciation at circus games, which included a march past of the Guard; Nero wore the dress associated with triumphant generals (his *imperium*, though operative outside the city, did not expire when he crossed the boundary), and so with the successes in Britain that were celebrated in 51;

ironically, Britannicus had to appear still in the toga worn by children. The summer saw Nero brought forward in another way. It was probably in June, while Claudius as consul was celebrating the Latin Festival on the Alban Mount, that Nero acted as Prefect of the City — the task that had been denied Claudius himself during Germanicus' consulship of 12. Only routine jurisdiction had been envisaged by the Emperor, but litigants clamoured to come before what must have been a model court.[17]

The year was one of portents, at the time not attributed to Nero's advancement, but reflecting political tension; their growing prominence in Tacitus' narrative is noticeable. In 51 they included a grain shortage at Rome due to a bad harvest; people reacted sharply, holding Claudius responsible. The famine was relieved by the arrival of shipments from overseas, made possible by an unusually clement winter. Jerome sets a famine in 50, probably a slip, but Suetonius does speak of 'continued' droughts, and it is worth asking if the festivities were not designed to take men's minds off a persistent shortage and whether the grant of *imperium* to Nero was intended in part to show commitment to easing the problem. After the riot, according to Zonaras, Claudius was induced to issue an edict proclaiming to the people Nero's readiness to take over; the same information was conveyed to the senate by letter.[18]

The restriction of Nero's *imperium* to territory outside the city was made less significant by another move of 51, which secured a single commander of the Praetorian Guard to replace those appointed in Messallina's time and temporarily replaced when Messallina was destroyed. Sex. Afranius Burrus of Vasio in Narbonensis had served as manager of estates belonging to Livia, Tiberius, no doubt to Gaius, and to Claudius, and must have been known to Agrippina in that capacity. Tacitus claims military distinction too; perhaps he owed it to his mutilated hand, a constant reminder of valour however long past. When the change of Emperor came, real power within the city, as exercised in 41, would be in the hands of a reliable friend.[19]

The seriousness of Nero's claims to power, and his good use of it, were demonstrated in 53, the year in which he married the Emperor's daughter. He spoke on behalf of the people of Ilium and their plea for tax exemptions. This speech also drew attention to Nero's claim to descent from Trojan Iulii, through his mother. Nero also spoke on behalf of Bononia in Cisalpine Gaul, which had suffered a fire, and won it a million HS. That city had been exempted from the oath taken to Octavian before the campaign of Actium because it had ties with Antony: Nero was deploying all his ancestral connexions. Rhodes too benefited from Nero's eloquence and had its freedom restored, reversing a decision of 44 — a gesture calculated to impress the Greek world. More routinely Apamea Celaenae secured a five-year remission of tribute in consideration of its losses in an earthquake.[20]

Nero showed astute concern for popular opinion at Rome just before his marriage, during an illness of Claudius. He entered the senate and offered a vow for the Emperor's recovery: circus games, the people's favourite diversion. They were celebrated at the time of the wedding.[21]

Agrippina's plans were not quite unopposed. A desperate effort had been made in 51 to indict the ageing, perhaps already dying Vitellius on a charge of diminishing the majesty of the Roman people (*maiestas*), which since the last decade of Augustus had often meant disrespectful language towards the Emperor or other persons of rank. The accuser Junius Lupus also claimed that Vitellius was aiming at supreme power. Such charges, brought in a year when the Emperor was consul and presumably presiding over the senate, were calculated to arouse Claudius' anger; but Agrippina intervened and it was Lupus who was exiled and banned from fire and water, for malicious prosecution. He was years too late. He was a young man, an ex-aedile at most, and his attack probably no more than a suicidal demonstration of loyalty to L.Silanus and Junia Calvina, of whom he may have been a distant connexion. When Vitellius died soon after his life could be presented as one of unswerving devotion to the Princeps. In the field, against Parthia at the end of Tiberius' principate, it had been unambiguously distinguished; at court Vitellius attached himself directly to the source of power, the Princeps, without having either the independent mind or the high ambitions of an Agrippa; he did not believe that his influence was strong enough to prevail against that of Claudius' wives, and refrained from testing it.[22]

The main resistance to Agrippina's plans for the sole succession of Nero is attributed by Tacitus to Claudius' freedman Narcissus, while Suetonius and Dio see Claudius himself battling for his son. Hostility between Narcissus and Agrippina was not inevitable, even if he had supported another candidate for matrimony with Claudius. Dio has Narcissus as much a creature of Agrippina as Pallas was; Nero might have saved him from Britannicus' vengeance, which Tacitus twice has him claiming to be willing to risk if he can only save his master. Another factor must be brought in: Narcissus' own declining prestige after he had engineered the destruction of Messallina: it was he who was responsible for the low repute of the imperial house in 48. Agrippina had restored it, and her chief associate among the freedmen, Pallas, benefited. Narcissus found himself losing his position of special intimacy with the Emperor. In January, 52, Pallas won the insignia of a praetor with his proposal on liaisons between free women and slaves, which the Emperor promoted in the senate. It was bad luck for Narcissus that in the same year his scheme to drain the Fucine Lake involved the Emperor in a fiasco by failing to work when it was first inaugurated and in danger from drowning at the second try. This may be the beginning of open hostility between him and Agrippina: he had made the enterprise, and the regime, look silly.[23]

Ill health and the second Fucine fiasco confronted Claudius with the possibility that he might not survive to give even Nero an unassailable position. There were still senators who would be glad to see neither boy in power. One malcontent was sent into exile in 52, probably *pour décourager les autres*: Furius Scribonianus, son of the rebel of 42. His mother had been exiled, but she now attracted renewed attention. The charge was a plausible one during Claudius' last years and likely to succeed with a frightened Emperor: consulting astrologers about his death. The whole tribe was accordingly expelled from Italy, a sure sign of political instability.[24]

The last case before Claudius' death in 54 ruined a woman of great significance: Nero's aunt Domitia Lepida, mother of Messallina. Tacitus, having things both ways, calls the reasons for her destruction 'typical of women'; but the circumstances are serious enough: her birth as a child of the elder Antonia, a great-niece of Augustus, a first cousin once removed of Agrippina herself and a sister of Agrippina's first husband, Cn. Domitius Ahenobarbus , all made her Agrippina's equal, as she nearly was in beauty and wealth, and (according to Tacitus) in age and depravity. If Claudius were to remove Agrippina (and Tacitus gives us to believe that Claudius in his cups had let out the portentous claim that it was his destiny to put up with the misbehaviour of his wives and then punish it), here was the alternative. Worse, young Nero had spent the time of Agrippina's exile, 39-41, in Domitia Lepida's house, and, like any aunt or grandmother, she spoilt him and so was a rival of Agrippina for his affections. Tacitus does not add that she was also the grandmother of Britannicus, with a closer interest in Messallina's son's claim to power than in Agrippina's, and that this may have been the reason for her destruction. The charge brought against her was of magic against her rival and of allowing slaves to run wild in Calabria (shepherds on the transhumance trails had been troublesome for more than a century). Nero appeared as a prosecution witness, persuaded perhaps by knowledge of her partiality for Britannicus. In the face of that the Emperor's sentence had to be death. Narcissus significantly is said to have been strongly opposed to it.[25]

If Britannicus' claim to power were to be sustained he must take the toga of manhood at least at the normal age of fourteen (in March 55 then), and, to match Nero, before he was thirteen and three months. This fact could have given rise to increasingly sharp disputes between Claudius and Agrippina in the last months of Claudius' life, from May 54 onwards, as Britannicus reached that age. Suetonius has it that in his last months Claudius began to rue his advancement of Nero (hence his tirade against unsatisfactory wives), repaired relations with the neglected Britannicus, and made his will. That is unconvincing. As Dorey insisted, Claudius is unlikely to have changed his mind about an established heir whether at the urging of Narcissus or on his own account: that would have been to invite civil war. Dorey suggested that the 'change of mind' was part of Agrippina's propaganda after she fell out with Nero (55–9); but the story would have its most natural genesis among her original opponents, adherents of Britannicus. Most plausibly, the rows were caused by Claudius' determination to keep to his original plan.[26]

Superstitious speculators, or those who believed that a person may know intuitively about his own state of health and imminent death, pointed out that Claudius had not provided for any consuls beyond the month in which he died; both the regular consuls were still in office on 18 June. Perhaps it was not presages that inhibited Claudius but uncertainty as to who should take on the last two months of 54; perhaps himself, exceptionally as suffect. Or, more probably, he thought of taking the regular consulship of 55, an idea that would have met resistance from his wife, because of what he would do with it in those last weeks of Britannicus' fourteenth year. Even with Nero installed as Princeps, it was as he approached that significant birthday, after the Saturnalia of mid-December 54, that Britannicus was taken ill at a banquet, died, and was given a speedy funeral.[27]

Murder cannot be proved, any more than it can in Claudius' case. Our earliest extant sources for Claudius' death, the author of the *Octavia* and the elder Pliny, assume murder without offering convincing detail: Pliny says only that a comet was seen when Claudius Caesar died by poison, leaving Nero heir to his power, and again during Nero's principate. The diverse accounts of Tacitus, Suetonius, and Dio show that nobody knew when, where, or by whom poison was administered; they built on the known facts that Claudius presided at a priestly banquet on the Capitol (for the Augustalia of 12 October) at which his taster, the eunuch Halotus, was in attendance, and that his next and last dinner was in the Palace. Tacitus and Dio have Claudius poisoned at home — Tacitus says by Halotus — with a mushroom treated on Agrippina's orders by the convicted poisoner Lucusta. Tacitus adds that after the first attempt failed, C.Stertinius Xenophon, Claudius' doctor, put a poisoned feather put down the Emperor's throat; Suetonius mentions both places, Halotus or Agrippina (with the mushroom) administering the poison, without deciding between them. Like Tacitus, he writes of a lingering death and a second attempt at poisoning, by gruel or enema.[28]

The timeliness of Claudius' death, and Britannicus', affords circumstantial evidence that both were murdered, although the fact that Halotus survived Nero inclines me to acquit him. Further, the absence of Narcissus at the time of Claudius' death — sent to Sinuessa by Agrippina, it was claimed, for his gout — fosters suspicion. He could not have guaranteed Claudius' safety; rather his absence made the smooth accession of Nero easier — at noon, at an astrologically favourable time — while the death was still concealed, the body under wraps in the Palace and the consuls and priests offering vows for the Emperor's recovery. Admittedly Claudius, always weakly, was in his sixty-fourth year, drank, and had been ill, perhaps in the autumn of 51, certainly and gravely in late 52 or early 53; and the year of his death seems to have been unhealthy: every magistracy lost a member. The strain of his dispute with Agrippina over the future of Britannicus may have brought on the heart attack that one modern scholar has diagnosed. But the death toll by judicial murder was already high, and on balance it looks as if Claudius' departure was brought about by Agrippina rather than due to her good luck.[29]

In any case, the movements of Britannicus and his sisters were monitored or checked, the Praetorian Guard lined up outside the Palace to receive its new Emperor and carry him to the barracks like his father. There Nero delivered an appropriate and presumably ready-prepared speech composed for him by Seneca, promised the same donative as Claudius had given, and was duly saluted *imperator*. Proceeding to the senate, the party found no hesitation. The necessary decrees launched the processes that would endow Nero with *imperium* and tribunician power. Nor did the provinces demur, governors, armies or subjects. They had been well prepared by the advancement of Nero during Claudius' later years: epigraphic monuments, coins, and sculpture made the position clear.[30]

Claudius died on 13 October and if the protocol of Augustus' and Tiberius' obsequies was followed, there would have been a lying in state of five days, followed by cremation on the 18th, a vigil by the widow, supported by members of the equestrian order, and insertion of the bones in the mausoleum on 24th. The first senate meeting at which Nero could establish Claudius' cult and outline his future plans would take place on the following day, 25th.[31]

Unfavourable facts were suppressed. Tacitus tells us that the will was not read in public, to prevent the fact that Nero had been preferred to Britannicus causing an upset. He is wrong about the reason. Nero's position depended heavily on a favourable will. What the public must not know was that Britannicus and Nero had been instituted equal heirs in it. In his last address to the senate Claudius had commended both youths to them. It would not have been the senate alone who prevented the reading of the will: the family's interests (that is those of Agrippina and Nero) were paramount.[32]

Scholars have been unwilling to accept the interpretation of court politics presented by ancient writers. The unscrupulous savagery of the participants is incredible. Some scholars have set themselves to redress the balance in favour of the rulers, shifting blame on to advisers, on to the victims themselves, who out of discontent or ambition offered provocation, sometimes on to an emperor's predecessor or successor. For the stress under which the participants lived scholars should recall other closed élites wielding unauthorized power over vast empires; and they should pay less attention to law. It is only occasionally that a clear decision is possible on legality in favour of the ruling clique, as for instance when there is a rising in a province like that of Scribonianus, or when an emperor is assassinated. Conversely, the guilt of the rulers is clear only from their blatant calumnies, such as the incest alleged between Silanus and his sister. Usually the grey area between innocence, through discontent, criticism, wishful thinking, magic, manoeuvring, and planning to active treason is too wide and too much open to interpretation to be charted successfully in legal terms. The area we are in is one where power is so important that legality, stretched to breaking point by the very existence of the Emperor, was only a weapon in the struggle. The first century of the Principate was part of a revolution and there were innumerable aftershocks as the new constitution established itself. It does not matter so much whether subversive action was contemplated, taken, or anticipated, whether Valerius Asiaticus was plotting against Claudius or was merely too successful for the courtiers or Claudius himself to permit. The level of envy, anxiety, or fear that each player was able to tolerate is what counted. The game must be analyzed essentially in terms of power and interest.[33]

Nor is it profitable to ask whether Claudius was the dupe of wives and advisers, when their interests coincided so closely with his, and his political position was so weak. Enduring ties based on blood and marriage, as well as on loyalty, favours, and obligations, had always been a feature of Roman politics, designed to mitigate the ruthlessness of individual ambition. On each critical occasion a group acted together or was fissured by divergent interests, each individual considering where his own interests lay. Such fissures occurred in the court in 47 and 54.

# 8

# THE POLICY OF THE EMPEROR

Can an Emperor be credited with 'policy'? More initiative may be allowed him than F.Millar permits. He is not a mechanism, but a person familiar with history and able to assess consequences beyond the immediate future. Only the backward-looking posture of the ancients, their view of a golden age in the past, made them more passive, less likely to initiate change, more content with remedying abuse, than modern politicians. Claudius had principles, even ideals, to be applied as long as the prime condition of his own survival was met.[1]

But the policy most commonly credited to Claudius was not one of which he had anything to say. The notion that the usurping Emperor Claudius undertook a systematic policy of 'centralization' has had a long run since it came into fashion in the heyday of the Dictators, and will need examination before we can pass to any others. The word 'centralization' entered written English in the first third of the nineteenth century, and means increasing the control of a geographical centre, depriving local authorities of power, responsibility, and funds; in Britain, for example, the transfer of administrative functions from local councils to Whitehall.

Applied to the Roman Empire, the word has been been assigned a different meaning. Relations between 'local' government, cities and tribes, with the central Roman administration, are not stressed, although 'any tendency to set up or to revive regional autonomies was always decisively suppressed'. What is cited as centralization of this kind, the refusal to allow the city of Alexandria a city council, was not a novelty of Claudius' reign but inherited from Augustus. Claudius' 'centralizing policy' is supposed to be signalled by his opening of the Senate to Gauls from Comata in 48: the claim is that he disregarded the privileges of Rome and Italy and set himself to achieve uniformity and equal status for the provinces, a reversal of the Augustan conception and intended to bring the Empire under the single control of the Emperor; governing and governed were to be reduced to the common level of the subject. There is no evidence for any such plan on Claudius' part, nor on that of Caesar who has been credited with the same idea a century previously.[2]

Another interpretation of 'centralization' predominates: it was a 'frontal attack' on the power and prestige of the aristocracy. But here it must be said at once that the word is less appropriate: senatorial decisions themselves emanated from one body in Rome. The issue, genuine enough, was the relative powers of that body and of one of its members, the Emperor.

The materials for constructing the theory of Claudian 'centralization' as an attack on senatorial power and prestige are of three kinds: allusions in the ancient sources to the Emperor's proneness to intervene in matters that might have been left to take their own course; recognition of his political difficulties with the Senate, and of tussles for power with them; and minor administrative changes made for diverse reasons. Together the materials are mutually supportive. Looked at more closely, however, the changes seem scrappy and even inconsistent. Sometimes the knights are favoured, sometimes they are attacked with the Senate. They were becoming functionaries who took their orders from freedmen, or were being paralyzed by the concentration of wealth, and so of trade, in the hands of the Emperor. Gaps in the construction have to be papered over or excused. Neither together nor separately do they provide reasons for believing that Claudius had any policy that could be called by a name so comprehensive and so modern.[3]

The Emperor's indubitable taste for doing things himself is attested by the ancient writers and provides a core for this version of 'centralization' in impeccable Latin: Tacitus accuses him of concentrating all legal and magisterial functions on himself. But this refers specifically to his passion for sitting in court; Tacitus happens to apply a very similar expression to Augustus, with a far clearer reference to the concentration of political power in the hands of an individual.[4]

Actions and reforms are cited in support of 'centralization', especially the claim that Claudius created or organized a secretariat of freedmen, a 'ministry' or 'cabinet', even a 'civil service', to direct operations throughout the Empire and above all in Rome and Italy where Principes had had little executive machinery at their disposal. Now, it is claimed, each private secretary was allotted a defined task and each department was established in a special office. New officials were created: a Procurator of Libraries, a Patronage Secretary (a studiis), Polybius. The imperial court became the executive headquarters of the administration, securing the Emperor's independence of the senate and enabling him to establish control over the procurators in the senatorial provinces and to involve himself in all business. Hence the unusual judicial activity remarked on by the ancient writers. Further, it is claimed that because the chief offices fell to men outside the Roman tradition the whole 'Italic' base of the Empire began to collapse, although the cosmopolitanism of freedmen uprooted from their native soil and committed to the service of one man gave no representation to provincial interests.[5]

The conception of a departmentalized administration was destroyed by Millar when he showed that the freedmen were advisers and friends like Cicero's Tiro, whose influential counsel often had nothing to do with any 'departments' of which they were in charge. Sulla and Pompey had had influential freedman, while Tiberius had laid himself open to their encroaching power by retiring from Rome; in 28 he was already complaining of an attempt to bribe them; and it was worth while for the aspirant to the Jewish kingdom, Agrippa, to spend his all on them. Even Gaius, so jealous of his power, had influential freedmen, especially Helicon, who could be blamed for his hostility towards Alexandrian Jews; their importance is clearly shown by the part that Callistus played in Gaius' assassination.[6]

Claudius should never have been given the credit of organizing and assigning the members their 'departments'. Augustus needed secretaries to deal with his paper work. Tiberius had an '*a rationibus*' (accountant) and other servants with specific titles; indeed, a memorial tablet commemorating his slave Musicus Scurranus, cashier at the Gallic Treasury in the province of Lugdunensis, was erected by Musicus' own slaves, all of whom except the woman at the end, Secunda, had titles and so defined functions: secretary, cook, footman, and so on. Private individuals also possessed servitors with titles.[7]

These men did become more important under Claudius, and their importance was more openly acknowledged. There were three related reasons for this. First, the level of society in which Claudius moved before his elevation: the freedmen were men he trusted. Second, the development of the monarchical side of the Principate and of the court, in part a consequence of the way Claudius was elevated against the wishes of the senate. And third, Claudius' honesty in giving credit where he thought it due; he prided himself on the trait, as the *SC* of 53 set up in honour of the leading freedman Pallas demonstrated, speaking of 'the Emperor's generous promptitude in acknowledging and rewarding merit'. The same can be seen in his frank recognition of the services of the Alexandrian Greeks on the delegation that came to him in 41; of the knight of Vienna, Vestinus, whose son he commended to the senate in 48; and, to a point where honesty became an inability to keep his mouth shut and avoid giving material to critics, precisely in his acknowledgment of Pallas as the author of the *SC Claudianum*. Pallas' position in charge of the Emperor's accounts (*a rationibus*) gave him knowledge of and power over State finances. The other freedmen were disliked for their incidental political influence, not for their control of a bureaucracy.[8]

Advocates of 'centralization' have made extravagant claims for Claudius' enhancement of the judicial powers of his procurators, so that their decisions were treated as equivalent to his own: it liberated the imperial treasury from senatorial control and gave administrative effect to the concentration of finance in the hands of the Emperor. The beginning of this process, the usurpation of power by procurators such as Lucilius Capito, certainly meant lowering the power and prestige of the senatorial governor in comparison with those of an imperial official. But if the final outcome in Claudius' reign was to deny the right of appeal from procurators to himself, the result was to devolve his own power on to the men on the spot in the provinces — the reverse of 'centralization'.[9]

Claudius notoriously intervened in financial matters and inserted procurators into senatorial boards, such as the Curators of the Tiber or of Aqueducts, where an additional imperial slave force was provided, larger than the original senatorial body. Certainly such changes had the effect of discrediting past senatorial efforts, perhaps of diminishing the boards' freedom of action, though not its scope; the formal shape of the administration was unchanged, and the responsibilities of the boards were not altered. The aim was evidently to increase efficiency and dispatch. Claudius' conduct was pragmatic, not politically motivated. Senatorial curators of roads under Tiberius were said to have misappropriated funds earmarked for road construction, or to have entered into shady deals with contractors. Gaius encouraged Cn. Domitius Corbulo (suff.39) to force the curators to disgorge alleged profits. Claudius restored the money, perhaps only for political reasons, perhaps because the charges were ill-founded.[10]

Another change that has been canvassed as evidence of 'centralization' is the transferring of responsibility for the payment of grain distributions from the State to the imperial Treasury — from the Aerarium to the Fiscus — and of the organization of the distribution to a Procurator Porticus Minuciae. These are better examples since the introduction of a new official involved an administrative reform and the Emperor was on hand to observe what was done — and to suffer from it if his arrangements failed. But there is no evidence for a once-for-all transfer of the cost, and the procurator in charge of the Minucian distribution centre, itself not certainly a Claudian creation, did not supersede any senatorial official: the first attested Procurator ad Miniciam belongs to Trajan's reign, and the view that the senators previously in charge of distribution, the Praefecti Frumenti Dandi, did not operate between the reigns of Claudius and Nerva is mistaken.[11]

Momigliano regarded the enlargement of the port of Ostia as 'a frontal assault on senatorial authority'. The office of Quaestor Ostiensis, who had judicial functions in the town and had long been responsible for securing the transport of grain up to Rome, was abolished in 44, and the freedman Procurator Portus Ostiensis emerges; there was no replacement for the other naval quaestor, the Quaestor Gallicus, who was probably stationed at Ariminum (Rimini) and whose post went at the same time; in Momigliano's view the supervision of shipyards and bases under these quaestors was taken over by the Prefects of the Fleet at Ravenna and Misenum, with the Ostian procurator charged only with the construction of the new harbour and of merchant shipping: this abolition of the quaestorships in favour of imperial officials carried Augustan policy, which was to avoid stationing quaestors at the headquarters of the fleet, to its extreme. More recently it has been argued that even after the Prefect became the official who dealt with the grain shippers (essentially a book-keeping job, according to G.Rickman), the Quaestor continued to see to the storage of grain and its transport upriver, and the organization of the harbour and market, as well as retaining control over shipping and even responsibility for the Ostian naval squadron. It is conventional to hold that in 44 these duties were assigned to the newly created Procurator, a subordinate of the Prefect of the grain supply. Yet neither places nor timing fit. Ariminum is not Ravenna, nor Ostia Misenum; and the Procurator should have been created as soon as the construction of the harbour was put in hand in 42, so that it is not clear that the Ostian quaestorship was abolished *in favour of* the freedman Procurator. No ancient source claims that it was, and the Procurator's title suggests a particular concern with the new harbour and its construction. What Claudius saw of the quaestors' activities in 43–4, when his travels took him both to Ostia and to north-east Italy, may be more relevant. He wanted to employ them in a more useful, and equally traditional way, as State Treasurers. Jurisdiction in the town, previously in the Quaestor's purview, might be left to the local magistrates, who could not be expected to submit to a freedman.[12]

New procuratorships, which have been said to show the tightening of imperial control in financial matters, need careful scrutiny. According to Momigliano Claudius had to supplement the *a rationibus* with a whole class of special superintendents, such as the procurators in charge of the 5% tax on inheritances and on the freeing of slaves. There is no evidence for the existence of these procuratorships before Claudius' reign, but absence of evidence cannot prove that there were none.[13]

At the heart of State finances, Claudius is accused of destroying the independence of the State Treasury: in 44 he transferred it from the two praetors selected annually by lot since 23 BC to quaestors chosen by himself. They were to hold the post for three years and then enjoy preferment in the next stage of their career. They were to advance immediately to the praetorship or take command of a legion even before they held the praetorship. (It depended on achievement in the office.) Ancient writers do not interpret the change of 44 as a threat to the independence of the State Treasury; nor do they see political significance or a concession to senatorial tradition in the return twelve years later, in Nero's 'senatorial' period, his 'golden age', to selected prefects (also to hold office for three years). On the face of it the backward-looking move was Claudius': the State Treasury had been in the charge of two quaestors (under the supervision of the consuls) during the Republic. What was wanting under Claudius, as Tacitus makes quite clear in his discussion of the change of 56, was firmness in the quaestors, in spite of their three-year term. It was not demands made by the Princeps on the Treasury that they failed to resist, but those of superior magistrates. Praetors showed firmness in 15 by refusing a senator's demand for compensation for the roadway and aqueduct that were being driven through his property; Tiberius solved the problem by paying it himself. Claudius, then, was redeploying magistrates in a conservative sense, and misconduct by the Treasury praetors of 42 in connexion with sales and leases of State property was probably a precipitating factor, just as a quaestor's excessive zeal in collecting debts precipitated the change of 56.[14]

It is hard to take seriously the next plank in the case: a campaign against a senate terrorized and shorn of its power. Several items are adduced: the introduction of new members and the creation of patricians to alter the senate's character; even its surrender of control of permissions for its members to leave Italy. The changes Claudius made, when examined individually, will take on a less sinister aspect. Here it is enough to note that the reputations of other emperors who paid attention to making up the numbers of senate and patriciate — notably Augustus and Vespasian — stood high in the ancient world. It is alleged that irregularities in the appointment and renewal of proconsuls showed them becoming the Emperor's servants: but irregularities due to need, favouritism, or inertia had already made the reign of Tiberius notorious.[15]

Another attempt to strike at senators, through their military privileges, has been seen. Claudius reversed the normal order of the two posts in the equestrian military career, those of the Tribunus Militum (Military Tribune) commanding one of the six cohorts in a legion, each notionally of a thousand men, and the Praefectus Alae, commander of an independent auxiliary cavalry squadron of 500 men. Claudius made the tribunate the second and senior post. This is seen as an attempt to boost the authority of the knights who predominated five to one in the legionary tribunates. They would now come to the tribunate after experience in two preliminary positions, the prefecture of the auxiliary infantry cohort of 500 men, and that of the cavalry squadron; their senatorial counterparts would be tiros. The change undermined the authority of the senatorial legionary commander himself, by showing that he was superfluous. Complementary was Claudius' introduction of supernumerary tribunates, which made it possible for a man to hold the required military posts without going near the army; again senatorial influence would be diminished. Resistance on the part of the Senate prevented the reforms from surviving their author.[16]

This explanation of the reforms is far-fetched. Their alleged purpose, the abolition of the senatorial legate, was not achieved. The legionary tribunate was no place to fight a political battle against the senate: it was a desk-borne job of little military or political importance. A more likely explanation is that Claudius was taking two separate measures. First, he was insisting on the seniority of the more distinguished — as Statius calls it — legionary post, which involved commanding Roman citizens. It was a pedantic change, given the tactical independence of the auxiliary command that he was demoting. But it was made in the context of a shortage of tribunes of senatorial rank; they had been becoming rarer in the last century of the Republic and under Augustus only a token one — perhaps an irreducible minimum, rather than a standard number — was left in each legion outside Egypt. Now Claudius was enhancing the qualifications required by knights for the military tribunate and so its senior status, making it more worthwhile a post. On the other hand, there were young men of good birth and promise for senatorial or equestrian posts but unsuitable for military duties (some Greek intellectuals, perhaps; and it is worth remembering Claudius' own disabilities). These were now enabled to take an honorary position as a qualification for further service. C.Stertinius Xenophon has been suggested as one instance, along with Ti. Claudius Balbillus. We are not told that holders of honorary posts were all of senatorial origin.[17]

There is another area in which Claudius has been credited with a unified policy: that of religion. The evidence is disparate, though much of it belongs to the middle years of the reign. The fact that each item has a religious dimension has caused them to be taken together as evidence of Claudius' preoccupation with religion — as if that could be separated from Roman public life generally. But these items, though interlinked, are to be treated separately. Three concerns emerge: first, with the conduct of subjects; second, with the stability of Roman society; third, with his own position. The second and third were both to be secured by using the ballast of history, legislation, and divine sanction. The clustering of relevant material round the years 47-9 reflects political anxiety: Claudius' fear for his own position and general fear for Rome's security. They surfaced in an expression of apparent optimism connected with one of the proposals: in the present universal well-being, the Emperor urged that gratitude for the beneficence of the gods be shown; rituals devised for times of crisis should not be neglected in prosperity.[18]

Claudius' attitude towards the Jewish communities of Rome and elsewhere resolves itself into concern for order amongst Rome's subjects. His dealings with other non-Roman cults are connected with his interest in maintaining the stability of Roman society. The high repute of the Eleusinian Mysteries, which he is said to have considered transferring to Rome, made them a more acceptable alternative to Judaism and its offshoot Christianity for Romans who were looking for fresh religious experience. Interest in alien cults went with political unease. Frequent portents, revealing that the peace of the gods (*pax deorum*) had been broken, made it desirable to regulate the familiar operations of the *haruspices*, diviners originally from Etruria who attended magistrates and private individuals and indicated the likely outcome of courses of action by examining the entrails of sacrificial animals. When they interpreted untoward signs as they did in 65 BC, just before the Catilinarian conspiracy, it was often in disturbing terms of political disaster. These diviners seem to have been achieving ever greater importance compared with official augury as politics became detached from the formal proceedings of public assemblies. In 47 Claudius promoted an *SC* to organize or reorganize them in a college, bringing them under official scrutiny.[19]

In the same year Claudius publicized his own confidence in the future of Rome by holding Secular Games (it was Rome's eighth centenary), and in 49 he revived after a lapse of seventy-five years the Augury of Security (*Augurium Salutis*), an inquiry made in peace-time as to whether the gods would be propitious to a prayer for the safety of the state; venturing to take the augury was itself a display of assurance. Bad omens had prevented Cicero from accomplishing it in his fateful consulship of 63 BC. Even Augustus does not seem to have repeated it after 28 BC.[20]

Claudius' extension of the Pomerium, the sacred boundary of the city, in 49 referred to Rome's past achievements, but also to his own; it was a visible token of his success in war. His moderation in respect of the imperial cult, classified as another aspect of his 'religious' policy, was essentially political, part of a prudent conception of the Princeps' role in the Empire and a reaction to the autocracy of Gaius.

The evidence for the policies commonly attributed to Claudius proved unsatisfactory. That does not mean that enquiry should be given up. Claudius' principles emerge in his own words and in those of friends and flatterers. From them flowed courses of action undertaken in response to appeal or spontaneously. From Claudius' historical knowledge came real policies on such matters as how best to deal with Parthians or Germans. *Constantia*, consistency and firmness, was a quality on which Claudius prided himself.[21]

First Claudius had to adopt a stance towards the assassinated Gaius. He was in a delicate position because his title to rule came largely from kinship with Gaius' father. In 41 Claudius refused to allow decrees ordering the destruction of Gaius' statues, the erasure of his name from monuments, all the procedures that in the full form came to be known as 'condemning a man's memory' (*damnare memoriam*). Instead he had the images removed quietly by night. That left Gaius in the same limbo that Tiberius inhabited, neither damned nor deified: oaths were not taken to their acts, and they were not mentioned in official prayers. In 42 Claudius would not celebrate the day of Gaius' assassination, even though it was the anniversary of his own accession, only giving the Praetorians a tip of a hundred HS each on the day he was 'declared *imperator*'. Claudius' ambivalence is illustrated by a pun in the *Apocolocyntosis*, where he is accused of having 'prosecuted' his predecessor.[22]

Scholars who have stressed Claudius' repudiation of Gaius may have been misled by coin types struck in 41-2. *Constantia*, steadiness, has been seen as an attack on Gaius' inconsistency (*inconstantia*), or rather his destructive frenzy (*furor*); *Pax* and *Victoria* are taken to represent a victory over tyranny; the legend commemorating citizens saved (*ob cives servatos*), which is accompanied by an oak crown reverse and an obverse portrait of the new Princeps wearing it, is taken for a reference to his having saved them from Gaius, who had neglected the vital grain supply. Claudius was often outspoken about Gaius' failings: damage to public works, even insanity. But the coins are more plausibly to be connected with Claudius' forbearance after the assassination (citizens saved), his refusal to take hasty measures (steadiness), the peace that his accession assured, and the victory in Mauretania soon after his accession. These themes persist in the coinage. Claudius quietly remedied what he could of Gaius' abuses: exiles were brought back, extravagant expenditure on games (and the consequent cost to magistrates) was avoided, works of art plundered by his predecessor returned.[23]

It was not until 43 that the senate decreed that Gaius' bronze coinage was to be melted down — only for Messallina to have statues of her lover the actor Mnester made of the metal. That is a good joke that Dio or his source has taken seriously. Claudius' own *aes* had been coming into circulation over the past two years, but whether the senate intended to annihilate a massive coinage seems problematical: no more than a token sample, perhaps what was in the State Treasury, as Sutherland suggested, can have been dealt with. But the declared intention may have been more sweeping.[24]

Claudius' prime task as Princeps was, as he saw, to heal the wounds of seventeen years, in particular those of Gaius' reign, and of the terror of 24-5 January, 41. Restoring an empire scorched and ruined was how Seneca put it, but Claudius, so often in the hands of physicians, favoured the metaphor of healing. Claudius left nothing undone to wipe away those memories.[25]

The immediate step was to exercise clemency. Claudius advocated an amnesty to those involved in Gaius' assassination, referring to the amnesty accorded the oligarchs by the Athenian people at the end of the Peloponnesian War in 403 BC. The comparison of his régime with the Athenian democracy suggests Claudius' political sympathies. Closer to home was his allusion to the attempt by the senate, under Cicero's guidance, to bring about an amnesty for the assassins of Julius Caesar — made fruitless by the zeal of Antony and Octavian. Here the point was not so much the merits of Cicero's policy as Claudius' superior restraint under provocation, outdoing the earlier dynasts.[26]

A claim to *clementia* does not imply supra-legal power; it had been made by Tiberius and was open to any office holder. However, it is the virtue of a superior to an inferior and its association with Julius Caesar gave it unwelcome monarchical associations. It shows Claudius with enemies at his mercy and prepared to let bygones go. Clemency was presented by the exiled Seneca as the Emperor's leading virtue — and singled out for mockery by Tacitus. Claudius himself boasted in 41 of tender care for his fellow human beings in his letter to the Alexandrians, warning them not to abuse it. Even the rebel Briton Caratacus was spared in 51, giving Claudius the right to claim that he would become an undying paradigm of clemency. Here he outdid Julius Caesar, whose great Gallic opponent Vercingetorix was executed in the Tullianum.[27]

In the long run another quality, civility, behaving like a citizen, was the keynote. Claudius was at pains not to raise fears of a second Gaius intent on self-glorification. The previous régime showed Claudius that high expenditure on honours for the Emperor and his close kin generated more offence than awe. He began by declining on grounds of expense all but one silver portrait of himself (presumably a bust) and two statues, one in bronze, the other in marble. Birth, marriage, and betrothal in the imperial family came weeks after his accession — and were quietly handled.[28]

Claudius' historical interests and his lack of experience make it particularly relevant for us to look for his models in Roman history. We have noticed the minor theme of giving Antony his due, which besides being an act of justice helped to enlist the loyalty of subjects in the east. Augustus (not Antony's opponent but the founder of the dynasty) is accepted as Claudius' prime model; swearing by Augustus was after all his most solemn oath. It would be surprising if Claudius had genuine regard for Augustus, considering the opinion that the Princeps had of him. And the part of Augustus' principate that Claudius had witnessed, say from the age of ten, had been far from happy. The theme of Augustus as Claudius' model is prominent in Tacitus. There is good reason for it. It served Tacitus' purpose, as K. Seif has pointed out, to juxtapose it to Claudian failures — the draining of the Fucine Lake, his attempt to put Meherdates on the throne of Parthia. But Tacitus' use of the Augustan model to expose Claudius' weaknesses shows how Claudius' deployment of Augustus' name should be interpreted. It was public; he used it as a gesture of good intent, and, as Tiberius had, for justification, as a knock-down political argument from precedent. It need not be sincere and it is also uninformative. 'Back to Augustus', like 'back to Lenin', was a safe programme, given the changes that the Augustan Principate had undergone in the founder's own time. For Claudius' true model for his political thinking we must look further back.[29]

Seeing the Principate in operation from the outside and resenting his exclusion made Claudius a severe critic. Tiberius the negligent absentee and Gaius, who not only let things slide but was out of his mind, did not get the respect that Augustus had to have in public. The model that Claudius' heart was set on was not Augustus but Caesar, murdered before he had time to carry his programme through (this left room for imaginative reconstruction). Being carried to power by the troops in face of senatorial resistance, taking the name Caesar, exercising clemency, would have put Claudius in mind of the Dictator. Impatience with Augustus and his maxim 'Make haste slowly' and irritation with the do-nothing absentee who succeeded him, as well as with Gaius' squandering of power, had probably done so long before. On 24 January, 41, the senate, summoned elsewhere than to the Curia Julia, considered motions advocating the erasure of memorials bearing the name of the Caesars and the destruction of all temples devoted to the extinct clan (Gaius was the last C.Julius Caesar). Claudius immortalized the name.[30]

With normality restored, the *quies* and *pax* that Caesar had claimed he wanted for Italy, Claudius was free to seek achievement and fame, late in life and outdoing all his predecessors including Caesar, perhaps especially him. He lost no time. The harbour at Ostia that Caesar had shrunk from beginning was put in hand in the first year of his reign. The draining of the Fucine lake, a project that Caesar had not had time to undertake, was begun soon after; and the conquest of Britain, relinquished in 54 BC, was taken up before Claudius had been three years in power. He even deployed the same spectacular weapon that Caesar had used: the elephant; and his strikingly successful victory could be compared by Orosius with Caesar's unacceptable rebuff.[31]

Claudius conspicuously resumed another practice first developed on a large scale by Caesar: colonization in the provinces. Caesar had had to dispose of his veteran legionaries and members of the urban plebs: 80,000 men in all, and he was not willing to disrupt Italy with colonies in the way Sulla had done in 81 BC. But Caesar had also been aware of the need to win support in the provinces. Claudius shared his awareness. Seneca grossly misrepresented the policy after Claudius' death: Claudius wanted to see all the Gauls, Greeks and Britons in togas. Seneca expected a sympathetic hearing for that from his audience: Claudius had offended public opinion with his generosity. Further, Claudius advocated admitting wealthy Roman citizens from the provinces of Comata to the senate. In his speech Claudius, with unusual and conspicuous discretion, referred only to the precedent set by Augustus and Tiberius in bringing on Italian worthies. But it was Caesar's precedent in admitting Gauls that was relevant.[32]

Claudius could not display his emulation of Caesar: it was either damaging or ridiculous. But it fits in well with his strenuous activity in public life. As age advanced Claudius may have felt that he no longer needed to emulate a man who had died at 55 satiated with glory. Most of the initiatives belong to the first three years of the reign. Perhaps from 48 onwards self-defence and the succession preoccupied him. In the early period Claudius showed a realistic conception of his position and powers, which he intended to use to the full, for his own security, but benevolently when possible. On accession he passed from makeshift survival stratagems to longer term strategies, some perhaps long considered. It is important to distinguish conscious aims such as the material welfare of Rome and Italy from the mere means devised by the Emperor for achieving them, and from trends in political and social life that he can at most have observed only dimly.

# 9

# SENATE AND EQUESTRIAN ORDER: CLAUDIUS AND THE ARISTOCRACY

In 41 the senate had declared Claudius a public enemy, a version of his accession has him contemplating its extermination, and a civil war had been raised against him in 42 which resulted in the deaths of a number of senators. By forcing himself on the senate Claudius inflicted a deep wound in its authority and self-regard. Members felt that blow in varying degrees. He had many to fear, as his precautions against assassination show; some were maintained after the crisis of 41 was over, throughout the reign. He proclaimed his danger in the House itself, and his fears were justified by the abortive revolution of 42. Although the ambitions of individual senators and the outrage of the whole House are distinct, they are connected because rivals would offer a better deal than Claudius in return for support. How far Claudius could go to mitigate senatorial dislike, and how successful he was in the course of his reign, must be investigated in the light of his demeanour in the House, his use of office, his promotions, and the part played by the senate in decision-making.[1]

To behave as if the trauma of January, 41 had never been inflicted would do something to heal it. Claudius made immediate gestures: the amnesty for senators, conferment of consulships on Republicans and possible rivals, restoration to a Pompeius of his grand surname Magnus, which Gaius had forbidden him; the burning of denunciations made to Gaius, and the return of exiles, not just Gaius' sisters, but senators who had fallen victim even before Gaius' accession to him and his allies.[2]

Claudius also went out of his way to placate the senate by displaying positive merits. First, unassuming deference (*civilitas*). Courtesy cost nothing: Claudius was interested in real power, not trappings and insolence, and he had learned from his predecessor what impression lack of respect made. When in the House Claudius made a point of rising to address the consuls, doing better than Julius Caesar, who had caused offence when 'indisposition' prevented him greeting members on his feet. In 42 he began remitting the readings of speeches by Augustus and Tiberius that had become obligatory at the opening of the year. Further, although he took an oath to the acts of Augustus, he wasted no time while the entire body of fifty-six magistrates went through it: one man from each college was enough. Again unlike Caesar, and before him the anxious upstart Marius, both of whom entered the House as consul wearing triumphal dress, Claudius was sparing in his use of it. Courtesy was extended to individuals as well. Claudius was sensitive to physical weakness and allowed a senator who could not hear the debate, L. Sulla, to sit on the praetor's bench. He himself would remain seated to respond to queries, but rose if his peers had been on their feet for any length of time. The courtesies had their social side. Claudius visited the sick and gave a banquet for senators and their wives, for knights and the people in their tribes. The Emperor made a point, perhaps early in the reign, of sharing senatorial festivities.[3]

Second, *libertas*. Claudius could not trump the consuls' proclamation in 41, but he could offer something approaching it, for which the same word would do: *aes* coins struck at Rome bear on their reverse a liberty cap (worn by slaves on their liberation) and the legend LIBERTAS AUGUSTA S(enatus) C(onsulto). The view that this *Augustan* liberty is a riposte to unqualified, that is, Republican liberty, is surely correct. Claudius continued to be presented as a champion of freedom on later coins and on the Cyzicus arch of 51. Claudius was an eager participant in meetings of the House, more so than any other emperor between Augustus' prime and the reign of Vespasian, at least until the last years of his reign, and we shall see him trying to involve the senate in discussion and decision-making — where practicable — to mitigate damage to the relationship. He could present himself as one of the senate when he chose, as in 48 when he was trying to persuade the House to look with favour on would-be members from Comata, though he is not found reiterating Tiberius' claim to be just a senator invested with peculiar power.[4]

Unlike Augustus and Tiberius, Claudius came to power having held only one suffect (replacement) consulship. Young Gaius, needing *auctoritas*, had come in as suffect in 37 and returned as one of the regular consuls of 39, though only for thirty days. In 40 he held the consulship without a colleague until 13 January and in the following year gave up the *fasces* after less than a week. This repetition, and tenure for only a few days (not to mention the depositions of 39 and the lack of a colleague in 40), were offensive to senatorial opinion. Claudius, also lacking *auctoritas* and needing the office, had to find a compromise. He showed self-restraint in refraining from holding the consulship for a second time until 42, leaving in office the men who had presided over the accession debates of 24-5 January. In 41 he was 'designated consul for the second time'; designation to the fourth consulship (47) came in the year of the third (43); to the fifth (51) only in the previous year. In 42, 43 and 47 Claudius held office for a respectable but not greedy two months, on the last occasion doing honour to L. Vitellius who was himself holding office for the third time and about to share the censorship with the Emperor. Claudius' last consulship, of 51, went on for much longer, at least to the end of October: it was his decennial year, and the one in which he celebrated his sixtieth birthday (1 August).[5]

Emperors since Augustus had exercised a strong though usually concealed influence on the election of qualified individuals to the consulship. Scrutinizing the known consuls shows Claudius' reign in line with the decade before he came to power and with the Principate of Nero. The proportion of consulships held by men descended from the Republican nobility declined markedly under the Julio-Claudians (Augustus 50%, late Tiberius and Gaius 27%, Claudius 21%, Nero 15%), although their grip on the two leading posts of each year relaxed more slowly (Augustus 64% of *ordinarii*, late Tiberius-Gaius 41%, Claudius 25%, Nero 23%). In the advancement of parvenus Claudius' reign is slightly out of line: 27% as opposed to 36% in the ten years that preceded it; under Nero it was nearly 42%. The reason may be that Claudius was preoccupied with honouring his own close supporters and their sons and with placating potential rivals. The proportion of men from the Republican nobility who held suffect consulships under Claudius was relatively high: 21% as against late Tiberius-Gaius 14%, Nero 12%. They may also have been squeezed out of the regular positions.[6]

The honour done Vitellius by Claudius' use of the consulship is clear; no other senator had held the *fasces* three times since M.Agrippa; indeed, the only private individuals to occupy a second consulship between 27 BC and 41 were the military man T.Statilius Taurus and Q.Sanquinius Maximus, the Prefect of the City who succeeded Gaius in the year of crisis, February 39. Claudius allowed second consulships as a mark of distinction to outstanding members of the order, such as C.Sallustius Passienus Crispus (44), M.Vinicius (45), Valerius Asiaticus (46), and C.Antistius Vetus (50). A lesser distinction was to be allowed the office for a whole year: C.Caecina Largus (42), M. Silanus (46), L.Vipstanus Poplicola (48), and Faustus Sulla (52). The claims of the first three rested on their connexion with the imperial family. Vetus was a special case: he had succeeded Valerius Asiaticus, who had resigned unexpectedly, and was himself replaced by Sulpicius Camerinus, having served only fifteen days; so he was given a second run. The reign also saw the consulship deployed between fathers and sons, as with the Vitellii (47 and 48) and Suillii (41 and 50), and brothers, the younger Vitellii (48) and the Flavii, Sabinus and Vespasian (47 and 51), highlighting the favour their families enjoyed. Honour was not the only purpose of these promotions. The men would be useful, both as leaders of the House when they were in office and amongst the consulars afterwards.[7]

It had been Augustus who in 5 BC introduced what became a regular system of suffects, making it possible for four or even more men to hold the *fasces*, ennoble themselves if they were new men, and qualify for high posts in the provinces; in Flavian times the regular number reached six. Originally it was accepted that each magistrate should hold office for six months. The Princeps' consulships, changes of régime, and other political upheavals disturbed the system, and there was constant pressure to increase the number of consuls, making more men available for further work and maximizing imperial patronage; the danger of cheapening the office was a restraining factor. Claudius inherited the scheme when it had been working nearly half a century, but in Gaius' reign every year except 38 (two pairs for six months each) had been irregular. Two new factors, Claudius' own need to accumulate consulships and his wish to confer second consulships on specially favoured persons, presented a problem, solved by giving the regular consulship for two months to a man holding it for a second time and allowing a suffect to hold office for the next four months, so that their combined terms lasted six. Towards the end of the reign pairs of suffects enjoying only the last two months of the year occur, to be explained by the pressure on the office from deserving men (especially after the crisis of 48), new protégés being advanced under Agrippina's auspices, and increased habituation to irregularity and short-term office. These November and December suffects may imply that the second and less honorific six months of the year were subdivided for the benefit of up-and-coming, if not well born servants of the régime. 51, when the new man, and later Emperor, Vespasian held his first consulship, was a case in point. November and December suffects were not infrequent in Nero's reign, and in the Flavian period three sets of consuls a year became the norm.[8]

The system made it easier for Principes to promote new and able but sometimes unprepossessing men to the highest office. Claudius sometimes did this. He continued the advancement of a man allegedly the son of a gladiator, Q.Curtius Rufus ('he's his own father', commented Tiberius when his support for Rufus' candidature for the praetorship met with criticism). The truculent Curtius was suffect in 43, a safe man during Claudius' absence because a nobody. He went on to command the Upper Rhine armies in 47, winning the *ornamenta triumphalia* for an engineering feat, and passing eventually to the proconsulship of Africa — where he had begun his career as a self-made man, and where he was to die. Claudius may have had an additional reason for favouring Curtius: a shared interest in history. The consulship of the deadly prosecutor and former exile P. Suillius at the end of 41 was controversial, but was probably due to Gaius. He had once been Germanicus' quaestor, and he was half-brother to Corbulo and Gaius' wife Milonia. Another recalled exile, T.Vinius Rufinus, who reached the praetorship, was observed filching plate from the Emperor's dinner table, but kept his place there as well as in the senate, though henceforward he had to be content with earthenware souvenirs.[9]

Claudius was willing to sacrifice senatorial tradition in making appointments, then, if it were in conflict with loyalty and efficiency. Nor were magistrates left entirely to their own devices. The activities of the praetors in fixing contracts were subject to supervision and correction. Such checks, admirable in themselves, were rightly seen by Tacitus as an erosion of the authority of the magistrate. Then Claudius intervened in the working of senatorial machinery, as when Ser. Galba was sent to Africa *extra ordinem* and retained there for a second year, probably because the province required a competent military man, as it had in 21 when Tiberius asked the senate to choose an effective commander. Besides proroguing in Africa, Claudius did so in Achaea and Crete with Cyrene, slowing up the careers of the men involved; but there was nothing like the extensions of Tiberius' sluggish régime. In 44 Claudius made permanent alterations in the administrative machinery, putting quaestors in charge of the State Treasury for a three-year stint; he was careful not to discourage them by retarding their future advancement excessively; it is significant that those known to have held this post were new men, and presumably amenable. Some were allowed to move directly to the praetorship, others received a salary according to the repute they had won while holding the junior magistracy, which must mean that they were given an imperial post (a legionary legateship was not uncommon).[10]

Claudius knew not only that in some sense he had to work with the senate, but that the great consultative and legislative body had to be seen to be effective. In spite of the complaints about the limited role of the senate which Nero made in his accession speech of October, 54, Claudius seems to have made free use of the senate as a forum and of senatorial decrees (*Senatus Consulta, SCC*) for legislation. Claudius' reign has a higher apparent fecundity in *SCC* and imperial addresses to the senate than that of any other Princeps; an average of one every nine months. Only Hadrian (117–38) and Marcus Aurelius and his colleagues (161–80) come near it (nine and a half months).[11]

Foreign affairs and matters concerning Rome's 'allies', traditionally the business of the senate, are found being dealt with in the House: in 41 Claudius struck a treaty with his friend Agrippa I of Judaea, which the king commemorated numismatically as being with Senate and Roman People; the House debated the subjection of Lycia in 43, heard a Parthian embassy in 49 and the cases for tax relief for Cos and Byzantium in 53. Two related suspicions arise. First, that there was an element of theatre in the proceedings, not always impeccably managed (the Lycian affair involved Claudius in a real scene): the Parthians were lectured, the grant to Cos was an occasion for lauding its distinguished citizen, Claudius' doctor C. Stertinius Xenophon. Second, that Claudius was fatally attracted to this mode when he had made up his mind but sensed objections in the offing, as there were against the men from Comata, and probably against the enhancement of procurators' powers in 53; the idea was to convince the opposition and commit it to his schemes; so he asked the senate to confer the title 'Claudian, loyal, and true' on the legions in Dalmatia after Scribonianus' revolt. Even unspoken objections, as to the adoption of Nero, were sometimes voiced by the Emperor himself. On one occasion Claudius scolded senators for not giving their opinions freely. That was not realistic, if the history of the generation before he came to power is considered — let alone his own elevation. The basic problem was lack of a firm constitution, or rather the fact that the constitution was continuing to develop. Where the boundaries were, nobody knew, nor the limits of what might be said by a senator or done by an emperor. Imperial Rome could have no Bagehot.[12]

A prerequisite of an effective senate was that it should be kept well manned. As we have seen, there was no difficulty in filling the higher magistracies. The number of praetors every year in Claudius' reign is said to have been between fourteen and eighteen; that is a rise from the time of Tiberius who began with efforts to keep to twelve but sometimes had to allow sixteen. Pressure was coming from the senate itself: the praetorship was the utmost distinction that many men could reasonably hope for, and an essential preliminary for would-be consuls; they were prepared to put up a struggle for it, with support from backers in the senate.[13]

On the other hand, Claudius encountered a problem that Augustus had also tried to deal with: a shortage of candidates for junior posts. Especially in the middle years of his principate, in the 'teens BC just after his final political defeat of the senate and at the time when the capital required by a senator rose from 400,000 to a million HS, there had been embarrassing vacancies in the *vigintivirate* (the group of twenty preliminary magistracies, normally held in the late 'teens), the aedileship (optional under the Republic), and even the once glamorous tribunate, which had lost its teeth when Augustus took tribunician power. Claudius encountering similar shortages. He adapted an Augustan remedy, one based on the traditional position of the tribunate as something outside the normal magistracies that could be held as a one-off post: knights might stand for it, take their place in the senate at the end of their year if they wished, and proceed to further office. Claudius may have had difficulty in filling the quaestorship; successful candidates had until 47 to contribute to the paving of roads, thereafter to offer gladiatorial shows, and that was not the end of their obligations. Praetors in 41 had been exempted from providing gladiatorial combats, but were still obliged to offer scenic games and races.[14]

Some ninety senators out of a roll conventionally taken to total 600 were away at any given time on public duty. Claudius wanted to secure the attendance of the rest, and he wanted ex-governors at Rome and available for prosecution after their term abroad. It was such a case that prompted him to act in 45, perhaps off his own impulsive bat. The right of granting leave of absence from Italy had hitherto been the senate's, and indulgently exercised (if members troubled to ask). The *SC* that secured Claudius the right may have censured a senator who had taken French leave; it was reiterated in the following year and achieved permanency, for in 49 senators from Narbonensis were granted the exemption for trips home that Sicilians already enjoyed. For those not abroad attendance was expected. Consequential 'suicides' are recorded, which might mean one suicide with more behind it than a distaste for senatorial debate or Claudian oratory.[15]

To replenish the senate and to make the wealth, talents, and loyalty of his own day available to it, Claudius took an obvious step: he assumed the censorship, once the crown of the Republican career. There were other reasons. The supervisory nature of the office probably appealed to him and it enhanced his prestige, this time on the domestic front. It was also a token of self-confidence: Claudius had conquered Britain, which his predecessors had failed to do; he was now to be censor, for which they had also lacked courage. This was a revival of an office which had been controversial: one of its functions was to control the composition of the senate, removing dead or discredited wood rooted in the House. The two holders had sometimes fallen out and resigned, leaving their work incomplete. Between 84 and 70 BC and again between 50 and 22 BC it had lapsed. In this last period Caesar, the Triumvirs, and Augustus had taken powers that made it redundant, incurring odium even though they avoided the actual office. Then, after Augustus' quarrel with the senate, two ex-consuls had been elected; their work immediately proved impossible, and when Augustus returned in 19 a revision of the senate's roll was carried out under his auspices. There were no more censors until Claudius entered office in 47, probably in April, with L. Vitellius as colleague. The years 45 and 46 had been politically turbulent, but the censorship was a slow, clumsy weapon against malcontents, more useful in dealing with long-term problems. The roll of the senate had not been pruned systematically — only by storms of political upheaval and sporadic action on the part of *principes* — since 13–14, perhaps not since 4. Now Claudius was going to work using the appropriate magistracy. As always, impoverishment was a factor: it is mentioned in connexion with the resignation of Valerius Asiaticus in 46; and the shortage of ready cash at least among young men is attested by the law against loans to minors that the censor passed in 47 — the latest in a long series, and not the last. Claudius seems to have been less ready than either Tiberius or Nero to have poverty alleviated by capital grants or supplementary income from state funds, although he tried to help magistrates burdened with expensive games. But there were also men of notorious character who would have to go. Claudius hoped to avoid humiliating unacceptable members and was pleased to announce a moratorium, each man to take stock of himself. It was a decent method, leaving the censor leeway if advice given in private were ignored.[16]

The poverty that was a common and acceptable reason for senators resigning was connected with changes in Italy's position in the Empire. 'Extravagance' (*luxuria*) was imputed to the Roman aristocracy; it needs interpretation. It is associated with intensifying political competition: conspicuous consumption showed power and willingness to use it. Sumptuary legislation, a feature of the last two centuries of the Republic, passed too by Caesar and Augustus, failed to check expenditure, until under Tiberius the senate took fright and asked the Emperor to act. Tiberius disdainfully told his peers that the remedy was self-respect, and declined to legislate. Tacitus comments that a change of personnel (the entry of men from Italian country towns and from the provinces) brought about a change of habits in the upper class. Another factor was the end of free elections and the ever-tightening control of public office by the Emperor. The agitation under Tiberius is the last conspicuous appearance of 'luxury' as an issue. That is instructive for the political climate of the reigns of Gaius and

Claudius. The political rivalry that flourished in open elections under Augustus did not return. Competition did not end altogether but public display was less useful; it was going out of fashion, was even looked at askance and found vulgar. Nero's extravagance was its final expression; in Vespasian the Romans were to have a frugal emperor from the Sabine country and it would not be sensible to upstage him.[16]

Claudius developed new methods for the advancement of deserving knights, more quickly than if they had to stand for the quaestorship. Before this, rulers had normally encouraged protégés, supported them for office, and let them make their own way up the ladder; the new method of offering new men a seat at a given rank was speedier, a more effective form of patronage, and useful for the running of the Empire; and the Emperor and his protégés need not suffer the loss of face of having their candidates criticised in the House like Curtius Rufus. From Claudius onwards, the expression 'adlected into the senate at the rank of ex-tribune', or 'ex-aedile', or 'ex-praetor' becomes familiar; with this came a logical concomitant, promotion within the senate to a certain rank. Not all were willing to be volunteered. Surdinius Gallus was a man whose wealth qualified him for membership of the senate. Whether or not he came from Carthage, he tried to remove there when Claudius made to elevate him; he was recalled to Rome, to be bound with the Emperor's 'golden fetters'; other recusants were simply struck off the roll of knights.[17]

We have already seen resistance to the advancement of some individuals. Gaius had promoted 'worthless' men and thereby provoked indignation. Some of these promotions were probably of senators, for Claudius undertook at the beginning of his Principate not to allow anyone whose great-great-grandfather was not a citizen to enter the senate. He made at least one exception, for the son of a freedman, whom he required to seek adoption by a Roman knight. He tried to justify himself to the House, but his interpretation of what Appius Claudius the censor, had done in admitting the sons of *libertini* (freedmen) was rejected by senators: they argued that *libertini* were properly themselves the sons of freedmen. The unsoundness of the argument shows how strongly they felt.[18]

There was resistance to men from outside certain geographical limits as well as to those originating from the lower strata of society at Rome. Men from the provinces were not a novelty: Augustus had been very cautious, but even Tiberius had admitted eleven. While new men roused suspicion and jealousy, and might indeed be subservient to the Emperor, their funds and interest in getting on made them an asset to the House, and their admission the work of Emperors who cared for its welfare. The increasing wealth of the provinces made the admission of provincial senators inevitable. Seven years into his reign Claudius was still attentive to the distinction between Italy and the provinces, acknowledging the novelty of what Augustus and Tiberius had done by admitting men — of good will and high standing — from all over Italy. In the provinces there is little evidence that Claudius took much initiative: a handful of new senators are known from reputable Narbonensis and Baetica, possibly the colony of Carthage; no easterners however distinguished followed in the footsteps of Augustus' protégé Q. Pompeius Macer of Mytilene or M. Calpurnius Rufus, the man from Attaleia (Antalya) in Pamphylia admitted by Tiberius or Gaius.[19]

But now during the censorship of 48 volunteers presented themselves in numbers: magnates of northern Gaul, representatives of sixty or sixty-four tribes who sat on the provincial assembly at Lugdunum in a system of proportional representation. Claudius met formidable opposition on his advisory council, some of whom had hardly accustomed themselves to the idea of senators from the whole of Italy. Provincials admitted in the past were individuals: numbers were the problem for the men from Comata, and the memory of struggles with the Gauls. There could have been as many as 120 men involved; given the right to wear the broad stripe on their tunics that signified that they were entitled to stand for senatorial office, they might with their wealth swamp the lower magistracies and block advancement for less well-off Italians. Old fears and prejudices lent respectability to these apprehensions. Claudius brought opposition into the open and summoned the senate for discussion, or at least to hear an oration from himself. The embarrassment of the speaker is evident, if not from his silence about the shortlived revolt of 21, then from feeble jokes and personal references intended to ingratiate him with his audience but inevitably irritating to the unconverted, and from his blurting out, not the name — that would have been going too far! — but an unmistakable reference to the disgraced Gaul Asiaticus. Nor did the Gauls quite win their case: as a first step the broad stripe was granted to the leaders of one tribe only, the Aedui, faithful and allied. M.T.Griffin points out the wider interpretation given the issue by Tacitus two generations later; it would have been strange, however, if Claudius had been at pains to demonstrate how far-reaching the consequences might prove.[20]

In 48 Claudius also endeavoured to strengthen the prestige of the senate in an uncontroversial way by honouring men whose parents had distinguished themselves, such as Q. Veranius, or whose families had a long history of membership, like T. Sextius Africanus and P. Pulcher. He added about fourteen *gentes*, perhaps thirty-three men, to those of the depleted patricians. It was a good reward and kept the structure of the House satisfactorily traditional, as well as providing persons qualified for indispensable ceremonials. Caesar in 45 BC and Augustus in 30 BC had done this too, with authority of a law behind them. There is no evidence for a law under Claudius, he being censor and as Pontifex Maximus qualified also to carry out the ceremonial. The Emperor enjoyed this, and let everyone see it. Claudius' numbers were in line with the score of *gentes* advanced by Augustus (over 60 individuals were involved); Vespasian adlected 19 *gentes*, up to 26 men.[21]

Whatever Claudius did, however, he could not abolish his accession.

Insistence on *libertas* (*Augusta*) and exhortations to senators to offer their views in debate were futile, given the fear that the usurper caused. His advent was represented as the securing of peace: in 41 the percipient inhabitants of Alexandria thought to offer him a statue of the 'Augustan Peace of Claudius' (Pax Augusta Claudiana). The word *pax* implies pacification and so force. The Praetorians were always there, a threat of renewed violence, ready to take an oath of Homeric vengeance as their watchword, escorting the Emperor, theoretically a Princeps among *principes*, even to evening parties. When Nero came to power the prophecy put into the mouth of Faunus presented the reign just over as 'a usurpation ... maintained by military force in what amounted to a continuous civil war. With the accession of Nero the Caesars returned to their rightful place, and the rabid Claudian war-goddess was bound and caged.' In down to earth terms, Nero's accession speech promised limits on the activities of the Princeps and real functions for the senate, and it was legitimate to imply criticism of the ignorance in which the senate had been kept even in routine matters of administration.[22]

There was little that senators could do to vent their feelings at their loss of real power. Irony was one weapon still available. One may see it operating in the decree of 44, that agreements struck with British tribes by Claudius and his legates should be binding, and perhaps in the financial rewards to Pallas that Barea Soranus proposed in 52 in recognition of Pallas' work on the *SC Claudianum*. But not every extravagant motion is to be taken as intended ironically: the consul of 48 was surely just jacking up the honours due to an outstandingly painstaking Emperor when he proposed at the end of Claudius' censorship that he should be known as *Pater Senatus* (Father of the Senate). It was true, as he said, that the standard title *Pater Patriae* had become worn out: it had been 'given to others' (he meant Gaius). Claudius had the sense to refuse the offer. It was not taken up until the reign of Commodus, which ended the Antonine dynasty (180–93): the senate needed no 'father' and, as a body, detested intervention in its composition, even if individuals were glad to see opponents removed or protégés brought in. Claudius' dealings with the senate must be seen as worthy, even heroic efforts to cope with an unquenchable fire of resentment.[23]

Under the Republic, senate and equestrian order had struggled against each other for privileges, notably that of staffing and so controlling the jury courts. Essentially though they were segments of the wealthy Roman upper class, senators who chose to participate in public life and win the dignity that it brought, *equites* who did not. Tacitus, writing of precisely that narrow area of dispute, treats it as past. Under the Principate the upper classes drew together. Claudius did not hesitate to stress his friendship with L.Julius Vestinus, the knight from Vienna, when he was speaking in the House. Other honours to knights were probably less acceptable: not only consular insignia to equestrian prefects, but a seat in the House whenever they accompanied the Emperor there. Claudius knew that this request would cause talk: his search for and production of an Augustan precedent show it. It was prudent to maintain outward differences. Although the orders had already been supposed to sit apart at spectacles, Claudius reaffirmed the distinction, assigning regular places.[24]

Before his accession Claudius had enjoyed cordial relations with the equestrian order, of which he was the most distinguished member; he had acted as its spokesman before both his predecessors. As Princeps, he enhanced the status of knights who entered his service. Yet relations deteriorated. First, and most obviously, he brought freedmen into the positions of high confidence that knights had once enjoyed, at that time to the disgust of senators. Less conspicuously, the philhellenism sometimes imputed to Claudius resolves itself, not only into favouritism towards Greek freedmen, but into the advancement of cultured *equites* from Greek-speaking provinces, men such as Balbillus and Xenophon, of Ephesus and Cos. In a less intimate relationship Vergilius Capito of Miletus and the Alexandrian Ti. Iulius Alexander found employment in posts that had previously been monopolized by Italians and men from the western provinces; yet knights from the Greek east were not undertaking the military posts open to *equites*. Nothing is heard against this development, but it may have rankled. Resentment, at least on the score of the freedmen, found its outlet in the activities of C. Silius and his many equestrian associates in 47-8. When the reign was over a horrific casualty list was totted up by Claudius' opponents: 35 senators, 321 knights.[25]

# 10

# THE PEOPLE OF ROME AND ITALY

The fabulist Phaedrus writes of an ass invited by his master to run away with him from hostile soldiers. On hearing that he would still carry only one pack for them, the ass declines to move. Phaedrus is referring to the turnover of masters that the Roman people had during his lifetime, the Julio-Claudian age: it meant no real change for the people. How they behaved is revealed not only by historians but by another poet, Juvenal, who gibes at the fickle mob for fawning on Sejanus, only to abuse him on his fall as an enemy of the state and of Caesar. An even better-known passage sneers at their only interest, 'bread and circuses'.[1]

Phaedrus was essentially right: the lot of the deprived and destitute could be improved only marginally with the resources available to the ancients, and the upper classes detested or were indifferent to them. As to Juvenal, modern writers have pointed out that poverty-stricken city dwellers, especially at Rome, had every reason to be concerned about bread; and they needed stirring entertainment to distract them from their privations. In the theatre, too, in the presence of the Emperor, they could protest against all deprivation. Even marginal improvements in life were worth fighting or rioting or fawning for; that made the urban plebs a factor to be taken into account by politicians.[2]

Augustus had found them useful allies between 23 and 19 BC, as had his daughter the elder Julia, when she made a bid for the advancement of her sons Gaius and Lucius, and his grandchildren Agrippa Postumus and the younger Julia in the next decade. Contrast with the disdainful Tiberius enhanced their popularity and that of the affable Germanicus and Agrippina. Once Tiberius came to power it was not only a suspect political attitude that alienated the people, but his actual conduct. Conscientious as he was in guarding against shortages of grain, these were significant in 18, amongst other complaints: he was slow in paying Augustus' legacies to the people (the explanation was probably shortage of cash in hand); and parsimonious over expenditure on banquets and shows. Tacitus' description of the anguish felt at Rome as varying news of Germanicus' last illness was brought from Syria is telling. So too is the absence of the imperial family from the interment and Tiberius' emphatic display of his appreciation of Germanicus' merits (he read a eulogy in the House). He was nervous about the people's reaction.[3]

In the twenties the affection of the people continued to be something for ambitious politicians to take into account: Tiberius' minister Sejanus had already exploited the unpopularity of Drusus Caesar. Fire was one of the terrors of life at Rome, and Sejanus showed up Drusus' inadequacy at fighting it in 15, proving conspicuously successful himself seven years later. After Drusus' death Sejanus was confronted with the immense inherited popularity of Germanicus' widow and children; his efforts to counter it and present himself as the champion of the people, a new Marcus Agrippa, culminated in a popular demonstration in his favour when he was elected to the consulship of 31. The people should have ratified his election by meeting as the Comitia Centuriata in the Campus Martius outside the city — for the Centuriata was the people under arms and forbidden to meet within the sacred boundary. Instead the election took place on the Aventine Hill, which had strong associations with the people. It was the site of temples of Ceres, goddess of grain, and of Liber Pater, the Roman equivalent of Bacchus; a place of retreat in the early Republic, when the plebeians struck against the ruling class; and in 121 BC the base of the people's champion, Gaius Gracchus. The Aventine was still conveniently outside the sacred boundary, and so available for the Comitia. This was something that even Tiberius could not ignore, and he made an ungrammatical reference to 'this outrageous hustings' (*improbae comitiae*) in a letter ingratiatingly addressed to his 'fellow-tribesmen' after the fall of the minister.[4]

Gaius Caesar, the last of Germanicus' sons to survive, embraced the role of people's favourite. A grand swell of joy greeted his accession, and even his severest judges admit that in spite of some unpopular taxation (probably not impinging on the least well-off) and of his well-known wish that the people had one head, so that he could wring its neck, he remained a favourite to the end. Their affection was still reciprocated after the senate had offended him in 39. On his return the following year he said he would greet the knights and people, but not the senate.[5]

Feelings that arose from near-hunger and a craving to be distracted from it took on a distinctive existence, to be illustrated from the 'shortlived and ill-fated affections' of the imperial populace, as Tacitus called them, referring to others besides Germanicus. The plebs particularly favoured young, or at least second generation, and relatively down-trodden members. In preferring the young they were doing what Phaedrus warned against: looking to the future, unlike the articulate, possessing upper classes who give the impression that the ancients all looked back to a golden age. The plebs had history too, and heroes, such as King Servius Tullius and, centuries later, the Gracchi. Changes resisted by the ruling classes had usually meant amelioration for the underprivileged: political rights, tribunes to protect plebeians, publication of the laws. In each generation the young had done nothing to disappoint the people, and still might help them. Sympathy with young or apparently less-successful members of the imperial family had sound political and historical sense behind it: it was alienated aristocrats who had proved the most faithful and energetic champions of the plebs. The memory of the Gracchi lingered, and affection for certain branches of the imperial family was inherited by one generation from another.

Claudius had witnessed the part played by the people in recent political upheavals. He was not young when the people saluted him in the theatre as the brother of Germanicus and uncle of the emperor, but he was still a member of the family who had never had his due. His position rather than any suspected intrinsic merit may have won Claudius these greetings, and the very dimness of his life made it easier for sympathetic crowds to project on him whatever image they chose. Starting with the hopes of the people behind him (for all Phaedrus' warning), he also had an historian's awareness that the people's support was vital to a politician at odds with the senate, which he certainly was. C.E.Stevens' characterization of Claudius as 'the last of the *populares*' brilliantly illuminates an important feature of his rule. He and the people needed each other.[6]

Claudius exploited this political position, using tribunician powers. Dealing with important matters in the senate he sometimes had the tribunician bench placed between the curule chairs of state occupied by the consuls, instead of using the chair himself, as he was entitled to do as possessor of consular power. His awareness of the right of the people to a spokesman, and to the right of the rank and file to rise in the world through the practice of eloquence, was revealed when the senatorial aristocracy tried in 47 to limit the rewards payable to advocates: the Emperor was warned not to forget the plebeians who had won distinction at the bar.[7]

The tribunes themselves showed a high profile. In 42 they summoned the senate to hold an election when one of the board died, a breach of etiquette when the consuls were in Rome. They may have been a particularly independent-minded set, but it is significant that they thought forward behaviour worth while. Under the Principate, licensed, almost ritualized freedoms normally took the form of disputes between praetors and tribunes: in 15, after hooliganism in the theatre, a proposal that praetors should be given the right of flogging actors was successfully vetoed by a tribune (other measures were taken); there was a replay in 56, when tribunes defended fans from the praetors' attempts to impose law and order — and had their own activities restricted. All three incidents came near the beginning of a reign, helping to set its tone, in Claudius' case populist.[8]

In 49 Claudius did something that unmistakably showed his populist stance — and in a more veiled way his determination to be the people's master: on the strength of his extension of Roman territory, he extended the sacred boundary of Rome, the Pomerium, and in doing so incorporated not only the Pincian Hill but the Aventine, the scene only seventeen years previously of Sejanus' hustings. His act symbolized the full recognition of the plebeians' claim to consideration within the state — there need be no secessions now. Nor could there be any repetition of Sejanus' act either, since the Comitia Centuriata had to meet outside the Pomerium.[9]

Suetonius stresses the Emperor's modesty in his private life: the idea of winning golden opinions with all sections of the public must have played a part. There was a puritanical streak in the people that allowed their embittered envy a decorous and righteous outlet. Prudent legislators responded to this with sumptuary legislation limiting ostentatious expenditure (although such legislation had the additional advantage of securing fair play between competing politicians with differing resources). Claudius significantly made few alterations to the imperial residence and showed circumspection when he was contemplating marriage again — to his niece Agrippina. That could have been unacceptable. If so, the repercussions could shake the state; but Vitellius was able to assure Claudius that he was positively commanded by the people to make the match. Given Agrippina's family history of ties with the people, it was probably true.[10]

For the minimizing of discomfort and for amenities the people depended on the Princeps. Cicero divided building activities into two groups, applying austere criteria: he approved of walls, docks, harbours, aqueducts, but not theatres, colonnades and new temples. Gaius produced some of the former, a harbour and aqueducts (unfinished), but continued restoration of the Theatre of Pompey, built an amphitheatre near the Saepta (unfinished), a race course (the Gaianum) and the Circus Vaticanus; there were also at least three temples to himself, shrines to his sister Drusilla and ambitious extensions to the Palace, the Domus Tiberiana (the bridge of boats at Baiae was a temporary assemblage). Claudius took note and, in his desire to be 'useful' to the state, built little without a practical purpose: the colossus of Jove and the marble arch of Tiberius next to the Theatre of Pompey, a work probably begun in 22 after a fire and still incomplete; repairs to the Theatre itself were also in all probability a continuation of Gaius' work. The structure carrying the Aqua Virgo over the Via Lata became a triumphal arch in 51, celebrating his success in Britain and drawing attention at once to domestic and foreign achievements. All repairs were excusable; the Aerarium was invited to sustain the cost of restoring the temple of Venus on Mt. Eryx in the senatorial province of Sicily.[11]

Claudius' magnificent utilities (the Emperor's taste for old-fashioned rugged travertine masonry has been noticed) provided as much work for free labourers as the directly self-regarding activities of Gaius. That was a factor in public thinking about an Emperor, though rarely explicit. Porterage through the narrow streets was another important means of livelihood, but the spreading of cash through the population was very largely due to expenditure on public building at Rome and a prime reason for popular interest in it. P.A.Brunt has shown, by analogy with late sixteenth-century Rome and late eighteenth-century Paris, that a substantial portion of the free, wage-earning population might have been engaged in construction. Popular politicians had been associated with great public works, and, as Brunt points out, most emperors were builders on a grand scale, with the middle of the first century AD, from Claudius to Vespasian, particularly remarkable in this respect.[12]

Most of the constructions were of direct benefit to the population. Claudius' attention was dominated by the problem of food supplies, especially for the free distributions to which about 200,000 citizens of Rome were entitled (a mark and privilege of citizenship rather than poor relief, though of greatest importance to the near destitute). Claudius' own greed may have made him more sensitive to hunger among his subjects. When he came to power in January, 41 he had an immediate chance to show how seriously he valued the support of the people. It was during a grain shortage in which it was claimed that only eight days' supply remained: the shipping season ended in October and would not begin again until March. This was at once countered by emergency measures: insurance money would be paid by the Emperor himself to persons who took the risk of bringing in winter supplies and lost their vessel; and the new Emperor's efforts were noted on the coinage: the goddess of grain appeared as CERES AVGVSTA, and a new quadrans obverse showed a grain measure (*modius*).[13]

Claudius determined to take permanent measures to avoid further shortages, and Suetonius insists that the supply of grain always remained high on his list of priorities. Dio reports a food shortage, apparently of the year after Claudius' accession, as the occasion for embarking on the construction of the harbour at Ostia. In Egypt irregularities in the Nile flood caused a shortage from autumn 44 or 45 to spring 46 or 47, and there was a shortage of grain in Judaea and all Syria in 46 or 47 when Christians of Antioch sent grain to Jerusalem. In Greece in 49 the price of grain rocketed, which means that profiteers would divert supplies in that direction, and two years later the troops in Armenia were in straits. A shortage at Rome in 51 (one of a series, to judge by Suetonius' language) led to a riot from which Claudius was lucky to escape into the Palace.[14]

The supply to Rome would take priority, though even that might be affected in the end, but even if supplies were available some of the main problems for the city seems to have been connected with conveyance from the source, reception, and storage. The extraction of grain from Egyptian farmers and its collection at Alexandria had long since been brought to a fine if ruthless art. Apart from ensuring that the post of Procurator Annonae was in the hands of a man who (at least according to his son-in-law Seneca!) was able to make himself popular in a post that normally brought odium on its holder (and who came from a town that was itself an important port and shipyard) Claudius' measures were concerned with conveyance and distribution.[15]

To secure imports to Rome he offered special privileges to those who built vessels of a minimum capacity of 10,000 *modii* (c. 70 tonnes) and kept them in service for six years: citizens were exempted from the Lex Papia Poppaea that penalized celibacy and childlessness by limiting the right to inherit; aliens, who were not subject to this law, were offered the citizenship itself. At Rhegium on the toe of Italy Gaius had begun harbour improvements for the security of the Alexandrian corn fleet; R.Meiggs was inclined to believe that Claudius completed them, but there is no evidence for it. In 52 Claudius established a colony at Ptolemais in Palestine. It had other functions but may also have served as a strong staging point for the grain run against prevailing northerly winds.[16]

Next, Claudius assisted safe reception of grain by developing the harbour at Ostia, the destination of the transports from Africa which according to Josephus brought two-thirds of Rome's supplies. Picking up a scheme of Caesar's and jettisoning Gaius' overall plans for improved Italian harbours, he defied opposition, began to build in the first year of his reign, and had made substantial progress by 46. Claudius appointed an equestrian Procurator Portus Ostiensis, whose name shows that his main charge was the harbour itself. The entrance was protected by a huge mole based on the ship that had brought a huge obelisk from Alexandria in Gaius' time. This was kept in place by serried ranks of piles and was surmounted by a lighthouse. Channels linked the harbour to the Tiber, a remedy against the river floods. For storage ashore granaries were constructed, and a police force *cum* fire brigade of 500 men was established at Ostia to protect them. The same was done at Puteoli, which served the Alexandrian fleet. Claudius took a personal interest in the works, which is why he seems twice to have been at Ostia when a political crisis developed (the more famous occasion being in October 48 when Messallina celebrated her 'marriage' to Silius), and on another occasion took part in a whale-hunt in the harbour. Claudius was not able to bring the great work to a completely satisfactory conclusion: in 62 a storm destroyed two hundred ships within the harbour, and Trajan had to cope with the silting up of the channels (102-114). Even so, Nero thought it worth appropriating the work by renaming it Portus Augusti.[17]

The final problems were those of transporting the grain up the Tiber and distributing it to entitled beneficiaries. The Quaestor Ostiensis, who had been responsible for the transport of grain, had often proved ineffective. His position had already been eroded when Augustus created the post of Praefectus Annonae (Prefect of the Grain Supply), and the Quaestorship was abolished in 44 when a junior magistrate was required elsewhere. As to the outlet in Rome, it was probably Claudius who facilitated distribution by creating the Porticus Minucia Frumentaria (Minucian Portico for grain distribution), equipping it with forty-five arcades with numbered outlets corresponding to applicants' tickets. C.Nicolet has pointed out that a late source connects the number with a vow ascribed to King Servius Tullius to create as many grain outlets as the years of his reign. Claudius admired the radical king and it may have been he who publicized the connexion.[18]

Claudius' second great construction project was also aimed at alleviating food shortages. It too was one that Caesar had contemplated and Claudius began it at once, in 41: draining the Fucine Lake into the Liris. It involved driving a water channel 5651m (6180yds) long, about 2.44m (8ft) wide and with side walls more than 2.84m (9ft 4in.) high, partly under the 240m (787ft) high Monte Salviano, and according to Suetonius took 30,000 men eleven years to complete; a modern estimate, accepting the length of time required, reduces the work-force by a factor of ten. Besides ending the danger and nuisance of flooding, it was intended to provide 607 sq. km of farmland within 85km of Rome. This project too has been criticized because its execution was not wholly successful (corruption was alleged). Pliny considers it to have been one of Claudius' most remarkable achievements, but it is clear from the way he writes that it is controversial; Trajan attempted to improve the scheme, and the Lake was not finally drained until the nineteenth century.[19]

The supply of pure water was almost as important as that of grain, and Claudius' efforts were unstinting. Besides repairing M.Agrippa's Aqua Virgo between 44 and 46 (this is the water that feeds the Trevi Fountain), Claudius completed the 6.6km long Aqua Claudia and the 87km Anio Novus, which Gaius had begun in 38, bringing them in over the Praenestine Gate (Porta Maggiore) and finishing them off with a lavish set of extremely elaborate basins. The elder Pliny, a more friendly observer than Suetonius, notes the high standard of the work, which supplied all seven hills of Rome, and claims that there was none more remarkable in the entire world. Claudius also advertized his success, this time on inscriptions celebrating the restoration of the Aqua Virgo, which Gaius had allowed to decay, marking the entry point of the other two aqueducts at the Praenestine Gate (52-3), and proclaiming that he himself had borne the cost.[20]

Here again Claudius modified the organization as well as undertaking construction work. The senatorial commission in charge of the water supply was afforced by a freedman procurator who had 460 slaves at his disposal, nearly trebling the force of 240 that the senatorial commissioner could deploy. The senators who held the post of Curator of the Water Supplies (Curator Aquarum) were men of consular standing. A.Didius Gallus (suff. 39), appointed in the second half of 38, held office for eleven years, to be succeeded by another able and trusty servant of the Emperor. Cn. Domitius Afer (suff. 39). However, it is clear from Frontinus that at least some curators neglected their duties; and Gallus was away from Rome in Moesia for at least three years. The original complexion of the post was not altered, but Claudius stimulated its activities by associating his procurator with it in exacting repair and construction.[21]

The flooding to which Rome remained liable until the present century caused hardship under the Republic and well into the reign of Augustus, though it was not so widespread as the suffering from hunger and lacked the political dimension (grain was every peasant's birthright). Besides digging the channels at the river mouth to keep the Tiber in check, Claudius imposed minimum distances from the river within which buildings could not be constructed and again brought in an additional equestrian official, the Procurator of the Tiber Bank, to give backbone to the senatorial commission of five that Tiberius had characteristically established to deal with the problem.[22]

Fire was an even more serious hazard. Resources in the city itself remained unchanged, but Claudius learnt his lesson from the political capital that Sejanus had made out of personal attention to fire-fighting. The tenements of the Aemiliana district, where the conflagration of 64 was to blaze and which had already caught fire in 38, were the scene of an almost uncontrollable blaze, probably in 53. The Emperor (with his consort) remained on duty for two nights in a nearby public building, recruiting additional firefighters and paying cash on the spot for their services.[23]

To elementary precautions for the material welfare of the people of Rome, Claudius added attention to their morale. Prudence, and his own tastes, prevented him from going to Tiberian extremes in reaction against the extravagance of Gaius' shows. He provided 'lavish and numerous games of many types'. There were new presentations marking fresh holidays, games in honour of Livia, Nero Drusus, and Antonia; shows commemorating the dedication of the theatre of Pompey and the British victory; and the secular games of 47. Shows were given in places not used for the purpose before, and the Circus Maximus was decorated with gilt turning posts and marble stalls for the animals. The number of races offered now reached its maximum of twenty-four a day. Then were various types of gladiatorial shows, one held annually in the praetorian barracks, as well as war games in the Campus Martius re-enacting the storming of a town, probably Camulodunum. Most notable was the sea battle that Claudius staged (although he had difficulty in getting the doomed participants to fight) on the Fucine Lake in 52, a silver Triton rising from the centre of the Lake to herald the battle; the unsuccessful outcome of the opening of the sluices meant that Claudius later had to offer a second celebration.[24]

To celebrate the victory in Britain the people were not only given a festival but a tip (*congiarium*) of 300 HS each. This was a standard sum, bequeathed by Principes in their wills to those qualified for the grain issue. Suetonius claims that they were tipped 'rather frequently' under Claudius. The claim simply reflects Claudius' populist image, even though he cannot have failed to distribute the same sum when he came to power; certainly he gave 300 HS each for Nero's coming of age in 51.[25]

Z. Yavetz holds that relations between Claudius and the urban plebs were simply 'correct'. That underestimates the needs of both parties. Relations were normally warm. Claudius' edicts offering homely tips on making the best of the vintage or medical matters were couched in homely language, and his free mixing with the people at shows right from the beginning won him praise. Picnic parties with exchanges of jokes are not signs of formal correctness. Claudius' care was reciprocated. When a rumour went round early in the reign that the Emperor had been assassinated, the people were furious. They knew whom to blame: the senate; and the Praetorians had betrayed him. Even when Claudius was caught in the Forum in 51 by a hungry, abusive mob and pelted with a shower of stale crusts, it was only a tiff: Octavian had once been stoned for the same offence.[26]

The truth was that Claudius' precarious position disturbed the people. The portents that marked the reign, increasingly towards the end, are an indication of that as well as of a wish for change. The Emperor took care that they should not be alarmed by an eclipse of the sun on his birthday in 45, explaining it in an edict beforehand, but there was more in this edict than the pleasure of teaching. More than any Princeps before him Claudius depended, after the Praetorian Guard, on public confidence and support. Claudius' needs made him sensitive to ingratitude. The people of Ostia once neglected to greet him with the customary flotilla. He noticed the failure and told them what he thought of it. That was not the only incident in which he had to draw their attention to his services — which, in addition to those we have already considered, included stocking the sea off the town with a new kind of fish, the *scarus* (parrot-wrasse).[27]

Another limitation in the relationship was that Claudius was dealing *en masse* with a recognized class, and was determined to maintain the stability of existing structures. He showed consideration beyond the frigid discharge of a noble's duty (Tiberius' view of it), but it did not enter his or any other emperor's head to change the status that determined the rights of individuals. And their economic position, which in practice governed their status, was not in his control. This meant that in some lights an emperor was indistinguishable from other predators. Phaedrus reveals that taverns displayed a picture of mice pursued by weasels scampering safely into their holes — except those who hampered entry with the distinctive horns they were wearing (probably these were prominent plebeians rather than members of the aristocracy). That sheds light on tavern society, which Claudius knew and loved — especially the meaty snacks they sold — and helps to account for his attempts at restriction and closure and his ban on popular clubs.[28]

The warmth between Claudius and the populace survived in the affection that they felt for his daughter Octavia. The early years of Nero's rule had little to offer; when the Emperor went among them it was at night, in disguise and for his own purposes. They may, as always, have been disappointed in their new patron; it was not until 60 that Nero took his first steps on the stage and needed their patronage. When Octavia was divorced and sent into exile in 62 they demonstrated in sympathy, to no effect. 'The power of the people is great', says the Nurse in the anti-Neronian tragedy *Octavia*; and receives a true reply: 'The Emperor's is greater'.[29]

If Claudius felt genuine compassion for his subjects it extended beyond those who could makes themselves immediately felt: to Italy and the provinces. In the *SC Hosidianum*, which probably belongs to 22 September, 47, Claudius is given credit for foresight (*providentia*) and for caring not only for the private buildings of the city of Rome but also for the conservation (*aeternitati*) of Italy. Strictly speaking, although the consular power that Augustus and his successors possessed legitimized intervention in the affairs of Italian towns, they preferred to work through the consuls and senate, rather than detracting from their authority. Claudius did not shrink from direct intervention, as his edict on the boundary disputes of Comum shows. After his death Nero renounced such activity. In Rome the special relationship of Princeps and plebs, embodied in his possession of tribunician power, overrode delicacy.[30]

In 47, however, Claudius chose to suggest action to the consuls, and they legislated against speculators who bought up property and resold it after pulling down buildings on it. There are similar Republican enactments dealing with the City, which are echoed by provisions in Republican and imperial municipal charters. Legislators' motives were complex. At Rome they seem to have been concerned in case the destruction of slums and the rebuilding on the same site of modern blocks of flats deprived existing inhabitants of accommodation: the *SC* refers to an 'utterly brutal type of transaction'. Both E. Phillips and P. Garnsey mention salvaging as a motive for these demolitions, and forcing up property prices. Claudius' personal concern is stressed in the *SC*, and it chimes in with his avoidance of grandiose private building, which also aggravated Rome's housing shortage. In the municipal documents care for the physical integrity of the all-important cities is paramount: when an exemption from the *SC* was granted in 56 the warning that is issued is against allowing derelict buildings to make any part of Italy hideous. In country towns the practice may also have caused alarm because it betrays a declining population and so a threat to Italian economy and society and to the supply of men suitable for service in the legions. Lucan, writing under Nero, notes the ruinous condition of Italian cities, attributing it to manpower loss suffered in the civil wars. Claudius is concerned for Italy's survival to Eternity (*Aeternitas*); so too were Trajan when, with recruiting in mind, he established schemes for funding the upbringing of Italian children, and Mussolini. There is also a moral element in the *SC*: the wealthy are not to make money out of an undesirable practice. This is an upper-class offence: speculators to pay a fine of double the price they paid and be reported to the senate; to penalize sellers the sales are to be invalid. (An exception is made in favour of owner occupiers, who are allowed to make alterations.)[31]

If city amenities were something that belonged to the whole Roman people, not just to the wealthy, so did Roman territory. It had been a plank in the populist programme since the Gracchi to restore public land and its revenues to the state, for the benefit of the whole people rather than of a few individuals. Cyrene, part of a senatorial province, contained lands that had been royal property of the last king, Apion. Bequeathed to the Roman People in 96 BC, they had become public land (*ager publicus* — an emotive phrase under the Republic). At the end of the reign reclamation was begun in Cyrenaica, and it was only Nero's care for the propertied classes of that province that made the work of Claudius' commissioner ineffective.[32]

# LAW, JUSTICE
# AND THE STABLE SOCIETY

Under the Empire the administration of justice centred on the holder of supreme power. The fact was resented, though diligence was admired: both Caesar's preoccupation with it, and Augustus', are noted. Augustus sometimes sat until nightfall, if his strength failed working from a litter on the tribunal, or reclining at home. Augustus took measures to combat the backlog of cases public and private. He removed the names of accused men from the docket if their accusers failed to appear; prosecutors who wished to take up the case later did so at a risk of being penalized if they were unsuccessful. Augustus also added more than thirty days previously devoted to games to those on which cases could be heard. Jurymen were now enrolled at the age of twenty-four, five years earlier than before, and their leave restricted. Augustus added a fourth panel of jurymen to the existing three, Gaius a fifth.[1]

For criminal cases there were still the standing courts of the Republic (*quaestiones perpetuae*), in which any male citizen might prosecute such offences as murder, extortion, bribery, *maiestas* (diminishing the majesty of the Roman people), and adultery, still staffed by juries of senators and other propertied men, and presided over by praetors. There was also the senatorial court. Under Augustus the consuls began to take cases involving the same offences by members of the upper classes in the Senate itself. It was a pernicious development, turning legal into political issues and infringing laws designed to protect Roman citizens against condemnation on capital charges in courts not established by the people. It went unchallenged because it seemed to make the senators masters in their own house. Further, the consuls had the right to take cognizance of actions, even if they were not laid down as criminal in any law. It was on this basis that the senate sometimes acted in political crises, as in the case of Sejanus in 31: Tiberius' accusing letter was read to the House in the morning, the Prefect was dead by the end of the day. It was like Cicero's execution of the Catilinarian conspirators in 63 BC. Thus senatorial jurisdiction was well established long before Claudius came to power.[2]

The senate sometimes avoided responsibility by referring cases to the Princeps, to be heard with the advisers who traditionally assisted magistrates in the use of their powers. Accusers sometimes aimed for this court. The trial of Cn. Piso in 20 for the alleged murder of Germanicus was properly a case for the standing court, as Tiberius admitted. The accusers tried to get Tiberius to hear it; he declined and it was taken in the senate. Augustus had already heard cases actionable under statutes dealing with the forgery of wills and with parricide; he too declined a murder case, in 10. Justice was tempered by recognition of superior political and constitutional power.[3]

Accused from the non-senatorial classes (equestrian or even lower?) may have been brought before the standing courts; but most plebeians and slaves must have been dealt with summarily by consuls, praetors and City Prefect. The tribunes had the right to command obedience, if they exercised it in person (in 43 a knight was thrown from the Tarpeian Rock by tribunes and consuls for conspiracy), and the Prefect of the Guard, holding office close to the emperor, was acquiring jurisdiction. In provinces governors had powers of life and death (in some provinces there were jury courts available if governors chose); but Roman citizens might could appeal against sentence to the Emperor (in Rome his tribunician power gave him the right to intervene). Augustus delegated appeals from the provinces to men of consular rank, one for each province. So Paul 'appealed unto Caesar'.[4]

Private litigation was dealt with at Rome in the courts of the praetor and lower magistrates according to the subject matter and along lines laid down by statute and by the praetor's own edict regulating his conduct, which followed his predecessors' guidelines. Augustus had delegated appeals against civil decisions taken at Rome to the court of the urban praetor, those from the provinces to ex-consuls *ad hoc.*[5]

Tiberius, following Augustus here as elsewhere, dispensed justice from a tribunal in the Forum, with an advisory body. That ended when Tiberius left Rome in 26. After that the only justice he can have dispensed was by indirect influence on presiding magistrates, by fiat from Capri, or in cases taken by him in private, with or without advisors. Writing of 39 onwards, Dio speaks of trials before Gaius alone and before the whole senate, which also conducted cases itself; but there were frequent appeals from the senate to the Emperor. In 39 and 40 Gaius was in the north, and although he began there by conducting the sensational trial of Gaetulicus and his sisters, little more is heard of judicial activities.[6]

Claudius' intense activity attracted notice after the sluggishness of Tiberius' last decade and Gaius' inattention. Taking on his functions in middle age, he was in a hurry; and there was a real backlog of cases. He showed himself totally committed to the practical administration of the law in person, not giving up even for his daughters' betrothal in 41 or for the festival for his victory in Britain in 44. He sat almost daily, either with the senate or alone, on a tribunal in the Forum or elsewhere; few cases were remitted. And if he did not preside he sat as member of the magistrate's advisory board. From concern for public business, trials and litigation as well as senate and assembly meetings, he cut down the number of days assigned to festivals. Claudius was keen to settle matters in courts other than his own, and urged the senate to go further against absentee litigants: the cases were to be decided against them.[7]

Claudius then was particularly diligent — yet his conduct on the bench was one of his most severely criticised activities. True, he seems to have renewed the traditional practice of sitting with advisers, which evidently had not been revived by Gaius, or not for long; there were assessors present when he tried Valerius Asiaticus in 47 and in a fictionalized hearing of charges against Alexandrian offenders there is a *consilium* of sixteen consulars and twenty other senators. Women of the court are also present. But reputable assessors are not conspicuous in accounts of Claudius' day-to-day juridical activity, and the inconsistency and savagery charged to him (for parricide he used the hideous penalty of immersion with animals in a sack, which Augustus had been at pains to avoid, enough for it be commented on by critics, and allegedly went beyond the law in condemning serious offenders to the arena) may have been due to his ignoring advice. Mitigation as well as excessive severity is noted, for example in allowing plaintiffs who had lost their cases to sue again for a smaller sum. Claudius cared more for equity and the merits of an individual case than he did for principle and precedent. That made both for inconsistency and for bad law; he preferred his own judgment. Then there was interpretation of precedent. Antiquarian material in the *Annals* that comes from Claudius' work is betrayed by 'particulars either unique or discrepant from standard versions'. It was not only in style that Livy influenced his pupil but in his choice of subject matter. Emotionalism made him liable to come to anomalous, even unfair decisions, and to take other matters into account than the case in hand, so it was alleged: men who had insulted him before he became Princeps were not punished for that, *unless they were brought to court for other reasons.* Further, Claudius' wilful — and inappellable — interpretations detracted from the role of the honoured profession of expert jurisconsults, who loom large in Nero's new regime as they creep from their dark hiding-places.[8]

Claudius' originality sometimes seems refreshing. A woman persisted in denying that a young man was her son: Claudius decided she should marry him. She refused and lost her case. At first this looks like a judgment of Solomon. Not so. The son was probably seeking access to his mother's property; if he had been an unrelated fortune-hunter should she have been expected to marry him? If the story is genuine, Claudius had already made up his mind about the case, and the order was a silly game.[9]

The lack of predictability in Claudius' proceedings meant that his court sometimes lacked dignity. The Roman bar was never a decorous institution. Cases were taken out of doors, turning them into public theatre. The scripts of Christian and Alexandrian *Acta* alike show that lively exchanges between examining magistrate and accused were normal. But Claudian incidents passed beyond that. There was something homespun about Claudius' administration of justice. The fact that in 51 the entire proceedings were disrupted by a bread riot and the Emperor had to flee the bench for the Palace shows how his jurisdiction was perceived, perhaps correctly. Normally he was long-suffering and litigants were not afraid of him: one threw his heavy brief into the Emperor's face. Claudius was prone to quote Greek; it was probably meant to add to his intellectual stature or had the same function as Tiberius' irony, that of allowing him to give vent to feelings without crushing his inferiors. But it exposed him to the ripostes of native Greek speakers. In one anecdote (*ben trovato* and a variant on 'Claudius the Gaul') he had the pleader Julius Gallicus thrown into the Tiber. It was a traditional punishment in Gaul for unsuccessful speakers. This left the client without an advocate. The great Narbonensian pleader Cn. Domitius Afer, applied to for help, asked the litigant if he thought that he, Afer, was a better swimmer than Gallicus. A more convincing story, involving another Gallic pleader, is that of an orator of equestrian status, this time from Vasio, who was executed for practising magic on the Emperor when a Druidical egg — carried for luck! — slipped from his toga.[10]

In the *Apocolocyntosis* Claudius is accused of hearing one side of a case or neither before delivering judgment. (It is a charge that he seems to anticipate in his Letter to the Alexandrians, where he claims to have heard both sides.) The accusation might refer to the penalizing of defaulters, but the gravamen probably relates to political cases. Men and women died when the charge was uncertain and with no opportunity of defending themselves: Suetonius lists Appius Silanus, the two Julias, Cn. Pompeius, and L.Silanus. This is close to the complaint put into the mouth of Augustus in the *Apocolocyntosis*, that Claudius had killed Augustus' two great-granddaughters, one by the sword, the other by starvation, and one great-grandson, Silanus. He asks, 'Why did you convict many of these men and women whom you killed, before you could examine the case, before you could hear the evidence?' In his later, formal charge he lists Claudius' relations, adding Crassus Frugi, Scribonia, and Messallina to the victims. Claudius himself is tried in the skit before the standing court on a regular charge of judicial murder (35 senators, 321 knights, countless others) and when defence counsel attempts to reply he is cut off and Claudius himself is condemned with only one side of the case heard. Modern writers put more stress on trials held, like that of Valerius Asiaticus, 'in the Emperor's private apartments' (*intra cubiculum*), which are complained of in Nero's accession speech. Augustus heard cases at home, but they were already on the docket, and conducted in reception rooms with regular advisers.[11]

Analyzing complaints shows a wide variety of proceedings, from a person allegedly being caught in the act and despatched; a denunciation made in private and instantly followed by an order for execution (or a demand for suicide); such a denunciation made in the presence of the accused and of members of the household, when some sort of reply might be made; and finally to a case taken in private Palace apartments or in the Praetorian barracks, but with advisers present who were not only members of the household but senators and hence (since respect for senatorial dignity demanded it) under a procedure that allowed the accused person to be heard by them. The form of these various proceedings is a function of the monarchical element of the Principate, which also made them necessary.

For the senatorial outsider or victim there is little to choose between any procedure beyond jury court and senate, but for the dominant clique the types classify the situations in which they find themselves: those requiring instant and silent action; those in which one segment is not strong enough to deal with opponents in public; and those in which a defeated element has put itself into the wrong so manifestly that the aftermath is like mopping up after a civil war.[12]

The status of the victims is also significant. Whether Appius Silanus underwent proceedings in the Palace is unclear: he was dead before the senate knew of his intention of assassinating Claudius. Pompeius Magnus, allegedly caught *in flagrante delicto* with a male lover, was despatched without question. His parents may have been forced to suicide. Of the Juliae, Drusus' daughter was 'driven' to her death by Suillius, perhaps another enforced suicide like that of Poppaea who is mentioned in the same breath. Germanicus' was exiled for adultery (her lover Seneca condemned in the senate) and then killed ('with the sword' for some additional offence?); L.Silanus was expelled from the senate by edict and committed suicide. The case of Valerius Asiaticus is a clear and outrageous specimen of the trial in the Emperor's private apartments, although an advisory council was present and two senators attested (Suillius and Vitellius). The drumhead courts martial in the barracks that followed the uncovering of the Messallina-Silius 'plot' were reminiscent of those that followed decisive battles of the Civil Wars, in which death or mercy were dealt out arbitrarily; Messallina herself was not even brought before the Emperor but died like a fugitive. After the exile of Livilla in 41, Claudius, in a gross extension of paternal power, far beyond the kind practised by Augustus against his erring children and grandchildren, was keeping family offenders in particular from any public hearing that would show up dissension in the ruling clique; Asiaticus could not be treated like that, but the trial was kept as private as possible.[13]

By contrast the great trial of Scribonianus' fellow-conspirators in 42 was held before the senate, and the consuls presided. It was a show trial of persons known to be linked with a manifest rebel, with the senate publicly sanctioning the actions of the victors. The senate met for the occasion in the Library attached to the temple of Apollo on the Palatine, next to the imperial palace. The place was innocuous, but some of the players were unacceptable. Freedmen were present, and Narcissus cross-examined.[14]

At first sight it is paradoxical that Claudius was one of the emperors said to have abolished the hated charge of *maiestas* that had featured so prominently in the last decade of Augustus' reign and increasingly during that of Tiberius. 'Diminishing the majesty of the Roman people', naturally including that of its magistrates, under Augustus of the senate or illustrious individuals, was a matter of interpretation, from Augustus' time onwards to be determined by a vote in the senate, which was inclined not to dismiss such charges lightly, especially when they affected the Princeps and his family. From the last decade of Augustus it could be words written or spoken as much as threatening actions. P.A. Brunt has shown that it is only this type that is likely to have been renounced at the beginning of a reign: emperors could not be expected to do away with a means of deterring treasonable *acts*. But Dio does insist not only that Claudius speedily released prisoners, especially those detained for *maiestas* (after careful examination) but that he promised to abolish the liability of *actions* to the charge. These would be actions that could also be interpreted as implying disrespect, such as relieving onself while bearing the Emperor's image on a ring. The charge had been so widely abused for slander and libel that it had become closely associated with them. Crises in 16, 31 and 39 had not been dealt with on this charge but had been hastily treated *ad hoc*. That did not come to an end. It was just such *ad hoc* treatment that was found objectionable in Claudius' régime, and it was as a clerk dealing with such cases that Claudius was assigned work in the underworld of the *Apocolocyntosis*.[15]

Claudius' legislation, unlike his judicial activity, has escaped unfavourable comment, indeed has won praise; it was less hasty and less self-regarding. His activities as censor, though criticized for inconsistency by Suetonius, show the underlying principles. The censorship was a traditional regulating mechanism: the citizen population and its property were assessed and men's names were added to or removed from the lists of privileged members of society, with birth, wealth, and character the official criteria. The attempt to make rank coincide with wealth and propriety of behaviour itself demonstrated that the fabric of society was still being cared for. Claudius did not wait until 47 to punish knights who had appeared on the stage under Gaius: in 41 he forced them to appear once more, as a disgrace. In the audience, senators and knights were once more allocated to special places, the privileged seating arrangements of the two orders reflecting privileges in society of which they must be worthy. Restraints imposed on the upper class checked the envy of the lower, and attention paid to rank gave those who survived in it something to cherish. In 47-8 Claudius counted the citizen body (it had increased reassuringly since Augustus' census of 14), removed the unqualified, even inflicting capital punishment on some offenders. He defined the limits of the body politic as in 49 he defined the limits of the city of Rome.[16]

Claudius' efforts to reinforce the structure of society by deploying religious ritual have already been mentioned. It was ironical, perhaps not a coincidence, that his efforts of 47-9, like Augustus' acceptance of the ultimate accolade, the title 'Father of the Fatherland' in 2 BC, came at the same time as a crisis in party and state, in Augustus' case culminating in the disgrace of his own daughter and her lovers, in Claudius' the fall of Asiaticus, leading to that of Messallina. In a censorial edict Claudius told his subjects to get on with pitching their wine casks ready for a bumper vintage. Messallina's festival in October 48 celebrated that in a way that contrasted with Claudius' solemn rituals. There was resistance to restraints on the upper class. The reign of

Nero was still to come, and Rome was not to approach its 'Victorian' age until the mid-second century.[17]

Contemporaries more sober than Messallina's friends savoured the debate that Claudius' activities engendered. Was Claudius entitled to hold the Secular Games at all? A hundred years had not passed since the last had been held, let alone the hundred and ten that would have guaranteed that no person who had witnessed one showing could be present at another. Some of the performers of 17 BC were still fit for the boards in 47. Again, how was he entitled to extend the Pomerium? The Emperor could say that the Games were held within a year of Rome celebrating her eight hundredth birthday, on the reputable computation of Varro (21 April, 48). As to the Pomerium, it was ancient custom: Claudius had fulfilled the necessary conditions by extending Roman territory.[18]

The stratification of Roman society became increasingly formal and hereditary with time. By the second century its division into *honestiores* and *humiliores* (the more solid citizens and men of humbler rank) was legally recognized. Claudius' personal contribution to the process was infinitesimal. But he has been credited with the creation of one social hierarchy. Before his reign, cohorts of auxiliary infantry and cavalry squadrons had sometimes been commanded by senior centurions (*primi pili*), who could have risen from the ranks, as well as by knights and young men of senatorial family. Claudius reserved those posts for moneyed *equites*; senators took only the post of legionary tribune, while the *primi pili* went on to the city forces. This development may not have been a conscious policy. While young aspirants to the senate had long been becoming reluctant to undertake military service (Augustus had tried to encourage them to embark on it), there were increasing numbers of knights, coming from Italy and elsewhere and eager to qualify through army service for prestigious administrative posts. Naturally their claims came before those of *primi pili*, so that they came to monopolize junior auxiliary commands as well as take all but one of the tribunates available in a legion.[19]

Order was always a prime concern. Even members of the Jewish community, whose right to practise an ancient and national religion had been explicitly acknowledged, were berated in an edict and finally expelled from Rome and Italy when internal dissent led to public disorder. In 41 synagogues at Rome were closed and in 49 at least some Jews were expelled. The circumstances are uncertain. Suetonius' phrase 'impulsore Chresto' ('Chrestus was the instigator of it') leaves open the bare possibility that Claudius was facing clashes between orthodox Jews and members of a new Jewish sect, the 'Christians'. To claim that Suetonius, writing in the second century, misunderstood a reference to Christians in his source is unconvincingly economical; to build on this view of the text a further hypothesis, that the disorder at Rome provoked Claudius to issue the so-called 'Decree of Caesar' that came to light at Nazareth and threatens violators of tombs with capital punishment (the disappearance of Christ's body from the tomb being taken by the Emperor for a device of his followers to win credence for their seditious sect), is gross extravagance. The precise cause of the expulsion remains obscure.[20]

The lowest strata of society were certainly to be kept in place by legislation and coercion; that was not new. Claudius exacted the respect due from freedmen to their former masters as best he could, confiscating property if they posed as knights, revoking freedom if they showed themselves ungrateful, or (worst of all) brought charges against their masters; their defence counsel were informed that any complaint of ingratitude brought by them would not be entertained. But all this was not enough to allay indignation.[21]

Early in the reign a slave who had insulted a man of distinction was sent into the Forum for a conspicuous flogging. Slaves posed a threat of actual violence. No murder of a master by his slaves is known from Claudius' reign, but an *SC Claudianum* reinforced the earlier enactment on the subject, the *SC Silanianum*, which provided for the torture of slaves when their masters were murdered, and prevented the opening of the will until the culprit was found. The danger was more serious because of the fellow-feeling for slaves amongst the free population; many remembered their own slave origins. When 400 of his household slaves were executed after the murder of the City Prefect Pedanius Secundus in 61 violence threatened. Augustus, in saving the slaves of another victim, Hostius Quadra, may have acted to avoid the danger of rioting. There was another factor in these murders, apart from the inevitable unpopularity of a City Prefect with the lower classes: the immorality and brutality of these and later victims roused the populace against them.[22]

More generally, hooliganism directed against persons of quality in the theatre, as it was in 47 against the poet P. Pomponius Secundus (suff. 44), who produced a tragedy not to popular taste, was severely rebuked in edicts. Claudius tried to encourage respect to the presidents of games by ostentatiously showing it himself. And in spite of having been a tavern-owner, he closed them down, banned the sale of hot refreshments and disbanded unlicensed clubs, all in the first year of his reign: there was to be no cosy getting together of malcontents. Control of cookshops was removed from the aediles, probably to the consular Prefect of the City.[23]

Like Augustus Claudius was active in adjusting the status and rights of corrosive elements in society. Each item noted below may have been brought in as a response to a distinct problem, or as a refinement of previous enactments. But two distinct lines of thought can be distinguished, which proved of unequal strength when they conflicted. First, and traditionally, he devoted attention to keeping property in the control of the *paterfamilias*, and to preserving his authority over dependents, children and freedmen, including, in particular, care for the interests of the Princeps himself. But the other line of thought was discrepant, amounting to consideration of underprivileged individuals: for women there was an advance, on the whole, of the so-called 'emancipation' that they had achieved in the late Republic and Augustan age; next, an advance in the treatment of slaves; third, but less clearly discrepant, measures to protect minors.

To start with the traditional defence of property rights, vested primarily in fathers of families, there are several new enactments:

**1** A property-owner's right to dispose of what he had as he wished in his will had been limited by the prior claims of children, restrictions on the right of women to inherit, bars on the unmarried and childless, inability to institute an heir after the death of the immediate heir. The institution of trusts enjoining heirs to provide for third parties (*fideicommissa*), had at first been unenforceable in law. Augustus provided them with protection through the consuls, affording testators greater freedom. Claudius had two praetors to spare after the State Treasury was transferred to quaestors (44), and assigned them the task of regulating trusts, so putting the institution on a level with other praetorian functions; in the provinces it was to be discharged by the governor.[24]

**2** The Lex Papia Poppaea of 9 limited the rights of unmarried or childless persons to bequeath and inherit. An *SC Pernicianum* (of 34?) had withdrawn dispensation from the Lex for men of sixty and women of fifty who had not married before they reached those ages. An *SC Claudianum* relaxed this severe interpretation: a man over sixty who married a woman of less than fifty would be deemed to have satisfied the law, on the grounds that he was capable of procreation.[25]

**3** A property owner technically owned his slaves' 'property' (*peculium*), and his slaves' children, who would be home-born slaves (*vernae*) of his. But free women were consorting with slaves, and the offspring, like those of all unions not recognized as legitimate marriages, had their mother's status and ranked as free. Some of these women may have been the freedwomen of the very owner of the male slave, making it seem even more iniquitous that the owner was being deprived of his due increment of *vernae*. The *SC Claudianum* of 52 secured the offspring to the owner. The Emperor was master of particularly well-off and eligible slaves; so it was appropriate that the proposal was devised by the freedman in charge of the imperial purse, Pallas. The *SC* provided that women who formed such liaisons without the consent of the owner became liable to enslavement themselves; the offspring, taking the mother's status, were also slaves. If, however, the union took place with the owner's consent the woman was reduced to the status of his freedwoman, but the children were still slaves. This provision was anomalous and was removed by Hadrian. And not mere ignorance of the owner but his formal refusal of permission came to be required for the woman's enslavement. Another characteristically Claudian provision, that if a free man unwittingly cohabited with a slave woman, the children were to follow the status of the parent of their own sex, was abandoned by Vespasian, who adjudged them all slaves.[26]

**4** A property-owner had continued to enjoy a vested interest in the property of his ex-slaves; Claudius strengthened it, approving two measures on the subject before he had been Emperor for two years. The first (probably of November or December, 41) permitted a patron to make a particular child or grandchild the patron and statutory heir to his freedman. The second, the *SC Largianum* of the second half of 42 established the order of succession to the estates of Junian Latins (informally emancipated slaves who, after fulfilling certain conditions, were admitted to full Roman citizenship, but whose estates meanwhile would fall to their ex-owners): the interests of the patron, his descendants and other heirs were secured.[27]

**5** Augustus had freed women with three children from all guardianship. They could then act as surety for their husbands, perhaps dissipating the property of their own family. Augustus issued an edict forbidding the praetor to accept an action against a wife who was the creditor of her husband, making her surety valueless. Claudius' liberation of all women from agnatic guardianship, discussed below, brought more women into the same supposed peril, so he reiterated or strengthened Augustus' edict. The senate in an *SC* Velleianum of Claudius or Nero's reign, 'aided' all women, unmarried as well as married, by forbidding them to offer surety on behalf of any debtor.[28]

**6** Another measure, fully in accord with traditional thinking, banned loans at interest made to minors and repayable on the father's death. Like the penalty of the sack, which Claudius employed too freely for Seneca's taste, it was designed to protect both father and son, from parricide. According to Tacitus it took the form of a law passed in 47. This has been doubted: Suetonius claims that Vespasian dealt with the offence, and this may have been through the *SC Macedonianum* of the legal texts. I am inclined to accept Tacitus' categorical statement and treat the *SC* as interpretation, introducing the provision that no action for recovery would lie even after the son became independent.[29]

These measures are grouped together as being in the interest of property owners, although there is a difference between protecting inheritance within a *gens* (**4** and **5**) and protecting the rights of the individual owner and his freedom to dispose of his own possessions as he wished (**1**, **2** and **3**). The measures that follow seem to show a genuinely humane attitude towards slaves, women, and minors, that is towards individuals and away from the interests of the clan.

**7** In 47 Claudius granted irrevocable freedom with Junian Latin status to sick slaves abandoned by their masters on the island of Aesculapius in the Tiber (if they survived), with a murder charge threatening masters who took an alternative way out. This measure has caught the imagination and sympathy of historians; it shows Claudius sensitive to a change in attitudes towards slaves which, if loudly opposed by some senators, was accepted and promoted by the most humane men of the first century (many of Claudius' best friends had been slaves). The edict created a new kind of manumission, justified by the master's refusal of care, and avoided disputes over ownership if the slave recovered. It did not, however, deprive the master of his property rights over the ex-slave's possessions.[30]

**8** Roman women, except those who had produced three children, legally required guardians (*tutores*). Those assigned to a woman by a father under his will, or chosen by the daughter herself, might be dismissed if the woman appealed to the praetor; 'statutory guardians', who included fathers who had 'emancipated' their daughters, releasing them from *patria potestas*, and the former owners of freed female slaves could not; nor could the agnatic guardian (the nearest male relative): J. Crook describes this as the only form of guardianship in Augustus' time that had any teeth. The Lex Claudia releasing all women from agnatic *tutela* was thus of some importance. (If it was indeed a law that would be explicable because of the novelty of the enactment.) Claudius left only fathers and former owners as statutory guardians, able to prevent a woman willing property away from them. From their *tutela* a woman could escape only as a fecund mother, under the provisions of the Lex Papia Poppaea. Doubts about how many daughters had been emancipated by their fathers and how likely freedwomen were to bear the requisite number of children after their emancipation are justified; but given the high mortality of the ancient world there may have been many women in agnatic guardianship.[31]

**9** Women entered their husband's family (as a kind of daughter) only if through a form of marriage that brought them into *manus* (his power). That had long been evaded. Hence wives and mothers, not counting as their husband's and children's agnate relatives, had no title to intestate succession; the praetor's edict allowed them rights as cognates (*bonorum possessio unde cognati*). Claudius upgraded the mother's right to inherit. This concession to her contribution to the family was also a move into line with what Crook calls the 'cognatic' principle of wills, which tended to spread goods beyond the male line of agnatic succession. It was left to the *SC Tertullianum* of Hadrian's reign to make fuller provisions, treating a woman (if she had the requisite number of children, which would, as J.Gardner points out, shorten the odds in favour of the property returning to the original family) as an agnate: the mother came in on the same basis as the sisters of the deceased.[32]

**10** Interest in protecting the young emerges during the reign. When a youth aged from puberty to 25 was to be adopted (a move that entailed loss of his independence and his property), the consent of his guardian had to be secured. Equally, the 'property' (*peculium*) of a boy in his father's power, which would previously have passed to the Imperial Treasury if the parent's property was confiscated, was ruled to be safe from pursuit.[33]

The arguments used in favour of all these measures reveal the postures acceptable in public. Traditional *mores* and the upholding of status were certainly invoked when the *SC Claudianum* (**3**) was passed. The measure treated of 'the penalty to be imposed on women who consorted with slaves' and it was introduced amongst debates on senatorial dignity. Repugnance for such unions was a justifying argument, even a reinforcing motive; illogically, since no penalty was attached to women who consorted with their own slaves. With the *SC Velleianum* (**5**) the justificatory argument, certainly in line with ancient thinking, was that offering surety was something that required male responsibility and was a task (*officium*) inappropriate for women, who would not understand what they were doing. The dominant idea is of 'protecting' women, but their intrusion in a male sphere is a secondary theme. Suetonius' language suggests that the measure against loans to minors (**6**) was a means of checking either youthful extravagance (the occasion of the *SC Macedonianum* seems to have been a parricide), or, in Tacitus' words, 'the unscrupulous greed of money-lenders', just as the *SC Hosidianum* forbidding pulling down buildings and selling the site at a profit was presented as an attack on brutal business methods. Acceptable argument for tradition was thus couched in terms of 'protection' and resistance to illegitimate financial gain, combining the images of antiquity, propriety, and tenderness. Occasionally there are independent appeals to human values: (**9**) was supported by an appeal to the natural feelings of a mother and her right to solace on the loss of children.[34]

Claudius discoursed on novelties that had become familiar, making the strongest claim at the end of the speech on the admission of Gauls to the senate: innovation at Rome was traditional. The same theme is heard from a supporter. Vitellius, promoting the marriage of uncle and niece, also in 48, told the senate that much that had once seemed extraordinary was now taken for granted. At the adoption of Nero in 50 Claudius remarked that there had previously been no adoptions amongst the patrician branch of the Claudii. A whole string of novelties is offered by Seneca in the *De Brevitate Vitae* as specimens of vain erudition. The date of the work is uncertain, but the topics were of interest during Claudius' censorship. This preoccupation with the abandonment of custom, with novelty and acclimatization is important as a symptom of changes in society and government, feared and only half-understood. The discussions represent attempts to come to terms with it. The shift of emphasis from tradition towards the welfare of individuals was imposed on the Emperor, who had to try to live up to his promise of an age of felicity. Claudius' combination of concern for traditional values and public order with pragmatic methods and innovation may be seen as the reaction of one individual in power to those changes.[35]

# 12

# FINANCE AND THE ECONOMY

Roman imperialism and the Roman Empire, begun in plunder, were sustained by taxes exacted for the State Treasury (Aerarium). Tiberius said that he wanted his sheep sheared, not flayed, but Rome's subjects were certainly to be sheared, supporting what was the main cost of further conquests, the army and its supplies, so that the system was self-perpetuating. The persuasive model of K. Hopkins suggests more than 824 million HS p.a. as the product of taxation under the early Principate, with about 445 million HS (54% of Hopkins's tax-revenue) going on army pay and bounties. Tribute was for the army, but loot and extortion enriched the ruling class beyond what they could make from their holdings in existing Roman territory and indirectly provided the plebs too with land, entertainment, public works, and employment in constructing them.[1]

The Princeps was dominant in the finances of the Empire in two ways. First, as a governor of provinces. Most legions were in the imperial provinces and expenditure there was correspondingly great. Territories relatively newly acquired, like northern Gaul, were his responsibility and proved an additional drain: they had to be controlled and offered enough encouragement in the process of 'Romanization' for them to be amenable to Roman domination. The Princeps developed an organization to manage the massive public funds that passed through his hands, the Fiscus. Second, as the leading member of the aristocracy, Augustus, with wealth estimated at 1000 million HS, was already the richest man in the Empire, and so were his heirs.[2]

Problems emerged. The greatest was the cost of maintaining Empire and army. In spite of riches acquired when Egypt was annexed in 30 BC, strain began to show twenty years later. Augustus found land for veterans less easy to come by and had to find money (12,000 HS to each man discharged). Failure caused outbreaks amongst the troops in his last, dark decade, and led to the creation in 6 of a special Military Treasury, funded by new taxes. The mutinies that broke out when he died in 14 showed that men were still being detained even after the twenty-year period that had finally been set as the limit.

Shortage of cash and land was aggravated because the services rendered by the army in the latter part of Augustus' principate, from 12 BC onwards, were not profitable. Undeveloped territories acquired beyond the Rhine were unlikely to produce much revenue, while hasty exploitation of the wealth and manpower of the Balkans and elsewhere provoked the Pannonian revolt of 6-9 and unrest in Gaul. After three legions were annihilated in 9,

Augustus and Tiberius reconsidered the cost-effectiveness of the operations in Germany. Tiberius as Princeps deployed troops only when he had to, as in 17-24 to maintain Roman control in north Africa, and he created provinces only when there was no risk involved. Reducing the profitable kingdoms of Cappadocia and Commagene to provincial status in 17-18 created revenues that enabled him to announce a halving of one of Augustus' new taxes, although it was back at its original level by 31. This caution, and the 10.7% reduction in the legionaries' stipend and discharge bounty bills resulting from the reduction of 28 legions to 25, must have brought down costs.

The problem of imperial expenditure had political dimensions apart from the danger of unrest in the army. One of the taxes feeding the Military Treasury was a novelty that caused outrage for nearly a century after its introduction: the 5% inheritance tax, reviving claims on private property that Romans thought they would never know again after tribute was abolished for Italy in 167 BC.[3]

The second problem was that of the distribution of public wealth within the Empire. Peaceful, well-developed provinces such as Asia continued to ship taxes to Rome. In high-cost provinces taxes circulated between tax-payers, collectors, and troops; if the tax produced did not meet the cost of maintaining the army and other services there, resources had to be diverted from tax-producing provinces to make up the shortfall. Overall, given Rome's commitment in the provinces, Rome and Italy benefited less from imperial revenues than in the last two centuries of the Republic, when one hellenistic monarchy after another had fallen to Rome. There was less to spend on games and buildings. Augustus said that he had subsidized the State Treasury three times from his private purse, Nero claimed in 62 to be doing so annually. Most of Augustus' public works belong to the earlier part of his principate; his successor Tiberius was notorious for economising on shows (it was a miserable occupation to be a gladiator in his reign!), public feasts (half-boars were served, with the explanation that the whole beast had no more to offer) and construction works, especially after 25, which depressed employment and income among the plebs and helps to account for Tiberius' unpopularity. The demand for manpower at Rome peaked in the last decade BC, and was not to reach the same level until the period 38-51.[4]

A result of this retention of funds in the provinces was that the Fiscus, the imperial financial organization, became increasingly important, dealing as it did with the major item of expenditure (the army). It was a bigger organization than the State Treasury of which it was a part, and eventually achieved an autonomy that made it possible in 100 to contrast the two treasuries.[5]

Further, funds expended by the Romans on public works and those circulating between the inhabitants of provinces and their garrisons contributed in the *Pax Augusta* to the economic development of those provinces.

Those with the best natural resources and communications or best placed to supply the troops began to rival Italy in prosperity, indeed to outstrip her. A Gallic magnate like Valerius Asiaticus could buy up many an impoverished Italian senator.[6]

In particular, the Italian propertied class, their wealth mainly in land, suffered from lack of liquidity, especially as a significant quantity of precious metal was going abroad to pay for the luxuries that élite status demanded. The price of landed estates fell and interest rates rose. Hence a crisis of credit in 33 which Tiberius solved by offering interest-free loans. Some members of the upper classes reacted to the long-term problem of cash shortage by engaging in prosecutions to restore their fortunes. Hence in part the 'frenzy of accusations', as the contemporary Seneca calls it, that marred the principate of Tiberius but was under way before 14. Hence also intense competition for the governorships of lucrative provinces like Asia.[7]

The third main problem was wholly political: the size of the Princeps' personal funds; their relation to those controlled by him in his official capacity through the Fiscus; his unaccountability in administering those funds; in short, his overall control of public finance, even over the starved and shrunken State Treasury, were a source of two different grievances against the wealth and power at the disposal of the Princeps. Private wealth put him far ahead of other politicians as patron and builder, while his ever-tightening grip on public finance limited the activities open to the senate as a whole. The provincials were the *Princeps'* sheep, and the goods of condemned persons, forfeit to the state, and of those who died intestate without natural heirs, began passing, not into the State Treasury, but to the Fiscus — which bore the greater burden of expenditure. Even the Princeps found it difficult to resist supplementing his own funds when there was nobody to challenge it; Nero in 62 used estates confiscated from Rubellius Plautus as alimony for his divorced wife Octavia. Confronted with the poverty of the State Treasury, he established a senatorial commission to check extravagance. This and later such commissions achieved little to restore the fortunes of the Treasury.[8]

It can be argued that the slow development of the Principate itself constituted a fourth problem, one of intelligent management of Rome's resources. Emperors, in handling financial matters, were too much affected by the conception of themselves as *primi inter pares*: they behaved not like statesmen but like private senators hoarding money or disbursing it in acts of praiseworthy liberality. Tiberius made a virtue of saving money like a good housekeeper, and patriotic senators followed his example of hoarding by contributing plate to temple treasuries, when judicious expenditure on public works would have been more beneficial to the economy of the Empire and to their subjects. Senators correspondingly and sometimes rightly regarded Emperors as motivated by the same greed or extravagance that had allegedly contributed to the ruin of morals and the end of the Republic.[9]

The principate of Gaius offered lessons on the problems we have noticed. First, the costs of Empire and those of maintaining the Principate itself rose again after 37 because, unlike Tiberius, Gaius felt bound to present himself as a commander in the line of Nero Drusus, an open-handed ruler and a manifest monarch. He raised a pair of legions for his projected expedition to Britain, increasing the annual cost of the legionary army by 8%. There were enormous expenditures in Rome and Italy on shows and tips for the people and demonstrations of his own high status, on villas, yachts, statues, and banquets (the annual revenues of three provinces were said to have been consumed on one dinner), most remarkably on bridging the bay of Baiae; it was claimed that in his first year he ran through the entire 2,700 million HS that had accumulated under Tiberius. Gaius found that he needed an increase in revenue, public and personal, and is said to have instigated prosecutions for gain, to have left nothing untaxed in the way of goods and services, and to have auctioned off his condemned sisters' furniture — in wealthy Gaul. He seems also to have been the first emperor to succumb to the temptation of legacy hunting, that is, of expecting testators to remember him in their wills.[10]

It has been claimed in his defence that Claudius' ability to spend large sums freely makes it unlikely that Gaius had really dissipated the balance left by Tiberius. However, this does not allow for Gaius' unusual methods of fund-raising. Again, the assertion that 'the grandiose schemes of Claudius and the well-attested peculations of his underlings were more serious in depleting Tiberius' hoard' is not convincing: the underlings were not a novelty of Claudius' reign, and most of their gains seem to have come from bribes rather than from peculation. In the reign of Gaius, high expenditure abroad and autocratic behaviour at home aggravated the first, third, and fourth problems that we have noticed. Only his expenditures in Rome and Italy, which gave work and increased the buying power of at least some Italians, seem at all praiseworthy.[11]

Claudius, however, usually comes off well in modern writing on financial management — by attracting little attention. 'There was substantial public expenditure ... ; but it was made possible by a rationalization of financial and fiscal administration and by confiscations.' That judicious recent summary requires explanation: there were changes through time, and several areas were involved.[12]

As far as keeping the costs of running the Empire down (the first problem), Claudius made a bad beginning in 41, outbidding the senate with his donative of 15,000 HS to each Praetorian, in comparison with the 2,000 they had received from Gaius (Tiberius' bequest of 1,000 and his own gift equalling it). For cohorts of five hundred men each the total of Gaius' benefaction would be 9 million HS, that of Claudius' $67\frac{1}{2}$ million HS; it was followed up with an annual tip of a hundred HS per man, totalling 450,000 HS. Claudius gave other troops a donative in 41, probably distributed in the same proportions as Augustus' bequests, so expending 747 million HS, more than 90% of one year's tax-revenue. Augustus' bequests must have amounted to about $51\frac{1}{2}$ million HS, which Tiberius had doubled on his own account; in 37 Gaius followed suit. Claudius set an expensive precedent: in 54 Nero had to repeat it, and the usurper Nymphidius Sabinus in 69 offered 30,000 HS to the city troops and 5,000 to legionaries. But the Romans' failure to establish a firm method of succession simply raised running costs. And expenditure on the Praetorians and other city troops, spent in Rome and their native Italy, had the same beneficial effect on the Italian economy as Gaius' Roman and Italian projects.[13]

Claudius' need to deal fairly with the mass of the people led to a temporary rectification of the weight standard of gold and silver coins, which had fallen under Gaius. That is what seems to be signalled by one of the two *quadrans* obverses of 41-2 (the other displays a *modius*, used for measuring volume). A hand holds a balance, with the legend PNR TI CLAVDIVS CAESAR AVG — perhaps *Pondus nummorum restitutum* ('the weight of the coinage restored'). A broader interpretation, proposed by Willers and accepted by A. Wallace-Hadrill, connects the two types also with the checking of all weights and measures, which took place in 47. That seems too late for the *quadrantes*.[14]

Besides working at the grain supply, Claudius had to make distributions of money, *congiaria*. Those of the years 45 and 51, when 300 HS were given, make a total of 45 million HS each (5.5% of annual tax-revenue). But Claudius ought to have given something to the people in place of the legacy of 260 or 300 HS they might have expected from a deceased emperor. If we allow for a distribution at the beginning of the reign, Claudius' total outlay under this head is still modest at 9.6 million HS p.a. compared with Gaius' 22.5 million HS. However, expenses fell more heavily at the beginning of a principate, so these figures do Gaius an injustice. Taking the first four years of their reigns, Tiberius distributed 84 million HS to the people, Gaius and Nero 60 million, and Claudius 45 million.[15]

Suetonius is more specific and better justified in what he writes about Claudius' lavish and numerous games. Neither on these nor on his numerous building projects in Rome and Italy, which Suetonius seems to criticize (the cost of provincial enterprises could be defrayed or diminished by exploiting local financial resources and local and military manpower), is Claudius likely to have spent less every year than Gaius did.[16]

The vast cost of two new aqueducts (perhaps 350 million HS or 42.5% of annual tax-revenue; the text is uncertain) is acknowledged by the elder Pliny; but this according to the epigraphic record was borne by Claudius himself. Even more ambitious were the port at Ostia and the draining of the Fucine Lake, which took eleven years to complete and an 'indescribably large' sum of money, much of it going on the upkeep of the men working on it. Here the deployment of labour between lake and aqueducts (the headwaters of Claudia and Anio Novus were only a few km from the site of the Fucine project) has won Claudius high marks as a manager: the force engaged on preparations for the aqueducts (38–42) was available for transfer just as the cutting of the tunnel was begun. All the same, the expenditure on the Fucine work-force alone, if Suetonius' figure is correct, must have put between 6.9 and 8.3 million HS into circulation yearly (up to 1% of annual revenue), depending on the cost of grain and the calorific needs of the labourers. There was also the financial bleeding normal with ancient construction contracts, probably on a scale here that was proportional to that of the work. All these schemes must have had the same beneficial effect as Gaius', that of providing a market for construction materials and employment for labourers willing to take it. Once complete, the constructions would require upkeep (on modern buildings 10% of outlay is allowed), and so would continue to provide work. Thought was given to recovering costs, and not all the expenditure came from imperial funds: the newly drained land was to be acquired by men who had subscribed to the operation.[17]

Such high expenditure may well have led Claudius into difficulties. He complains in an anecdote about the funds available to him and is assured that he will be perfectly well off if a couple of his freedmen take him into partnership. But Claudius was aware that if he had to use unorthodox methods of recovery there would be political repercussions. He is not known as a predatory Emperor, nor as as a legacy hunter, any more than the distasteful word *largitio*, with its connotations of squandering and bribery, attaches itself to him, as it was to do to Nero, Otho, and Vitellius. The fact that there were other faults to attract attention may be part of the reason. The political struggles of the reign resulted in a number of deaths, those of thirty-five senators for a start. Estates certainly accrued to the Fiscus as a result, including granaries at Rome belonging to the Lollii. But with Claudius this was evidently incidental: resentment focused on the deaths themselves or on Claudius' wives' interest in town gardens, not on any rapacity of his. In financial matters, the main grievance was status dissonance, the wealth of the freedmen, necessarily acquired by corruption, especially in sales of privilege, or by outrageous gifts from the Princeps.[18]

Claudius' self-restraint in extracting money from individuals is clear from the ancient writers, who have nothing to say of any exactions. He declined the gifts that had been accepted by Augustus and Gaius and like both Augustus and Tiberius he excused himself from accepting legacies from anyone with surviving relatives to inherit. The novel taxes that Gaius had imposed Claudius abolished piecemeal, and he returned confiscated property to its former owners, including road commissioners mulcted of gain alleged to be ill-gotten. Most of this belongs to the beginning of the reign, when Claudius was anxious to distance himself from Gaius. There is a hint of rapacity towards the end. Calpurnius Siculus, writing early in Nero's reign, implies that Claudius had pounced alarmingly on treasure trove — surely only in one instance.[19]

Minor economies were practised. Much as he enjoyed shows, and knew that the people shared his enjoyment, Claudius changed the proportion of expensive equestrian to gladiatorial events, which were cheaper because only condemned criminals and captives were used. Claudius' boast of the number of men he 'expended' in the games that celebrated his British victory may mask consciousness of economies being practised elsewhere. Furthermore, it was noticed in 44 that when Claudius undertook to produce as many races as could be shown on one day, that turned out to mean only ten, because of the number of other events crammed into the intervals. (Admittedly a large number of animals were killed on this occasion.) Again, some of the property that Claudius returned to his predecessor's victims was made up by taking back presents made by Gaius to his favourites (a plan borrowed by Galba in 68 after the death of the improvident Nero). One ingenious item on the plus side was the selling of monopolies, although it had the undesirable consequence of forcing up prices and causing shortages. It was in the same year as he notices these shortages, at the beginning of 43, that Dio fixes a wave of economies on holiday periods and of attempts to recover anything that Gaius could be said to have given away for frivolous reasons. Claudius may now have been experiencing cash-flow problems, particularly in connexion with his forthcoming campaign in Britain, which required long-term planning and preparation of supplies and equipment. Certainly Claudius could expect higher expenditure during 43 and for (he may have thought) two or three years to come.[20]

But Claudius probably intended to take a short-term profit from Gaius' new legions. The occupation of Britain in the long run did not pay for itself, but after a hundred years in immediate contact with one of the most rapidly developing areas of the Roman Empire the island was economically advanced enough for there to be substantial booty and instant tribute. In its first decade as a province Britain must have paid enough in captives, plunder, tribute, and the exploitation of raw materials to make up for the cost of the invasion in equipment and manpower. The Romans lost no time in bringing the lead of the Mendip mines into play: pigs stamped with the names of the consuls of 49 show that. The exploitation of British resources and labour is a recurrent theme in Tacitus.[21]

Military success brought Claudius a bonus: the crowns of victory-gold (*aurum coronarium*) that subjects paid to a Roman general in recognition. Claudius boasted of what the three Gallic provinces and Tarraconensian Spain had apparently contributed: a combined 16,000 pounds of gold or 67 million HS (8% of annual tax-revenue). As the province settled down its inhabitants' demand for amenities certainly brought profit to entrepreneurs, but mainly those from nearby Gaul rather than Italians.[22]

Tribute also came in from the other four areas annexed by Claudius (Mauretania, Lycia, Thrace, and Noricum, only the last notably prosperous) but Thrace and Mauretania were permanently troublesome and required military attention; and it is unlikely that the previous rulers of these regions had got away without paying subscriptions for their privileges.[23]

Adequate funding of the State Treasury and the solvency of individual members of the Italian upper class (both factors of the second problem mentioned above, the greater economic dynamism of the provinces as compared with Italy) were also of interest to Claudius, not only because he would become politically vulnerable if they were unsatisfactory, but because a well-funded Treasury at least would obviate the need for disbursement from his own fiscal and private resources. Without establishing a general commission of inquiry, Claudius immediately scrutinized the activities of consuls and praetors. In 42 Claudius showed concern in two ways: he went down to supervise the activities of the praetors, whose management of sales and leases of state property was unsatisfactory; and three ex-praetors were assigned the task of collecting debts due to the state, with the additional authority that attendant lictors gave them and the help of assistants in carrying out their duties, more efficiently, presumably, than before. They will have held office until the quaestors were given the work in 44.[24]

Nero was to berate his predecessors for anticipating revenue due to the State treasury. There is no evidence that Claudius was guilty of this. Like Augustus and Tiberius, Claudius was ready to make substantial *ad hoc* adjustments between the funds owned or administered by himself on the one hand and the State Treasury on the other. When he more than doubled the number of men working on the maintenance of aqueducts he made, by paying for them himself, a concealed subsidy to the State Treasury. That was by no means a perfect solution from the political point of view, because of the invidious patronage it conferred, but it helped to deal with what was, after all, a minor technical hold-up in the financial system as a whole.[25]

To concern for the solvency of the State Treasury Claudius added concern for the pockets of the governing class of Rome, which had suffered not only from confiscations but also from an unfavourable economic climate due to the retention of cash in the provinces. Heavy financial burdens fell on senators as they passed from one magistracy to another. Unlike Augustus and Tiberius, Claudius did not offer financial grants to individual senators, but he paid attention to the cost of other officials' games, as well as his own. He immediately clamped down on the practice of prolonging them artificially by making 'mistakes' in the accompanying ritual, which meant that they had to be repeated. When there were second performances, equestrian events were restricted to one day. Individuals seeking popularity this way must have been able to afford the additional expenditure, but their rivals might not. Praetors were among the magistrates who were expected to give games during their term of office; Claudius forbade them to add to their expenses by offering gladiatorial shows on his behalf, but in the speech advocating the admission to the senate of Gauls from Comata that Tacitus puts into his mouth the Emperor is made to look forward to the Gauls contributing their gold and wealth instead of keeping it to themselves. Again, though, this was politically unsatisfactory, because it was precisely the wealth that the newcomers could deploy that was a cause of fear to

Italian senators. Trajan met that fear in about 106 by providing that provincial newcomers should invest one-third of their capital in Italian land.[26]

Although Claudius did not have a financial policy, only projects that had to be financed, and a political position to maintain, he noticed all the problems we listed except the fourth. He tried to meet them not only by economy and management but by reviving the grand old means of replenishment, which may indeed have served him well for a number of years: foreign conquest.

The achievements of his reign look different according to whether they are seen from Italy or the provinces. In the Empire as a whole the reign provided opportunities for development that owed much to Tiberius' policy of quietude. For nearly a quarter of a century equipment and men were no longer being lost at the same rate as they had under Augustus; the peace established by Augustus and maintained by Tiberius encouraged economic development in the provinces, a rise in the population of the Empire, higher production, an increase in the volume of trade, and a greater quantity of tax collected. When Claudius took his census in 48 he found a million more Roman citizens than there had been on the last occasion, according to Tacitus: 5,984,072 against 4,937,000 in 14, a rise of 21%. That does not prove an increase in the overall population, but it suggests how many grants of citizenship had been made in the interval, presumably to well-qualified, respectable persons. The Empire was beginning to enter the steady state that it was to enjoy for nearly a century and a half after Claudius' death, even though Rome and Italy were in reduced circumstances by comparison with some other areas (southern Spain, southern and central Gaul, Asia Minor, and soon Africa). Further, Claudius' reign positively boosted the prosperity of the regions that fed the administration of Britain and the aspirations of its inhabitants to live like Romans.[27]

One phenomenon gives striking reality to this bright picture: much bronze coinage of the time, found in the Rhineland, Gaul, Spain and Britain, was not struck by official mints. When in the Julio-Claudian period the mint at Lugdunum closed down is a matter of controversy; the years 37-8 no longer seem certain. The loss of its contribution, and of the issues of the Spanish colonial mints, closing under Gaius, diminished the supply of bronze coinage available in western Europe, and the unofficial issues represent attempts to fill a gap which remained until Nero set up an *aes* mint at Lugdunum. Unofficial issues are significantly found in the areas most favourably affected by the spurt of economic activity associated with the invasion of Britain. Official supplies were unable to cope with the demand for currency (a fact which was acknowledged, for the unofficial issues seem to have been tolerated); private enterprise made more available.[28]

With these developments, on the other hand, no permanent improvement in the position of Italy could be expected, rather the reverse. From the point of view of Italians, and especially of the Roman upper class, Claudius' attempt to make the wealth of prosperous provincials available in the capital and his enhancement of the spending power of the plebs through public construction deserve recognition. On the political side, however, only the conquest of Britain and his abstention from confiscation were marks to Claudius' credit. Our third problem, the Emperor's ever-increasing control of State funds, was only intensified by economies, subsidies, and acquisition of new revenue. M.Corbier traced the formal division of State Treasury and Fiscus to the first year of Claudius's reign, part of the general reform of financial administration. It was a more gradual process than that, but the Fiscus grew more conspicuous under Claudius, as in its financing of the new labour force for the aqueducts. The evidence that it was Claudius who created a separate office to deal with the imperial properties (*a patrimonio*), as well as the procuratorship that handled the inheritance tax imposed on Roman citizens (*procurator vicesimarum hereditatum*) is purely negative: they are not heard of previously. But his reign did nothing to diminish their importance. Likewise the poverty of established senatorial families came out into the open as a political issue under Claudius. Others besides the friends of Messallina must have held the view that the ruling class should be free to enjoy its privileged position, refusing to accept the relatively straitened circumstances that Italy's position in the Empire imposed.[29]

# 13

# THE ARMY AND
# THE INVASION OF BRITAIN

Claudius' dealings with the forces outside Italy are marked by sensitivity to the men's rights as citizens, actual or potential, and by public recognition of their service. There was a longstanding ban on marriage for serving legionaries, which he could hardly rescind and which remained in force until the reign of Septimius Severus. Instead, in 45, probably in response to an attempt to challenge a bequest, he granted privileges that the Lex Papia Poppaea of 9 denied voluntary bachelors and the childless. Legionaries obtained the right to give and receive bequests on the same basis as married men with children.[1]

The mainly non-citizen auxiliaries also had their wishes heard. In 44, when he annexed Judaea, Claudius gave way, perhaps unwisely, in the light of their later misconduct, to the demands of units stationed there not to be transferred to Pontus. Under Claudius too begins the series of bronze *diplomata*, certificates that give evidence of honourable discharge for auxiliary troops and praetorians and, for the former, the award of citizenship. Formerly thought to be accorded to all auxiliaries after twenty-five years' service and originating perhaps in the census of 47-8, they have recently been seen as an honour awarded for particular campaigns, and beginning naturally with the great British expedition of 43. There is a doubt about this: it is surprising that *diplomata*, unlike honorific inscriptions mentioning military decorations, say nothing of the occasion of the award.[2]

In 41, the Romans were fighting for control of Mauretania. Upon the successful conclusion of the campaign of 40-1, Claudius accepted triumphal insignia from the senate, an award devised by Augustus for successful generals who were not members of the imperial family. A studied insult, one might think. But Dio claims that his freedmen persuaded Claudius to take the insignia. It was a compromise between passing over the chance to glorify the Emperor in his first months and assuming honours that would be ridiculously disproportionate to a minor campaign that had begun under Gaius. For the German campaigns of 41, Claudius accepted the normal salutation as *Imperator*, the second of 27 such salutations.[3]

During 42, Claudius discovered that he had the troops in the provinces behind him. Scribonianus revolted in Dalmatia. His legions, VII and XI, refused their support and earned the title Claudia Pia Fidelis ('Claudius' own, Loyal and True'). Detachments of VIII Augusta may also have taken part: an officer was awarded a golden crown 'on return from service' — as it was discreetly put. When the revolt was over the men killed disaffected

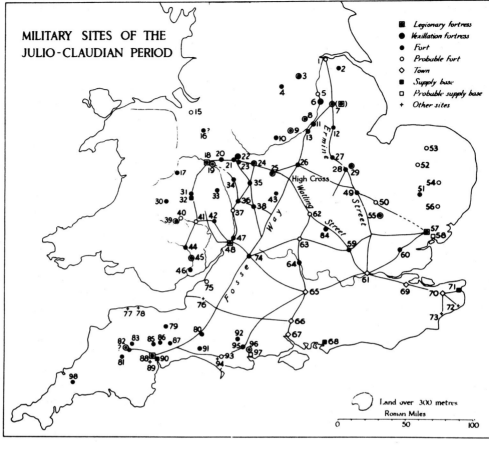

MILITARY SITES OF THE
JULIO-CLAUDIAN PERIOD

■ Legionary fortress
● Vexillation fortress
• Fort
○ Probable fort
◇ Town
■ Supply base
□ Probable supply base
+ Other sites

Land over 300 metres

Roman Miles
0    50    100

| | | | | | | |
|---|---|---|---|---|---|---|
| 1 | Winteringham | 27 | Great Casterton | 52 | Saham Toney | 76 | Charterhouse-on- |
| 2 | Kirmington | 28 | Water Newton | 53 | Swanton Morley | | Mendip |
| 3 | Rossington Bridge | 29 | Longthorpe | 54 | Scole | 77 | Martinhoe |
| 4 | Templebrough | 30 | Nantmel | 55 | Great Chesterford | 78 | Old Burrow |
| 5 | Marton | 31 | Leintwardine | 56 | Coddenham | 79 | Wiveliscombe |
| 6 | Newton on Trent | | (Jay Lane) | 57 | Colchester | 80 | Ham Hill |
| 7 | Lincoln | 32 | Brandon Camp | 58 | Fingringhoe | 81 | Okehampton |
| 8 | Osmanthorpe | 33 | Walltown | 59 | Verulamium | 82 | North Tawton |
| 9 | Broxtowe | 34 | Greensforge | 60 | Chelmsford | 83 | Bury Barton |
| 10 | Strutts Park | 35 | Metchley | 61 | London | 84 | Dropshort |
| 11 | Thorpe by Newark | 36 | Droitwich | 62 | Towcester | | (Little Brickhill) |
| 12 | Ancaster | 37 | Worcester | 63 | Alchester | 85 | Tiverton |
| 13 | Margidunum | 38 | Alcester | 64 | Dorchester on | 86 | Cullompton |
| 14 | Number not used | 39 | Clyro | | Thames | 87 | Hembury |
| 15 | Chester | 40 | Clifford | 65 | Silchester | 88 | Exeter |
| 16 | Whitchurch | 41 | Kenchester | 66 | Winchester | 89 | Ide |
| 17 | Llwyn-y-Brain | 42 | Stretton Grandison | 67 | Bitterne | 90 | Topsham |
| 18 | Wroxeter | 43 | Baginton | | (Clausentium) | 91 | Waddon Hill |
| 19 | Leighton | 44 | Abergavenny | 68 | Fishbourne | 92 | Hod Hill |
| 20 | Red Hill | 45 | Usk | 69 | Rochester | 93 | Dorchester |
| 21 | Stretton Mill | 46 | Coed-y-Caerau | 70 | Canterbury | 94 | Maiden Castle |
| 22 | Kinvaston | 47 | Kingsholm | 71 | Richborough | 95 | Shapwick |
| 23 | Eaton House | 48 | Gloucester | 72 | Dover | 96 | Lake Farm |
| 24 | Wall | 49 | Godmanchester | 73 | Lympne | 97 | Hamworthy |
| 25 | Mancetter | 50 | Cambridge | 74 | Cirencester | 98 | Nanstallon |
| 26 | Leicester | 51 | Ixworth | 75 | Sea Mills | | |

officers. Such loyalty was something to consolidate: conquests would raise the morale of the entire army, even of the legions who took part, if booty were to be had.[4]

Claudius and his advisers must have decided to invade Britain at latest by the end of 42. It was the obvious place for the acquisition of real military glory. The dream of conquering it was one of Julius Caesar's legacies. Nearly a hundred years before, in 54 BC, he had received the surrender (*in deditionem*) of tribes in the south-east and had required the Belgic Catuvellauni of Hertfordshire to refrain from aggression against the Essex Trinobantes. Even taxation, a *vectigal*, was imposed. The Romans could claim that by surrendering, the tribes left them with the option of imposing direct government. Rumours circulated that Augustus would take it up, and when he failed to do so the official claim was that Britain was virtually part of the Empire already: revenue from customs was larger than what would have come in from direct taxes, especially with the cost of maintaining troops in the island. Strabo, writing in the early years of Tiberius, estimated that one legion, with some cavalry, would be required.[5]

Augustus chose a harder and more relevant option: the conquest of Germany. But the setback he met there in 9 prompted him to advise Tiberius in his political testament not to try to advance Roman power any further. Tiberius concurred, and followed Augustus' line in Britain also. In effect Augustus aimed at keeping the south coast of Britain friendly and checking the expansion of the Catuvellauni. The coasts of Gaul were to be free from contact with independent peoples hostile to Rome (Strabo emphasizes close links between Britain and Gaul) and make the threat of a full-scale invasion plausible. The key to this policy was the other Belgic kingdom, that of the Atrebates in Berkshire and Hampshire, centred on Calleva (Silchester), although it had been founded by a refugee from Caesar's Gaul, Commius. One of his sons, Tincommius (25/20 BC-AD 7) was overthrown by another, Epillus (7-15), and he by a third, Verica (15-42). Augustus records his reception of Tincommius, but significantly was willing to recognize usurpers who showed respect to Rome. They were even permitted the style 'Rex'.[6]

Roman preoccupation with Germany from 12 BC onwards made it possible for the Catuvellauni, centred on Verulamium (St. Albans), to continue their encroachments. Some at least of the leading Trinobantian tribesmen were probably glad to join them. With superior agricultural techniques and political cohesion they were in a powerful economic and so political position as well as being the British end of a trade link with the continent. The two tribes were unified under the Catuvellaunian Cunobelin ('Cymbeline'), who finally took over the Trinobantian centre Camulodunum (Colchester) for his capital in 9, just after the Romans lost the legions in Germany. Catuvellaunian power extended from Northamptonshire to the Thames and eventually west as far as Gloucester. Their horse emblem may be seen in the chalk above Uffington in Berkshire, as well as on coins struck at Camulodunum. Cunobelin also moved into Kent, and put one of his sons, Adminius, in charge. The two men quarrelled, and in 39 Adminius took refuge with Gaius in Gaul. Not long afterwards, Cunobelin died, and his sons Caratacus ('Caractacus') and Togodumnus took the chieftaincy.[7]

In his dealings with Roman imperialism Cunobelin saw that effective power, combined with distance from areas under direct Roman control and a friendly stance, made for acceptability in Roman eyes. He set up offerings on the Capitol and in 16 returned Roman troops shipwrecked on the coast of Britain. His sons Caratacus and Togodumnus, however, showed no good will to Rome, and moved on the south coast. Cunobelin's brother Epaticcus had already been pressing on the Atrebates, and Calleva fell in 25. Pressure became irresistible after Caratacus took over. Verica fled to Claudius, and Rome had lost her suzerainty over the south coast. One of the reasons offered for Claudius' invasion was that the Britons were 'causing trouble because the refugees had not been returned to them.'[8]

According to Tacitus, Gaius had already mooted the idea of invading, but had given it up without taking active measures. An expedition to Britain posed dangers: unrest in Gaul, invasion from Germany, treachery at home. The conquest both of Britain and of Ocean was left for Claudius.[9]

The minimum response to the insults offered Rome and her subjects was to send an expeditionary force to restore Verica. But he could not survive alone against the Catuvellauni. There would have to be a full-scale invasion, establishing economical dependent rulers where practicable and direct control over the Catuvellauni. Claudius emerges as a predecessor of Domitian and Trajan in throwing the weight of his own presence into the scale when a changed situation on the outer limb of the Empire demanded active intervention.[10]

Whether the object of the operation was the conquest of the whole island, or only of the south is a tempting question, but, like questions about Augustus' objectives in Germany (the Elbe as the border aimed at, or indefinite expansion?), it proffers a false dichotomy: the Romans did not yet have to decide. It presupposes knowledge that the Romans may not have had in 43 (though ignorance was likely to be exaggerated in the aftermath of success): according to Tacitus and Dio it was not until the governorship of Agricola that the circumnavigation of Britain proved it an island. In 43, Claudius was simply going to 'open Britain up'.[11]

The immediate objective was probably the subjection of the fertile lowland, south of Severn and Trent, with ultimate conquest of the entire island as the optimum outcome. It was politic to revive the powers overrun by the Catuvellauni, and so to establish a loyal chieftain over the Atrebatic kingdom in place of Verica (who may have died or been discredited by flight). This was Ti. Claudius Cogidubnus, who probably landed with the main invading force, or even with a separate division, to be established at Noviomagus (Chichester). As king in his headquarters at nearby Fishbourne he set the example of the loyal and well-heeled magnate for many years.

Setting up the chieftain gave additional legitimacy to the invasion, and, as Tacitus said precisely in connexion with Cogidubnus, a dependent monarch was an efficient means of control.[12]

Gaius' two new legions, XV and XXII Primigeniae, were not experienced. Instead, II Augusta and XIV Gemina were withdrawn from the upper Rhine army, XX from the lower, and IX Hispana from Pannonia. A section of the Praetorian Guard took part, and the numbers of auxiliary troops, including Batavian and Frisian cavalry, made up for the fact that Claudius used one legion less than Caesar in 54 BC: Caesar had had only 2000 cavalry. Claudius' forces totalled about 40,000 men, Caesar's 27,000. The British may have reached 80,000. Claudius' commander-in-chief A.Plautius came straight from the Balkans, and the legionary commanders included the experienced Cn. Hosidius Geta, T.Flavius Sabinus, and his younger brother the later Emperor Vespasian. This was a show-case display of Roman military might; nothing must go wrong.[13]

The expedition was not expected to be a walk-over. Preparation was intense. The services of the procurator in northern Gaul, Graecinius Laco, in organizing pay and commissariat were recognized as equivalent to those of senatorial officers: he won a statue at Rome, like senators who were awarded the triumphal ornaments. Even so, Caesar's difficulties, his failure to return to the island, interpreted as a virtual defeat, the decades that had elapsed, Gaius' evasion of the job, all increased the troops' fears. They refused to embark — or wanted heroism recognized. The efforts of the freedman Narcissus to urge them on board appealed to their sense of humour (an ex-slave ordering them about: it was like the Saturnalia!) and they gave in. Plautius divided his invasion force into three, perhaps to divide the Britons or stagger disembarkation, and was able to land without resistance. The Channel itself, 'Oceanus', though a link between Gallic and British traders, was a formidable psychological barrier. Pro-Claudian sources still claimed that Britain was unknown before Claudius, and the fleet played a highly regarded role. (Caesar's expedition had required 800 ships.) Claudius was deemed to have earned a naval crown (*corona navalis*) for his efforts.[14]

The army's lack of discipline at Gesoriacum (Boulogne) delayed the expedition; for how long hinges in part on whether Narcissus was on the spot already, as one would expect for such a crucial enterprise. The wording of Dio suggests that he was sent for from Rome when trouble began, but it is not clear what generals on the spot thought a freedman could accomplish that exemplary executions would not. The delay is unlikely to have lasted long. An expedition planned, say, for the beginning of May could have put out by the end of the month at latest.[15]

The course from Plautius' probable landing place at Richborough was not easy. The Britons had to be brought to battle. A preliminary success was followed by the establishment of a fort at the crossing of the Stour. The Gloucestershire Dobunni, who had been conscripted against Rome, declared for the invaders, but there was fierce resistance at the Medway on the way to London, dealt with by a feint crossing by auxiliaries. The main crossing was accomplished by legionaries and both Vespasian and his brother distinguished themselves. Once over the river the Romans still had difficulty in maintaining their bridgehead, and Hosidius Geta's attack ended a two-day struggle. The way was clear to cross the Thames near London; this operation was helped by the capture of a bridge upstream, but over the river the marshy ground proved as much of a hazard as the enemy.[16]

Dio's story, based on official dispatches, is that Claudius was summoned because Plautius was afraid to advance any further. That is wholly implausible. Plautius must have been instructed to pause when he had established a firm bridgehead. Claudius is equally unlikely to have been waiting at Rome, as Dio implies; initiative could be lost over the weeks that it would take Claudius to reach Gesoriacum with his entourage. At latest, the announcement of a successful landing would be the signal for Claudius to set out. Reinforcements were probably assembling for embarkation while he travelled up from Ostia. As far as Massilia (Marseilles) the sea route was followed, with a stop at Luna. It was normally the quicker way, but Claudius' ship was endangered by bad weather. From Massilia the journey was made by road (the route from Arelate (Arles) to Lugdunum was under repair in 43) and perhaps by river, the Saône-Seine route described by Strabo as an artery for commerce with Britain. At Gesoriacum the Emperor waited for the moment to take command. Claudius was probably across the Channel by the end of July; it is unlikely to have been later because of the equinoctial gales feared by the Romans, especially since Germanicus' campaigns, that he then expected to meet on return.[17]

The importance of this campaign to Claudius is shown by the political risks he was running by leaving Rome and hazarding life and reputation in Britain. A galaxy of consulars distinguished for high pretensions or military talent accompanied him. They shared the glory — and were kept from mischief at Rome: M.Licinius Crassus Frugi, cos. 27, and his son Cn. Pompeius Magnus, L.Iunius Silanus, all three close to the centre of power; M.Vinicius, cos. 30; D.Valerius Asiaticus, suff. 35; Cn. Sentius Saturninus, cos. 41, was probably already in the island. In Rome Claudius entrusted everything to Vitellius, including command of troops, probably appointing him Prefect of the City, even of the Guard as well. One Guard Prefect, Rufrius Pollio, seems to have taken part in the expedition and Claudius had recently executed another, Catonius Justus, so there was probably a vacancy. The suffect consuls of 43 were all grateful new men.[18]

When Plautius' summons reached Gesoriacum, Claudius delayed a little himself, wishing to ensure that Ser. Sulpicius Galba, who had been unwell, was fit, then boarded with his retinue for Kent and Essex, the impressive advance, and the triumphant procession into Camulodunum. There the court, the parading troops, and the elephants with their mahouts, gave the Britons a sight of imperturbable Roman majesty. The most famous participant in the Durbar that Claudius held was probably a queen,

Cartimandua of the Brigantes in Yorkshire and Lancashire, already in 43 perhaps, certainly by 47 the paramount chieftain of a confederation of twelve peoples, the most populous in Britain, which reached across the country as far north as the future line of Hadrian's Wall, south from Mersey to Humber, including the Peak District. If their subsidies kept her in control of her people, the Romans could be sure of having a friendly power to the north of them as they established themselves in central and southern Britain, and on their right flank as they pressed on into Wales.[19]

Claudius' sons-in-law were sent home to report the victory; his own return was leisurely. The progress displayed new confidence, and gave some subjects their first chance to see the triumphant ruler — and to offer their tributes. We have a clue where he went, and can guess what he was doing. Pliny, discussing the river Po, its tributaries, and how its volume is diverted in channels for 120 miles between Altinum and Ravenna, writes of the mouth nearest to Ravenna and the vast harbour it forms that 'it was here that Claudius Caesar, celebrating his triumph over Britain, sailed out into the Adriatic on a vessel that was more of a floating palace than a ship'.[20]

Claudius had come from Gaul, probably over the Alps. A combination of filial piety and practicality diverted him from his short outward route. One of Claudius' achievements was the construction of a road mapped out by his father Nero Drusus during his conquest of the Alps in 15–14 BC: it led from Altinum up by the Adige valley past Tridentum over the Alps to the Inn and down towards the Danube, giving Roman troops quick and direct routes between Italy and the Voralpenland and Danube. Claudius probably followed that route in 43. He then had the road laid out to conform to Roman norms, completing it in 46. It is highly probable that before he left Gaul Claudius visited places of remembrance on the Rhine: the tumulus near Moguntiacum (Mainz) that Nero Drusus' soldiers had constructed for him in 9 BC, where Gauls had been required to pay homage on the aniversary of his death (September), and the corresponding monuments to Germanicus, where ceremonies were held on 10 October. The soldier Claudius cannot have missed the chance of being present on those occasions.[21]

There is nothing to associate the upgrading of the Alpine ruler Julius Cottius from Prefect to King with Claudius' journey, but the problems emerging in the region of Comum (Como) and the Val Bregaglia, and those concerning Roman citizenship in the Tridentum district (Trento) may have emerged during Claudius' journey or during surveys of the area, 44–6; Claudius describes his emissary Julius Planta as his 'companion'; he may have been with Claudius in Britain, or have accompanied him on the return journey south of the Alps.[22]

After an absence of five to six months, the most successful in his life, of which only sixteen days are said to have been spent in Britain, Claudius entered Rome with some of the senators who had played their part in his progress, celebrating his triumph in 44 (the first for the personal success of a Princeps since 29 BC), and having raised his tally of imperatorial salutations from three (the lowest number recorded for 43) to at least five, perhaps eight or nine. He ascended the Capitol on his knees, supported by his sons-in-law. That hid awkwardness in of his normal gait, but imposed physical strain. It is evidence of determination to emulate an act of Julius Caesar's. Arches in Rome and at the embarkation point in Gaul that were voted recall those set up in honour of Nero Drusus Germanicus his father and Germanicus his brother, just as his new title Britannicus recalls Nero Drusus' posthumous title of Germanicus. The success continued to be commemorated annually, once with a pageant representing the capture of a British town.[23]

Rewards to others also measure the euphoria. Plautius did not return until 47, but then enjoyed a unique honour: not *ornamenta* but a genuine ovation, the minor triumph in which the commander entered the city on horseback instead of in a chariot. Under the Principate it had been used only for members of the imperial family. Drusus Caesar held one in 20, and Tiberius refused one for what he scathingly called a 'suburban outing' to Campania in 21, but Gaius had accepted one in 40 when he returned from his expedition to the north. Claudius wanted to show particular appreciation of Plautius' successes from 43 to 47, perhaps tacitly to recognize his support in 42. This compromise gave Plautius a real military parade without eclipsing Claudius' own full triumph.[24]

The impact of the conquest on the public throughout the Empire was considerable, partly in response to Claudius' perceived wishes. Individuals offered works of art and verse, and the Guild of Travelling Athletes offered the Emperor a gold crown on his success, and Roman citizens domiciled in Cyzicus united with the people of the town in 51 or 52 in offering a triumphal arch to Claudius. Wealthy persons at Aphrodisias in Caria may have put up the relief representing Claudius' heroic subjection of Britannia in part because they knew it would please the court. But the arch and the reliefs made the victory more celebrated among people who might never have heard of it: peasants in town for market day, for example. And they continued to remind everyone of it. The conquest of the island beyond Oceanus was a stroke of elegance and power for a new and underestimated Emperor, and its effect on the minds of his subjects, as its fame washed through the Empire and rippled even into its remotest provinces, incalculable.[25]

The slow business of conquering southern Britain went on after Claudius' departure, first under Plautius, then from 47 to 53 under another well-connected general, Ostorius Scapula, who may already have been to Britain in Claudius' entourage. The Second Legion, Augusta, operated in the west under Vespasian, using Noviomagus (Chichester) as a supply base. Vespasian took the Isle of Wight and in a series of spectacular captures of hill fortresses subdued the Durotriges of Dorset and another western tribe, probably the Dumnonii, for he brought the site of Exeter under occupation before he left in 47. The Fourteenth moved along the line of Watling Street into the

**1** Claudius' uncle Tiberius during the lifetime of Augustus, 8-10, as Imperator for the fifth time; reverse: Altar of Rome and Augustus, Lugdunum. Ae. (sest.). *RIC* Augustus 240; Oxford, by courtesy of the Visitors of the Ashmolean Museum.

**2** Tiberius as Princeps (Imperator for the seventh time, in his seventeenth year of Tribunician Power, AD 15-16); reverse: female figure (Pax, Iustitia, or Julia Augusta?) seated with left hand resting on sceptre, holding *patera* (sacral dish) in right. Ae. (as). *RIC* Tiberius 33; Oxford, by courtesy of the Visitors of the Ashmolean Museum.

**3** Claudius' mother Antonia Minor, as Augusta; reverse: Claudius veiled and togate, holding *simpulum* (sacrificial ladle); *c*. 41-50. Ae. (dupondius). *RIC* Claudius 92; Oxford, by courtesy of the Visitors of the Ashmolean Museum.

**4** The praetorian barracks; above, shrine containing military standard and image of Fides (Good Faith), seated, with right hand supported on staff; on wall, 'the Imperator received (under the protection of the Praetorians' Good Faith); obverse: Claudius, wearing laurel wreath, in his fourth year of Tribunician Power (AD 44-5). Au. 2: 1. *RIC* Claudius 25; Oxford, by courtesy of the Visitors of the Ashmolean Museum.

**5** Claudius' brother Germanicus Caesar (son of Tiberius; grandson of the deified Augustus); reverse: letters S(enatus) C(onsulto) (by decree of the senate), with titles of Gaius (great-grandson of Augustus, in his fourth year of Tribunician power, 40-1). Ae. (as) *RIC* Gaius 50; Oxford, by courtesy of the Visitors of the Ashmolean Museum.

**6** 'Messallina the wife of Augustus'; reverse: Claudius' children Octavia, Britannicus, and Antonia (carrying cornucopia); 41-48. Caesarea of Cappadocia. Ar. (didrachm). 2:1. *RIC* Claudius 124; British Museum, by courtesy of the Trustees.

**7** Claudius clasping hands with a soldier of the Praetorian Guard holding an *aquila*, 'the Praetorians received (under protection of the Emperor's Good Faith)'; obverse: Claudius, wearing a laurel wreath; 41-2. Au. *RIC* Claudius 11; British Museum, by courtesy of the Trustees.

**8** Claudius' father Nero Drusus, wearing laurel wreath; reverse: two shields crossed, two spears and two trumpets crossed in front of vexillum, recalling Nero Drusus' victories DE GERMANIS; *c*. 41-5. Au. 2:1. *RIC* Claudius 73; Oxford, by courtesy of the Visitors of the Ashmolean Museum.

**9** 'To the Constantia (Firmness) of Augustus': Constantia standing, wearing breastplate and helmet, and holding spear in left hand; obverse: Claudius, bareheaded; *c*. 50-4. Ae. (as). *RIC* Claudius 111; Oxford, by courtesy of the Visitors of the Ashmolean Museum.

**10** Head of Claudius from Cerveteri, wearing oak wreath crown awarded for saving the lives of fellow-Romans. Ny Carlsberg Glyptothek; Cat. 648; V. Poulsen, *Les Portraits romains* 1 (Copenhagen, 1962) 92 no. 58.

**11** 'Augustan Liberty', standing with hands extended, holding *pileus* (liberty cap) in right; obverse: Claudius, bareheaded, *c*. 41-50. Ae. (as). *RIC* Claudius 97; Oxford, by courtesy of the Visitors of the Ashmolean Museum.

**12** 'The Augustan Ceres'; Ceres, seated facing left, holding corn ear in right and torch in left; obverse, Claudius, bareheaded; *c*. 50-54. Ae. (dupondius). *RIC* Claudius 110; Oxford, by courtesy of the Visitors of the Ashmolean Museum.

**13** Vessels in the Claudius' harbour at Ostia ('Port. Ost. Augusti'), 'At top pharos surmounted by statue of Neptune, left, left holding sceptre; at bottom, reclining figure of Tiber, left., right holding rudder, left dolphin; to left, crescent-shaped pier with portico … terminating with figure sacrificing at altar and with building; to right, crescent-shaped row of breakwaters or slips, sometimes terminating with figure seated on rock' (C. H. V. Sutherland, *RIC* p. 157); obverse: Nero, wearing laurel wreath and aegis; *c*. 64. Ae. (sest.). *RIC* Nero 181; Oxford, by courtesy of the Visitors of the Ashmolean Museum.

**14** Arch with DE GERM(ANIS) inscribed on architrave and surmounted by equestrian statue (of Nero Drusus) brandishings pear; on either side, captives and trophies; obverse: Nero Drusus as Imperator, wearing laurel wreath; c. 41-5. Au. 2:1 *RIC* Claudius 69; British Museum, by courtesy of the Trustees.

**15** Arch with DE BRITANN(IS) inscribed on architrave and surmounted by equestrian statue (of Claudius), holding spear in left hand and extending right in greeting; trophies on either side; obverse: Claudius, wearing laurel wreath, in his sixth year of Tribunician Power (46-7) and as Imperator for the eleventh time. Au. 2:1. *RIC* Claudius 33; Oxford, by courtesy of the Visitors of the Ashmolean Museum.

**16** King Agrippa I and King Herod of Chalcis placing a wreath on the head of the Emperor Claudius, who stands wearing a toga and with head veiled; reverse: 'Oaths of the great King Agrippa to Augustus Caesar and the senate and the Roman people, his friendship and alliance'; between the lines of the inscription, a wreath; all round clasped hands; countermark: laureate (?) head facing left (C. J. Howgego, *Greek Imperial Countermarks* (London, 1985) 134 no. 156). Ae. A. Burnett, *Mél. de Num. offerts à P. Bastien,* edd. H. Huvelin *et al.* (Wetteren, 1987) 31-7, Plate 4, 8 (ex Auction Bank Leu 45 (1970), Lot 358); cf. Y. Meshorer, *Anc. Jewish Coinage* (N.Y., 1982) 2, P1. 9, 5b. 1½:1.

**17** Messallina Augusta (an error, perhaps due to the Roman form
Messallina Augusti, as on next illustration) as New Hera at Nicaea, Bithynia;
in front of her head, corn ears; reverse: colonnade, on base of which is
inscribed the name of the Nicaeans, all surrounded by the name of the
incumbent governor, C. Cadius Rufus, proconsul. For the colonnade, see
M. Price and B. Trell. *Coins and their cities* (London and Detroit, 1977)
99. Ae. Paris, cf. W. Waddington, *Recueil gén. des monnaies gr. d'Asie
Mineure,* cont. and completed by E. Babelon and Th. Reinach, 1 (Paris,
1904-12) 401 no. 31 (Pl. 66, 7).

**18** Claudius' nephew Gaius, wearing laurel wreath; reverse: Gaius'
sisters Agrippina (holding cornucopia and resting on column, as Securitas),
Drusilla (holding *patera* in right and cornucopia in left, as Concord), and
Julia (Livilla; holding rudder in right, cornucopia in left, as Fortuna);
37-8. Ae. (sest.), *RIC* Gaius 33; Oxford, by courtesy of the Visitors of the
Ashmolean Museum.

**19** Cameo of Messallina, Octavia, and Britannicus (emerging from a cornucopia): 41-8. R. West, *Römische Porträt-Plastik* 1 (Munich, 1933), 216f.; Plate LIX no. 257; Bibliothèque Nationale, by courtesy of the Trustees.

**20** Claudius subduing Britannia. From the Sebasteion, Aphrodisias.
See Smith 1987, 115-7. By courtesy of Professor K. T. Erim; photographs
by Mr Ali Döğenci.

**21** Detail from fig. 20.

**22** *Right* Milestone from the Via Claudia Augusta, AD 46 or 47, recording Claudius' building of the 350 m.p. road from the Po to the Danube that his father Drusus had laid out after his military operations had opened up the Alps (15-14 BC); *Docs*. 328, in Städtl. Müs., Bozen; photo by the Museum.

**23** Porta Maggiore (the Praenestine Gate). The top register (cut in 52) records that Claudius saw to the bringing in of the Aqua Claudia from the springs called Caeruleus and Curtius, a distance of 45 m.p., and of the Anio Novus, 62 m.p. The central and lowest registers record restorations by Vespasian (71) and Titus (81).

**24** Bust of Claudius. Ny Carlsberg Glyptothek; Cat. 650; Poulsen 93 no. 59.

**25** Bust of Agrippina. Ny Carlsberg Glyptothek; Cat. 636; Poulsen 96 no. 61.

**26** Claudius, crowned with an oak wreath by togate figure of the Roman People or Senate, and clasping hands with Agrippina. From the Sebasteion, Aphrodisias. See Smith 1987, 106-10. By courtesy of Professor K. T. Erim; photographs by Mr Ali Dögenci.

**27** Detail from fig. 26.

**28** Jugate portrait of Claudius and Agrippina (TI. CLAVD. CAES, AVG. AGRIPP(INA) AVGVSTA); reverse: Diana of Ephesus. Ar. (cistophoric tetradrachm). Ephesus. *RIC* Claudius 119; Oxford, by courtesy of the Visitors of the Ashmolean Museum.

**29** Nero Claud(ius) Caes(ar) Drusus Germ(anicus), Princ(eps) Iuvent(utis), bareheaded; reverse: Nero a supernumerary member of all four major priestly colleges, by decree of the senate, with four sacral implements shown: *simpulum* (ladle) and *lituus* (augur's staff), over tripod and *patera* (sacral dish). Au. 2:1. *RIC* Claudius 76; Oxford, by courtesy of the Visitors of the Ashmolean Museum.

**30** Busts of Nero and Britannicus, wearing laurel wreaths. Sinope (see M. Amandry, *RN* Sér. 6 Vol. 28 (1986) 72-82). Ae; British Museum, by courtesy of the Trustees.

central Midlands, first to Mancetter, eventually to Wroxeter (Viroconium); the Ninth advanced on the Trent, probably along the route of Ermine Street, on its way to the occupation of Lincoln. The Twentieth stayed with Thracian cavalry in reserve at Colchester.[26]

Scapula had a formidable task. Togodumnus had been killed in 43, but Caratacus proved troublesome, fleeing to south Wales, where his status as Cunobelin's son and resistance hero won him the military leadership of the Silures in Monmouth, Glamorgan, and Hereford. Scapula had to secure the 'midland triangle' abutting on the Severn. Friendly tribes, on the upper Severn the Cornovii and lower down the Dobunni, were targets for Caratacus' raids in 47. Scapula arrived at the end of the season, perhaps to take charge of an army that did not know him, certainly to find that his legate had suffered a reverse and that the allied tribes were under pressure. His reaction to the trouble on the borders of Wales was to disarm the tribes in his rear, even allies like the Iceni in East Anglia. Insurrection broke out among these last, and Scapula has been severely judged for his mistake. It may have been during this insurrection that Cogidubnus also found himself under attack at Calleva, which was fortified in this period.[27]

After reducing the Iceni, Scapula returned to the attack in Wales. His plan for 48 was to advance northwards through the Cheshire gap, and he made first for the Deceangli in Flint. But Cartimandua was unable to carry out her duties as a dependent ruler: some of the south-westerly members of her conglomeration had religious and cultural connexions with the tribes of north Wales, and there was an insurrection amongst the Brigantes on Scapula's right flank that made him abort the campaign and turn his attention to the recalcitrant Silures.[28]

Before the Silurian campaign, Tacitus puts the foundation of the colony of Claudia Camulodunum, which was to be for Britain what Lugdunum had been in Gallia Comata since 43 BC. The colony created a commitment that Rome could never give up, while the natives saw it as a fortress to guarantee the perpetual subjection of Britain (although it was apparently left unfortified between the departure of the legion and the revolt of Boudicca (Boadicea) in 60). The governor's duty of encouraging the natives to pay due respect to their conqueror was fulfilled here, too. Like Lugdunum, Camulodunum was chosen for the site of an altar, erected to Claudius and Rome, which on his death took the form of a massive and costly temple to the Deified Claudius. Even without the temple, the cult had to be maintained along lines set out long before in wealthy Gaul, with its sixty or sixty-four tribes, by the fourteen (if Welsh tribes and those north of the line of the Wall are excluded) of the less advanced Britain. The burden gave rise to grievances, but from Claudius' point of view his new status, comparable with Caesar's in Gaul, had to be matched by new dignity, such as accrued to Queen Victoria when she became Empress of India.[29]

The foundation of the colony freed the Twentieth to support the advance into Wales. It was probably Scapula who assigned them a fortress at

Kingsholm near Gloucester. Other preparations against the Silures included posts on the north coast of Devon overlooking the Bristol Channel. But Caratacus, avoiding encirclement, moved north to the Ordovices in Caernarvon and Merioneth. Now he had to risk a pitched battle, offering his conglomeration of allies the prospect of decisive success and booty. They were entrenched on heights, perhaps near Caersws, and Scapula's victory was against the odds. Caratacus' kinsmen were taken, but he reached Cartimandua — and was handed over to the Romans — the price they could demand for protecting her. At Rome Caratacus was paraded, compared with Syphax or Perseus, formidable opponents of two centuries past, who had been brought down by two of Rome's greatest generals, Scipio Africanus Major and L. Aemilius Paulus, and, unlike Caesar's great opponent in Gaul, Vercingetorix, allowed to live. But it was also Scapula's last throw against Wales; beyond the Usk the tribes remained free for the moment, scoring successes against legionary detachments and isolated foraging parties who did not keep on their guard, even east of the Severn. The governor's exhaustion showed, if he allowed himself an ill-judged expression of his intention to exterminate the Silures or deport them to Gaul, and he died in the summer of 52, having secured the area between Severn, Fosse Way, and Watling Street.[30]

In the preceding year Claudius had dedicated his triumphal arch on the Via Flaminia. This has been taken to show that the capture of Caratacus was regarded as the real end of the war. But it was only the end of an important early stage, stressed for domestic political reasons. The arch claimed that Claudius was the first to receive the submission of eleven kings without loss. Some of the eleven were allies since 43, others then still remained to be brought in; Caratacus was just in time to be included. Later tradition flattered Claudius by crediting him with the submission of a king from the Orkneys; possibly a chieftain involved in local feuding did make contact, but Roman writers discussing Roman achievements in Britain tend to glorify them by moving them northwards. A poet writing under the Flavian dynasty (69–96) has Vespasian sailing the Caledonian Ocean (he crossed the Solent!).[31]

Scapula's successor hurried to his province, arriving late in the campaigning season of 52. If the Silures could not be decisively crushed, at least the military position must be consolidated. A. Didius Gallus (suff. 39) may have been on Claudius' staff in 43; since then he had seen action against hostile tribes over the Danube and north of the Black Sea. But Tacitus notes his advanced years. Quaestor in 19, he must now be rising 57 at least. The appointment suggests that Claudius and his advisers had concluded that it was time for a pause in the strenuous advance: a period of military consolidation south of the Trent and the Severn and of acculturation wherever Roman influence had penetrated was in order before the move forward into the highland zone, the Pennines and Wales. During the latter part of his governorship, too, in 54–7, offensive war against Parthia was being prepared; Britain was best kept quiet. Accordingly Gallus never tried for the final conquest of the Silures, although he may have extended Roman military control further into Wales; they dispersed and he kept the enemy on the far side of the Usk, bringing up the Second Legion to Glevum (Gloucester), the Fourteenth to Viroconium (Wroxeter), and the Twentieth perhaps to Usk; garrisons may also have been planted among the Brigantes, if a fort at Chesterfield is Claudian. Gallus held on to Rome's gains, and even planted forts in advanced positions in Wales and Brigantia. By the time he was succeeded the province was ready for the next push.[32]

First Q. Veranius (cos. 49), and then when he died after only one campaign against the Silures (claiming in his will that two more years would have seen the province subjugated), Suetonius Paullinus (suff. 42 or 43) took Wales on. Both were qualified for work in mountain country, Veranius by his takeover of Lycia in 43, and Suetonius, whom Tacitus calls the most distinguished soldier of the age, by his campaign in the Atlas at the beginning of Claudius' reign.[33]

But even the Silures were to be left free until after the civil wars of 68-70: the Romans as often underestimated the difficulties of holding down subjugated areas and began exploiting the province too quickly and too brutally. No sooner had Paullinus captured Mona (Anglesey) in 60 than Boudicca of the Iceni rose. When the rebellion was over in 61 the Romans acknowledged that further consolidation was needed before the advance into the highland zones was resumed. At the end of Nero's reign Cartimandua of the Brigantes was overthrown and the Romans found themselves once again, as in 43, confronting a free and defiant power. It was under Vespasian and his sons (70-83) that Wales and the Brigantes were subjugated and the conquest of the Scottish highlands attempted.[34]

It can be held that, in spite of its apparent success, Claudius' invasion was a mistake. The peace of the Channel coast could have been kept by other means. In the next century and beyond, Britain continued to be a drain on manpower beyond anything it could contribute in taxation or materials, as the historian Appian pointed out. There were gains: lead and silver, the rewards of victory, as Tacitus calls ore, were indeed being obtained six years after the invasion; and luxuries such as hunting dogs and pearls were exported. Any idea that Britain was invaded for its grain lacks support: Tacitus has grain being requisitioned, but for military purposes. Grain could have been obtained without invading. On the debit side, Britain's defence demanded the personal attention of Emperors such as Hadrian (122) and Septimius Severus (died at York in 211) who had bigger problems; and its own contribution to the manning of the Roman army — let alone the higher echelons of the imperial service — was minimal, except at the level of non-citizen auxiliaries.[35]

But Claudius' successors could not give up the acquisition that had won him such glory. Only Nero is said to have considered withdrawal. If this item from the deliberations of the emperor's *consilium* is to be trusted (and a Cabinet is not always leak-proof), the date is uncertain. The death of Claudius in 54, when his plans were under reconsideration and military operations were looming in Armenia, remains the most likely occasion. The frigid line that Nero or rather his advisers took over Claudius' achievements in Britain may be seen from the eulogy that Nero delivered on his late father: no disaster had been inflicted by people outside the Empire. Vespasian had taken part in the original invasion and enjoyed his first real success there. His unleashing of a new phase in the conquest was only to be expected. Vespasian's son Domitian, who had severe problems in Germany and on the Danube, shrank from the final push that his general Agricola's victory at Mons Graupius (83) had made possible, and Roman fortresses in south Scotland were not maintained long beyond the accession of Trajan. Hadrian's Wall showed how far the Romans were prepared to fall back.[36]

For Claudius himself his invasion of Britain was the greatest event of the reign, and one of his prime claims to rule, as his systematic exploitation of it shows. It was celebrated when the news of it arrived in Rome, and when he returned to triumph; A. Plautius' ovation of 47 renewed the mood; when Claudius enlarged the Pomerium in 49 the advance of the Empire was made symbolically visible at Rome; and the parade of Caratacus in 51 gave Claudius virtually another triumph. The repeated and heroic self-assertion failed only in the face of insuperable political problems.

# 14

# WARFARE ON THREE CONTINENTS

When Claudius came to power Rome was involved in fighting in Mauretania. Spain could be invaded from north Africa, as Q.Sertorius had shown in the seventies BC. Augustus' client ruler, Juba II, and his successor Ptolemy kept Mauretania quiet and served Rome well against rebels. Ptolemy may have been too successful: political, cultural, and economic advance prepared the way for direct Roman rule. The change comes naturally at the end of a reign, but Ptolemy, who was a descendant of Antony and Cleopatra and so a cousin of Gaius, was summoned to Rome and executed. The era of the new province shows that it was formally taken over in the first seven months of 40, and the timing of Ptolemy's death suggests that it was connected with the execution of Cn. Gaetulicus, whose father had campaigned in Africa and would have known Juba. Rebellion broke out: Ptolemy's freedman Aedemon, and presumably the rest of his court, faced loss of position and perquisites, and an inquiry into past financial management, but there were fair reasons for rebellion too: revenge for the king's death, hellenic patriotism. That rising seems to have been put down in 40-41 by M. Crassus Frugi; there was some damage: destruction and fire at Volubilis belong to this time, and evidently much loss of life, as there seems to have been also at Lixus and Tamuda (Larache, Tetuan); a leading citizen of Volubilis (Ksar Pharaoun), who commanded cavalry in the war against Aedemon, won rewards from Claudius in recognition of the town's services and sufferings.[1]

Crassus and Claudius were both awarded triumphal insignia, Claudius taking what credit he could for a success won mainly in Gaius' principate and allowing every possible distinction to the aristocratic Frugi; in the British triumph of 44 he was allowed to wear an embroidered toga and enter Rome on horseback, the animal itself heavily bemedalled. A fresh outbreak followed, this time of native tribesmen. C. Suetonius Paullinus and Cn. Hosidius Geta (suffects 42 or 43 and 44) were sent as praetorian commanders to deal with the Moors in successive campaigns, probably of the years 41-2 and 42-3. So Germanicus had despatched praetorian legates to deal with the annexation of Cappadocia and Commagene in 17-18. Suetonius' campaign made him the first Roman commander to penetrate the Atlas mountains and emerge into the Sahara; but his victory was not complete, even if he attained triumphal insignia: he did not annihilate the tribesmen nor capture their leaders. Geta was left to pursue the elusive commander Salabas — thankless police work that recalls P. Dolabella's achievement in Africa in 24, when Tacfarinas, a rebel who had lasted seven years, was finally trapped. Geta found himself with a severe water shortage, and only a cloudburst saved him and induced the enemy to come to terms, probably in 43. Their mobile forces had been able to operate on a wide front, and Numidia had also been involved in the attacks, to be restored to peace only with the defeat of the Moors. Mopping up may have continued in 43, even into 44; it is to that year that Dio dates the recall of Umbonius Silio, governor of Baetica presumably 43-4, and his expulsion from the senate for failing to send sufficient grain to the troops serving in Mauretania, presumably in that winter.[2]

The long strip of land was already divided in Claudius' fourth year of tribunician power (January, 44-5), perhaps early in 43, into two provinces, Tingitana, its capital Tingi (Tangiers), but also embracing Sala (Rabat) and Volubilis, and Caesariensis, centring on Caesareia (Cherchel), near which the garrison was stationed. They were insignificant in size, and were assigned to equestrian governors, a procurator *pro legato* (acting legate) in possession of legionary detachments in case of further trouble. It soon broke out: Galba, proconsul of Africa 44-6, won triumphal decorations for dealing with unrest in his province and the incursions of free tribesmen. It was not ruled out at the time of Claudius' death.[3]

Claudius' arrangements remained in force until 68, and with a considerable garrison: nineteen auxiliary infantry cohorts and squadrons of auxiliary cavalry (five hundred men each), beside local levies. Galba united the two provinces under a senatorial governor, and so it was under Vespasian, when an ex-praetor was sent to reorganize them. The end of modern colonial régimes, and the contribution of scholars from colonized as well as colonizing nations, have changed perceptions of Roman imperialism, in Mauretania as elsewhere. How acceptable was it? The heavy garrison and the upgrading of the governor a quarter of a century after annexation support Rome's critics: her rule was unwelcome in western north Africa.[4]

Compared with operations in Mauretania, the annexation of Lycia on the south-west corner of Asia Minor seemed a mere police operation, but the senator in charge of it, Q.Veranius (*cos.* 49), is thought to have been accorded the *ornamenta triumphalia* for his success. Lycia was too small to be run on its own so was made into a province with the plain of Pamphylia to the east. The Lycian federation had remained 'free' until 43 because it was well-governed, hard to get at, and strategically unimportant. Civil disorder involving the deaths of Roman citizens was the pretext. For the purpose of Veranius' operations and ease of access to the mountainous area, there was a temporary boundary change, Cibyra being taken out of Asia and put under Veranius' charge. Veranius held the post for five campaigning seasons, 43-7, and claimed military successes: he reduced Lycia into Claudius' power, pacified it, and pulled down walls of recalcitrant communities. He also operated further east, on the mountain ranges at the eastern end of Pamphylia, and destroyed a fortress belonging to the people of Rough

Cilicia. Probably Veranius was operating against the Cietae; they had already been up in arms in 36 when a census had been imposed on them, and they rose again in 52.[5]

On the Rhine as in Mauretania Claudius had to sanction military action almost as soon as he was in power, and two years later, besides opening up Britain, he was to 'pacify' Germany, in Seneca's cautious formulation. But in Germany there was no intention of annexing territory, and Claudius' reign has rightly been seen as a turning point in Rome's dealings with the Germans. It was in his reign that wooden legionary fortresses began to be rebuilt in permanent stone. Turbulence among the free peoples of Germany was the prime reason for the opening campaigns, but previous Roman intervention under Gaius played a part.[6]

Augustus' political testament advised Tiberius to keep the Empire within its boundaries. This policy for Germany had indubitably been thought up by both men, and Tiberius faithfully maintained it. He did not give up Roman ambitions in Germany (Tacitus was still nurturing them in 98, with his complaint of the length of time that the conquest was taking) but adopted cheaper, slower, indirect methods, based on setting one tribe, one chieftain, against another. Social changes in free Germany made that easier. They were themselves due in part to the proximity of the Empire and all it could offer in return for amber and slaves. The result was instability: old lineages lost place, new men arose with the help of newly acquired riches, resentment was engendered; at the tribal level the more settled peoples became a target for needy marauders.[7]

Above all, the Romans feared the development of a large stable power east of the Rhine. In the time of Augustus and Tiberius the kingdom of Maroboduus in Bohemia presented that threat. Maroboduus was overthrown by rivals in 19, to the joy of Tiberius, who compared him with two classic bogeys of Roman history, Antiochus III and Philip V of Macedon. When Maroboduus was expelled Drusus Caesar installed a modest client king, Vannius, on the north bank of the Danube, between the Morava and a more easterly tributary, the Waag. In Britain Augustus had accepted friendly usurpers; in Germany and Armenia, sometimes in Parthia, the Romans were able to put their own pieces on the board. Puppets had small chance of success, because they were only requested when trouble was well started; but at worst they would keep it going.[8]

Tiberius' policy had not meant any hasty weakening of Roman forces. There were still eight legions on the Rhine in 23 and a Roman presence on the east bank. New fortresses shortened gaps between the existing ones, and there were fresh outposts. So Ad Confluentes (Coblenz) at the mouth of the Moselle intervened between Bonna and Moguntiacum (Bonn, Mainz). On the other hand, between 30 and 40 it was found safe to evacuate Ara Ubiorum (Cologne), the Twentieth Legion moving to Novaesium (Neuss), the First to Bonn. There was also to be a diminution of strength, which meant that from 43 onwards the upper Rhine army consisted of only three legions: II, XIV, and XX were withdrawn for Britain in 43; the last two were replaced, but Argentorate (Strasbourg), which lost II, now had no legionary garrison until 70; XIII Gemina, which had been at Vindonissa (Windisch) went to Pannonia in 45-6, although it was replaced by XXI Rapax. Auxiliary forces would to some extent have made up for the loss, but Roman thinking seems plain. Germany sinks from view in Tacitus' *Annals* after the year 50. It provides no triumph between 17 and 83. Gaius was the only emperor personally engaged there in that period.[9]

After replacing Gaetulicus in the late summer of 39 Gaius took the ill-disciplined legions over the Rhine on at least one expedition in search of the enemy, who may have been marauding in Gaul, and led them on long route marches if the enemy failed to appear. Gaius was repeating what his father Germanicus had done a quarter of a century before to the month, after the mutinies amongst the Rhine legions: he too had raised morale with an attack on an unsuspecting German tribe celebrating its autumn festival. Gaius also operated in lower Germany, on the coast, perhaps against the Canninefates (on a coastal strip of north Holland still called Kennemerland) and it was at one of the mouths of the Rhine or even at the mouth of the Ems rather than at Gesoriacum (Boulogne) with an invasion of Britain in prospect that he instructed his troops to pick up seashells, 'spoils of Ocean due to Capitol and Palace': Gaius was celebrating his father's expeditions of 15 and 16, on both of which he had suffered severe losses at sea.[10]

There were repercussions: northern tribes, the Chauci (between the mouths of Ems and Elbe) and Canninefates, and the more southerly Chatti (east of the Moselle-Rhine confluence), began or went on raiding. Gaetulicus' successor Ser. Galba and his colleague on the lower Rhine, P.Gabinius Secundus (suff. 35), were coping with them in 41, perhaps winning Claudius a welcome salutation as *imperator*. Gabinius, who recovered what may have been the third of the eagles lost with the legions in 9, was allowed to assume the name Chaucicus, the last time such a name was acquired by a man in a private station.[11]

The Chatti were the tribe to watch — it was they who were to give Domitian his triumph of 83, by that time having become Rome's prime opponents east of the Rhine in place of the Cherusci. They were already beginning to assume that role in the time of Claudius. In 47 the once great Cherusci, Varus' and Germanicus' main opponents from the middle Weser to the Elbe, between Hanover and the Harz mountains, were reduced by a quarter of a century's internal feuding and fighting with the Chatti to asking Rome for a chieftain (Tacitus calls him 'king'). Italicus was a distinguished protégé to deploy, son of a loyal supporter of Rome, Flavus, nephew of the resistance hero Arminius who had destroyed the three legions in 9, and on his mother's side of Chattan descent. He had been raised, not in captivity as a hostage, as Claudius pointed out in his valedictory speech, but as a Roman citizen (as Arminius and Flavus, who had served in reconnaissance, probably as a troop commander, had both been). In 47 Italicus became chieftain of the Cherusci, the first Roman citizen, born in the city, as Claudius also pointed out, to go abroad on such a mission. Struggles within the tribe had destroyed the nobility; perhaps the unknown of Arminius' blood was seen as an acceptable compromise; as a trained fighter, hard drinker, and good horseman he possessed all the qualities that the Germans admired. But his impartiality made enemies of some of his fellow tribesmen, and their defeat in battle only postponed his first expulsion. Italicus returned to power with support from the neighbouring Langobardi (Lombards) of the Elbe valley, who being relatively few in numbers needed allies, or may have wanted to set the Cherusci at loggerheads with each other. Tacitus implies that that was just what Italicus continued to do.[12]

The occupation of Britain entailed renouncing aggressive ambitions beyond the Rhine. Costly achievements were becoming exceptional in this period: other methods, including *glacis* across the Rhine, were developed. In Cn. Domitius Corbulo (suff. ?39) Claudius had a general to watch: the ambitious half-brother of Gaius' wife. Fresh in post in 47 after the death of his predecessor Q. Sanquinius Maximus (suff. 39), he reacted sharply to an opportunist raid of the Chauci by land and sea, which may have involved the burning of an auxiliary fort on the lower Rhine. Not only did Corbulo take military action; he used the eastern branch of the Chauci, beyond the Visurgis (Weser), to trap Gannascus, the renegade Canninefatian auxiliary commander who was the ringleader. That was likely to start a war between the two branches of the Chauci, close to Roman territory, and Corbulo was criticised for it. The legions were recalled from the conquest that Corbulo's campaigns beyond the Rhine promised (or threatened), and garrisons were withdrawn to the west bank. Corbulo's angry exclamation on the happy lot of Roman generals of the distant past was preserved by Tacitus and Dio.[13]

Corbulo did succeed in cooling a problem that had been smouldering for nearly twenty years. In 28 the Frisii (west of the Ems to the Ijsselmeer, in the district still called Friesland) had rebelled against demands for tribute, and had got away with killing nine hundred Roman officers and men (Tiberius refused to gamble with more soldiers' lives). Now Corbulo marched in, took hostages, planted a garrison, guaranteed the Frisii their land, and reorganized them with council and leaders regularly appointed. One sector of the lower Rhine had been stabilized, and Claudius decided to allow the Frisii autonomy, withdrawing troops to the fortified west of the Rhine. Corbulo spelt out for Claudius the message that mischief might arise from idleness, as it had under Gaetulicus, by setting the troops to work constructing a canal between Rhine and Meuse. His execution of two soldiers for digging earth for a camp rampart without wearing side arms may have been part of the message.[14]

Idle soldiers were also profitless. The upper Rhine army under Q.Curtius Rufus (suff. 43) was meanwhile conducting a similarly salutary but in the end not very profitable operation: that of opening up a silver mine in the territory of the friendly Mattiaci, a branch of the Chatti centring on Wiesbaden north of the confluence of Rhine and Main. First Corbulo then Rufus were rewarded for their efforts with the *ornamenta triumphalia*, which prompted rank and file to compose a letter to Claudius requesting that the honour be accorded generals *before* they joined their troops. It suggests awareness on all sides that the non-military functions of the army would become more important.[15]

In 50 the Chatti reappeared, after plunder; they were easily enveloped and crushed by auxiliaries levied from tribes on the left bank of the Rhine, the Vangiones and Nemetes from the districts round Worms and Speyer, reinforced by auxiliary cavalry. The *glacis* was extended and the Chatti, caught between the waiting Roman legions and their traditional enemies the Cherusci, sent hostages to Rome. The commander, P.Pomponius Secundus (suff. 44), not only scored this point without wasting Roman lives but recovered prisoners of war lost in the Varian disaster of 9. His reward, the usual triumphal ornaments, must have seemed deserved even to his troops.[16]

In the same year Claudius sanctioned the foundation of a colony among the Ubii. The foundation came at about the same time as that of the colony at Camulodunum, but was of a different type. The native inhabitants of the region were not treated as barbarian slaves like those of the British town. Marcus Agrippa had brought the loyal tribe of the Ubii over the Rhine in about 38 BC. This method of defence continued into the late Empire, and its wisdom has been questioned; but the gains to both parties in this early period were indisputable: the settlers could be absorbed on the Roman side of a culturally ill-defined border zone and were fierce in defence of the land they were given. In 50, with the addition of discharged veteran soldiers, the Ubii acquired the rights of Roman colonists and their community, as Colonia Claudia Ara Agrippinensium, took the name of the Emperor's wife, granddaughter of their original benefactor, who had been born in the place. The grant of the name probably brought material gifts, such as public buildings, with it. Tacitus has it that the idea came from Agrippina, but she may have been no more than a willing intermediary, putting a well-timed request to the Emperor.[17]

That this is the last we hear of the Rhine under Claudius does him honour, given that he was following the Tiberian plan of maintaining ground with minimum loss and maximum profit. Movement among the German tribes in the forties and fities, especially on the part of Chauci and Chatti, makes the inexpensive Roman control of the Rhine and the tribes that bordered on it look all the more impressive. The Romans were aware of the disadvantages of their techniques of destabilization (disturbed tribes might cause disturbances of their own), as the defence of the *glacis* and Claudius' fears about the Chauci show; but they were clearly preferable to the risks of attempting to impose direct control. Tacitus, writing of events in Nero's reign, and giving credit for the policy to the commanders on the spot, has them deciding that as the triumphal insignia had been so cheapened they would win more recognition if they kept things quiet. Clearly Claudius' success had left Nero and his advisers nothing to do but imitate him.[18]

Students have observed a change in Roman military habits during the first century AD. At the beginning of the period the legions were mobile units whose power has been rightly defined in terms of their opponent's expectations. They carried a concentrated threat and were deployed as much with subjects as with external enemies in view: the Roman Empire extended as far as the Roman army could impose its will. Gradually static frontiers manned by legions in permanent fortresses at the outer edge of the Empire came into being and were fully operational by the reign of Hadrian, 117–38. His wall in Britain, begun in 122, exemplifies the thinking, as does the change in the meaning of the word *limes*. It had once been a route driven by a Roman expeditionary force through the enemy. By the second century it had made a right turn and come to be applied to the 'paths' that ran along Roman frontiers. Claudius' principate stands near the beginning of the process, and his annexation of Britain right outside it. The withdrawal of Corbulo from free Germany, certainly the stone-built camps on the Rhine, are signs of a change that took on real momentum only after 70.[19]

Events of Rhine and Danube are interconnected, as the switching of commanders from Augustus' family between Rhine and Balkans and the abortive two-pronged attack on Germany in 6 had shown. South of the Danube in the Voralpenland the Romans had subjugated the Raetians by 14 BC. East of the Lech development was quicker than on the west bank. The fort of Kastel Risstissen on the Danube 20 km (12.5 miles) south-west of Ulm belongs to Claudius' reign, and that period saw a marked advance, with signs of Roman occupation between Lech and Danube intensifying. The Via Claudia Augusta driven over the Alps in 46 entails a route along the Danube as its goal, and there was communication with the Rhine through the Black Forest.[20]

On the Danube too since Tiberius the Romans had preferred, while maintaining an increasingly strong military presence — the auxiliary fort at Arrabona (Győr) was constructed early in Claudius' principate — to use the methods of diplomacy; they found men to work for them amongst the tribes. But in 50 the Quadian Vannius, who had extended the kingdom given him by Drusus Caesar in 19 to include his own tribe and the Marcomanni in Bohemia and Moravia, was expelled. The rich kingdom, once organized by Maroboduus, with taxes and plunder concentrated in the king's fortresses, was a temptation to its neighbours, the Silesian Lugii (between the Oder and the Weichsel; they were better known later as the Vandals); and Vannius' successors, his nephews Sido and Vangio, impatient for power, enlisted the help of Vibilius, king of the Hermunduri who occupied the upper reaches of the Main on the western flank of Vannius' realm. The new chieftains needed Roman support as much as Vannius had, and the Romans indifferently kept them in power with subsidies and military support for another twenty years. Claudius simply instructed Sex. Palpellius Hister (suff. 43), governor of Pannonia in 50, to deploy on the south bank of the Danube, on which the fleet was also at the ready, in case the victors tried to range further for plunder, into Roman territory. In the event it was only Vannius and his dependants who had to be provided for; the Romans never threw away a card that might be played again.[21]

It was a significant stage in the development of the region north and east of Italy when Noricum was annexed in 46. Even after the conquest of the Alpine tribes by Drusus and Tiberius it probably remained a dependency, without a monarch: local silver continued to be struck at Magdalensberg until Claudius' reign. Noricum gave no trouble, but under pressure from tribes pushing in from the east and turning southwards as they passed the Black Sea, running the Danubian provinces became a growth industry for Roman military men, superseding the disappointing Rhine. The Danube basin was to be the scene of bitter Roman defeats before the end of the century, and of striking victories, culminating in the creation in 106 of the province of Dacia north of the river. The two key provinces were Pannonia and Moesia. Before A.Plautius (suff. 29) led the invasion of Britain he had been governor of Pannonia and commander of its three legions. The most important posting, however, proved to be Moesia. Tiberius had combined it with the governorship of Achaea and Macedonia in 15, and it had been held by the same reliable man for twenty more years. Poppaeus Sabinus (cos. 9) was replaced by P.Memmius Regulus (suff. 31), who kept his post for nine years. The army under his charge consisted of two legions, like the garrison of Dalmatia.[22]

Mobility was vital if Roman power were to be used economically in the vast area covered by the Balkan provinces. Hence attention paid by Augustus and Tiberius to road building, and Tiberius' concern to make the Danube navigable at the Iron Gates. Subjects had to be controlled as well as external tribes dealt with, as the disposition of the legions shows. Few were on the Danube itself. In Pannonia XV Apollinaris was stationed at Carnuntum (Petronell, 40 km. or nearly 25 miles east of Vienna) confronting the Marcomanni, VIII Augusta at Poetovio (Ptuj), IX Hispana, soon destined for Britain, perhaps at Siscia. Of the Moesian garrison IV Scythica may have been at Scupi (Skopje) and V Macedonica at Oescus (Ghigen) on the Danube watching the Dacians. The legions in Dalmatia, now no longer a front line or a front-rank province, were both stationed on river valleys leading into the interior: VII at Tilurium (Gardun) near the capital Salona (Solin, Split), XI at Burnum (Ivosevci). One concern of Drusus Caesar during his overlordship of the Balkans had been the dependant monarchy of Thrace, a mountainous area and overlooking the Bosporus. It was a cheap method of control but Roman intervention was often called for in a kingdom fraught with rivalries in the royal family and discontent among the common people of a harsh terrain who had to sustain the monarchy as well as provide the sovereign power with its cut.[23]

It was with the governorship of A.Didius Gallus (*suff.* 39) in Moesia, probably 44-7, that military activity opens up, significant for the future in its eastward orientation. Claudius probably thought that attention such as Achaea and Macedonia had had from Regulus would not leave the governor of Moesia time for his real duties. In 44 he severed the two parts of Regulus' province and transferred Achaea and Macedonia to proconsuls chosen by lot from ex-praetors. It was probably Claudius too who removed Legion VII to Viminacium (Kostolac) on the Danube in Moesia, after service in Thrace. In 45 troops were needed to suppress disorder there again after the death of King Rhoemetalces. Claudius decided to annexe. Didius must have been the man responsible for its subjugation in the following year, using V Macedonica, VIII Augusta, possibly VII Claudia, and auxiliary detachments. Annexation was soon followed by the foundation of a colony, Apri.[24]

Didius emerges in the pages of Tacitus stabilizing another dependency. His control of the Danube to its mouth and of the western shore of the Black Sea put that Roman lake, on which a forty-strong fleet was maintained, largely in his charge. The sea was important for the transport of grain from south Russia, and the terminal for its transport by river was in the Bosporan kingdom in the Crimea, a dependency of nearly a century's standing, its capital Panticapaeum (Kerch). There the Romans maintained a small military presence and shared customs revenues. Claudius had put Mithridates in power there in 41 and deposed him in favour of his younger brother Cotys five years later; details are lost in the missing portion of the *Annals*, but Dio tells how Mithridates intended to rebel against his Roman masters, and sent Cotys with a friendly message to Rome to lull suspicion. Cotys betrayed him. Dio's is probably the Roman version. Rebellion was improbable, but any story would be easy for Romans to believe if Cotys promised larger imposts. Serious fighting in 45 won Didius triumphal ornaments and Claudius salutations. It demanded the bringing up of Legion VIII Augusta from Poetovio and, more significantly for future siting of legions, its replacement by XIII Gemina from the Upper Rhine, the double move showing the urgency of the situation.[25]

When Didius and the main body left, detachments of auxiliary infantry under the command of the knight C.Julius Aquila had to defend Cotys against Mithridates' bid to recover the prize. Enlisting local tribesmen and deserters, he gained control of the Dandaridae, whose king, an hereditary vassal, he displaced. Cotys and Aquila were also threatened by an attack from an old enemy, the Siraci under King Zorsines. Cotys and the Roman were able in 49 to outbid their opponents with an offer of Roman 'protection', possibly also with material benefactions, and so secure the help of cavalry supplied by Eunones of the Aorsi, a tribe living north of the Sea of Azov. They took the initiative, captured two strongholds of Mithridates and Zorsines (siege warfare was a Roman speciality, difficult for the armies of the orient, because of the firm organization it required). They gave no quarter, and terrorized Zorsines into surrender and obeisance before Claudius' image. It was a cheaply won victory, only three days' march from the Don, it was said, and not to be depreciated because the returning troops suffered shipwreck and lost a substantial number of auxiliaries and a cohort commander at the hands of the Crimeans. Mithridates was sent to Claudius under guard and Aquila was deservedly awarded the insignia of a praetor. (The procurator who conducted the prisoner to Rome received consular insignia because of his higher standing.) Like the Briton Caratacus, Mithridates was put on public display at Rome and made the object of Claudius' mercy in a demonstration of power useful for the purposes of internal politics.[26]

Success in pacifying the area should not be over-estimated, although IV Scythica may have returned to Germany in about 50. Claudius' procuratorial governor of Thrace eventually proved inadequate, the new fortress of VIII Augusta at Novae (Staklen) was the furthest east in Moesia, and it was not more than eighteen years, perhaps only eight, before the Romans had to intervene again. Ti. Plautius Silvanus (suff. 45) was honoured by Vespasian for achievements as governor of Moesia in Nero's reign: achievements on the Danube and in the Crimea came in retrospect to seem more significant than they were at the time after the tribes had taken advantage of Rome's distraction to cross the river during the civil wars of 68-70.[27]

By 68 the Romans had to take note of Alans from further east: they were moving into the Caucasus and may have been one reason for Trajan's decision to annex Armenia Major in 113. Under the Julio-Claudians the Romans were preoccupied with Armenia rather as a bone of contention with the Parthians, the only rival great power that confronted them. Parthia had indeed scored successes against distinguished Romans such as the Triumvir M. Crassus (Carrhae in 53 BC) and Mark Antony (35 BC). But its Arsacid rulers were politically weak and the army too had weaknesses due to the independence of the nobility and their several contingents. Rome had found it feasible to leave the east without legionary forces north of Zeugma on the Euphrates (Balkis), putting large tracts into the hands of dependent monarchs or entrusting it to equestrian governors, as Tiberius did in 17-18 with Cappadocia, which commanded the river crossing at Tomisa (Komurhan), (although he united Commagene, annexed at the same time and dominating the crossing at Samosata, to Syria): the military routes between the two empires were those from south-east Anatolia and northern Syria into northern Mesopotamia. The four oriental legions outside Egypt were all in Syria after Augustus' time: VI Ferrata near Laodicea (Latakya on the coast); X Fretensis at Cyrrhus (Kuros) on the road from the capital, Antioch, to Zeugma, while XII Fulminata is found at Raphaneae (Rafniya) under Nero; the base of III Gallica is unknown. Significantly enough, the Third was transferred to Moesia in 68. By then Claudius had strengthened the Roman presence by founding colonies: Archelais (Ak Saray) in Cappadocia and Ptolemais (Acre) in southern Syria.[28]

The annexation of Commagene was not definitive. The client monarch Antiochus IV, after vicissitudes under Gaius, was reestablished by Claudius and outlasted the reign of Nero. He did good service in Rough Cilicia in 52 where a fresh rising of the Cietae that reached the coastal town of Anemurium (Anemur) and threatened merchant shipping had seen off an onslaught of auxiliary cavalry brought from Syria into unsuitable terrain. Antiochus' divisive tactics and and a naval squadron dealt with it.[29]

For both Rome and Parthia the diplomatic engagement was important: Roman rule was regarded without enthusiasm in parts of the east, while the Parthian king suffered from his arriviste dynasty's unpopularity and from potential rivals from the royal harem. Armenia was the sphere of action: it was useful to the Parthians, as a kingdom for younger brothers, but Rome had laid claim to it in Antony's time and would lose face if she gave it up. Augustus, instead of annexing it in 20 BC, was content to replace the Parthian incumbent with a Roman nominee, solemnly crowned. It was an honourable and economical solution but had drawbacks: if the nominee were unsuccessful in maintaining his position (not many long resident in Rome were as tough as Italicus) and were expelled, and in any case when he died, the whole process would have to be gone through again, sometimes at some military cost. Augustus lost Gaius Caesar in AD 4, and Tiberius Germanicus in 19, in the course of such missions, but the policy was continued by Tiberius when the successful candidate Zeno, crowned as Artaxias by Germanicus, died in 35, then by Claudius, with ill success, and by Nero until 62.[30]

The death of Artaxias tempted Artabanus of Parthia to try once more to take over Armenia. L.Vitellius (cos. 34) checked him; indeed, Artabanus himself was temporarily displaced by a Roman nominee, while in Armenia an Iberian called Mithridates was installed, whom Claudius reinstated in 41 after his removal by Gaius, intimidating the Parthians with a threat of war: a legion was brought up to Zeugma and a garrison installed at Gorneae (Baş Garni, north-east of Artaxata?) under a prefect and a centurion. (The crossings at Tomisa and Samosata (Samsat) were protected by dependencies to the east: Sophene, of which Claudius made Agrippa II monarch, and Edessa.) Roman sensitivity to the activities of vassals in the area is shown by the intervention of Vibius Marsus, governor of Syria, in a summit conference between the kings of Commagene, Judaea, Emesa, Chalcis, Pontus, and Armenia Minor just before the death of Agrippa I. That may have played some part in the Roman decision to annex Judaea in 44 and Ituraea in 49 when its ruler Sohaemus died after a ten-year tenure.[31]

Claudius had another opportunity to inflict a crushing humiliation on the Parthians at no cost by deploying a claimant to their throne. In 49 dissident groups asked him for a claimant, Meherdates, son of an earlier pretender, who was ceremoniously dispatched after a lecture from the Emperor. He was escorted to the Euphrates by the governor of Syria, C.Cassius Longinus, and let loose. Meherdates' failure in Parthia, if predictable, was unimportant: it was an expendable bonus. But in Armenia in 51 the Iberian Mithridates, after surviving for ten years, was expelled and killed by his nephew, Radamistus, egged on by a father who feared for his own throne in Iberia if Radamistus failed to find one somewhere else. The Roman strong-point at Gorneae proved useless to Mithridates: its commander Caelius Pollio surrendered it, under the protests of his subordinate Casperius and in response to bribes (he pleaded shortage of provisions to meet Radamistus' siege).[32]

Claudius' undistinguished governor of Syria, Ummidius Quadratus, who had been adequate in Dalmatia but had risen beyond his capacities, failed to take action to reinstate the Roman nominee and contented himself with a demand for Radamistus' withdrawal (the arguments would be that he had alienated his people and that Radamistus was no Parthian). Julius Paelignus, Procurator of Cappadocia, while ready to act to restore order and relieve the garrison at Gorneae (confident perhaps because of his friendship with the Emperor), was ill-armed for serious campaigning (Tacitus mentions local auxiliaries) and he failed to intimidate Radamistus and secure his allegiance. On the contrary, he was forced to witness and sanction the crowning of the man who had usurped Mithridates' throne. Quadratus now sent a legion to Armenia under Helvidius Priscus, only to withdraw it when the Parthians made representations. All Quadratus finally did was to place a squadron of cavalry at Europus on the Euphrates as an impediment to any attack on Syria, always an ultimate goal for the Parthians. Radamistus was not to keep Armenia for long: an Iberian prince could not stand up against the forces of Vologaeses, the new king of Parthia (his first known coin is dated to the late summer of 51), who saw Armenia as the placement for his brother Tiridates, since the Romans were apparently unwilling to defend their interests there. Ejected in late 51 or more probably 52, Radamistus made an attempt at a come-back after a hard winter (51-2 or 52-3) that forced the Parthians to withdraw. But his revengeful savagery now alienated his subjects, and at the end of 54, just after Claudius' death, reports reached Rome of a second Parthian invasion and of the Parthian nominee once more installed.[33]

Rome's reputation had to be restored without delay. The immediate appointment of Corbulo, who had been prevented from taking the military action in Germany that he had seen as correct, was a denigration of Claudius's arrangements, although Quadratus was kept in post. Nero's ultimate solution, which was always Corbulo's, was reached in 63: Armenia could indeed go to the Parthian king's brother, but it must formally be granted to him in Rome, as it finally was in 66 when he received his tiara from the hand of the Emperor.[34]

There is a marked contrast between Claudius' achievements in east and west, although in both spheres he had clear precedents to follow. In the west he showed himself decisive: conquest in Britain and containment on Rhine and Danube. In the east opportunities were lost and Rome's reputation smirched by incompetence, even though it was Radamistus who was in control of Armenia when Claudius died. Certainly four to six weeks might pass before Rome knew what was happening in eastern Anatolia and much depended on the initiative of men on the spot. Claudius' were not of the highest calibre (although some of the scandalous allegations of corruption made against them may be due to the disparagement of subordinates and successors early in Nero's reign), and he is accountable for that. His own interest in the west (perhaps stimulated by Caesar's achievements and Germanicus' first-hand accounts), was probably greater. Claudius had no personal knowledge of the east, although geographical details featured in his writings, and he may have underestimated the importance of maintaining face before the Parthians, even the nature of the engagement. In the west the issues were military and clear-cut; in the east the Romans were dealing with a major though vulnerable power sophisticated in diplomacy. The contrast may be illustrated from the courses pursued by Corbulo in Germany under Claudius (though he favoured a more aggressive approach to the Germans) and in the east under Nero. Here even he, and perhaps from the first years of his appointment, advocated rapprochement with Parthia after negotiations conducted from a position of strength.[35]

# 15

# CLAUDIUS AND THE PROVINCIALS

*Principles and structure*

Seneca speaks of Claudius' coming to power as his having dedicated himself to the entire world, like Atlas; the comparison is echoed by a small marble Atlas dedicated to Claudius in 49 and found in Baetica. Claudius' friend Paullus Fabius Persicus as governor of Asia issued an elaborate edict curtailing (he hoped) inefficiency, waste and dishonesty in the administration of the temple funds established for the cult of Artemis at Ephesus. He prefaced his edict with a paragraph on the example set by the Emperor who wanted every man to have his due. Claudius' own pronouncement on the Anauni also shows how aware he was of his responsibilities towards his subjects and to subordinates who dealt with problems on the spot.[1]

By the standards of Hadrian (117-38), with his four great tours, Claudius was no peripatetic emperor. He knew little of the Empire first-hand before coming to power. Augustus as Triumvir had campaigned in the east and in the Balkans, and once in sole power moved to Spain and Gaul; it was only after 8 BC that he became rooted in Italy. By 14, Tiberius had seen service all over the Empire except in north Africa, though he never left Italy again. Gaius, precluded by youth, and Claudius, by unfitness, had no experience. Even the evidence that Claudius visited Thessaly in 10-11 is fragile. Only the trip to Gaul in 39 is certain. As Emperor Claudius left Italy once, for six months in 43-4, and even in Italy we see him treading a worn track down to Ostia or Baiae, or visiting the Fucine Lake. Claudius did not need to travel, however, either to exploit the resources of Empire more widely, or to voice more demonstratively than ever before the care for the provinces that was a recognized part of the Princeps' duties. He showed brutality and sadism, but only where criminals were involved. To his dealing with provincials he brought freshness, conviction that he knew best, interest, and humanity.[2]

The Emperor's prime concern was decent government on a regular basis. He wanted officials to supervise the running of the Empire as conscientiously as he did. His 'friend' Gallio, governor of Achaea, did not care for the squabbles of Jewish sects in his province; on another matter, however, the welfare of Delphi, he received firm advice from the Emperor. How Claudius envisaged a governor's duties may be seen from his prohibiting legates from giving speeches of thanks on appointment: they had been given a task, not a prize. This conception foreshadows the conscious dutifulness of the younger Pliny in Bithynia and of other second-century governors. There

163

was less glory and gain to be had from provinces under the Principate. Some men were reluctant to accept posts, or to set out for them. Proconsuls, whom Tiberius had enjoined to leave for their posts by June, were now given only until mid-April. Inevitably there were still greedy offenders. Dio reports that Claudius exiled a governor for taking bribes, and confiscated his gains; nothing new, but the case seems to have given rise in 45 to the rule that 'assessors', that is legates who were assistant-governors, might not draw lots for their next province without an interval in which prosecutions could be brought. Dio also claims that tenure of another office or absence on public business (*rei publicae causa*) was not allowed to inhibit prosecution, and that was novel. Of the few trials for extortion recorded under Claudius, one was politically motivated: the trials were brought from Bithynia and Asia, two provinces commonly involved in such prosecutions because of their wealth, their articulate ruling circles, and the contentiousness of their civic politics, in which governors sometimes became involved. At a lower level, a citizen of Cibyra, Q. Veranius Philagrus, was able to get Claudius to remove an agent who had been extorting 12,000 HS from the city every year, perhaps in connection with exactions of grain; and Ventidius Cumanus, procurator of Judaea, succumbed to accusations brought by his subjects in 52. Claudius saw himself as contending with human depravity. He complains of it in an edict from Tegea (49-50) dealing with another deeply rooted problem: misuse of the official transport facilities for which subjects paid.[3]

It is probably a coincidence that the first firm evidence for regular instructions (*mandata*) issued to the incoming governors of senatorial provinces, as opposed to instructions on specific points given during their terms of office, such as Gallio received, comes from Claudius' reign; they began by being *ad hoc* and exceptional, as in the instructions that Tiberius gave the proconsul of Africa in 21 when a rebel had to be dealt with. A Claudian governor of Asia refers to them quite casually.[4]

Care for the provinces was in Claudius' own interest, as was his notorious generosity over granting the citizenship: benefits earned gratitude and established obligations. The more people who acknowledged them the more support Claudius enjoyed. The desire to 'maximize patronage' (C.E. Stevens' phrase) may have played a part in his care and in the grants. But the Emperor was not greedy for ostentatious recognition: new citizens did not have to take Claudius' name (some Lycians took that of their first governor, Veranius); this, and failure to make the Emperor a legatee, were made a grounds for prosecutions, but Claudius did not entertain them.[5]

There were both political and practical arguments for granting citizenship: increasingly the provinces were supplying the manpower that was Rome's main strength, and only citizen manpower could be recruited for the legions. On the other hand, those who had already fought for Rome were recognized as having a claim to the citizenship. The principle went back to the end of the third century BC, but Claudius stressed it more than any dynast since Caesar, partly because of his own need for support. The foundation of genuine colonies in the provinces was one means of building up usable provincial manpower, through intermarriage with local women of veterans possessing the right of contracting legitimate Roman marriages (*conubium*). Settlements of troops such as that at Siculi (Biac) in Dalmatia and Savaria (Szombathely) in Pannonia kept up the supply of recruits and incidentally helped to 'Romanize' a province. At Colonia Agrippinensis (Cologne), on the other hand, only a few discharged soldiers joined the loyal Ubii, but the children of all alike would be liable to the call-up. Grants of citizenship without military settlement were also made. Volubilis in Mauretania Tingitana had served Rome in war at the beginning of Claudius' reign and received citizenship in recognition. Communities or districts of attested loyalty were sometimes rewarded with Latin rights. Members of the ruling aristocracy then obtained Roman citizenship on holding local office. Entire districts, such as the Graian Alps, Belgica, as E.Wightman believed, and, under Vespasian, the whole of Spain, advanced in this way.[6]

Claudius' edict of 46 granting citizenship *en masse* to the Anauni and other tribes attached to Tridentum (Trent) shows that he liked to handle this subject himself, for principles might be involved. Citizenship was also awarded to individuals. Both communal and viritane grants were liable to cause alarm, the first because of the large numbers who benefited, foreshadowing the levelling of provincials and Italians to the same status, the second because corruption was passing unchecked, in spite of Claudius' determination to preserve distinctions between citizen and non-citizen (usurpers were executed). Hence protests on both grounds. Individuals allegedly were buying citizenship for mere broken glass vessels, and Claudius 'wanted to see all the Gauls, Greeks, Spaniards, and Britons in togas'. The numbers of Claudii exhibited in the indexes of epigraphic collections are modest in comparison with Iulii and even Flavii, which should indicate that Claudius was less generous than he has been supposed to be, and less generous than the Flavian dynasty. Complaints may have arisen simply because of the contrast with Tiberius' extreme caution over enfranchisement. But Latin rights given to communities would not show in the nomenclature. It may have been just these grants that caused alarm.[7]

Claudius' reign saw some increase of provincial territory governed by Roman officials over the alternative method of control, client rulers. Tiberius had annexed Cappadocia and Commagene when their rulers died, but Gaius reverted to a defensible policy of his great-grandfather Antony, that of conferring small and difficult areas on grateful dependent monarchs. He had friends and coevals of royal lineage who had been brought up in the house of Antonia, and was pleased to favour them. In 38 he entrusted Commagene and Rough Cilicia to King Antiochus IV, who reigned until 72, with an interruption at the end of Gaius' principate; Ptolemy of Mauretania was executed. Claudius annexed Britain, leaving only parts of it to dependent rulers, and provincialized Mauretania, Lycia, Noricum, and Thrace. On the other hand he reinstated Antiochus and dispatched Mithridates VIII to the

Bosporan kingdom, while Polemo II, its incumbent king or a claimant, is said to have been assigned Olba in Rough Cilicia. Politics and personal favour naturally still dominated such decisions. Antiochus of Commagene and Polemo of Pontus enjoyed warm relations with Claudius, and his friendship helped Agrippa I to an extension of his kingdom in 41.[8]

The extensive but poor area formerly administered by the tetrarch Philip, which extended north and east of the Sea of Galilee and included Paneas, Batanaea, Gaulanitis (Golan), Trachonitis (El Lejja), and Auranitis (Hauran), had been turned over to Agrippa by his friend and patron Gaius, along with the tetrarchy of Lysanias centring on Abila (Suk) north of Damascus; later Gaius added Galilee, west of the Sea, from which he removed Herod Antipas. By giving Agrippa Judaea in 41 Claudius made him a great king, ruler of as much territory as Herod the Great; and he awarded Agrippa's brother Herod a principality of his own in Chalcis. An additional sign of esteem was the consular and praetorian insignia that the brothers received. It was a good solution for Judaea in spite of the friction that developed between Agrippa and the governor of Syria, Vibius Marsus: the Idumaean kings might offend Jewish susceptibilities, but the Romans would not be directly involved. But the king died in 44, to the joy of his subjects, and Claudius did not entrust the kingdom to his son Agrippa II, who was only sixteen. Instead he revived the Roman province and returned Philip's difficult tetrarchy to the province of Syria. Agrippa II was appointed to Chalcis in 49-50, after his uncle Herod's death, though he lost it in 53, when he was given a larger realm including Batanaea, Trachonitis, and Gaulanitis. Until his death in about 92 Agrippa II loyally continued his father's work of policing without cost to Rome, indeed of conciliating Rome's Jewish subjects, and his family contracted marriages with leading client dynasts as well as with Claudius' freedman and last governor of Judaea, Felix.[9]

Agrippa's was not the only dependency to be enlarged. M.Julius Cottius, of the district still known as the Cottian Alps, was awarded additional territory in 44. This change may be seen as an expression of Claudius' judgment of what one man could now manage in an area close to which he had recently travelled; it was also a recognition of Cottius' forbears' success in bringing their realm into the Roman economic and political system, through feats of road-building. But the territories of successful dependent rulers tended to be taken under direct control as their culture and economy approached closer to those of neighbouring provinces. Twenty years later, when King Cottius, as he was allowed to style himself, died, his realm was provincialized under an equestrian procurator. Noricum, annexed in 46, looks like a similar case. It had been under Roman supervision since 15 BC, advancing materially and culturally. Now there was no reason for the anomaly, a dependency without a client ruler, to continue. In the new province the Celtic Magdalensberg was abandoned and a new capital, with Latin rights, Virunum near Klagenfurt, was established.[10]

In the Greek east there were comparable changes. The strategic motive for detaching Achaea and Macedonia from Moesia, Roman determination to bring unrest to an end in Thrace, and military operations in Lycia and Cilicia have already been mentioned. The occasion for annexing Lycia was politically interesting as well: the murder of Romans, possibly Italian business men who had misused their status in making a profit, more probably enfranchised natives deploying Roman citizenship as a weapon in local politics. Men trusted by Rome were assassinated or more probably became the victims of judicial murder, since the whole federation suffered. The Lycians sent an embassy but could not clear themselves, although some loyalists were rewarded with Roman citizenship. Rhodes too was deprived of its nominal freedom, in 44 just after Lycia, and likewise after violence: Roman citizens had been impaled. That could not have been a legal form of execution in civilized Rhodes, and it looks as if a mob had practised lynch-law — on money-lenders at a guess. It is tempting to ask if preparations for the invasion of Britain and the demand for 'voluntary' contributions, had caused financial difficulties.[11]

In extending the Empire Claudius was increasing responsibilities as well as revenues. Attentive governors were required. In Noricum four communities besides Virunum attained Latin rights, Iuvavum (Salzburg) in the north-west of the province on the Salzach valley, the others, Aguntum (near Lienz), Teurnia (near Spittal), Celeia (Celje), in the south and east in the valleys of the Drave and its tributaries. In the Mauretanias Claudius recognized urbanization and encouraged further 'Romanization' by grading the privileges he accorded. Of the two leading communities, Caesarea (Cherchel) and Tingi (Tangiers), one was made a Roman colony, the second enlarged, and Claudius gave full rights to the *municipium* of Volubilis (Ksar Pharaoun), Rusucuru (Dellys), and perhaps to Sala (Rabat), Latin rights to Tipasa.[12]

Old territories were not neglected. The Alpes Graiae and Poeninae became a separate administrative district under an equestrian governor in the first century AD, and Rome's takeover of dues that had been paid to the native inhabitants of the Alpine passes meant the decline of four separate tribes and their absorption into one community of the Vallenses, Octodurus or Forum Claudii (Martigny), which had first Latin and then full citizen rights. This title, and that of Forum Claudii Ceutronum in the Graian Alps, suggests that it was Claudius who accorded both districts the Latin right. In the Maritime Alps, too, there were grants that made the recruitment of legionaries possible.[13]

## Road-building and material advance in the the West

In the Gallic provinces Claudius' reign marked the start of a new spurt of development, especially in the north. Personal beneficence was one factor, in particular favouring Lugdunum, which received the aqueduct of La Brévenne and the style Colonia Copia Claudia Augusta. Another was the advancement of a handful of magnates to the senate. In the long run security achieved by a stable Rhine frontier was more important, and the development of the road system; then the region's role as base for the British expedition, its contribution of auxiliary troops, and its continued input into the island. De Laet notes the rise of pre-invasion centres at Tournai and Courtrai and the development of Gesoriacum (Boulogne) and Samarobriva (Amiens). Bagacum (Bavai) too was to flourish, receiving its town plan, a grid, under Claudius. Belgica was to be 'transformed' in the century between Claudius and the Antonines, most obviously by the substitution of stone for wood in construction. Claudius must have noted the nascent wealth of Gaul, that was to eclipse Italy, all other provinces of the west and all but Asia and Syria in the east, but scholars overestimate his personal contribution. The Rhine armies and their purchasing power were a permanency. From this and from the annexation of Britain northern Gaul acquired secure wealth to be spent on the amenities and education that carried the conquerers' prestige, and so became Romanized. The Gauls began to deploy natural resources and acquired expertise, offering goods for sale beyond the Channel, Baltic, and Vistula.[14]

All Gaul was favoured in the first six years of the reign with road construction and repair: Narbonensis alone shows more dated Claudian milestones than all other regions outside Gaul, 27 against 23; Comata has 17. In 41 there was a massive restoration of the old south-coast route, the Via Domitia, which may have suffered from sea flooding, as G.Walser suggests. Work on the Massilia – Lugdunum route took place in 43, as well as improvements to the road north from Lugdunum to Andematunnum (Langres), and in 44 restoration of the Moguntiacum (Mainz) – Oppidum Ubiorum (Cologne) highway, with attention west of it to the route from Durocortorum (Reims) to Augusta Treverorum (Trier), which was enlarged under Claudius and may have been made a colony: with the basic routes of Narbonensis restored to full efficiency, arterial roads to the Rhine, upper and lower, could be strengthened.[15]

In 45-6, when the flood of the British captives who were probably used in construction work was settling down into a steady stream, it seems to have been the turn of the south and west: a road is attested from Lugdunum to Augustonemetum (Clermont-Ferrand) and beyond, with a branch from Forum Segusiavorum (Feurs) towards Divona Cadurcorum (Cahors) and Burdigala (Bordeaux), and perhaps a route northwards from Augustonemetum towards Avaricum (Bourges). A stretch running south from Limonum Pictonum (Poitiers) to Mediolanum Santonum (Saintes) was also dealt with. The furthest-flung roads were constructed in the Brittany and Normandy peninsulas, between Condivicnum (Nantes) and Gesocrivate (Brest), and Augustodunum (Bayeux) and Coriallum (Cherbourg) respectively. The distribution of the milestones makes it possible to think of the systematic construction of connexions between Lugdunum and Atlantic harbours, and on the other side of the Channel early governors of Britain have been

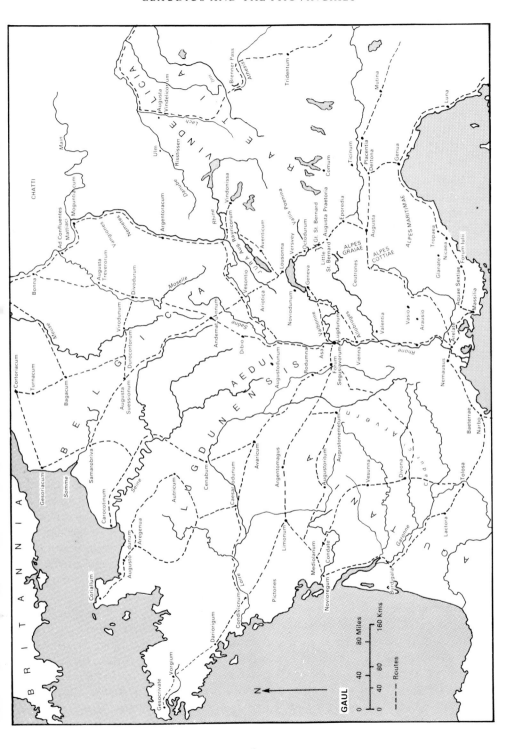

GAUL

credited with the construction of the road network in the south of the island. How far such roads conformed to specifications is unclear for lack of surviving milestones: the first known are Hadrianic (117-38). Commitment at an early stage would be surprising: the Romans could not be sure which would be the permanently important routes, and the advice of men on the spot after the initial stages of the conquest would be required.[16]

Even in Gaul Claudius' achievement should not be exaggerated, as it was in Scramuzza's claim that the provinces were 'literally criss-crossed with roads built or improved by Claudius' or that he 'threw a network of roads over' Gaul. Many stones are missing and it goes beyond existing evidence to credit Claudius with the whole system. Nor does the wording on milestones imply that the whole work was his, as does that of the stones from the Alpine Via Claudia Augusta, the Via Claudia Valeria in Italy, as those erected by Augustan and Tiberian governors in Spain, Dalmatia, Africa, and Galatia claim whole roads or stretches of them. Development may have been piecemeal, with Claudius improving existing routes and bringing them up to Roman standard. The position of several milestones, near the Brittany and Normandy coasts, is suggestive: Claudius was perhaps finishing off work begun, where it had petered out. British prisoners could easily be transported along the coast to work on these projects, and that too may be a relevant factor. Other stones belong to routes radiating from Lugdunum; how far did Claudius' builders get along them?[17]

The Gauls were be more closely connected with Italy culturally as well. Gaius established a competition in Greek and Latin eloquence to be held annually at the altar of Lugdunum to foster their intellectual gifts. But Claudius saw an impediment to progress. Augustus had forbidden Gauls who were Roman citizens to practise Druidism, while Tiberius banned Druids and 'that type of soothsayer and healer' altogether, according to Pliny, who had served on the Rhine and should have known what he was saying. Suetonius attributes the same ban to Claudius, who 'totally abolished the dreadful and savage religion'. Claudius may have been reiterating a neglected ruling issued by Tiberius after the revolt of 21, which certainly had native Celtic elements in it, but his measure may represent a hardening of Roman attitudes. In spite of his claim of long-standing loyalty among the Gauls, Claudius too may have acted after a disturbance, unless an ugly sacrifice came to his notice, or a use of magic against himself. A Gallic orator of Vasio (Vaison), an *eques* too, let a Druidical snake's egg, an object particularly valued for the luck it brought in law suits, slip from his toga during a speech before the Emperor. The timid Claudius had him executed. This is attractive as an immediate occasion for the ban. Tiberius perhaps dissolved the official priesthood, which up to then had been forbidden only to Roman citizens. Claudius in his fear made any such practice illegal. To claim, however, that he went further, demanding that the Gauls adopt Roman versions of their gods, goes beyond the evidence. By banning Druidical practice, Principes identified it with opposition to Roman rule

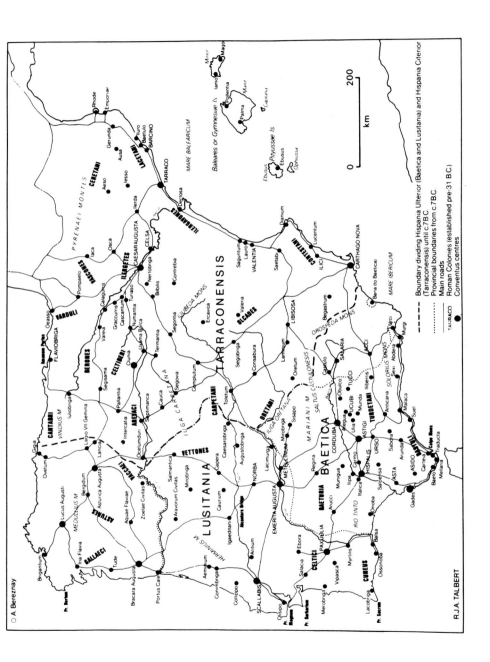

○ A. Bereznay

R.J.A. TALBERT

Boundary dividing Hispania Ulterior (Baetica and Lusitania) and Hispania Citerior
(Tarraconensis) until c.7BC
Provincial boundaries from c.7BC
Main roads
Roman Colonies (established pre-31 BC)
Conventus centres

and provided malcontents with a ready-made religious binding agent. Many upper-class Gauls had already turned their thoughts to more practical and up-to-date matters: the study of Classical Literature and History, which could win them employment in the imperial service.[18]

Although Claudius' attention inevitably focused on Gaul, Spanish routes were not neglected: Claudius comes next after Augustus in the roll of first-century road builders. The Via Augusta that led from the Pyrenees down the east coast to the Baetis (Guadalquivir), to the cities of Andalusia, and ultimately to the Atlantic at Gades (Cadiz) received attention in 43-4. To the main highway in the north a spur was developed in 44-5, the road to Ilerda (Lérida) and then to Osca (Huesca).[19]

Most work was done in the western, less developed parts of the peninsula. Bracara Augusta (Braga) was a focus of attention. Milestones of 43 on the road from Bracara via Aquae Flaviae (Chavez = 'Keys') to Asturica Augusta (Astorga) among the Astures, show the importance attached to maintaining easy access to the mountains of the north-west, conquered only in 19 BC and a prime source of minerals. The road north from Bracara towards Tude (Tuy) and on to Lucus Augusti (Lugo) was also repaired in 43, and the highway south to Olisipo (Lisbon) received attention. The last known work in the Spanish provinces came in 50, when a central artery was put in hand, the route from Emerita (Mérida) to Salmantica (Salamanca), which again led on to Asturica.[20]

In spite of the claim in the *Apocolocyntosis*, that Spaniards were excessively favoured with grants of citizenship, the name of the Emperor is not widespread in Iberia compared with some republican *nomina* and those of the Flavian dynasty and Hadrian. The relatively large number of dedications to Claudius made by individuals may be due to native custom. Ammaia committed itself to the annual discharge of a vow to Claudius, but only two towns bear his name, one, Claudionerium, on the north-west coast, probably south of Cape Neria, the other, Baelo Claudia (Bolonia) on the south-west near Gades, which developed markedly under Claudius and Nero. D.Nony convincingly connects this development with the need to supply Mauretania Tingitana, which took auxiliary troops from the peninsula, by way of the restored Via Augusta; and he connects the advance of Claudionerium almost as persuasively, given the Roman view of Ireland as lying between Britain and Spain, with the invasion. But the concentration of material in the west of the peninsula, like the construction of roads leading to Asturia, mainly implies tighter control of the north-west and intensified exploitation of its minerals; under Nero the the tribes were in revolt again, perhaps as a result.[21]

Given the limited impact that the reign made on Spain, the indifferent quality of governors, and the neglect that made it necessary for local enterprise to produce small denomination coinage, it remains puzzling that the *Apocolocyntosis* included Spaniards among the favoured provincials. Nony's solution, that the author (not to be identified with the Spaniard

Seneca) mistook the people of north Africa, formerly dependent on Baetica, for Spaniards, is unattractive; so is the idea that Seneca was making a joke at his own expense. The word Seneca uses is *Hispani*, native Spanish tribesmen; Seneca of the colony of Corduba was not that, but *Hispaniensis*, descended from Italian settlers. More than a non-Spaniard he might resent attention paid to the west and north. It would be good to know how senators from Narbonensis reacted to Claudius' willingness to allow the chieftains of northern Gaul to enter the senate.[22]

Claudius' greatest achievement as a road builder was the 350 Roman mile (525 km) route over the Brenner Pass to link Tiberius' foundation, Augusta Vindeliciorum (Augsburg) and the Danube basin with northern Italy at Altinum and, further west, on the Po at Hostilia, the road forking at Tridentum (Trent). The two branches were completed in 46. Further west, 47 saw the development of a comparable trunk road with its head at Forum Claudii Augusti (Martigny), part of the route from the Great St. Bernard Pass and Genava to Lousonna (Lausanne–Vidy) and Colonia Iulia Equestris (Noviodunum, Nyon), to Aventicum (Avenches), where in the reign of Claudius wooden houses were being replaced with stone, Ariotica (Pantalier), and Vindonissa (Windisch), the base of XXI Rapax; G.Walser notes the inscription commemorating its new doors. It may have been Claudius who continued the road over the Jura to Adematunnum (Langres) on the attested Claudian line from Lugdunum to Augusta Treverorum. The road tightened control of Raetia, conquered only in 15 BC, and brought the whole vital region of upper Rhine and Danube closer. There are few inscriptions, but Claudius has plausibly been credited with further road-building in Raetia — notably the road along the south bank of the Danube between Tuttlingen and Günzberg — Noricum, and Pannonia. It was the consummation of the Augustan conquest of the Alps which was commemorated on the Tropaeum Alpium (La Turbie) in 7-6 BC.[23]

In Dalmatia milestones of 47 bear indisputable witness to work on the road from Burnum (Šupka Crkva), headquarters of the Eleventh Legion, to the river Sana, with a fork northwards between Han Bravsko and Han Gliso; another attests a road running south along the coast from Salona (Solin, Split). Dalmatia had been a focus of attention at the end of Augustus' principate in what J.Wilkes calls 'a massive programme of strategic roads' aimed at linking Salona and other Adriatic centres with the military on the other side of the Dinaric Alps on the Save, where Siscia and Sirmium (Sisak, Srmska Mitrovica), were to come into prominence in the later Empire as stations on the main route west-east. The programme included a stretch of $77\frac{1}{2}$ Roman miles (116 km) to Mt. Ulcirus (Strmica) among the Ditiones, at the head of the River Una. This is the route from Salona and Burnum that Claudius extended to Bosnian Novi and to the upper Sana near Ključ and beyond. He was also responsible in 47 for the road leading inland from Epidaurum (Cavtat) and Ragusa via Vecchi to Trebinje, which Wilkes suggests was also part of the original scheme. Wilkes observes that the route

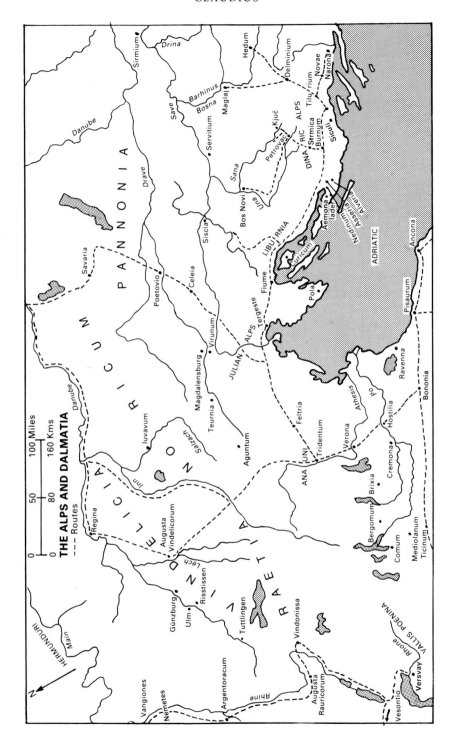

THE ALPS AND DALMATIA
--- Routes

north of the Strmica Pass was not later restored: it did not coincide with a civil and commercial route, as the Gallic roads did. On the coast urbanization continued, with Claudius adding at least three new Roman communities, Asseria (near Benkovac), Curicum (Krk), Fertinium (Omišsalj) and perhaps Nedinum (Nadin) and Alveria (?Dobropoljici), to some thirteen created by his predecessors.[24]

Elsewhere, in Sardinia, Pamphylia, Cyrene, and Egypt, road building under Claudius was moderate. What is surprising is its apparent cessation after 51. Did Claudius run out of energy, money, or labour? If prisoners of war were used in Gaul and on the Alpine project, as they were probably used on Tiberius' Dalmatian roads, they may have died off rapidly, especially in the Alps. Domestic factors may also have been at work, entailing diminished attention to the provinces.[25]

But what stimulated the original effort? For Scramuzza, Claudius was a planner on a large scale, and moved to action by what he saw; for Walser by contrast a man of the past, who read in the archives what his predecessors had in mind and continued it. On this view road-building in Gaul was intended to restore and continue the network that Agrippa had begun, and in the Alps Claudius was executing plans conceived by his father during the conquest of the mid-teens BC. Likewise, the Apennine routes had nothing to do with Claudius' return from Britain in 44, as Scramuzza believed (there is no evidence in Pliny's account that Claudius sailed from Ravenna on to Hadria (Atri), at which of one of the routes terminated). The Via Claudia Valeria from Cerfennia to the mouth of the Aternus connected Rome and the Adriatic, and was a continuation of the Via Tiburtina and Via Valeria; and the Via Claudia Nova led from Foruli (Civitatomassa) to the confluence of Aternus and Tirinus at Populi (Pópoli) on the Via Salaria ('Salt Road') through the territory of the Vestini. Together they linked the systems of northern and southern Italy, and the scheme was a continuation on the Italian side of the work in Dalmatia begun by Augustus and Tiberius.[26]

Claudius should not still be burdened with the dichotomy of his old reputations as innovator or obsessive scholar. Behind the operations multiple factors may be conjectured — and recognized as conjectures. Even the source of the initiatives is unclear. Did Claudius on his accession circulate a directive asking governors to examine roads in their provinces and report desiderata? That, though it would be the action of a man with a new broom, as Claudius was, seems implausible. Or did initiatives, heeded by a conscientius newcomer, come from the governors themselves? That fits the canal-building and mining activities of Corbulo and Curtius in Germany, enterprises that secured imperial approval. In Asia the road from Smyrna to Ephesus, Magnesia, and Tralles was repaired in 51; we should allow the peripatetic governor credit for noticing the condition of that busy route. In Bithynia-Pontus, where the proconsul was usually undistinguished, improvements were carried out by Julius Aquila at his own expense. So the energy and ambition of individuals was relevant; perhaps also rivalry between

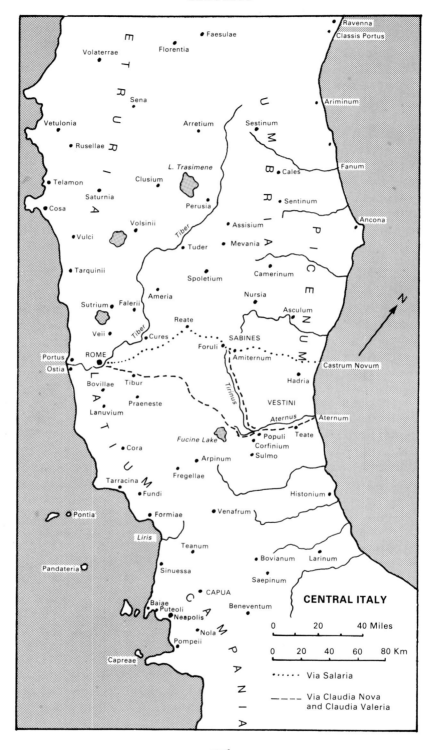

**CENTRAL ITALY**

| 0 | 20 | 40 Miles |

| 0 | 20 | 40 | 60 | 80 Km |

······ Via Salaria

– – – – Via Claudia Nova
and Claudia Valeria

governor and procurator. Procuratorial involvement, as in Pamphylia, is unsurprising, when it was these officials who were charged with transporting supplies and probably cash to the legions. Wherever the initiative originated, means too must present themselves: cheap labour (idle troops on the Rhine, captives from Britain) and materials.[27]

When the initiative came from the Emperor, the imperial archives are less likely as a source of inspiration than personal observation and the Emperor's perceived needs, with priority given to restoration over new construction, at least in Gaul and Spain. The invasion of Britain set off a significant train of events. Orders to refurbish the Massilia–Lugdunum highway may well have had the Emperor's progress in view. There was no direct connexion between the invasion of Britain and construction in Lugdunum and Aquitania, still less with road-building in the Alps, where there were other pressing strategic needs, but once the Channel was fully Roman it was reasonable to make communication with it as speedy as possible. On the return journey Claudius' attention was drawn to the campaigns of his father in the Alps and the importance of the Alpine routes, especially if as I have suggested devotion led him to visit sites associated with Nero Drusus and to travel by routes that he had used. With the road system of Dalmatia and of the Italian peninsula west of the Adriatic other factors were at work. First, the Dalmatian rebellion of 42 showed how important rapid communications with Salona were. And even if Claudius did not travel back to Rome via Hadria it was easy to ascertain that the difficult passage over the Apennines was where time was lost. Second, the campaigns of Didius Gallus in 45-6, hardly the first intimation of the importance of swift communication with Moesia and the capacity to move troops from the heart of the Balkans to the periphery. Tiberius knew it in 14; and Rome's involvement over the Danube, which had begun under Augustus, made it clearer as pressure grew from incoming tribes, while an immediate factor indicating the need for mobility was the repeated unrest in Thrace that led to its annexation in 45-6.

## The east; and the Imperial cult

In eastern provinces Claudius was dealing largely with developed regions and with Greek-speakers who knew that they were Rome's equals at least and were continuing diplomatic negotiations with the Principes as they had conducted them with the Republic and with hellenistic monarchs. Their envoys, equivalents of Gallic chieftains, were the men upon whom Rome depended for the internal stability of the eastern Empire. Material benefits conferred on such societies took a different form from those in the west. There was less need for road-building, because of existing systems, and most cities had basic utilities, except aqueducts. Restoration or the construction of new amenities were most appreciated; where cities did not exist, their creation gave rise to pride and gratitude.

Development was likely to be quickest in Asia Minor (Achaea and Macedonia we have already seen to be backwaters, although there were three or four exceptionally prosperous cities). Names such as Claudiopolis, which was the name Bithynium took (there was another in Galatia, and a Neoclaudiopolis in Paphlagonia), are familiar from Anatolia, though known elsewhere, as at Tyre. Requests for the change must have secured attention, even gifts, from the ruler. At least two native communities that formed part of double cities with Roman colonies, Ninica in Rough Cilicia and Iconium in Phrygia, were honoured under Claudius, securing the titles Claudiopolis and Claudiconium respectively. Central Asia Minor was particularly favoured, or Claudius was petitioned by a succession of rival cities: his name is compounded with those of Laodiciea Combusta, Derbe, Caesareia-Misthea, and Seleuceia, in recognition of advances in urbanization in the Galatian province made since the region had come under direct Roman rule in 25 BC; and Archelais in Cappadocia became a colony.[29]

Concern and aid is the keynote in Greece proper. To Delphi in 52 Claudius wrote of long-standing care for the livelihood of Pythian Apollo and his city and advised them to welcome settlers from other communities as citizens. At Athens he won more dedications than any other emperor between Augustus and Hadrian, including philhellene Nero. A whole series honours him in conventional terms as Saviour and Benefactor. Probably he paid for stairs leading to the Propylaea, not only adorning the Acropolis but providing work for quarrymen and craftsmen.[30]

Claudius could not fall behind in concern for material welfare. Both Augustus and Tiberius had showed solicitude, offering relief from tax payments for three or five years after earthquakes, and additional help. The surviving monuments show Claudius outstripping Tiberius. His first legate in Lycia, Q.Veranius, was looking after 'august works' in accordance with the instructions of the founder (that title is a sign of material benefaction), and those of the august senate, besides creating new citizens. Cibyra was not in Lycia: it was an assize centre of Asia under Gaius and the Flavians. One possibility is that it had been attacked and damaged by Lycians, but there is nothing of this in the ancient sources. The most plausible reason for the temporary annexation to Lycia is that it facilitated Veranius' military activities. Hit by earthquake in 23 and let off tribute for three years, besides receiving gifts from Tiberius, Cibyra may have suffered a fresh shock: later, in 47, there was a particularly severe one, and on Samos Claudius restored the ruinous temple of Dionysus, earning the title of 'New Founder'. Miletus, Smyrna, Ephesus, and Tralles, as well as Antioch in Syria and Crete (in the penultimate year of his reign), also earthquake victims, received help, Miletus becoming 'Caesarea' for a while. George Syncellus also mentions damage to Laodiceia, Hierapolis, and other cities including Antioch, and Claudius was one of the 'Saviour gods' at Sidyma in Lycia. But at Cibyra he may have been continuing restoration already undertaken. In the last two years of his principate, Claudius built an aqueduct at Sardis which may again have been a work of reconstruction after the earthquake of 17, and begun by Tiberius. The aqueduct was not the first he had built: Cerynia on Cyprus received one by mid-44 at latest.[31]

In 53 Apameia in Bithynia, also stricken in an earthquake, was let off five years' taxes on the Augustan or Tiberian model. But Nero's eloquence also secured tax exemption for Ilium, simply perhaps because it was the city of his putative ancestor Aeneas; the grateful city put up a portico in honour of the Emperor and his consort. For Cos there were local brokers, the Stertinii, to secure the privilege, and Claudius was duly added to the local pantheon alongside Tiberius as Zeus the Saviour. Imperial donations were valuable not only in themselves but for the stimulus they gave to local magnates. Claudius' gifts at Cibyra had the local Q. Veranius Philagrus vying with him. Similarly his gifts to Miletus spurred Vergilius Capito to acts of liberality.[32]

Earthquakes were simpler to cope with than grain shortages, which demanded speed and the organization of transport, not just funds for rebuilding. Imperial women were shown in eastern art as promoters of good harvests, but when a serious and 'worldwide' famine struck Greece and Judaea, raising the price of grain in Greece to six didrachms the *modius*, it is of a Queen of Adiabene that we hear, buying it at a high price in Egypt, which itself was recovering from a shortage due to an excessive Nile flood (probably autumn 45-spring 47).[33]

Although Claudius was generous as a benefactor, he did not let the outrage of provincial notables hinder him from asserting the rights of the Roman people. Like all popular politicians from the Gracchi onward, Claudius was preoccupied with the due exploitation of provincial territory for their benefit. Crete and Cyrene were senatorial provinces but contained lands that had been royal property of the last king, Apion. Bequeathed to the Roman people, they had become public land — an emotive phrase under the Republic. In Italy public land had been occupied by wealthy squatters who came to regard it as their own. The Gracchi had reclaimed some for distribution to landless ex-soldiers and their families. Towards the end of his reign it came to Claudius' attention that public land in Cyrenaica had also been taken over. In this province, five Greek cities lived off a native substratum, with a substantial Jewish community. Tensions had already emerged in the edicts that Augustus issued to the province: judicial murder of Greeks by Roman citizens, accusations of treason, and governors taking advantage of their position. The inhabitants were already accustomed to putting their case to the Princeps. Perhaps the occupation of public land by the wealthy was drawn to Claudius' attention by the poor; or he discovered it in connexion with the road-building of 45; or an officious procurator reported it, as Camurius Statutus reported to Claudius on his properties in the northern Italy. Claudius did not ask the annual proconsul to take on a lengthy enquiry, nor a procurator, but sent a special commissioner of the same praetorian rank as the governor but not 'pro consule', L. Acilius Strabo.

ASIA MINOR

0    50    100 Miles
0    80    160 Kms

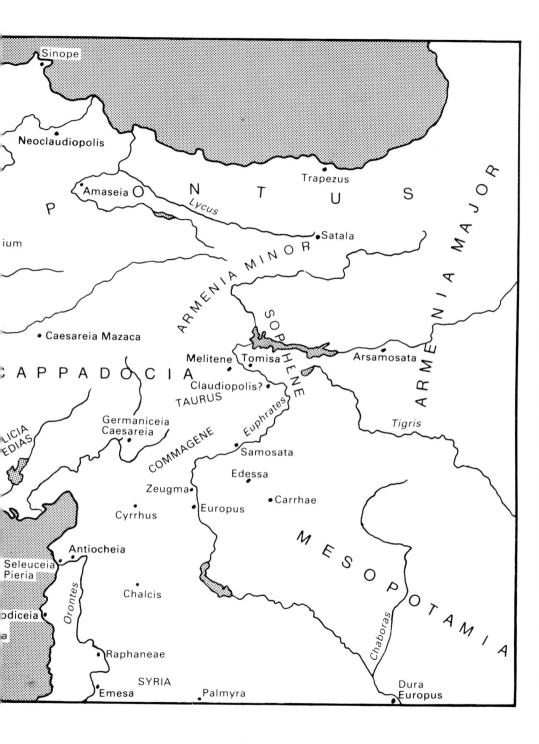

Powerful landowners of Cyrenaica must have hindered him, and it was not until 59 that he was in Rome for them to produce their charge of corruption against him. Nero acquitted him, left in place the boundary stones he had succeeded in planting — and equally allowed the previous 'owners' to stay on. 59 was a difficult year for Nero, who executed Agrippina in April. Claudius could afford to be more stringent in recovering state property. He was equally concerned also for the revenues of provincial corporations, as his confirmation of Augustus' grant of land to the temple of Aesculapius at Cnossus showed, and, in Asia, the regulations drawn up by Paullus Fabius Persicus for the temple of Artemis at Ephesus.[34]

Claudius has been thought of as a philhellene. When Agrippa I and his brother Herod were assigned their realms, they were allowed to deliver their thanks in Greek, even in the senate house, where Claudius himself would often address Greek-speaking delegations in their own language. But this does not mean that Claudius had any idea of treating Greek and Latin on equal terms, as H.Bardon suggested. His use of the language was a concession, and an occasion to show his own skill. And if Claudius was ever seen in Greek dress it was at Naples, once a free Greek city, where he was attending Greek games established in Augustus' honour or the literary festival at which he produced a play by Germanicus. The use of dress and language has to be taken in context, and Claudius did not go beyond existing convention or Augustan practice in that respect. Except for his gracious use of Greek in the House, his conservative uncle Tiberius, who distinguished sharply between private persons and holders of *imperium* on official business, would have been satisfied. In the view of H.-G.Pflaum, Claudius advanced Greeks in the second half of his reign, but the men he names are heterogeneous and cannot be taken to indicate policy; in any case some were favoured before 49 (Balbillus, for example).[35]

Claudius protected Greek institutions, in 43 reaffirming the privileges of the Guild of Hymnodi of Asia — choruses who performed at the celebration of the imperial cult — as he did those of the Athletic associations and actors. But he did not affect an interest in philosophy and its practitioners, beyond employing Ti. Claudius Balbillus, the astrologer and philosopher of Ephesus, on his staff in Britain, in official positions in Egypt, and at court. He cared for Greek culture and was in the company of educated Greeks, his freedmen. Pallas claimed Arcadian descent, but there is no evidence that it led him to take the district under his protection; perhaps it was more remote than the origin of Augustus' freedman Zoilus who did much for his native city Aphrodisias.[36]

The most serious problem that Claudius had to deal with in the provinces concerned the Jews, in Judaea proper as in Alexandria and other Greek cities, where anti-semitism had led to pogroms and in 41 to full-scale Jewish reprisals. What made the problem particularly serious was that there were Jewish communities throughout the east and in Rome itself. Moreover, Claudius had to cope with it before he was secure in his own power, a fact that the protagonists in the struggle probably tried to use.

In Judaea itself, after the annexation of 44, the governors, confronted at once by violent outbreaks, proved inept or corrupt, and were to lay an explosive trail that led to the Jewish revolt of 66. The third procurator, Ventidius Cumanus, failed to keep his troops under control, twice allowing rioting to develop. Finally, fighting between Jews and Samaritans threatened to develop into revolt against Rome. The Samaritans demanded redress from the governor of Syria, Ummidius Quadratus. His on-the-spot enquiry ended in 52 with executions of Jews and his dispatch of Cumanus and other offenders to Rome. There the freedmen supported the Samaritans and Cumanus, who had left the original Samaritan offenders unpunished, while Agrippina and of course Agrippa II, who happened to be at Rome, backed the Jewish cause. The rationale for the alignments is plain: some Greek freedmen shared the anti-semitism of Greeks of Antioch, Alexandria, and elsewhere, while Agrippina's ties with the dynasty of Herod, inherited from Antonia and M.Agrippa, claimed her support. Claudius, accepting the claim that the Samaritans had bribed Cumanus not to punish them for the original attack, found in favour of the Jews and banished Cumanus (52). His successor was Pallas' brother Felix. On the face of it this appointment was a concession to the anti-Jewish side, but in 53 or 54 Felix, who may have been on the staff of Quadratus, married Agrippa's sister.[37]

Claudius now strengthened the Roman presence in the area by founding a colony at Ptolemais Acco, already called Germaniceia after his brother. Colonia Claudia Stabilis Germanica Ptolemais Felix had four legionary standards shown on coin reverses and 'veterans' mentioned in its epigraphic record. In 56 the route from the colony to Antioch was developed as a military road with milestones. Ptolemais was both a base against insurgents and possibly a staging post for ships out of Alexandria, perhaps grain ships, struggling against northerly winds.[38]

An immediate problem for Claudius in 41 were the relations between Jews and Greeks in Alexandria, where Jews, though not citizens — and citizenship of Alexandria, as well as conferring exemption from the poll-tax, alone qualified inhabitants of Egypt for Roman citizenship — enjoyed corporate institutions and status. Their privileges and good relations with Romans, notably with Julius Caesar, infuriated the citizens of a defeated Hellenistic capital, who resented any attempt at their further advancement, whether it was a question of individuals seeking political rights within the *polis* or of the Jewish community trying for recognition as a separate entity. The Alexandrians had other, real grievances: that moneys due to the state were now rigorously exacted; that since 30 they had not been allowed the city council that any Greek city considered an essential part of its machinery of government (Claudius in his letter was to fob off a request that it should be restored by referring the question to his Prefect). Local politicians regarded themselves as betrayed, and unleashed mobs against the scapegoats. Trouble had broken out in 38 with the arrival of Agrippa (I) on his way to his tetrarchies. The Alexandrian Greeks took umbrage at his state and retaliated by setting up statues of Gaius in synagogues. The Prefect, Avillius Flaccus, was already in fear of the Emperor and in return for testimonials from the Greeks ordered Jews residing outside the original Jewish quarter of Alexandria to be removed. The act was accompanied by looting and violence. But Flaccus was relieved of his governorship in the same year and his successor Vitrasius Pollio referred the question to Gaius. Two deputations of five men each went to the Emperor in the winter of 39–40, the Greeks led by Apion, the Jews by the philosopher Philo. Before any decision was reached Gaius was assassinated. Seeing their chance, the Jews of Alexandria brought in co-religionists from outside Alexandria. The fighting had to be suppressed by the Prefect.[39]

On his accession Claudius, according to Josephus, issued an edict (dated simply by his tribunician power) confirming Jewish privileges in Alexandria and censuring the Greeks, and a second edict, that extended the guarantees to Jews throughout the Roman world. In the summer of 41 Claudius heard both sides in the dispute, not the original delegations but a fresh Alexandrian embassy sent with honours and fresh complaints for the new Emperor and a second Jewish delegation, possibly one with views divergent from Philo's. Claudius' letter to the Alexandrians was published in Egypt on 10 November. He wisely declined to pronounce on past rights and wrongs. Both sides were warned about future conduct under threat of what a benevolent ruler forced to anger might do. Jewish customs were to be respected (he held to the same principle in 46 when he wrote to the Jews and to the Procurator of Judaea, Cuspius Fadus, granting custody of the high priest's robes) and the Jews were not to be confined to one quarter of a city where they had lived for generations. But they are warned against infiltrating Greek games or (on A. Kasher's interpretation) breaking them up. If they brought in reinforcements from outside Egypt he would treat them as the source of a general epidemic (that is, of civil disorder: it was in 41 that violence at Rome caused Claudius to close synagogues there). Finally the Jewish community is forbidden to send 'two delegations as if they lived in two cities', referring to the successive embassies, Philo's and the embassy that matched the second Alexandrian embassy under Balbillus (it is less likely that they were being forbidden to send delegations separate from those of the Alexandrian Greeks).[40]

The Alexandrians continued resentful and anti-Jewish, and a martyr-literature dramatizing the exploits and sufferings of community leaders covers events nearly to the end of the second century. Under Claudius it includes a confrontation of two leaders, Isidore son of Dionysius (who had been in Apion's embassy) and Lampon, before Claudius and his advisers. The hearing, on 30 April–1 May, ended in their execution, and can hardly have preceded the hearing of the embassies in 41; a much later date, 53, is preferable. The target of the two men was Agrippa II, a 'twopenny-halfpenny Jew', who was at Rome in 53. Claudius himself came in for abuse before the two men were led off: he was 'the cast-off son of the Jewess Salome'. The ties between the imperial house and the Herods (especially Livia's friendship with Salome and Antonia's with Berenice) made any unfavourable decision automatically suspect to the Alexandrians. With cruel accuracy the gibe struck at Antonia's dissatisfaction with her son; and Herod the Great's sister Salome had both been in Rome in 10 BC and involved in an affair with Syllaeus the Nabataean vizir.[41]

The Prefect, introducing Claudius' letter, referred to him in different terms, as 'our god Caesar'. Similarly extravagant language is used by Claudius' doctor Scribonius Largus and by Seneca but does little more than stress the greatness of the man and his beneficence; it entailed nothing that sundered him from his human fellows. The temples that the Alexandrian delegation offered were a different matter. 'The imperial cult' was a galaxy of phenomena manifested over three continents and three centuries, but it operated by mechanisms that persisted from one reign to another in kindred societies. In Asia and Bithynia in 29 BC homage was offered as a means of securing the goodwill of a ruler whose supremacy was acknowledged as inevitable. Emperors, excepting Gaius, understood that acceptance entailed obligations, financial benefactions, favour against rivals, and the like. Hence a family resemblance in Emperors' responses, though no formula. In the letter Claudius lists honours offered to himself, deprecating but accepting some, such as celebration of his birthday and erection of statues of the Claudian Peace, declining the greatest, a high priest and temples. Tiberius had fudged at least one reply to an unacceptable offer; Claudius, the routine established, spoke out clearly, and by selecting from what was offered arrived at the till with a limited amount to pay and so able to speak his mind on the requests that filled the second half of the letter and on Alexandrian treatment of the Jews.[42]

The sudden elevation of an unknown to the Principate caused flutterings in the provinces. Cities and tribes found the Julii to whom they traditionally owed loyalty cut off, and a Claudius in place, though a brother of Germanicus. Declarations of loyalty, oaths and embassies, were normal at the beginning of a principate, coming naturally when the principate itself passed smoothly by inheritance. In 41 a fresh relationship had to be established after violence. That is one reason why we are so well informed about diverse forms of homage offered to Claudius, and his reactions. A special effort was necessary on both sides. In his own interest he stressed continuity and existing connexions with his house, as in the letter to the Alexandrians; prudence made him repudiate costly excess. Aphrodisias in the province of Asia had special links with Augustus and his family; it is no surprise to find fresh evidence for homage to the imperial dynasty there under Claudius and Nero.[43]

With homage part of a permanent relationship of give and take, it was offered either as an opening move or, as at Miletus, in response to favours. The sequence often has to be guessed at, as on Thasos, which had its cult in place by 42. No cult but an era rapidly established in his honour, counting both by years of the reign and from a connexion established thirty years previously, was devised by the Thessalians. Perhaps it was at games in which the youth had shown his appreciation of Thessalian bull-fighters that the relationship had begun; he brought some to Rome during his Principate. At Xanthos in Lycia Claudius enhanced his own position indirectly, as he had done at Rome, by doing honour to his dynasty. In the precinct devoted there to the imperial cult he erected a 'provincial shrine of the Caesars'. Perhaps Claudius paid for a shrine that the Lycians had offered the monarch of their own volition.[44]

In both east and west the cult was a means of mediating between Rome and her subjects: magnates established relations with the ruling powers which in turn enhanced their own prestige with their dependants. In Gaul and Britain the initiative came from Rome: the cult was an instrument of control and change, chieftains committing themselves to their new rulers. Even in Britain, however, Claudius seems not to have departed from his moderation by allowing a temple to be set up at Camulodunum rather than an altar on the Lugdunum model: the temple is mentioned first only in the *Apocolocyntosis* after his death; until 54 only an altar to Rome and the Emperor occupied the annexe to the former legionary fortress.[45]

No government can give its subjects all they wish. Ancient rulers had weaker means at their disposal than modern, for good and ill, but any power laid responsibility on them. Subjects who had seen famine, earthquake and faction had to look to the future: 'The Caesar owed to his ancestors and manifest god has passed to them; the Emperor of the known world, looked for and hoped for, has been proclaimed, good spirit of the known world who is the origin of all good things, Nero Caesar has been proclaimed. Therefore we ought all to wear garlands and offer sacrifice of cattle in gratitude to the gods.' So, perhaps with two alternative phraseologies included, runs the draft of the proclamation of Nero's accession in Egypt. There was nothing to be hoped for from the god gone to his ancestors; provincials pinned their hopes to the new epiphany.[46]

# 16

# AFTERMATH: THE REPUTATION
# OF CLAUDIUS

The ups and downs of Claudius' reputation since his death reveal more about those who have passed judgment on it than about the régime itself. Modern writers must make allowances for this when they form their own judgments. Claudius was deified in 54 because Nero's own position demanded it, although it dangerously enhanced Britannicus' standing as well. Nero needed to be 'Son of the Deified [Claudius]'. On the other hand, he needed to distance himself from a usurper whose accession and efforts to remain in power had alienated his peers. Hence on coins struck at Rome *Divi filius* did not survive Nero's second year of tribunician power. Even within a few days of Claudius' death Nero's eulogy, with its references to the foresight (*providentia*) of the deceased Emperor, drew permissible sniggers from the assembled senators. There was a little more mirth in them than even Nero and his advisers might have wished: foresight was the quality of a princeps who made satisfactory arrangements for his succession. Commemorative coins were issued, but a temple, provided for in the senate's decree, was left incomplete and was virtually destroyed after Nero's mother's death in 59, ironically giving place to a distribution station for the Aqua Claudia.[1]

Officials had to take deification at face value, and the deified Claudius received sacrifice in Arval rituals under Nero and in 69. He is given his title by the Prefect of Egypt Ti. Julius Alexander in his edict of autumn 68 and as Nero's parent even on monuments raised by private persons in Britain and Italy. Nonetheless the cult of Claudius, unlike those of the founders of the dynasty, Augustus and Livia, did not survive in the provinces — except where a city owed him a special debt of gratitude, as at Asseria in Dalmatia — and in Thessaly the era that probably dated years from a visit to the district did not outlive him. There was nothing to be gained from maintaining it under Nero.[2]

Literary men on the other hand safely ignored the deification. So clear is this that the date of Asconius' commentary on Cicero's speeches (54-7) has been inferred in part from the way he refers to C. Caecina Largus as a man who was 'consul with Claudius': no title, so the Emperor is dead; but he is not Divus. In court circles the deification was a subject of witticisms. Nero spoke of his father's ceasing to 'silly-sally' on earth, while according to Seneca's brother L. Junius Gallio, Claudius had been dragged to heaven on a hook, as criminals' corpses were dragged to the Tiber. Derision of Claudius was open enough to be recorded on paper: the splenetic *Apocolocyntosis* produced for the next Saturnalia by Seneca, who was the main influence on Nero's early government and in the reaction against Claudius.[3]

Seneca had reason to hate Claudius: he had suffered eight years of exile. His hatred showed in the *Apocolocyntosis*. There were also less personal and more creditable reasons for his antagonism: the usurper's style of government and the fatally irreconcilable clash of interest between him and the senate. From genuine conviction Seneca brought Nero to accept a policy of consultation and consensus and of preserving to each organ of state the functions that were traditionally its own, that is, Tiberius' policy of minimum principate adapted to a later stage of the principate's development. On the other hand, the policy was also designed to make Nero a more acceptable heir than the usurper's son Britannicus, and at the same time to render him amenable to advice from sources other than the usurper's widow who, as a woman of power, was no friend to senatorial government. The aims were compatible, and Seneca deserves credit for efforts which in the end alienated him from Nero and caused his enforced suicide. Seneca's dislike of Claudius, with which he was charged in the senate in 58, did not abate: in the *De Beneficiis*, written near the end of his life, he reports Claudius' friend Passienus Crispus, who died some time after 44, sneering at the Emperor for want of judgment.[4]

In his accession speech, drafted by Seneca, Nero painted a fair picture of his future principate, naturally singling out what had recently caused most outrage to the listening senators; a yet fairer prospect is put on view in contemporary literature, both political prose such as Seneca's *De Clementia* and court poetry, the *Eclogues* of Calpurnius Siculus. Even the *Octavia*, the tragedy preserved among Seneca's works, written towards the end of the seventies and bitterly hostile to Nero, presents him on his accession as a prince of peace, the enthusiastic choice of senate and knights, bringing an end to the grim rivalry for the purple.[5]

The list of Claudius' political failings in the speech is formidable: and if it had not been largely justified there would have been little point in drawing it up to recite before men who knew. Nero undertook not to make himself judge of everything and anything, nor to confer unlimited licence on a few favourites by hearing cases shut up in his palace. Nothing was to be for sale there either, or accessible to undue influence. He would separate his household from the state. The senate was to keep the functions it had enjoyed in ancient times; for example, petitioners and litigants from Italy and the senatorial provinces should approach the tribunal of the consuls, who would grant access to the senate. Nero defined his own role as looking to the running of the armies — it was the senate after all who had entrusted him with them.[6]

The first *Eclogue* of Calpurnius Siculus is more vivid and wider-ranging than Nero's speech and Seneca's other writings, but the claim of the poet was the same as that of Seneca in the *Apocolocyntosis*. They announced a new Golden Age. Senators would be released from prison, lawyers would be free to act. What we have in these documents is not a sober judgment on a dead emperor but a bid for support from his successor, or eager hope on the part of his supporters that a Golden Age has arrived. In any case, the talk does not mean that there was any serious chance of a fundamental change being made. The senate's position was still being eroded by the encroachments of the Emperor, and the succession had not been legitimized. A new generation was growing up, the struggle for power went on, and rivals continued to be eliminated, beginning with Britannicus early in 55.[7]

This is the significance of Seneca's *De Clementia* of 55. It promised surviving friends of Claudius that Britannicus' supporters had nothing to fear: the adviser of the all-powerful monarch Nero was committed to working for reconciliation. But it is also intended to remind readers of what had passed away: the excessive severity of a frightened, irascible, bloodthirsty old man.[8]

Where change was particularly hoped for was in the role of the senate, which could be allowed serious discussion on matters of substance remitted to them by Nero's *consilium* (absolutely excluding any discussion of the Principate itself, which was defined in Nero's accession speech). For popularity, Nero was given to understand by his mentors, he must give senate and knights, as well as the people, what they wanted. But disillusion set in over the triviality of the topics that were dealt with (the number of pairs of gladiators to be allowed in Syracuse was the one that first attracted unfavourable comment). The most practical of committed senators — P. Clodius Thrasea Paetus, the target of senatorial criticism — accepted that senatorial freedom of speech was precarious and was content with the concessions that Nero's weak position made possible. For Nero had his mother Agrippina, who as Germanicus' daughter was the favourite of the Praetorian Guard, to thank for his accession to power, and she precisely represented all that was resented in the Claudian regime: the domination of the imperial household and the eclipse of the senate, its functions and its officials. Nero's first measures included the repeal of a minor Claudian enactment, that quaestors should finance gladiatorial shows. Agrippina resisted the trivial but symbolic change as the overthrow of all Claudius' enactments.[9]

For all his promises, Nero did not keep freedmen in their place. In 61 he sent the freedman Polyclitus to Britain to discover what was really going on there between the senatorial legate and equestrian procurator, and when he left for Greece in 66 he left Italy in the hands of the freedman Helius. In 70 it was still plausible to show the new Emperor Vespasian being advised by the philosopher Apollonius of Tyana amongst other things that he should take care to keep the freedmen in check, advice as relevant in the author Philostratus' own day, the early third century, as in Vespasian's. The court remained, and equestrian pride was assuaged by the creation of equestrian posts within the household, offices that supervised the routine work of the freedmen in more than one department.[10]

Matricide, the execution of his divorced wife Octavia and others, and his appearance on stage, showed Nero's régime by no means preferable to his predecessor's. Nero's complicity in what had been accepted as Agrippina's crime, the timely death of Claudius, also came into consideration: had he not described mushrooms as 'food of the gods'? Attitudes towards Claudius began to change. When a replacement for Nero was sought in 65, C. Piso was to legitimize his claim by marrying Claudius' daughter Antonia; Nero himself was said to have considered her as a bride after Poppaea's death.[11]

In the Flavian period Claudius underwent a partial rehabilitation, corresponding to the denigration of Nero. It was not immediate: fierce debates took place in the senate during Vespasian's absence early in 70. Curtius Montanus, urging the House to take action against *delatores*, asked if members thought that Nero was to be the last of the tyrants. Those who had survived Tiberius and Gaius had believed it of them, but another, yet more hateful and more savage, had come to power. But Vespasian regarded Claudius as a reputable predecessor, and he appears in the 'Lex de Imperio Vespasiani' of 70 with Augustus and Tiberius as one whose practice legitimated actions that Vespasian himself was now to be permitted by law. Likewise Claudius had a place by Augustus' side in the epigraphic monuments set up in Vespasian's Capitol at Brixia (Brescia). Vespasian himself had received triumphal honours and reached the consulship (as Claudius' colleague in 51) during the reign, after a shaky start under Gaius. Vespasian did not do so well at first with Nero: his patrons Narcissus and L. Vitellius were dead, he was an unglamorous and dispensable figure, and may have been so closely identified with Claudius that he was acceptable neither to Agrippina nor to Nero's advisers Burrus and Seneca. More importantly, Vespasian sympathized with Claudius' political plight. He too was a usurper, lacking in prestige. Vespasian like Claudius kept on good terms with the people, exploiting the common touch; he even had a rustic Sabine accent to flaunt. Both Vespasian's success under Claudius, then, and his problems as Emperor, tended to produce a revised estimate of Claudius' régime in the period 70-96.[12]

Vespasian's son Titus had been educated alongside Britannicus, fourteen months his junior, notes Suetonius in Titus' biography. The Flavians made every effort to identify Titus with Britannicus, even propagating the story that Titus had been sitting near Britannicus at the fatal banquet in 55 when he was poisoned; he had even taken a sip of the poison himself. In their view Claudius was the legitimate Emperor, and his son the legitimate successor whose place had been usurped by Nero. Now Titus would eventually take the Empire that his dead friend had been cheated of. A further refinement illustrates the rehabilitation of Narcissus in the Flavian period: in Suetonius' biography of Titus, the freedman is made to prophecy that he, unlike Britannicus, would succeed his father. To keep Britannicus' memory alive and foster Titus' claim, statues of Britannicus were erected, one, gilt, in the Palatium, the other an ivory equestrian one which was still being carried in procession at the Circus in Suetonius' day. And when Titus was Emperor, 79-81, coins were struck in Britannicus' honour.[13]

Men who had faltered under Nero were now further advanced: M. Pompeius Silvanus (suff. 45), who had escaped conviction for extortion in 58, received a second consulship (suff. 71); Ti. Plautius Silvanus Aelianus became Prefect of the City and consul for the second time (suff. 74), receiving acknowledgement of old achievements in the Balkans; L. Acilius Strabo, who as an ex-praetor had early in Nero's reign produced an embarrassing report on the occupation of public land in Cyrenaica, came to a suffect consulship in 71.[14]

It was not only on the level of personalities that there was a harking back to Claudian times, showing a new appreciation of Claudius' achievements. The Flavians, besides repairing the Aqua Claudia, resumed and strengthened Claudian legislation, especially on social problems: on lending to minors (the SC Macedonianum), on liaisons between free women and slaves, and on the demolition of buildings. They also adopted Claudian techniques of management. The censorship was an office to enhance their position: so Vespasian and his son Titus were colleagues in it in 73-4 and at a few strokes brought into political life many new men, their supporters, and advanced families already senatorial to patrician rank, including Agricola and the father of Trajan. Domitian took the censorship again in 84 and in the following year had himself freed from the restriction of time that came with the magistracy: he was assassinated in 96 still holding the office.[15]

In token of this Flavian revisionism, Claudius' deification was taken seriously and his temple completed at the expense of Nero's Golden House, with a precinct planted along the same lines as that of Fishbourne Palace. Soon it would overlook the great gift of the Flavians to the people, the Colosseum. The hostility to Claudius in the senate that we have already noted at first caused some hesitancy in official circles: although the precedents of the reign are cited as valid in the 'Lex de imperio Vespasiani', Claudius is not given the title 'Divus'. M. Charlesworth explained this in terms of senatorial reaction against the dynasty now gone and the senate's aspiration to an equal partnership with Vespasian. That cannot be right. The Lex is absolutist, drawn up by Vespasian's partisans. These men must have been uncertain how far he was prepared to rehabilitate Claudius. Augustus, founder of the constitution as well as the dynasty, was firmly enrolled among the gods. Claudius, adoptive father of Nero, was different. The authors of the Lex underestimated Vespasian's appreciation of his dead patron. The designation 'Divus' was not obligatory, however, in private use, even for loyal writers such as the elder Pliny. He refers to an event as taking place 'during Claudius' principate' (Claudio principe); occasionally the late Emperor is 'Divus Claudius', usually 'Claudius Caesar', once merely 'Claudius'. Even an officer decorated by Claudius was able to neglect the title.[16]

The revisionist picture of Claudius could not be uniform and writers might still differ over the court. In the tragedy *Octavia* (*c.*79), Messallina is a misguided, passionate adulteress, a victim whose death begins to forge a chain of disaster. On the other hand, there is no doubt in the play of Agrippina's responsibility for Claudius' murder. This is hardly surprising, given that the work is designed to win sympathy for Messallina's daughter Octavia.[17]

In the Flavian period came most of the first generation of historians of Claudius' reign, although, as Syme has pointed out, Servilius Nonianus (suff. 35), who died in 59, may already have written about the early part of the reign. Each, besides paying attention to the ideology of his own time, had personal reasons for the line he took, or, as Tacitus put it, opening the *Annals*, 'grudges fresh in the mind'.[18]

First, the elder Pliny, an equestrian official and servant of Claudius, who had been impelled to compose his work on Rome's German wars by the apparition of Claudius' father Nero Drusus. He was out of favour with Nero, and was a loyal supporter of the Flavian dynasty. He was the biographer of the poet and soldier Pomponius Secundus, and that, like his own rank, will have coloured his historical narrative. The work of Pliny might seem likely to have been inoffensive, even dull. His enthusiasm for the draining of the Fucine Lake suggests that it is probably he who is attacked by Tacitus for displaying too much interest in material achievements, buildings and the like. But he refrained from publishing his history during his lifetime, clearly not because it failed to treat Vespasian and his family with respect but because it must have shed an unfavourable light on politicians of the Claudian and Neronian age who were still alive.[19]

Cluvius Rufus, a consular like Nonianus, has been denied the title historian at all. But he contributed a considerable quantity of historical material to the store, scandalous as it might be. Cluvius, a prominent but never malicious member of Nero's court (he had even acted as herald during the Emperor's performances) had some interest during the reign of Vespasian in showing that other courtiers had played a more discreditable role. Since Mommsen wrote he has been credited with being the source for Josephus' account of Claudius' accession in the *Antiquities of the Jews*, because Josephus recounts and exchange between a consular 'Cluvius', in on the assassination plot, and another member of the Palatine theatre audience on the morning of 24 January. Cluvius cannot have been a consular then (the title may be given him proleptically), and whether the 'Cluvius' of Josephus' narrative was the historian remains problematical: Syme has suggested Nonianus rather than Cluvius Rufus as the authority for this part of Josephus' narrative. For the rest of Claudius' reign after it had been rehabilitated and contrasted with Nero's he would not have been a hostile witness. Into the mouth of Vindex, the rebel of 68 who began Nero's overthrow, Dio puts a speech favourable to Claudius, in which the old emperor is compared with Augustus. That speech has also been attributed to Cluvius Rufus.[20]

Josephus has two accounts of the accession, illuminatingly divergent. The first and shorter, in the *Jewish War*, belongs to the second half of Vespasian's reign. Vespasian was Josephus' patron and gave him citizenship. Not surprisingly he shows no hostility to Claudius, rather stressing the danger he was in from the senate. Twenty years later, he wrote the *Antiquities* (published 93–4) in the reign of Vespasian's younger son Domitian, when the dynasty seemed well established and Domitian was deviating from the policies of his father and elder brother. In this work Josephus intended to show the part in Gentile affairs played by Jews. He was also under the influence of Agrippa II, and presents Claudius as a lay figure guided by Agrippa's father, Claudius' friend Agrippa I.[21]

Fabius Rusticus was the last well-known historian of the generation that knew Claudius' reign, though he survived until at least about 108. Like Pliny he was a man of equestrian rank. Tacitus' admired Rusticus' work, and used it as a source for his *Annals*, but not without one important reservation: it had at least one bias, the defence of Seneca. Whatever Rusticus wrote about Claudius after his master had made the crushing final claim in the *Apocolocyntosis* that Claudius had 'messed everything up' in a way all his own must have been hostile.[22]

It was upon these three Latin writers, then, as well as upon memoirs, oral tradition and senatorial records, directly consulted and including the Emperor's speeches, that Tacitus and Suetonius could draw in the first two decades of the second century. Suetonius' biography, published in the twenties, stressed the paradox constituted by the elevation to supreme power of such a man as Claudius. Tacitus, writing in the previous decade, but already in comparative freedom, more than sixty years after Claudius' death and twenty after that of the despotic Domitian, last of the Flavian dynasty, used the same sources but for a greater purpose. Indeed, his interpretation was part of his account of the tyranny and failure of the Julio-Claudian dynasty. What Tacitus owed to Pliny, Cluvius or Rusticus is a matter of debate; literary genius made the material entirely his own. Students of the narrative of *Annals* 11–12 have not only amply demonstrated its exquisite art and its independence of any one historical writer, but have defended what Tacitus made its central thesis, that ignorance of his wives' and freedmen's machinations led Claudius to despotism.[23]

For Dio, writing his large-scale *History of Rome* at the end of the second and the beginning of the third century, the reign of Claudius was only an episode. His admiration of such achievements as the harbour at Ostia, and his cool assessment of the failure of the attempt to drain the Fucine lake suggests that Pliny may be the main source of the narrative, with anecdotal details drawn from Cluvius Rufus. Lacking the power to create a unity from the sources, he presents an emperor capable of beneficent and well-thought-out acts, all his own, while the executions are differentiated as the work of freedmen and wives. Transitions between the two are abrupt and awkward. After a list of the Emperor's initial measures, social and foreign, Dio baldly remarks that these were his own, and universally lauded, but the freedmen and Messallina were also active; this leads into a section on their outrages. More elaborately, but very awkwardly indeed, we are told after a section on gladiatorial shows that Claudius' taste for them made him used to carnage, and prepared him for other forms of slaughter; but that was the responsibility of Messallina and the freedmen, who frightened him into it. Another clumsy transition reports on the pleasure felt at Claudius' firm treatment of slaves and its contrast with the regret caused by his own enslavement to his wives and freedmen. Equally awkward is his rendering of relations between Messallina and the freedmen: thus the unwillingness of Appius Silanus to sleep with her is alleged to have alienated them. One wonders how.[24]

It is natural to suspect that after the violent end of the Flavian dynasty in 96 Claudius' reputation had already declined in the world at large for want of champions to resist the strength of the early, Neronian accounts; the great work of Tacitus, and Suetonius' influential biography, must have done him further damage. Pliny the Younger, visiting Prusa in Bithynia in about 110, found a temple to Claudius, bequeathed to the city by Claudius Polyaenus, who must have received citizenship from the Emperor, in ruins. But this may reveal more about city finances than about the attitude of Prusans to Claudius. Trajan's reply to Pliny's enquiry about the site, although referring baldly to 'Claudius', is concerned with the 'religio' accruing to a place consecrated to a predecessor. Circus games were held on Claudius' birthday in 124, and he seems to be included in the Divi honoured by the Arvals in 183 and 218, but, as Charlesworth suggested, he had the ill luck to have the same birth date as Pertinax, the Emperor of 193. Pertinax was a useful founding figure to the Severan dynasty of 193-235, and in the early third century he ousted Claudius from the celebrations of 1 August. Claudius was not one of the emperors commemorated on a series of coins struck by Trajan Decius (249-51) and soon suffered another stroke of bad luck, that of being eclipsed by another Claudius, the great Claudius II Gothicus (268-70). At Delphi, for which he had shown care, his memory seems to have lingered, to judge by the reused statue base that bears his name. Only for the army, it seems, was the cult of Claudius was still required in the third century, for he features on the calendar of official military festivals from Doura Europus. On the calendar of Philocalus (354) Claudius has no place, and it is Gothicus who figures in the list of good emperors given by the *Scriptores Historiae Augustae* at the end of the fourth century.[25]

Writers who did not use the sources studied by Dio show that when knowledge of Claudius' work faded, what remained was mostly scandal. Dio's contemporary Philostratus assails all the Julio-Claudian rulers; even Claudius was no good, because of his subjection to women. The memory of Claudius that percolated into the writing of George Syncellus at the end of the eighth century is that he was a bloodthirsty man who showed some courage in subduing Germans, Britons and Thracians; falling in love with his own niece he became the first to legalize the marriage of uncle and niece. There were exceptions, made for reasons of special pleading. It was sheer opportunism in the early fifth-century writer Orosius, the 'Christian monarchist', to exploit Claudius' extraordinary and genuine clemency on his accession as a work of God, while the sixth-century chronicler Malalas, preoccupied with the fortunes of Antioch, naturally rated Claudius high for his generosity to stricken cities.[26]

The nineteenth century began a transformation. Critical historians would not take their ancient predecessors on trust, and revaluation of the Principate was undertaken by historians who admired the powerful autocracies of Prussia and Napoleonic France. New material came providentially to hand or began to be studied seriously for the first time: epigraphic documents and coins. Claudius more than any other Princeps spoke for himself through these documents, although he did not impress the greatest Roman historian of the nineteenth century, Mommsen, who found in his utterances only confirmation of the unfavourable verdict of the ancients. But in the thirties of the present century the sympathetic novels of Robert Graves, written in the first person, provided Claudius with an *apologia*, and the public works attracted more attention in the years of Mussolini's Italy and Roosevelt's New Deal. The view of the 'centralizing' Claudius that emerged, especially in the deservedly influential work of Momigliano, was favourable — though anachronistic.[27]

After the Second World War greater attention was paid to analysing masses of documentary material that could yield information about ancient society at levels hardly studied before. Interest began to shift towards the common people, away from details of an individual's life to long-term trends. The study of gradually evolving societies has brought a new significance to Claudius' reign, that of serving scholars as a turning point or a distinct epoch. Contributions recorded in *L'Année philologique* are ranged in archaeological, social, or art-historical periods covering 'Augustus to Claudius', 'the epoch of Claudius and Nero', or the Principate 'from Claudius onward', and Claudius is seen as 'the great establisher of norms'.[28]

Turning points in politics, society, art or literature are conveniently and genuinely marked when an emperor does give a lead or react consciously and effectively, as Augustus did to representations of himself in art, or as Nero may have done to the selection of his coin types. Claudius and his contemporaries were aware of change; only that can explain their interest in the past, in innovation and conservatism in Roman history. But not all change, material, cultural, or moral, elicited a reaction, or any known attempt to influence it. Hence a double problem. First, that of establishing a sound chronological framework and of fitting specific items within it. Changes in pottery fabrics, decline or advance in trade, the reconstruction of buildings in new styles or materials, all normally take place piecemeal and over a period of years. How sound are chronological schemes that often have to be based on incomplete evidence, or the criteria for assigning finds to a given period? Do long-held, sometimes untested beliefs play a part in establishing these schemes, as they did when it was assumed that Claudius abolished the senatorial Prefect in charge of grain distribution? Second, there is a problem of interpretation. Even archaeological evidence soundly dated in an unassailable framework may still be misinterpreted to fit preconceptions, as the purposeful role ascribed to Claudius in the development of northern Gaul illustrates.[29]

The personal role of a single emperor is significant to society at large only as far as he reacts to trends or initiates them. Did Queen Victoria shape Victorian England, or was she a product of it? Did parsimony in imperial Roman society really begin with Vespasian, as Tacitus implies? At present we can be sure that the reign of Claudius contributed to change under the principate in two ways: the manner of his accession, and his success in surviving in power and in arranging for the peaceful transmission of it to an heir. The first made his reign a turning point from the constitutional point of view, because of the open role played in it by a section of the army. Claudius was a usurper who depended for support on army and people. Their demand for his installation meant more than the constitutional powers conferred (*en bloc*, too, as they had been on Gaius) by the senate, which became a formal ratification of a unified power that Claudius already possessed. This advance towards monarchy was accelerated by the accession of Vespasian, who actually counted his tribunician years from his salutation by the eastern legions. As a usurper, and because of a long-checked wish to take matters in hand, Claudius yielded to the temptation to intervene more than was acceptable to the senate. And in struggling to stay in power he had to destroy potential rivals and confer favours and power on groups and individuals outside the senate to a degree unknown before. But, as Tacitus wrote, putting the claim in the mouth of a Roman general addressing Gauls a quarter of a century after Claudius' death, 'For all your distance, you have equal advantages from Emperors of good repute; it is their immediate neighbours who are the victims of those who lash out.' It was this second factor, the ruthlessness of Claudius' efforts to stay in power, that allowed the economic and social condition of the Empire as a whole to continue to improve and stabilize itself, particularly in Gaul, where his self-interested activity generated business and industry. But Claudius' personal contribution to the century and a half of comparative prosperity, confidence, and tranquillity that the Empire was approaching will be revised and assessed more soberly than it has been in the past.[30]

As to his conscious aims and achievements, the material considered in this book yields the portrait of an emperor who began his usurping reign with a heroic double effort, in conciliating the nobility, above all in invading Britain, to secure his position. Both proved inadequate against the resentment that his usurpation caused, and in 48 fissures developing among his own supporters weakened his political position still further. At no stage did Claudius dare to give up manipulation as his main political weapon or to assume the full weight of the Principate as he had helped to make it. To his credit must be put his very efforts to remain in power and secure it for the next generation, averting for nearly three decades the civil war that Orosius regarded as the worst of political evils. In dealing with Rome, Italy and the Empire, too, Claudius showed extraordinary initial energy, partly spontaneous, partly as an ostentatious reaction against the neglect or misdirected efforts of Tiberius and Gaius. Activity fell off towards the end of the reign, in part because the original plans were under way or already implemented and because here too the manpower and booty won from Britain was not enough for all that might have been achieved, in part too perhaps because Claudius recognized that he had failed to win on the political front in Rome itself.[31]

# REFERENCES AND NOTES

## 1 THE PRINCIPATE (pages 1–10)

TA 1, 1-12; 4, 1-9; Suet., *Aug.*; DC 52-56; Syme 1939, 227-524; the best recent study is N.Mackie, 'Rome's first Emperors: the birth of an Institution', *Internat. Journ. of Moral and Social Stud.* 2 (1987) 41-61. P. Cuff, 'Two cohorts from Camerinum', in B. Levick, ed., *The Ancient Historian and his Materials* (Farnborough, 1975) 75-91; P. Brunt, 'The Army and the land in the Roman Revolution', *JRS* 52 (1962), 69-86; *Italian Manpower* (Oxford, 1971); *Social Conflicts in the Roman Republic* (London, 1971); Yavetz 1969; Weaver 1967; P. Garnsey, *Social Status and Legal Privilege in the Roman Empire* (Oxford, 1970); K. Hopkins, 'Élite Mobility in the Roman Empire' in M.I. Finley, ed., *Studies in Ancient Society* (London, 1974) 103-120; G. Alföldy, *The Social History of Rome*, tr. D. Braund and F. Pollock (London and Sydney, 1985).

1. Republican plebs: F. Millar, *JRS* 74 (1984) 1-20; 76 (1986) 1-11; A. Lintott, *ZSS* 104 (1987) 34-52.
2. See Cuff 1975.
3. TA 3, 48.
4. TA 16, 17, 3.
5. TA 3, 30; 12, 60. Status dissonance: Hopkins 1974.
6. Suet., *Tib.* 29; *Cal.* 29, 1.
7. Suet., *Tib.* 25, 1.
8. Ael. Arist., *On Rome* 63; 66.

## 2 EDUCATION OF A PRINCE (pages 11–20)

SA 1-9; 30f.; 40-2, with Mottershead 1986; DC 55f. C.J. Simpson, 'The early name of the Emperor Claudius', *Acta Ant. Acad. Scient. Hung.* 29 (1981) 363-8. T. Frank, 'Claudius and the Pavian Inscription', *CQ* 2 (1908) 89-92; M. Stuart, 'The date of the Inscription of Claudius on the Arch of Ticinum', *AJA* 40 (1936) 314-22; Balsdon 1934, index *s.v.* Claudius; Scramuzza 1940, 35-50; A. Garzetti, *From Tiberius to the Antonines* (tr. J. Foster, London, 1974) 596-9. E. Leon, 'The "Imbecillitas" of the Emperor Claudius', *TAPA* 79 (1948) 79-86. Learning: Momigliano 1934, 1-19 (bibliography in repr. 1961, 128f.); Bardon 1940, 125-61; Heurgon 1953; Last and Ogilvie 1958.

1. Nomenclature: Stuart 1936, 318 n.7; *PIR*² C942; Simpson 1981 argues implausibly that 'Nero' was taken in place of 'Drusus' only in 4, to prevent the *cognomen* disappearing. But Claudius could not avoid being a Nero; the Claudii Nerones were the family to which he belonged. He took 'Drusus' perhaps only in 9 BC, when Nero Drusus' son dropped it for 'Germanicus', and relinquished it in 4, when Tiberius' son became Drusus Iulius Caesar and he himself, as head of the

Claudii, assumed 'Germanicus': see B. Levick, *Acta Ant. Acad. Scient.*, forthcoming.

2. Gaul: *Docs.* 369, col. 2, l.29; cf. *SC* 2. 1; *SA* 6, 1. Nero Drusus and Antonia's children ('*complures*'): *SC* 1, 6; Germanicus: 2, 1, not saying that it was only the head of the family that bore the name, with Groag, *RE* 3 (1899) 2781f. and Mottershead *ad loc.*; Simpson 1981, following Suetonius; DC 60, 2, 1; 5, 3.

3. Widowhood: Val. Max. 4, 3, 3; *JA* 18, 180. Health: see *PIR*² A 885. Berenice: *JA* 18, 143; 156; 165.

4. B. Levick, *Lat.* 31 (1972) 779-813.

5. B. Levick, *Lat.* 35 (1976) 301-39; R. Syme, *History in Ovid* (Oxford, 1978) 199-229.

6. *SC* 2, 2; cf. DC 55, 27, 3.

7. Diagnoses: Scramuzza 1940, 238; Garzetti 1974, 587; and 'infantile paralysis in some form' is postulated by M.P. Charlesworth in *CAH* X, 667; so H. Scullard, *From the Gracchi to Nero*, ed. 5 (London and N.Y., 1982) 288. Cerebral palsy: Leon 1948, 46; Griffin 1984, 30; Mottershead 1986, *ad* Suet. 30f. and p.145-7; Leon, 82 n.10, cites T.C.de Courcy Ruth, *The Problem of Claudius* (Diss. Baltimore, 1916), 131. I am greatly indebted to Dr J. Mellanby and to Professor G. Glaser, who examined the evidence, concluding that cerebral palsy was the most likely diagnosis, answered my questions, and revised my text.

8. *SA* 3, 1; Antonia: *SC* 3, 2, with Leon 1948, 81, and S. Dixon, *The Roman Mother* (London and Sydney 1988) 79. A prayer for easy delivery on an earlier occasion: *AP* 6, 244. Leon, 81, draws attention to Claudius' large head as a possible factor.

9. Limp: a phrase used by Virgil, *Aen.* 2, 723f., of a toddler is maliciously echoed by *SA* 1, 2; cf. *SC* 30: his knees let him down; *SA* 5, 3 '*insolitum incessum*'; 5, 2: '*pedem dextrum trahere*', with shaking head (cf. Juv. 6, 622); limbs shaking also: DC 60, 2, 1; limp hand: *SA* 6, 2: '*illo gestu solutae manus*'. Tiberius: Suet., *Tib.* 68, 1.

10. Voice: *SA* 4, 3; 5, 2f.; 6, 2; 7, 2, l.4; 7, 4; 11, 3; 14, 2; *SC* 16, cf. DC 60, 17, 9, with B.Levick, *Hist.* 38 (1989), 112-6. Repulsive delivery: *SC* 30; cf. Juv. 6, 622. Health improvement: *SC* 31; cf. 33, 1.

11. '*Stultus*' or '*μωρός*': Antonia, *SC* 3, 2; litigants, 15, 4; 'assumed by Claudius for self-defence', Claudius, taken up by a pamphleteer, 38, 3. Tacitus' use of his work: Syme 1958, 703-10; cf. Townend 1962, suggesting Aufidius Bassus as an intermediate source; De Vivo 1980, 68 n.1; 96.

12. Apathy: '*socordia*' implied by Antonia, *SC* 3, 2; '*segnitia*', 5, 1; *TA* 11, 38, 3. Judge: '*inconsultus et praeceps*', *SC* 15, 1; see below, Ch. 11. Ostia, '*ira*' and '*iracundia*': 38, 1f.; cf. [Sen.], *Oct.* 265; *TA* 11, 26, 4. Palsy the cause: Mottershead 1986, 146. Prodigy: *Docs.* 369, col. 2, ll. 14f.

13. *SC* 4, 1-5: '*motus habitus incessus*'; for the importance of appearance, see Mehl 1974, 69, citing *TA* 11, 12, 2 (C. Silius); A. Woodman *ad VP* 2, 69, 4.

14. DC 55, 22, 4. But he must not be rivalled or outdone by yet another member of Tiberius' house.

15. Arch: EJ² 61; Priesthoods: *CIL* III, 381; ILS 198; augurate: *SC* 4, 7, with Mottershead 1986, pointing out that it did not feature on the inscription. Betrothals and marriage: *SC* 26, 1f.

16. Letter and Augustus' 'model': *SC* 4, 5; barbarian: 2, 2; kindness: 40, 2.

17. Will: *SC* 4, 7. Family membership, strangely questioned by Frank 1908: Stuart 1936, citing *TA* 3, 29, 5f.; 4, 7, 3 (the betrothal of Claudius' son to Sejanus' daughter

was a mésalliance). '*Unius familiae quasi hereditas*': T*H* 1, 16.

18. Speech: above, n.11; Interest in oratory: Levick 1978, 101f. against Momigliano 1934, 6f. Defence of Cicero: S*C* 41, 3, cf. Quint. *Inst.* 12, 1, 22; P*Ep* 7, 4, 3; A. Gell., *NA* 17, 1, 1. Pollio had also attacked Claudius' master Livy: Quint. *Inst.* 1, 5, 56; 8, 1, 3; A.B. Bosworth, *Hist.* 21 (1972) 446. Keeping to the text: T*A* 13, 3, 6, with Bardon 1940, 146. Augustus' judgment: S*C* 4, 5f. Quaestor: D*C* 60, 2, 2. Livy: 4, 3-5. Last and Ogilvie 1958; E. Keitel, C*W* 71 (1977-8) 382f. (Livy 3, 56, 3, used by Claudius at T*A* 12, 52, 3. Lugdunum speech: *Docs.* 369 (esp. col. 1, 37-40; col. 2, 14-18). A critical appreciation and comparison with Tacitus: Fabia 1929, 73 n.1 (Livy), 118 (Cicero), 133-43; Miller 1956. See further Scramuzza 1940, 67; 103f.; 130f. (more favourable); Bardon 138-161; Benner 1975, 100-15.

19. Histories: S*C* 42, 2; perhaps J*A* 19, 213. Sallust: *Cat.* 3f. Etruria and Claudius' marriage connexions: Heurgon 1953, and *Arch. Class* 21 (1969) 88-91 (Etruscans under a Hamilcar). Origins: A. Holleman, *Hist.* 33 (1984) 504-8.

20. Roman History: S*C* 41, 1; Servilius: P*Ep* 1, 13, 3. Tarquitius and Caecina: Rawson 1984, 28 and 304; Veranius: 93 and 303; cf. Syme 1957.

21. S*C* 41, 3; T*A* 11, 13, 3, with R. Oliver, A*JA* 53 (1958) 113-39. For -ai-, see *ILS* III, p. 808.

22. Travels: S*C* 25, 5 (interest in the Eleusinian mysteries); Thessaly in 10-11?: A.v. Premerstein, *JÖAI* 15 (1912) 205. Naples: S*C* 11, 2; Greek: 42; J*A* 19, 213; for S*C* 15, 4 as a reply to a quotation, see B. Levick, *Hist.* 38 (1989, 112-4). Poetry: S*A* 12, 3, l.29. Precepts: Sen., *Cons. ad Pol.* 14, 1.

23. Tiberius: T*A* 6, 46, 9; Suet., *Tib.* 68, 4; Claudius: S*C* 16, 4; journey to Britain: Scrib. Larg., *Comp.* 163; vultures: John Lyd., *Mens.* 4, 104 p. 143 Wuensch (if this is Claudius I); note the letter of the physician Thessalus possibly to Claudius or Nero, prefacing treatises on astrological botany, A.-J.Festugière, *Rev. Bibl.* 48 (1939) 45-77; cf. H. Diller, *RE* 6A (1936) 180f. (apocryphal).

# 3 THE FRUSTRATION OF A POLITICIAN (pages 21–28)

S*C* 5-9; T*A* 3, 1-6; 49-51; D*C* 57-59; Balsdon 1934, index *s.v.* Claudius; Levick, 1976, 148-79; Levick 1978; C.J. Simpson, 'The "Conspiracy" of A.D. 39', *Stud. Lat. Lit. and Rom. Hist.* 2, *Coll. Lat.* 168 (ed. C. Deroux, Brussels, 1980) 347-66; Jung 1972.

1. Sodales: T*A* 1, 54, 2; *CIL* 3, 381; and will: S*C* 6, 2.

2. Tarracina and Rome: T*A* 3, 2, 4; 3, 2. Claudius omitted: 3, 18, 4; J. González, *ZPE* 1984, 58f., Fr. 1 lines 6f.; 19-21 (after sister); he is before her in EJ² 93 (14-19, from Ilium).

3. Priscus case: T*A* 3, 49-51; Urgulanilla: S*C* 4, 3; 26, 2, with Syme 1958, I 386; Etruscan connexions: Ch. II n.19. Betrothal to Sejanus' daughter: T*A* 3, 29, 5f. (in 20, but the corrupt text of S*C* 27, 1, emended by Bentley, has the betrothed a young man '*prope iam puberem*', and claims that he died a few days after the betrothal: a preliminary agreement to be followed by a solemn ceremony has to be postulated, especially as Sejanus' only known daughter died a child in 31: T*A* 5, 9, 2f.; 4, 7, 3 (agreement subsisting in 23); cf. 39, 4; D*C* 58, 11, 5; 60, 32, 1.

4. Fiancées: Ch. II. Fire: D*C* 57, 14, 10.

5. S*C* 6, 2, with Mottershead 1986 *ad loc*.: the senate decreed that he be appointed Sodalis Augustalis (14) '*et mox ut domus...restitueretur*', etc. Fires of 22: T*A* 3, 72, 4, with credit to Sejanus, but only the theatre of Pompey was destroyed; 4, 64, 1;

36: 6, 45, 1.

6. SC 3, 2.

7. Divorce: SC 26, 2; ; Syme 1986, 430, has it 'not long' after the marriage. Murder: TA 4, 22; cf. R. Graves, *I, Claudius* (London, 1934, repr. 1953) 307-13.

8. Claudius as envoy: DC 59, 6, 6. Downfall of Sejanus: Levick 1976, 171-9.

9. Dissipation: SC 5, 1; 33, 2 (monograph on gambling); 40, 1 (taverns); TA 12, 49, 1; SC 4, 5 (early boon companions); sadism: SC 34; DC 60, 13, 1-4. Last night: DC 60/61, 34, 2f.

10. Gaius' piety: Suet., *Cal.* 15, 1; DC 59, 3, 3-5 and 8; *Docs* 84a; 85a; cf. *ILS* 8789f.; *CREBM* I, 145, no. 44, 70f.; *CIL* V, 4953. Claudius: Suet, *Cal.* 15, 2; DC 59, 6, 5; *Fasti Ost., Inscr. Ital.* 13, 1, p.191; second term: SC 7, 1.

11. Claudius and the knights: SC 6, 1; *Cal.* 15, 2; DC 59, 6, 5. *Eques* of Alexandria Troas: *CIL* 3, 381, with B. Dobson, *Die Primipilares, BJ* Beiheft 37 (1978) 178.

12. Greetings: SC 7.

13. Threat: SC 9, 1. 'Conspiracy': Suet., *Cal.* 24, 1; DC 59, 22, 5-9; SC 9, 1.

14. Scepticism on conspiracy of 39: Simpson 1980. Marriages: Suet., *Cal.* 25. Death of Drusilla: DC 59, 11, 1.

15. Embassy: SC 9, 1; DC 59, 22, 9; 23, 2; Jung 1972, 372. Gauls dipped: Suet., *Cal.* 20.

16. SC 9, 2, with Mottershead 1986 on Claudius' lack of seniority. Tiberius and the order of speaking: TA 1, 74, 6 (15); 3, 22, 6 (Drusus in 20).

17. Jung 1972, 369, 372, on Claudius as a potential adviser to Gaius, and 375-8, seems to overestimate the importance of learning and decency.

18. Cronies: SC 4, 5: Sulpicius Flavus and an Athenodorus; TA 11, 49, 1. Properties: SC 38, 2. Losses and forged will: SC 9, 2 (8m. HS), cf. *Cal.* 22, 2-4 ; DC 59, 28, 5 (10m. HS). Clerk: SC 38, 2.

19. Pollux: JA 19, 13. Disrespect from Gaius and others: Suet., *Cal.* 23, 3; *Nero* 6, 2; DC 59, 23, 5; 60, 3, 9; SA 15, 2. Beatings: SA 15, 2, with circumstantial details. Claudius had his little revenge on the many who had insulted him: DC 60, 3, 7. Danger: JA 19, 221. Meise 1969, 101, rightly insists that Gaius did not envisage Claudius as his heir; as yet, however, he lacked another acceptable heir. Jung 1972, 373f., does not take sufficient account of the importance of blood.

20. SC 38, 3; alluded to in SA 1, 1; DC 59, 23, 5; 60, 2, 4. Brutus: Livy 1, 56, 7.

## 4 ACCESSION (pages 29–40)

Suet., *Cal.* 56-60; SC 10f., with Mottershead 1986; JB 2, 204-14; JA 19, 1-273; DC 59, 29f.; 60, 1; Aur. Vict., *Caes.* 3, 14-20; Oros. 7, 6. Scramuzza 1940, 51-63; D.Timpe, 'Römische Geschichte bei Flavius Josephus', *Hist.* 9 (1960) 474-502; Timpe 1962, 77-93; H. Ritter, 'Cluvius Rufus bei Josephus?' *RM* 115 (1972) 85-91. Swan 1970; Jung 1972, Garzetti 1974, 100-109; Wiseman 1982; T.P. Wiseman, 'Killing Caligula', *Pegasus* 31 (1988) 2-9.

1. Suet., *Cal.* 40; DC 59, 28, 11; JA 19, 25-7; indictment: Wiseman 1988.

2. JA 19, 98; Asprenas appears in MSS as Ἀσπρίνας (in margin), Ἀμβρωνᾶς, Ἀμπρώνας, Aspronas; see Jung 1972, 379 n. 45. Aponius, wounded by the Praetorians at a later stage (JA 19, 264), is identified in *PIR²* A 936 with Aponius Saturninus, Suet., *Cal.* 38, 4.

3. Capitol meeting: Suet., *Cal.* 60; DC 60, 1, 1. Extermination: Aur. Vict., *Caes* 3.16; Oros. 7, 1, 3; cf. JB 2, 205. Importance of the rule of law: Wiseman

1988, 3-9. Saturninus' speech: Timpe 1960, 482-6. Numbers of troops with senate: JB 2, 203 (3 cohorts); JA 19, 188 (4), with Timpe 1960, 502, and H. Freis, *Die Cohortes Urbanae, Beihefte der BJ* 21, *Epigraphische Studien* 2 (Cologne, etc., 1967), 39-42. Volusius: Eck, *Herm.* 100 (1972) 461-81. People: TA 1, 15, 1; DC 59, 20, 4f.

4. Tribunes: SC 10, 3; JA 19, 229-36; DC 60, 1, 4; JB 2, 204-13, replaces them with Agrippa as a go-between.

5. Second meeting: JA 19, 248.

6. On the text of JA 19, 251, see Swan 1970; the political conclusions do not necessarily follow from Swan's convincing treatment of the text. Vinicianus: DC 60, 15, 1.

7. Galba: Suet. *Galba* 7, 1; timing: see Ehrhardt 1978, 54, n.19. Danger from Pannonia: VP 2, 111, 1. Plautius and Scribonianus: DC 60, 15, 2, with Wiseman 1982, 62f.; Scribonianus: *id. ib.*, on the basis of DC 60, 15, 2. Memmius: *PIR*² M 468.

8. Donative: SC 10, 4 (with opposition to senate from their troops: '*multitudine quae circumstabant unum rectorem iam nominatim exposcente*'); JA 19, 247 (offer before second meeting; including the rest of the army); opposition to senate: 249; 254-9); DC 60, 15, 1.

9. DC 60, 1, 3 (a member of the imperial family, and decent). Scramuzza 1940, 54-63, and Jung 1972, 381f., overstress Claudius' personal merits as an influence on the Praetorians, while Ehrhardt 1978, 52, underestimates Claudius' dynastic claims. Heirs: GI 2, 152-63.

10. Claudius' message: JB 2, 207f.; JA 19, 246f.

11. Agrippa's role: Jung 1972, 381 n.50. Official account: DC 60, 1, 3a; Jung 1972, 381f., cites JA 19, 217ff. and 162-5; SC 10 3; cf. 4 ('*iurare passus est*'); JB 2, 207; 209.

12. Three conspiracies: JA 19, 17 (for Regulus, see Ritter 1972, 89 n 34); Vinicianus: 20; Asprenas: 98; spattered: 87; killed: 123. Norbanus: 123f. Anteius: 20; 125. Suet., *Cal.* 58, 3, has them all innocent.

13. Prefects: Suet., *Cal.* 56, 1, plural and without names; DC 59, 29, 1 ('έπαρχος); JA 19, 37 (Clemens, Papinius); 46; 48f. (bringing in Vinicianus); 110 (Aquila).

14. Callistus: JA 19, 64-69; DC 59, 29, 1; cf. TA 11, 29, 1. Alcyon: JA 19 157; PNH 29, 22.

15. Claudius' fear: JA 19, 218, with Jung 1972, 379f. Theatre: JA 19, 102-4; DC 60, 1, 3, says that Claudius was with Gaius when he left the theatre. Josephus has Gaius follow with Paullus (Faustus?) Arruntius (cf. *PIR*² A 1128, 1135).

16. Whole family to go: JA 19, 258; DC 60, 3, 4. Soldiers' intentions: JA 19, 162-5 (vehement that they had decided); 221-6 (not all were in the know; so SC 10, 2), with Jung 1972, 377f.

17. Declaration of war: JB 2, 205, a passage drawn to my attention many years ago by Mr. C.E.Stevens; for *hostis/bellum* (war) see *Dig.* 49, 15, 24. Claudius' capture of Rome: SA 6, 1. It was Mrs A.M. Dabrowski who in conversation first suggested Claudius' complicity; Jung 1972 argues strongly for it.

18. Executions: JA 19, 268-73; SC 11, 1; DC 60, 3, 4f. Casperius: Syme 1958, 35.

19. Callistus: JA 19, 64-9. Agrippa: JA 19, 265 with Scramuzza 1940, 12f. and 57-9, and Jung 1972, 381 n.50. Sabinus: DC 60, 28, 2.

20. 'Antius': *PIR*² A 727, with R. Syme, *JRS* 39 (1949) 9. P. Anteius Rufus: 731, with *CIL* 3, 1977, TA 13, 22, 2, and 16, 14, 2-6.

21. Praetors: DC 60, 12, 4; 17, 9 (it is just possible that Veranius belongs to 43); Gordon 1952, 244f. For Veranius' career in general, see also Rogers 1931, 175f.; Birley, 1981, 50-4. The elder Veranius: *TA* 2, 56, 4; 2, 72, 2 (etc.), with *AÉ* 1981, 824, for Nero Drusus.

22. Gaius and the Prefects: Suet., *Cal.* 56, 1; DC 59. 25. 7f. Attitudes of the Prefects: Jung 1972, 384f. Clemens: JA 19, 37; not trusted: 47; implicated by Lupus: 190f. Younger Clemens' success: T*H* 4, 68; Suet., *Dom.* 11. Marriages of Clemens' daughters: Suet. *Tit.* 4, 2, with G.B.Townend, *JRS* 51 (1961) 56-8 (suggesting a longstanding connexion between the families) and 62, and B.W. Jones, *The Emperor Titus* (London, etc., 1984) 18. Age of Clemens: JA 19, 45.

23. Plot generally known: JA 19, 19. Seneca as the source of the picture of Claudius at his accession, Timpe 1960, 480f.; Jung 1972, 381, discusses the working up of Josephus' essentially friendly source by a hostile or dramatizing writer, identified by Timpe, 500f., with Fabius Rusticus or Cluvius Rufus; Ritter 1972 shows Rusticus at work.

24. *Docs.* 370, ll. 35-7; Messallina: S*A* 11, 1.

25. *RIC* I², 122-4, no. 15f. (41-2); no. 48-50f. (49-59); no. 53f., 59f. (50-1); no. 63f. (51-2).

26. Boycott of senate: Caesar: DC 60, 3, 2; Suet. *Iul.* 14, 2; 16, 1. Coins: *RIC* I², 122f., nos. 7f. (41-2); 19f. (43-4); 25f. (44-5); 36f. (46-7) (IMPER RECEPT); nos. 11f. (41-2); 23f. (43-4); 29 (44-5) (PRAETOR RECEPT). The small figure with the *aquila* is now recognized, not as a soldier but as Fides herself, and the legends interpreted 'in fidem praetorianorum' and 'in fidem imperatoris' respectively: C.H.V. Sutherland, *Roman History and Coinage 44 BC–AD 69* (Oxford, 1987) 76f., following C.L. Clay, *NZ* 96 (1982) 43. Use as donative: B. Campbell, *The Emperor and the Roman Army* (Oxford, 1984) 167. Note Claudius' eye on the Praetorians when he grants citizenship to the Alpine tribes in 46: Millar 1977, 64; Frézouls 1981, 249.

## 5 FROM PRINCEPS TO EMPEROR (pages 41–52)

P. Brunt, 'Lex de Imperio Vespasiani', *JRS* 67 (1977) 95-116; R.Syme, 'Imperator Caesar: a Study in nomenclature', *Hist.* 7 (1958) 172-88 = *RP* I, 361-77; N. Mackie, 'Rome's first Emperors: the Birth of an Institution', *Jrnl. Mor. Soc. Stud.* 2 (1987) 41-61; B. Levick, 'Julians and Claudians', *G and R* Ser. 2, Vol. 22, (1975), 29-38. A.H.M. Jones, 'Procurators and Prefects in the early Principate', *Studies in Roman Government and Law* (Oxford, 1960), 115-25; D. Stockton, 'Tacitus *Annals* XII.60, a note', *Hist.* 10 (1961) 116-20; R. Seager, 'Tacitus Annals 12.60, a note', *Hist.* 11 (1962) 377-9;; F. Millar, 'Some evidence on the meaning of Tacitus *Annals* XII. 60', *Hist.* 13 (1964) 180-7; 'The Development of jurisdiction by imperial procurators: further evidence', *Hist.* 14 (1965) 362-7; Brunt 1966; M.Ghiretti, 'Lo "status" della Giudea dall'età Augustea all'età Claudia', *Lat.* 44 (1985) 751-66; P. Weaver, *Familia Caesaris* (Cambridge, 1972) 199-294.

1. Lugdunum: *AÉ* 1976, 424. Tiberius: DC 57, 8, 2; EJ² p. 52; Gaius: JA 18, 234. Lex: Brunt 1977. I hope to return to this topic elsewhere, and take the view here that the Lex conferred by law powers that previous Principes had exercised *de facto*.

2. Baiae: *Docs.* 368 l.2, cited by Millar 1977, 27 n. 32. *Pater patriae* (6-12 January, 42): DC 60, 3, 2; SC 14; *Docs.* 13; *ILS* 201; *CIL* 6, 2032; *CREBM* 190 nos. 181-4, with PP COS II; note 185 with EX SC PPOB CIVES SERVATOS. Claudius' *dies*

*imperii*: SC 11, 3; Vespasian's: Suet., *Vesp.* 6, 3. Scholars hesitate: B. Parsi, *Désignation et investiture de l'empereur romain* (Paris, 1963) 118, citing M. Hammond, *MAAR* 15 (1938) 25f., but the tribunician day is of academic interest only; Timpe 1962, 90, is firm for 24th.

3. *Imperator*: SC 12, 1; Suet., *Tib.* 26, 2; cf. DC 57, 2, 1. Augustus: Syme 1958. See L. Lesuisse, *AC* 30 (1961) 421f.

4. 'Caesar': Levick 1978; claim dismissed: SA 5, 4; 6, 1. It does not do Claudius' claim justice to hold that it was based on the adoption of his grandmother Livia by the will of Augustus (so Wiseman 1982, 58, n.7): the name came closer when acquired by his brother Germanicus in 4.

5. Activities in Britain: Ch. XIII. Grant: DC 60, 23, 6.

6. DC 60, 23, 4.

7. 'Uncles': *Docs.* 368, 1.11; 369, col 2, l.1 (strictly Augustus was Claudius 'avunculus magnus'); 369, col.2, l.1. Wiseman 1982, citing (58) SA 10, 4, has valuable discussion of Calp. Sic., *Ecl.* 1 ('maternis Iulis' at 45); perhaps he accepts too many of its claims. Ehrhardt 1978, 54 n.21, rightly stressing the importance of Augustan descent, identifies it with belonging to 'the Julian house'; see Levick 1975.

8. Claudius: 1/8; Nero: 5/32. (I am indebted to Dr Mellanby for advice.)

9. Augustus as Gaius' grandfather: Suet., *Cal.* 23, 1; P. Ceaușescu, *Hist.* 26 (1973) 270-73; as Claudius', *Anth. Pal.* 6, 235 (Thallus), with A. Cameron, *GRBS* 21 (1980) 49f. The rumour about Nero Drusus' birth was not taken seriously: see W. Suerbaum, *Chiron* 10 (1980) 345, and M. Flory, *Herm.* 114 (1986) 365-71.

10. Will: Suet., *Cal.* 24, 1; intestate succession: *Tit. ex Corp. Ulp* 26, 1; Papia Poppaea: 14, 1. Exemption: Ulp., *Reg.* 16, 1; *Vat. Fr* 216-9. Livilla's marriage: Griffin 1984, 27. Tiberius' will: Levick 1976, 220. Property: Suet., *Nero* 6, 3; DC 60, 4, 1.

11. SC 7.

12. SC 11, 2 (circus games for Drusus, a *carpentum* for her image at the games for Antonia; 'Augusta': see *PIR²* 885); cf. DC 60, 5, 1 (birthday games for both). Meise 1969, 139 n. 59, cites numismatic and sculptural evidence; *RIC* I² 124f., nos. 65-8 and 69-74 (issues in names of Antonia and Nero Drusus respectively, 41-5). Nero Drusus' arch was matched by Claudius': *RIC* I², 122-30: Drusus': nos. 3, 35 (DE GERMANIS: 41-2, 46-7, Claudius on obv.); nos.69-72 (similar legend, *c.* 41-5, Nero Drusus on obv.); no.98 (Nero Drusus' name as legend, *c.* 41-50, Claudius on obv.); no. 114 (similar, *c.* 50-54); Claudius': nos. 30, 33f., 44f. (DE BRITANN: 46-7, 49-50). See D. Nony, *MÉFRA* 92, 2 (1982) 893-8. 'Drusi f.' goes from Gallic milestones in 48: Le Glay and Audin 1976, 17.

13. Livia: SC 11, 2 (42, Mottershead 1986) ; DC 60, 5, 2 (41); cf. *Acta Arv., Docs.* 13: '[ob consecr]ationem divae Aug. i[n] tem[plo novo?]' (43-8); *ILS* 4995; coins: *RIC* I², 128 no. 101 (41-2?); Persicus: *Docs.* 380; presumably a decision taken early in 41 was implemented at the beginning of 42; *Pietas* dedication: *ILS* 202 (43). Altar: R. Bloch, *MÉFRA* 56 (1939) 81-120; I. Ryberg, *MAAR* 22 (1955) 64-80; Demolition: G. Koeppel, *Röm. Mitt.* 89 (1982) 453-5.

14. Coins: *Pietas* is securely identified with Livia only on provincial coins: Sutherland 1951, 192. Drusus: TA 3, 56f.; 59, 2. Claudius' *pietas*: SC 11, 2.

15. SC 11, 3; Sen., *Cons. ad Pol.* 16, 1f.

16. Inheritance: TH 1, 16. Agrippina: TA 12, 37, 6. Crassus: SA 11, 2. *Paludamentum*: PNH 33, 63.

17. *Ornamenta*: TA 12, 21, 2 (Chilo and Aquila): DC 60, 33, 6 (Chilo); SC 24, 1

(this case according to Furneaux: the procurator of Bithynia-Pontus was a *ducenarius*, *CIG* 2509); *PIR*2 I 744; S*C* 24, 1. Laco: DC 60, 23, 3; *ILS* 1336. See Talbert 1984, 367f.

18. Freedmen: T*A* 11, 38, 5 (Narcissus); 12, 53, 2 (Pallas). Disgust: P*NH* 35, 201; Pliny, *Ep.* 7, 29; 8, 6. Polybius and Posides: S*C* 28.

19. Military decorations to equestrian Greeks: *Docs.* 261a; 262. Posides: S*C* 28; cf. V.Maxfield, *The military decorations of the Roman Army* (London, 1981) 86: the *hasta pura* is a weapon never used.

20. Egypt: T*A* 12, 60, 1; Jones 1960, 120-23. *Ius gladii:* e.g., *ILS* 1372.

21. Mauretania: *Docs.* 407a. Sardinia: *Docs.* 343 and 392, l. 6. Raetia was under a procurator (*pro legato*) who is commemorated on a stone that employs Claudian orthography and cannot be earlier than 47: *Docs.* 256; in Thrace in 61 it was a procurator who was constructing buildings on the main roads: *Docs.* 351. Pilate: EJ² 369; J.-P. Lémonon, *Pilate et le Gouvernement de la Judée* (Paris, 1981) 54, dating the change *c.*46, suggests (56) that the prefect's job had widened in scope. Claudius on Pollio: *Docs.* 370, l. 44; cf. Philo, *In Flacc.* 2; *Leg. ad Gaium* 132; Pliny, *NH* 36, 57; Musurillo 1954, 1 l.9; Judaea: Philo, *Leg.* 299; J*B* 2, 117 and 169; J*A* 20, 2; 14 (Claudius on Fadus); see Jones 1960, 124. Pacification: P. Garnsey and R. Saller, *The Roman Empire* (London, 1987) 23.

22. Caesar's friend: *John* 19, 12.

23. Alps: Strabo 4, p.203; P*NH* 10, 134; EJ² 166 (Cottius) and (Maritime and also Moesian districts) 243 (= *Docs.* 258), 244; esp. note EJ² 241: a local chieftain in the Alps as '*praef. cohort.*' under a legate; *ILS* 1348. Survival of Noricum: below, Ch. XV; procurator: *Docs.* 258. Spain: *ILS* 6948; *CIL* 2, 3271. Sardinia: DC 55, 28, 1; EJ² 249. Corsica: *CIL* 12, 2455. Later Mauretania and Sardinia: *CIL* 2, 1120; *ILS* 5350; Alps: *ILS* 9011.

24. T*A* 14, 38f.

25. T*A* 12, 60, with Stockton 1961; Seager 1962; Millar 1964, 1965; Brunt 1966 (best); summary, Lémonon, *op. cit.* 66 n. 71.

26. Short formulation: Griffin 1984, 291 n. 36, citing Pliny, *Pan.* 36, for reform. Brunt 1966, 477, asks whether Claudius is not promising also to be bound by *executive* decisions (cf. *Dig.* I 19, 1 pr.). Vipasca: E. Smallwood, *Docs. illustr. the Principates of Nerva . . . Hadrian* (Cambridge, 1966) 439f. Tiberius: T*A* 4, 15, 3f., and 6, 6. Nero: T*A* 13, 4, 3.

27. S*C* 12, 1: '*utque rata essent quae procuratores sui in iudicando statuerent*'. Return of exiles: DC 60, 4, 2 (41). Guard in senate: 16, 2 (42); cf. 23, 2f. (44).

28. Appeals only to emperors from procurators: *CIL* 8, 10570, with D. Flach, *Chiron* 8 (1978) 489–92 (Commodus); DC 52, 33, 1; *Cod. Iust.* 2, 46, 1 (215); *Dig.* 49, 1, 25 (Alexander Severus, 222–35).

29. Presence: S*C* 30, 1; rowdy litigant;: 15, 3f.; humour: 21, 5; Precautions: 35, cf. DC 60, 3, 3; Augustus; Suet., *Aug.* 35, 1f.; Vespasian: *Vesp.* 12. Assassination: T*A* 11, 22, 1; S*C* 36. Galba's escort: T*H* 1, 24; Suet., *Otho* 4, 2; Plut., *Galba* 20, 7. Ring: P*NH* 33, 41; Vespasian: Suet., *Vesp.* 14: '*ex officio admissionis*'. Trajan: Pliny, *Pan.* 47, 3f. Gracchus: Sen., *De Ben.* 6, 34, 2. Attendants: Millar 1977, 61–9; 465–77.

## 6 POLITICS AND THE COURT: I: 41–48 (pages 53–68)

T*A* 11; S*C* 26-9; DC 60-60/61, 31, 8. Saller 1982, 41-78. Scramuzza 1940, 80-98; Mehl 1974; J. Colin, 'Les vendanges dionysiaques et la légende de Messaline', *LÉC*

24 (1956) 23-39; Meise 1969, 123-69 (methodical analysis of ancient and modern interpretations); Ehrhardt 1978; Grimal 1978; Oost 1958.

1. Court: Griffin 1984, 31; its apogee and moving with the Emperor: Millar 1977, ch. I.
2. *Potentia/potens*: Mehl 1974, 67, draws attention to T*A* 11, 5, 3 (Silius); 26, 3 (Messallina); 28, 1 (freedmen); 31, 3 (Claudius); 12, 42, 4 (Vitellius); 13, 12, 1 and 19, 1 (Agrippina); cf. 14, 39, 3 (freedmen); 3, 30, 4 (*equites*). Pallas, Narcissus, Callistus worth more than 200m. HS each: P*NH*: 33, 134f., where they are sovereign ('*rerum potiantur*'); Pallas: T*A* 14, 65, 1; Juv. 1, 109; Front., *De Aquis* 19; S*C* 28; offered 15m. HS in 52: P*Ep*. 8, 6, 8; T*A* 12, 53, 2 and 5. Callistus: P*NH* 36, 60; Narcissus: DC 60/61, 34, 4; Juv. 14, 329-31; Sosibius received 1m. HS in 47: T*A* 11, 4, 6; Claudius' hand: T*A* 12, 1f.; Jews: J*B* 2, 245; J*A* 20, 135. 'Brokers': Saller 1982, 74f. Vespasian owed his legionary legateship to '*Narcissi gratia*' and as Emperor took the broker's tip (Suet., *Vesp*. 4, 1; 23, 2); citizenship sold for 'broken glassware' (DC 60, 17, 6).
3. Succession problem: Griffin 1984, 189-96.
4. Octavia's birth: P. Gallivan, *Lat*. 33 (1974) 116f. Ehrhardt 1978, 54 n.22; Paetina: T*A* 12, 2, 1; 'ex levibus offensis', S*C* 26, 2; her kinship with Sejanus was not close. Messallina: T*A* 4, 52, 1-6; pedigree: see Table 2. Character and aims: Meise 1969, 138f.; 148.
5. Syme 1958, 437; 1986, 150, 164-6; 178; *contra*, Meise 1969, 152 n.122. Ehrhardt 1978, 55, still considers the marriage to Claudius her first.
6. Power: [Sen.], *Oct*. 949: '*partuque potens*'. 'Augusta' denied: DC 60, 12, 5; *carpentum*: S*C* 17, 3; DC 60, 22, 1 (permanent use or only at the triumph? See Meise 1969, 151f., and for her honours in general, 149f.) Britannicus: S*C* 27, 2, erroneously implying 42; cf. T*A* 13, 15, 1; see Mottershead 1986 *ad loc*. SPES: *RIC* 1² 118f., 128 no. 99.
7. Seneca and Livilla: *Schol. Juv*. 5, 109; Sen., *Cons. ad Pol*. 13, 2; S*A* 10, 4; T*A* 13, 42, 3; S*C* 29, 1; DC 60, 8, 5; 61, 10, 1. See Meise 1969, 139-41. Grimal 1978 holds unconvincingly that Seneca and Agrippina stood for a less monarchical position than Messallina.
8. Julia: S*A* 10, 4; 13, 5; [Sen.] *Oct*. 944-6; T*A* 13, 32, 5; 43, 3; S*C* 29, 1; DC 60, 18, 4; Plautus: T*A* 13, 19, 3-20, 2; 14, 22, 5; 57-9. See Meise 1969, 142f.
9. Justus: T*A* 1, 29, 2; cf. Ehrhardt 1978, 65f.; Messallina is credited with the deaths of Justus and Julia in 43 by DC 60, 18, 3f., Claudius with that of Justus in S*A* 13, 5. Justus' colleague Rufrius Pollio, appointed in 41, appears among Claudius' victims in the *Apocolocyntosis*, but as an emendation: there is no other evidence, and Crispinus' name suggests that he was a relative of Pollio's: 41: J*A* 19, 267; victim: S*A* 13, 5; cf. T*A* 12, 42, 1.
10. S*C* 13, 2; DC 60, 27, 5; S*A* 13, 5. Sceptical appraisal: Syme 1986, 183; Mottershead suggests that it was the death of his brother Ser. Celer, suff. 38 (S*A* 13, 5) that inspired Gallus' plot, but see *PIR*2 A 1225; McAlindon (*AJP*) 1956, 129f.; 1957 282, n.35.
11. Freedmen listed: Nony 1968, 53f. Who freed Narcissus is uncertain; Claudius probably emancipated Polybius, securing a formal obligation of duty; cf. S*C* 40, 2. Pallas: Oost 1958; Antonia: Nicols 1975.
12. Syme 1986, 181. D. Silanus: B. Levick, *Lat*. 35 (1976), 333-6.
13. Frugi: *Docs*. 224; Magnus: DC 60, 5, 7-8.

14. Prospects: Ehrhardt 1978, 54f., 59-61, rightly stressing their equal treatment. Appius: DC 60, 5, 7f.; 14, 3; TA 3, 68, 3; Syme 1986, 181; 193f.; Table XIII; legions: R.F.S. Jones, *JRS* 66 (1976) 49-51.

15. Syme 1986, 185 (on Messallina); Wiseman 1982, 64 (differences between Claudius and his entourage).

16. SC 37, 2; DC 60, 14, 2-4; TA 11, 29, 1 (Narcissus leading); Domitia Lepida blamed Messallina: 37, 4; Dorey 1966, 147, suspected that Appius Silanus was already involved in Scribonianus' plot. Gaius: Suet., *Cal.* 26, 2. Gaius' assassination: Ch. IV.

17. Revolt: SC 13, 2; DC 60, 15, 1-16, 8. Scribonianus' family: Weinrib 1968, 274f.; Arruntius: TA 1, 13, 2.

18. Pomponius: TA 13, 43, 2, with Wiseman 1982, 59-63, on Calp. Sic., *Ecl.* 1, 49-53, and the seriousness of the revolt; *CIL* 6, 2015 (name erased); Arria: TA 16, 34, 3; DC 60, 16, 6f.; Vinicianus: 15, 1. Praetor: 4. Cloatilla: Quint. 8, 5, 15f.; R. Rogers argued, *TAPA* 76 (1945) 264-70, that Claudius having pardoned her, Domitius defended her at a second trial concerned with sureties (Ch. 11).

19. Watchword: DC 60, 16, 7, from Hom. *Il.* 24, 369; *Od.* 16, 72; 21, 133. Trial: DC 60, 16, 3. Arria's husband: 16, 6; torture: 15, 6. Outsiders in senate: Talbert 1984, 156f.

20. Aims: DC 60, 15, 3; SC 13 ('*novum imperatorem*'); Swan 1970, 162f., sees restoration of the Republic as at least a front. Narcissus: DC 60, 17, 4.

21. Amnesty for sons: DC 60, 16, 2. Arvals: *Docs.* 12: 20 May, 43. Scribonianus and his mother: TA 12, 52, 1 ('Vibia' Furneaux, for 'Vivia' Med.; 'Iunia', 'Vinia' *alii*; cf. Syme, 1986, 258 n. 37: 'Vinicia'), and P*Ep.* 3, 16, 7-9, with Sherwin-White *ad loc.* for the political descent.

22. Vinicius: DC 60, 27, 4; his 'murder' is strangely accounted for: 'suspicion' is given as the reason, as well as 'anger' because of his refusal to sleep with Messallina; see Syme 1986, 279.

23. 'Magnus': Suet., *Cal.* 35, 1; honours to Frugi: SC 17, 3; Magnus' execution: 27, 2; 29, 1; DC 60/61, 29, 6ᵃ; 30, 6ᵃ; unacceptability of Magnus to Messallina: Ehrhardt 1978, 67f. (two of Dio's epitomators blame her for his death, but there was a gradual deterioration in his position; McAlindon (*AJP*) 1956, 126f., denies her involvement); death of his parents: SA 11, 2, with Meise 1969, 145-7 (date n.90). Galba: TH 1, 15.

24. TA 11, 1, 1; DC 60, 27, 1-3; 60/61, 29, 4-6ᵃ. Gardens of Lucullus and Taurus: Blake 1959, 31.

25. Difficulties in Tacitus' account, see Mehl 1974, 35-7; possible *Putsch*: A.Bergener, *Die führende Senatorenschicht im frühen Principat, 14-68 n. Chr.* (Bonn, 1965) 35, 124-6, 140-2; Dorey 1966, 146. Citizenship: L. Ebel, *Transalpine Gaul* (Leiden, 1976) 94f. Vienna: Strabo 4, p.186. Antonia: TA 11, 3, 1; Saturnina: *PIR²* L 329; their wealth included a residence at Baiae and an enterprise at Puteoli: Camodeca 1982, 20f.; his claims: JA 19, 252; Saturnina and Gaius: Sen., *de Const.* 18, 2.

26. *Latro*: *Docs.* 369, col. 2, l. 19f.; Cic., *In Cat.* 1, 33. Definition: Sen., *De Ben.* 5, 14, 2. Vienna and Asiaticus' brother: *Docs.* 369, col. 2, ll. 9-19.

27. Supplies: cf. TA 1, 71, 3. Of 32 Narbonensian legionaries known Augustus-Gaius, 8 are from Vienna; of 58 under Claudius and Nero, 12: G. Forni, *Il Reclutamento delle legioni da Augusto a Diocleziano. Pubblic. della Fac. di Lett. e Filosof. della Univ. di Pavia* (Milan, 1953) 164f., 173f.; *ANRW* 2, 1 (1974) 366-9.

28. Claudius a *gallus* : SA 7, 3. Allobroges: *Docs.* 369, col. 2, ll. 24-6; Sall., *Cat.* 40, 1; Vell. Pat. 2, 121, 1. Local importance of Asiaticus: G. Townend, *AJP* 83 (1962) 125-8, citing TH 1, 59 and 2, 94.

29. Resignations and circus games: DC 60, 27, 1-3; '*pauper e Latio*': TA 11, 23, 5.

30. *Intra cubiculum* trials: Ch. 11. Vitellius: TH 1, 59, with Townend, *art. cit.* 127; if Vitellius' role is put in an unfavourable light, one may look to a Flavian historian as the source, perhaps to Cluvius Rufus.

31. TA 11, 22, 1f.

32. TA 11, 5; Suillius' defence: T. Dorey, *CP* 60 (1965) 265 (over-subtle).

33. Politically destructive madness: TA 11, 12, 1, with Seif 1974, 69 n.8; so the sympathetic [Sen.], *Oct.* 258f. Discrepancies: Seif 111. Silius' passivity: TA 11, 12, 3; Juv. 10, 329-33.

34. Mehl 1974, 62 n. 334, points to the political tone of TA 12, 65, 1, citing recent works for the view that Silius had political aims. Motivation: Meise 1969, 162-66. Agrippina motive: 166, citing Messallina's attacks on earlier 'rivals'. Games: TA 11, 11, 5. Nero's age: see *PIR*² D 129 (p.35).

35. Freedmen killed: SA 13, 5; Passienus: P*NH* 16, 242; *Schol. Juv.* 4, 81, with Syme 1958, 328f.

36. Silius: TA 11, 5, 2; DC 60, 31, 3; consulship: Camodeca 1982, 18. Knights killed: SA 14, 1; TA 11, 35, 6f. List of those involved: Meise 1969, 154-8. *Éminences grises*: TA 12, 60, 5f.

37. Claudius' authorization: SC 29, 3. Privacy: TA 11, 29, 1; Juv. 10, 337, with Meise 1969, 136f. Conspiracy, 152-4. 'Bacchanalia' theory of Colin 1956: 128-32. Marriage: 132-7. Adoption: 159. Obscurities of divorce: P. Corbett, *The Roman law of marriage* (Oxford, 1931) 143, doubting the possibility of bigamy (224f.; 226 n.1). I am greatly indebted to Professor S.Treggiari for help, and especially for her kindness in allowing me to read a draft chapter of her forthcoming work. Nero: TA 15, 37, 7-9; DC 62, 28, 3.

38. Courtiers passive: Meise 1969, 161.

## 7 POLITICS AND THE COURT II: 48-54: (pages 69-80)

TA 12; SC 39; 43-6; DC 60/61, 31, 5ª-35; Timpe 1962, 94-105; Meise 1969, 176-87; Melmoux 1975; Griffin 1984, 23-33. G.Bagnani 'The case of the poisoned mushrooms', *Phoen.* 1.1 (1946) 15-21. M.S. Smith, 'Greek Precedents for Claudius' actions in 48 and later', *CQ* NS 13 (1963) 139-44. See also bibliography to Ch. VI.

1. Rivalry: TA 11, 12, 1. Contrast: 12, 7, 5-7. Literary purpose: Ehrhardt 1978, 70f.; cf. Meise 1969, 151f.; Mehl 1974, 122-5.

2. Alexander: TA 2, 73, 2-4. The elder Agrippina: TA 1, 69.

3. Conference: TA 12, 1f. Antonia: cf. Ehrhardt 1978, 69. Dorey 1966, 154, implausibly interprets Narcissus' opposition to Agrippina as due to a feud begun in 48.

4. TA 12, 5-7; SC 26, 3. Nerva is said to have forbidden uncle-niece marriage, but it was probably extension to sisters' daughters that he forbade: DC 68, 2, 4; Dio's 'αδελφιδή does for a niece on either side. GI 1, 62, distinguishes Claudius' from the forbidden marriage to a sister's daughter (it would not help preserve the family).

5. Murder attempts: Suet., *Nero* 6, 4.

6. Consort: Sen., *Cons. ad Pol.* 12, 5, cf. Ovid, *Tr.* 2, 165f. Phaedrus 3, 2, might

be a hopeful reference to Agrippina's attitude to those who had not damaged her, 3, 15, to the relationship of Agrippina and Britannicus. Failing powers: H. Scullard, *From the Gracchi to Nero*, ed. 5 (London and N.Y., 1982) 290.

7. TA 12, 3, 2-12, 4; 8, 1.

8. TA 12, 9.

9. Seneca: TA 12, 8, 3; Lollia: TA 12, 22; 14, 12, 6.

10. Adoption: TA 12, 25, 1; *Docs.* 21, l. 58f.; Suet., *Nero* 7, 1 (antedating). Colonia Agrippinensium: TA 12, 27, 1f. Augusta: DC 60/61, 33, 2a; fire at 12, after Nero's marriage; Agrippina had Livia's privileges and all Claudius' power, but 'wanted his title outright' ('ἀντικρυς 'ονομάζεσθαι). Imperial duty at fires, including women, see Ch. III. Gazetting: Dio 60/61, 33, 1 (*Acta Diurna*); cloak: PNH 33, 63; DC 60/61, 33, 3; tribunal: TA 12, 37, 5 (51); DC 60/61, 33, 7 (with ambassadors, cf. 1); both: 56, 5 (53). Vows: *Docs.* 14: '*subolem Agrippinae Aug., Ti. Claudi Caes. Aug. Germ. divini principis parentisque publici filium*'.

11. TA 12, 25f.; SC 39, 2. Novelty: *Docs.* 369, col. 1, l.5; col. 2, l. 2. Octavia adopted: DC 61, 33, 2[2.]

12. Caratacus: TA 12, 36-8. Ninth year: 36, 1. Arch: *Docs.* 43b. *Carpentum*: TA 12, 42, 3; DC 60/61 33, 2[1].

13. TA 12, 25, 3 (ages); 26, 2 (Britannicus deserted, 50); 41, 5 (officers and friendly freedmen dismissed in 51); 6 ('Domitius'), preferable to Suet., *Nero* 7, 1; cf. DC 60/61, 32, 5 (51); 33, 10 (52-3). Gaius and Gemellus: Levick 1976, 201-21.

14. Claudius designated: *Docs.* 347; Gallivan 1978, 425. Nero's birth: Griffin 1984, 241 n.11. TA 12, 41, 1: '*maturata*'. *Liberalia* and age for toga: B. Levick, *Lat.* 35 (1976) 310, 39. Appointments: *Docs.* 21f.

15. Claudius consul: Camodeca 1983-4, 60-62; Agrippina and Nero: Rome: *RIC* I[2], 129 no. 103 (*carpentum*); 125f. nos.75-83; 129 no. 107f.. Balkans: *CREBM* p.195 n.. Ephesus: *RIC* I[2], 130 no. 117 (50-1); Pergamum: 131 no. 121. Britannicus and Nero at Corinth: M. Amandry, *Le Monnayage des duovirs corinthiens, BCH Suppl.* 15 (1988) 73f., 195 (50-51); Sinope: M. Amandry, *RN* Sér. 6, vol. 28 (1986) 72-4 (54-5) (I owe this reference to the kindness of Dr Howgego); Judaea: *BMC Palestine* 264f. nos.21-33 (54). Subtle analysis: Sutherland 1951, 143-7.

16. Claudius' view: Mottershead 1986, p.139. Sodalis: *Docs.* 132b (first half of 51); cf. TA 1, 54, 1f. Other priesthoods: *RIC* I[2], 125 no.76f.; 129 no. 107. Octavian's consulship: A. Woodman *ad* Vell. Pat. 2, 65, 2. Gaius and Lucius: B. Levick, *Lat.* 31 (1972) 786f.; anomalously Gaius was elected consul before taking the toga: DC 55, 9, 2. *Princeps Iuventutis: RIC* I[2], 125 nos. 75, 78f.; 129 no. 107f.. *Imperium*: TA 12, 41, 2. Tiberius' views: Levick 1976, 157f. Agrippa's *imperium*: EJ[2] 366.

17. Tips: TA 12, 41, 3f.; (and Prefecture) Suet., *Nero* 7, 2, cf. SC 4, 3; Van Berchem 1939, 147.

18. Portents of 51: TA 12, 43, 1, omitting the three suns of PNH 2, 99 (cf. DC 60/61, 33, 2[2] and 2[c] (the sky on fire on the day of the adoption; earth tremors); John Lyd., *De Ost.*, Proem 4); 53: Phlegon, *Mir.* 7, FGH 2, 1179 (an androgyne born on Agrippina's steading in Mevania); 54: TA 12, 64, 1-3; see J.H.W.G. Liebeschuetz, *Continuity and Change in Roman Religion* (Oxford, 1979) 155f.; the loss of the narrative of 41-47 must be allowed for, and a possible change of source. Bread: DC 61, 33, 10 (riot instigated by Agrippina; Nero's capability); TA 12, 43, with '*modestia hiemis*' (3). 50: Eus.-Jer. 181 Helm; cf. SC 18, 2.

19. TA 12, 42, 1f.; DC 60/61, 32, 6[a]; Burrus' career: *Docs.* 259; Pflaum, *Carrières*, 30-32 no. 13 (a different justification of his reputation).

20. TA 12, 58, with Furneaux's comment; SC 25, 3; DC 61, 33, 11 (marriage; Ilium; Apamea). Ilium had evidently lost privileges: Strabo 13, 593; 595. Significance: D. Braund, CQ 30 (1980) 420-5. Bononia: Suet., Aug. 17, 2; Rhodes: DC 60, 24, 4; Anth. Pal. 9, 178. A. Stein, PIR² D 129 (p.37), doubts the date; Suet., Nero 7, 2, has him speaking before Claudius as consul (51); E. Koestermann, ad TA 12, 58, 2, suggests that the speeches belong to various years.

21. DC 60/61, 33, 9; 11, with W. Huss, AC 47 (1978) 131 n. 15.

22. Lupus: TA 12, 42, 4f.; maiestas: Ch. 11. 'Pietatis immobilis erga principem', Suet., Vit. 3, I; cf. Dorey 1966, 144-7.

23. All leading freedmen Agrippina's: DC 60/61, 31, 8; 33, 3a; Seif 1973, 151-3; Pallas' honours: TA 12, 53; Pliny, Ep. 8, 6, 13 (date). Lake: TA 12, 57: 'nimias spes eius arguens' (5).

24. Scribonianus: TA 12, 52, 1-3; astrologers: DC 60/61, 33, 3b. Misunderstood by R.Bauman, Impietas in Principem. München. Beitr. zur Papyrusforsch. u. ant. Rechtstgesch 67 (Munich, 1974) 65. I interpret the case of T. Statilius Taurus, cos. 44, in 53 as one of a poverty-stricken legate attacking his exceptionally rich commander for the financial reward. When Taurus committed suicide the House wilfully declined to continue the case; nothing for Tarquitius, who then came into the category of impoverished senators liable to expulsion because they lacked the decency to resign (he had been in Africa when the resignations had been requested): TA 12, 59, with Furneaux ad loc. for a different interpretation; 14, 46, 1 (Tarquitius after money again); cf. 12, 52, 4 (expulsions in 52).

25. TA 12, 64, 4-65, 2; he seems mistaken (64, 5) about their ages: Syme 1986, 165f. Threat: TA 12, 64, 4; SC 43, 1; DC 60/61, 34, 1. Shepherds: Sall., Cat. 46, 3 (63 BC); TA 4, 27 (24); CIL 9, 2335 (c.29). Nero's evidence: Suet., Nero 7, 1. Narcissus and Domitia Lepida's relationship with Britannicus: Seif 1973, 268-70; cf. Griffin 1984, 31.

26. DC 60/61, 34, 1 (toga virilis). See Dorey 1966, 155. Will: SC 44, 1. Analysis: Scramuzza 1940, 91f.; cf. Timpe 1962, 97f.

27. Consuls: SC 46; Britannicus' death: TA 13, 15-17.

28. [Sen.,] Oct. 164f.; PNH 2, 92; SC 44, 2f., where Mottershead collects references to poison and to the mushroom; for Suetonius on Halotus offering Claudius a poisoned drink (cf. Suet., Nero 39, 3), following Cluvius Rufus, see the acute analysis of G. Townend Herm. 88 1960, 109f.; TA 66, 4-67, with P. Wuilleumier, RÉL 53 (1975) 3f. (boleto not cibo boletorum), and Mehl 1974, 285, on the 'Dramatisierender Künstler' using rich sources; DC 60/61, 34, 2f. Sources: see also Momigliano 1975, 818-20.

29. Halotus: RE 7 (1912) 2283f. Heart attack: Bagnani 1946, with unacceptable elaborations. Fatalities of 54: TA 12, 64, 3. Scepticism: Griffin 1984, 32f. Poisons reviewed: Heller 1985, 70f.

30. Accession: TA 12, 69; Suet., Nero 8; Narcissus TA 12, 66, 1; 13, 1, 4; SA 13, 2; DC 61, 34, 4-6; Nero in the barracks: TA 12, 69, 1-3. Celebrations on 13 October: Docs. 21f.; 26.

31. Parallels: Levick 1976, 68-81; 219f.; M. Sage, Anc. Soc. 14 (1983) 293-321.

32. Suppression: TA 12, 69, 5 (hence the story of a new will?); DC 61, 1, 1f. Senatorial action: Timpe 1962, 104, criticised by Seif 1973, 292-4, who cites SC. 46. Britannicus probably preferred: H. Bellen, ANRW 2, 1 (1974) 104.

33. McAlindon 1956 is persuasive on provocation.

# 8 THE POLICY OF THE EMPEROR (pages 81–92)

SC 11f.; 16; 18-25; DC 60, 3, 5-7, 4. Momigliano 1934, 20-73; Scramuzza 1940, 80-98; 145-56; F. Millar, 'Emperors at Work', *JRS* 57 (1967) 9-19. Chilver 1949; H. Pavis d'Escurac, *La Préfecture de l'Annone, service administratif impériale d'Auguste à Constantin, BÉFAR* 226 (Paris, 1976); Rickman 1980, 73-9; 213-17; Chandler 1978; Devijver 1970. Levick 1978; E. Ramage, 'Denigration of predecessor under Claudius, Galba, and Vespasian', *Hist.* 32 (1983) 201-14.

1. Passivity: F. Millar, *JRS* 56 (1966) 166.
2. Momigliano 1934, 63, with 67 for local autonomy. H. Scullard, *From the Gracchi to Nero*, ed. 5 (London and N.Y., 1982) 292-5, has a section 'Claudius' centralized administration'; De Vivo 1980, reviewed by M.T. Griffin, *JRS* 72 (1982) 188f. Caesar: M. Gelzer, *Caesar the Politician and Statesman*, tr. P. Needham (Oxford, 1964), 312f.
3. Wealth concentrated: Momigliano 1934, 53; cf. Ch. XII.
4. TA 11, 5, 1: '*cuncta legum et magistratuum munia in se trahens*'; 1, 2, 1: '*munia senatus magistratuum legum in se trahere*'.
5. Momigliano 1934, 46; Bardon 1940, 169, on the Library Procurator (*ILS* 1587; but cf. Suet., *Caes.* 56, 7, for an Augustan librarian) and the *a studiis*; Scramuzza 1940, 83-87, esp. 86: Claudius created the 'secretariat'. Polybius' post: Sen., *Cons. ad Pol.* 5, 2; SC 28. It was formerly held that he combined the posts of *a studiis* and *a libellis*: but see Millar 1967, 16f. with n. 108: Callistus is referred to by Zonaras as *a libellis* before he mentions Polybius' death; the *a studiis* was not a research assistant but a patronage secretary. Dorey 1966, 153, suggested that Narcissus was responsible for Claudius' safety.
6. Millar 1966; TA 4, 70, 1; JA 18, 145; Philo, *Leg.* 166-78.
7. Officials: *CIL* 6, 8409; 8412; 5181 = *ILS* 1676. Scurranus: EJ² 158. L.Volusius Saturninus had an *ab hospitis* at Rome: *ILS* 7446.
8. Monarchy: Ch. V. Greeks: *Docs.* 370, ll.105-7; Vestinus: 369, col. 2, ll. 10-12. Pallas: TA 12, 53; quotation from Pliny, *Ep.* 8, 6, 13.
9. Momigliano 1934, 45. Capito: TA 4, 15, 3f.. See Ch. 5.
10. Aqueducts: Front., *De aquis* 105. Tiber: *Docs.* 265. *Curatores viarum*: TA 3, 31, 7; DC 59, 15, 3-5; 60, 17, 2, with Balsdon 1934, 148; Bourne 1946, 40; Syme 1970, 29f.
11. Momigliano 1934, 49f., 107 n.21 (earlier bibliography); Fiscus' role: M. Rostowtzew, *Röm. Bleitessarae, Klio, Beih.* 3 (1905) 14-16; Scramuzza 1940, 169. Praefecti continued: Chilver 1949, 7f.; R. Syme, *JRS* 67 (1977), 49; Rickman 1980, 192-5; 213-7. Minucia: *Docs.* 174, a freedman of Claudius, '*curator de Minucia*'; but he is not an official, only in charge of a burial club: see Van Berchem 1939, 37f.; first known Procurator: *ILS* 2728 (Trajanic). On transfer of cost, see Pavis d'Escurac 1976, 33-39, against Van Berchem 72; Rickman 1980, 77f.; Mottershead 1986, ad SC 18, 1. Continuity from Republic to Empire is stressed by C. Virlouvet in *L'Urbs. espace urbain et histoire. Coll. École fr. de Rome* (Rome 1987) 175-89; see also Ch.10.
12. Duties of Quaestor: Pavis d'Escurac 1976, 105f.; difficulty of freedman in dealing with municipality: 107; 121. Book-keeping: G. Rickman, *MAAR* 36 (1980), 270. Change of posts: SC 24, 2; DC 60, 24, 3, with Momigliano 1934, 51, and 108 n.23; Meiggs 1973, 55 and 299, suggesting that the first known Procurator, Claudius Optatus, was identical with a Claudian Prefect of the Fleet at Misenum: *Docs.* 173 and PNH 9, 62. So Chandler 1978, 332f., and G. Houston, who argues for

'replacement', *MAAR* 36 (1980), 157 and 159. But the prefect was a Julius: Pavis d'Escurac 1976, 397. Quaestors could hold office at 24; it would be surprising if Augustus cared about keeping them off naval bases.

13. Claudian freedman '*proc. XX here*' (Achaea): *Docs.* 172; '*a patrimonio*': 176.

14. *TA* 13, 29, 2f.; *SC* 24, 2; *DC* 60, 24, 1-3; *Docs.* 233f.; Momigliano 1934, 46; cf. the judicious comments of Griffin 1984, 56f. Praetors: *DC* 60, 10, 3; debt: *TA* 13, 28, 5; roadway: *TA* 1, 75, 3f.

15. Momigliano 1934, 43-52. For the senate, see Ch. IX. Tiberian irregularities: *TA* 1,80; 3, 32-5, with W.Orth, *Die Provinzialpolitik des Tiberius* (Diss. Munich, 1970), 71-81; 131f.

16. *SC* 25, 1; *Docs.* 280; after abolition of the reform: 265. Momigliano 1934, 47-9 and 106 n.19, scouts the view (A.v. Domaszewski, *BJ* 117 (1908) 129) that Claudius considered the quasi-magistracy, the tribunate, senior.

17. Tribune commanding Roman citizens: so Miss J. Annas (Mrs Owen) as an undergraduate, and not incompatible with Domaszewski's view; cf. Devijver 1970, especially 77, arguing persuasively that Claudius thought the tribunate a good preparation for civilian administrative posts. Mottershead 1986 cites *Docs.* 261f. Tribunes deskborne: P*Ep* 7, 22. Statius: *Silv.* 5, 1, 97.

18. 'Religious policy': Momigliano 1934, 20-38; Scramuzza 1940, 145-56; H.Scullard, *From the Gracchi to Nero*, ed. 5 (London and N.Y., 1982) 294f. Cf. May, 1936, 254 n.I: '*politique réligieuse ... plus hésitante*'. Legislation: Ch. XII. Optimism: *TA* 11, 15, 2.

19. Jews: Ch. XIII. Mysteries: *SC* 25, 5. It is said of Hadrian '*initia Cereris Liberaeque, quae Eleusin a dicitur, Atheniensium modo Roma percoleret*' (Aur. Vict., *De Caes.* 14, 4); P.Graindor, *Athènes sous Hadrien* (Cairo, 1934) 120, citing Arrian, *Disc. of Epict.* 3, 21, 13f., for the impiety, thinks of such ceremonies as the procession of the *calathos*; Claudius (*Athènes de Tibère à Trajan* (Cairo, 1931) 102) went further, initiating discussions with the priestly families: he venerated the cult, in which he had not been initiated (cf. Ch. 2); but also wanted to raise the prestige of Rome and was acting within the tradition of annexing alien cults. Claudius' alleged favour to the cult of Cybele (J.Carcopino, *MÉFRA* 40 (1923) 135-59; 237-34; R.Bloch, *MÉFRA* 56 (1939) 103f.) was adequately refuted by Scramuzza 1940, 152-5. *Haruspices*: *TA* 11, 15; 65 BC: Cic., *Cat.* 3, 19; see J.H.W.G. Liebeschuetz, *Continuity and Change in Roman Religion* (Oxford, 1979) 8; 22f.; E.Rawson, *JRS* 68 (1978) 139-49; *Intellectual life in the late Roman Republic* (London, 1985) 27f., suggesting that Claudius identified the sons of Etruscan *principes* encouraged by the senate of the second century BC to study their traditions, the *haruspices* summoned on occasion, and the *collegium* (= *ordo*?); the *ordo* proper may be Augustan. Note the preoccupation of Etruscan lore with *saecula*.

20. Secular Games: *TA* 11, 11, 1-4; Scramuzza 1940, 284 n.12. Pomerium and *Augurium Salutis*: *TA* 12, 23, 3f., with Furneaux on the calculation; Cicero: *DC* 37, 24-5, 1; *De Div.* 1, 105; Augustus: Suet., *Aug.* 31, 4. See Momigliano 1934, 87 n.10; Scramuzza 1940, 285 n.14.

21. Statements: preambles to *Docs.* 365 and 380.

22. *SC* 11, 3; *DC* 60, 4, 6. '*Memoria damnata*': *Dig.* 24, 1, 32, 7 (Ulp.). 'Prosecution' of Gaius: *SA* 11, 2.

23. Coins: *RIC*[12], 121-31: CONSTANTIAE AVGVSTI: nos. 2, 13f.; repeated 46-7, 49-50: nos. 31f., 42f.; on gold and silver, 41-5: no. 65f.; undated *aes*, *c.* 50-4, no. 111. OB CIVES SERVATOS: nos. 5f., 15f.; repeated 46-7, 49-52: nos. 40f., 48-50, 53f., 59f.,

63f.; on undated *aes c.* 41-50: no. 96; at Caesarea, no. 123. PACI AVGVSTAE: no. 9f.; repeated 43-7, 49-52: nos. 21f., 27f., 38f., 46f., 51f., 57f., 61f. VICTORIA AVGVSTI: no. 17f. Ramage 1983, 204f., cites Sen., *Cons. ad Pol.* 17, 5, for *inconstantia*, and *De Brev. Vit.* 18, 5f., for grain. Attacks on Gaius: *Docs.* 308b; *JA* 19, 284. Games: R.F. Newbold, *PACA* 13 (1975) 30-5; statues: DC 60, 6, 8; *IG* II/III² 5173-9 (Athens).

24. DC 60, 22, 3, with C.H.V. Sutherland, *Roman History and Coinage* (Oxford, 1987) 79f., citing partial obliteration (Domitian) and a decision to continue issues (Vitellius).

25. SC 11. 1. Medical metaphor: Sen., *Cons. ad Pol.* 13, 1; 14, 2; 17, 3; cf. *Docs.* 370, l.100.

26. DC 60, 3, 5; Oros. 7, 1, 6, 1-5, with A. Mehl, *RM* 121 (1978) 185-94.

27. Constitutionality: Mehl 1974, 30; cf. Levick 1976, 252 n. 20. Claudius: Oros. 7, 6, 4f.; Sen., *Cons. ad Pol.* 6, 5, cf. 12, 4; 13, 2-4; *Docs.* 370, l. 81; Caratacus: *TA* 12, 37, 5; cf. 11, 2; 52, 2. Mockery: 11, 3, 1. Caesar: Suet., *Iul.* 75, 1; S. Weinstock, *Divus Iulius* (Oxford 1971) 240-3.

28. *Civilitas*: SC 35, 1; A. Wallace-Hadrill, *JRS* 72 (1982) 32-48. Marriages: SC 12, 1, with Mottershead 1986 for the birth of Antonia's son after 46 (DC 60/61, 30, 6a); her first marriage: 60, 5, 7. Octavia and Antonia: Ehrhardt 1978, 59. Britannicus: DC 60, 12, 5. 43: 17, 9. Expense: 5, 3; see Ch. 12.

29. Antony: *Docs.* 370, ll. 24f.; 100-4; Ch. V. Augustus: Mehl 1978, 41, citing *Docs.* 369, col. 2 ll.1-4; *TA* 12, 11, 1; precedents: 11, 11, 1; 12, 23, 2; 25, 1; *SA* 10f. (Augustus Claudius' judge; but this may be the author's standard rather than Claudius'); see also Sen., *Cons. ad Pol.* 12, 5. Claudius trying 'to co-operate with the Senate on Augustan lines': H. Scullard, *From the Gracchi to Nero*, ed. 5 (London and N.Y., 1982) 290. Tacitus: Seif 1973, 259-62.

30. Caesar: Levick 1978, 96-105; comparison, though '*auf die hellenistische Monarchie des Caesar zurückgehenden Claudius*' in connexion with the imperial cult: E. Kornemann, *Klio* 1 (1902) 104. 'Make haste slowly': Suet., *Aug.* 25, 4; A.Gell., *Noct. Att.* 10, 11, 5; Tiberius' absenteeism, and Gaius dangerous: *Docs.* 368, ll. 11-13, cf. 308b; *JA* 19, 284; cf. Sen., *Cons. ad Pol.* 13, 1; Suet., *Cal.* 60.

31. Ostia: SC 20,1, with Pomp. Porph. *ad Hor.*, *Ars Poet.* 65; DC 60, 11, 3-5; Fucine Lake: *TA* 12, 56f.; SC and DC *locc. citt.*; Britain: Oros. 7, 6, 11: '*tempus et tempus, bellum et bellum, Caesar et Caesar ... hoc felicissima victoria, illud acerbissima clades fuit*'; *Docs.* 43b. Elephants: Polyaenus 8, 23, 5, with C.E. Stevens, *History Today* 9 (1959) 626f.;'confusion' according to S.Ireland, *Roman Britain, a Sourcebook* (London and Sydney, 1986) 36; but see C. Hawkes, *Proc. Brit. Acad.* 63 (1977) 161 n.2, 170 n.3 (I am greatly indebted to Professor Hawkes for this reference). Claudius: Meiggs 1973, 49, citing *ILS* 1578; Juv. 12, 102-7; *PNH* 8, 22.

32. Colonies: F.Vittinghoff, *Römische Kolonisation u. Bürgerrechtspolitik unter Caesar u. Augustus, Akad. der Wissensch. u. der Lit. in Mainz. Abhandlungen der Geistes u. Sozialwiss. Klasse* 14 (Wiesbaden, 1951, publ. 1952) 63-91. Claudius: Ch. XV. Togate subjects: *SA* 3, 3. Gallic senators: *Docs.* 369, col. 2, l. 1-4; *TA* 11, 23-5; Suet., *Iul.* 80, 2. Birley 1981, 359, comments on the amusement for Claudius in having a Cn. Pompeius Magnus with him in Britain as a subordinate; it was equally titillating for Caesar's admirer to have a Cn. Pompeius Magnus as a son-in-law.

## 9 SENATE AND EQUESTRIAN ORDER: CLAUDIUS AND THE ARISTOCRACY (pages 93–104)

SC 11-16; TA 11f.; Bergener 1965; Talbert 1984; Gallivan 1974, 1978; 1979; H.-H.Pistor, *Prinzeps und Patriziat in der Zeit von Augustus bis Commodus* (Diss. Freiburg, 1965); McAlindon 1956, (*AJP* and *Lat.*) 1957; Swan 1970; Chandler 1978. Daube 1969, 117-128.

1. Accession: Ch. IV. Assassination attempts and civil war: SC 13,1; fear proclaimed: 36, 1; precautions: 35 (all with Mottershead 1986); DC 60, 3, 3.
2. Amnesty: DC 60, 3, 5-4, 1f.; denunciations burnt, a 'poisoner' executed: 4, 5; restitution: 6, 3; Magnus: 5, 9. D. Laelius Balbus, exiled 37, was suff. 46: TA 6, 47f., with Levick 1976, 216, for Balbus as a victim of Gaius' ally Macro.
3. Civility: SC 12, 1f.; '*iactator civilitatis*': 35, 1; DC 60, 6, 1; 12; honours: SC 12, 1; DC 60, 5, 3-5; 7, 3; rising: 6, 1; oath and speeches: 10, 1f.; 25, 1. dress: 6, 9; Sulla: 12, 3; sick visits: 12, 1; socializing: 7, 4. *Libertas*: *Docs.* 367, col. 3, ll. 10-23; Cyzicus: *Docs.* 45, with G. Walser, *Hist.*, 4 (1955) 362f. Coins: *RIC* 1², 128 no. 97 (*c.*, 41-50); 130 no. 113. (*c.* 50-4), with Swan 1970, 163 n. 54. Attendance: DC 60, 11, 8; Talbert 1984, 176f., citing DC 60, 2, 2, for less regular attendance at the end of the reign. Claudius as senator: *Docs.* 369 col. 2, l. 29, cited with other claims by R. Syme, *Historia Augusta Papers* (Oxford, 1983) 115f. Tiberius: Suet., *Tib.* 29.
4. Gaius: Suet., *Cal.* 17, 1; DC 59, 13, 2. Designations: 'Cos. des. II': *CIL* 12, 5493; IV: *Docs.* 338; V: 347. Length of term: DC 60, 21, 2, assigns him six months in 43; cf. SC 14, 1, and *PNH* 10, 35 (suffects took office in March). 51: *AÉ* 1973, 161; Gallivan 1978, 425 ('12 months'); SC 14, 1, gives six months; see Mottershead 1986 and on 16, 1, arguing for a six-month term in 47; but that means rejecting TA 11, 25, 8, and 12, 4, 4 (censorship ends *c.* Oct. 48).
5. Figures are highly uncertain (there are many gaps and the origins of attested consuls are not always known); they are based on the papers of Brunt, *JRS* 51 (1961), esp. 74-6, 79-81; Gallivan 1974, 1978; Camodeca 1982. Carney 1960, 103, gives declining figures for patrician consuls: from 53% (Augustus), 37% (Tiberius), 19% (Gaius), to 30%; his figures for new men (not necessarily parvenus) show a rise from 35% (Augustus), 42% (Tiberius), 50% (Gaius), to 53%.
6. Caecina and Silanus: DC 60, 10, 1; 27, 1. Vetus: see *PIR*² A 773.
7. System: Gallivan 1978, 412, citing 42, 43, 45, 46, ?47, 49, ?50 for two-month *ordinarii*. Vespasian: Suet., *Vesp.* 4, 2; see Townend *AJP* 83 (1962), 114.
8. Rufus: *PIR*² C 1618f.; TA 11, 21; PEp. 7, 27, 2. For his identification with the historian of Alexander, see J. Atkinson, *A Commentary on Q.Curtius Rufus' Hist. Alex. Magn. Books 3 and 4* (Amsterdam, 1980), 19-39, accepted by Syme 1986, 438 n. 110; scepticism: U. Vogel-Wiedemann, *Acta Class.* 17 (1974) 141f. Note Wiseman's Neronian date, 1982, 67 n. 95, for 10, 9, 1-6. Consuls with scholarly forbears: Ch. I. Suillius: Gallivan 1974, 419. T. Vinius: TH 1, 48, with Chilver's commentary; Plut., *Galba* 12, 2.
9. Political interpretation of administrative changes: Ch. VIII. Praetors: DC 60, 10, 3; cf. TA 1, 75, 3f. Galba: Suet., *Galba* 7; cf. TA 3, 32; 35f.; prorogations: DC 60, 25, 6: Martius Macer *extra sortem* in Achaea (44-5?): *PIR*² M 343; M. Iulius Romulus in Macedonia: *Docs.* 237; Talbert 1984, 505f., also cites Q. Soranus (suff. 34) in Africa, 41-3; ?Caesernius Veiento in Crete, 46-7. Quaestors: DC 60, 24, 2f.; *Docs.* 233f.

10. *SC* rate: Talbert 1984, 438-59.

11. Role of senate: *TA* 13, 4, 3. Agrippa I: *JA* 19, 275, with Talbert 1984, 429, n. 41; he adds *TA* 12, 23, 2 (consultation in 49 about the annexation of Ituraea and Judaea to Syria). Lycia: DC 60, 17, 3f.; Parthians: *TA* 12, 10f.; tax relief: 61-3; see Talbert 1984, 423. Gauls: see below, n. 20. Procurators: *TA* 12, 60; legions: DC 60, 15, 4. Nero: *SC* 39, 2 (significantly transferred to the audience, *TA* 12, 25, 4). Debate required: *Docs.* 367, col. 3, ll. 10-23; Talbert 1984, 499f. (Claudian authorship: cf. Millar 1977, 350 n. 59).

12. DC 60, 10, 4; cf. *TA* 1, 14, 6.

13. Knights as tribunes: DC 60, 11, 8; cf. 54, 30, 2 (12 BC); 56, 27, 1 (12); Suet., *Aug.* 40, 1. (12 BC). Quaestorship: *Docs.* 234, *PIR* T 34f., with McAlindon (*Lat.*) 1957, 254; new men hold the prestigious quaestorship attached to the Princeps.

14. *SC* 23, 2; penalties imposed by Claudius as censor: 16, 2; DC 60, 25, 4-6 (45); cf. 29, 7$^a$ = *Suda s.v.* κλαύδιος (7 mile limit). Narbonensians: *TA* 12, 23, 1, cf. DC 52, 42, 6 (29 BC, in a context of replenishing the senate.)

15. Other censorial activities: Ch. 10f. History: T.P. Wiseman, *JRS* 60 (1970) 59-75 (bibliography); A.H.M. Jones, *Studies in Roman government and law* (Oxford, 1955) 19-26. Chronology: designated censor: *ILS* 208, 209 = *Docs.* 329; he was *cos.* IV with Vitellius III (two months at least), so can hardly have entered office until 1 March: see I. König, *Die Meilensteine der Gallia Narbonensis* (Bern, 1970) 78. The term could have run from 1 March 47 to 31 August 48, but unless Tacitus' juxtaposition of the Lustrum (closing of the censorship) with Claudius' discovery of his wife's 'marriage' is artistic licence, this is a little early. E. Groag, *RE* 3 (1899) 2802, using *TA* 11, 25, 8, and 12, 4, 4, dates the censorship back the statutory 18 months from Messallina's death (October 48) to immediately after the Secular Games celebrating Rome's birthday (21 April). Like Furneaux *ad TA* 11, 13, 1, he rightly denies them a quinquennium in office: when Vitellius used his edict to expel L. Silanus in 49 the census was over; the indignant senate authorized the act. Loans: *TA* 11, 13, 2, and see Ch. XIf. Resignations: *TA* 11, 25, 5; 12, 52, 4; DC 60, 11, 8; 29, 1. Senators' property and expenses: Talbert 1984, 49-53; 58-64. Gladiatorial show imposed on quaestors designate in 47: *TA* 11, 22, 3-10; remitted in 54: 13, 5, 1; previously they had contributed to the paving of roads: *SC* 24, 2. Praetors let off gladiatorial shows in 41: DC 60, 5, 6. Claudius paid for L. Silanus' praetorian games: 31, 7.

16. Luxury and sumptuary legislation: Daube 1969, followed by B. Levick, *G and R* 29 (1982) 53-62. Tiberian debates: *TA* 2, 33; 3, 54-5, with Tacitus' comments. Italy's changing position: Ch.11f.

17. A. Chastagnol, *RHDFÉ* Sér. 4, Vol. 53 (1975) 375-94; C. Nicolet in F. Millar and E. Segal, edd., *Caesar Augustus* (Oxford, 1984) 104. Individuals, at tribunician level: M. Iulius Romulus of Narbonensis: *Docs.* 237 ('*adlecto [trib. p]lebis*'); M. Calvius Priscus of Cora: *PIR*$^2$ C 362; ?C. Salonius Matidius of Vicetia: *PIR*$^2$ M 366, following G. Alföldy, *ZPE* 39 (1980) 255-66. Gallus: DC 60, 29, 2; cf. *CIL* 6, 1442, with *PIR*$^2$ L 171 ('*inter quaestorios?*'); recusants: *SC* 24, 1.

18. Gaius' κίβδηλοι: *JA* 19, 174. Claudius' undertaking: *SC* 24, 1, where Claudius' interpretation of *libertinus* is rejected without reference to a source, causing problems to scholars. Swan 1970, 160.

19. Italians: *Docs.* 369, col. 2, l.5. Excluding Eprius Marcellus from the *adlecti* (R. Syme, *ZPE* 53 (1983) 202f.) saves his claim. Provincials: De Laet 1941, 279f.; westerners encouraged, and value of new men: Talbert 1984, 490; H. Halfmann,

*Die Senatoren aus dem östlichen Teil des Imperium Romanum bis zum Ende des 2.Jh. n. Chr.* (Göttingen, 1979) 101f., inclines to accept M. and Q. Sergius Paullus as natives of Pisidian Antioch.

20. Tiberius: Levick 1976, 98f. Gauls: T*A* 11, 23-5; see De Vivo 1980, reviewed by M.T. Griffin, *JRS* 72 (1982) 188f., and Griffin 1982. U. Schillinger-Häfele, *Hist.* 14 (1965) 444, holds that the Gauls were to be adlected.

21. Criteria and past history: T*A* 11, 25, 3. Patricians: see De Laet 1941, 225; 251-63 (18 men advanced; 7-10 *gentes*); Bergener 1965, 32-41 (36; 17 *gentes*). They agree on Acilii (3; 2); Helvii (1; 1); Nonii (1; 7); Plautii (2; 3); Salvii Othones (3; 4); Sextii Africani (1; 1); Vitellii (4; 3); Pistor adds (XIV) Q. Veranius, whom J. Reynolds, *CR* NS 4 (1954) 313, dates to 49 (but all others known were advanced when Claudius was censor); C. Ummidius Durmius Quadratus (XIII), Camillus Surdinus (IV), and C. Fisius Po... (III), and Al...(II) are admitted on a tenuous basis, *CIL* 6, 2002. De Laet has 3 unknowns: nos. 1048 (C. Salonius Matidius Patruinus) = Pistor VIII, who should be deleted, 1169 (L.f. Camilia...anus) = Pistor III, and 1170 (?C. or better Cn. Hosidius Geta?) = Pistor VII. The Volusii may have been patrician before 48 (W. Eck, *Herm.* 100 (1972) 483f.); so Ti. Plautius Aelianus, by adoption from the Aelii: Birley 1981, 357f. Add ?P. Memmius Regulus (suff. 31): *PIR*² M468, add. p. 329, following R. Syme, *ZPE* 53 (1983) 203. Augustus and Claudius: Talbert 1984, 30; Vespasian's adlections: W.Eck, *Senatoren von Vespasian bis Hadrian, Vestigia* 13 (Munich, 1970) 108f. (16 certain, 10 uncertain; 19 *gentes*).

22. *Pax* (*Augusta*): *RIC* 1², 122-4 nos. 9f., 21f., 27f. (41-4); no. 38f. (46-7); nos. 46f., 51f., 57f., 61f. (49-52); P. Jal, *RÉL* 39 (1961) 210-18. Praetorians: DC 60, 16, 7; S*C* 35, 1. Nero: Wiseman 1982, 67, on Calp. Sic., *Ecl.* 1, and Q. Curtius 10, 9, 1-6. Ignorance: T*A* 14, 18, 3.

23. Treaties: DC 60, 23, 6. Pallas: T*A* 12, 52. Pater Senatus: T*A* 11, 25, 7; Mommsen, *St.* 2, 895 n.3.

24. Senate and *equites* draw together: T*A* 12, 60. Vestinus: *Docs.* 369, col. 2, ll. 10-14. Decorations: Ch. V. Equestrian officials in the House: DC 60, 16, 3; 23, 3. Seating: 7, 3.

25. Philhellenism: Pflaum 1950, 172-4. Casualties: S*A* 14, 1.


## 10 THE PEOPLE OF ROME AND ITALY (pages 105–114)

S*C* 18-22. Z.Yavetz, 'The Living conditions of the urban plebs in Republican Rome' *Lat.* 17 (1958) 500-17 = *The Crisis of the Roman Republic*, ed. R. Seager (Cambridge, 1969) 162-182; Yavetz 1969; B. Baldwin, 'Rulers and Ruled at Rome: A.D. 14-192', *Anc. Soc.* 3, (1972) 149-63; D. Daube, *Civil Disobedience in Antiquity* (Edinburgh, 1972). Gapp 1935; C.Virlouvet, *Famines et émeutes à Rome des origines de la République à la mort de Néron*, Coll. Éc. fr. de Rome 87 (Rome 1985); A. Scobie, 'Slums, sanitation, and mortality in the Roman world', *Klio* 68 (1986) 399-433. H.Pavis d'Escurac, *La Préfecture de l'annone: Service administratif impérial d'Auguste à Constantin, Bibl. Éc. fr. d'Ath. et de Rome* 226 (Rome 1976); Rickman 1980; P. Garnsey, *Famine and food supply in the Graeco-Roman world: Responses to risk and crisis* (Cambridge, 1988). Bourne 1946; Blake 1959; Meiggs 1973; Brunt, 'Free labour and public works at Rome', *JRS* 70 (1980), 81-100; Thornton 1983 and 1985. E. Phillips, 'The Roman Law on the demolition of buildings', *Lat.* 32 (1973) 86-95; P. Garnsey, 'Demolition of houses and the law', in *Studies in Roman Property*, ed. M. Finley (Cambridge, 1976) 133-6.

1. Phaedr. 1, 15, cited by Daube 1972, 54f.; Bardon 1940, 162f., arguing against *c.* 43 for a date under Gaius. Juv. 10, 81; *TH* 4, 38.
2. Yavetz 1958; Rickman 1980, 67-93; Garnsey 1988, 240-3.
3. Augustus' house and the people: Levick, *Lat.* 31 (1972), 798-801; 35 (1976) 326-339. Tiberius: see Bourne 1946, 31f.; Levick 1976, 117-124. Obsequies: *Tabula Siarensis*, fr. 2b, ll.11-19, González, 1984, 75f.
4. Fire-fighting: Sen., *Cons. ad Marc.* 22, 4f. Sejanus on the Aventine: EJ² 53, with Syme 1956 and Levick 1976, 118-20.
5. JA 18, 225; Suet., *Cal.* 13-20; cf. 30, 2 (hostile to people); 49, 1 (alienated from senate but favours others); DC 59, 28, 11.
6. People's need for Claudius against the senate: JA 19, 160; 228. *Popularis*: see Levick 1978, 89f., citing C.E. Stevens.
7. Bench: SC 23, 2; DC 60, 16, 3; see Levick 1978, 89 n. 30, and Mottershead 1986, suggesting ' <sella> *tribuniciove subsellio*' and bringing Suetonius' account into line with what Dio says happened at trials. Advocates: TA 11, 7, 7; Mehl 1974, 47 n. 235.
8. Tribunician election: DC 60, 16, 8 (it was C.E. Stevens who showed me the significance of this passage). 15: TA 1, 77; 56: 13, 28, 1-4.
9. TA 12, 23, 4f.; M.T. Boatwright, *CJ* 80 (1984), 36-44, citing G. Lugli, *Fontes ad topographiam veteris urbis Romae pertinentes* 1 (Rome, 1952) 128f. for survivors of the *cippi* planted (one numbered 139 and including *Docs.* 44). Blake 1959, 30, suggests practical considerations, such as tightening control over a commercial area.
10. Palace: Blake 1959, 30f. Marriage: TA 12, 5f.
11. Cic., *De Off.* 2, 52-60. Bridge: Virlouvet 1985, 52 n. 46. '*Utilem rei publica ostentare se*': Oros. 7, 6, 9. Blake 1959, 25f., discusses the evidence for Claudian arches; the arch associated with German victories and with Nero Drusus may already have been in existence in Germany: cf. González 1984, 60, ll. 26f., suggesting that Germanicus' honours were based on his father's; but there was probably a structure at Rome also, Claudian according to Blake; the relationship of the Aqua Virgo arch to the triumphal arch previously shown on coins of 46-50 is also unclear. Claudian structures: PNH 34, 40; SC 20f.; 11, 3, with Mottershead 1986; fire of 22: TA 3, 72, 2. Minucia: Ch. 8. Venus: SC 25, 5.
12. Travertine: Blake 1959, 32. *Popularis* builders: P. Brunt, *Social Conflicts in the Roman Republic* (London, 1971) 58, 63, 86, 144, and 146. Porterage: G. Rickman, *Roman Granaries and Store Buildings* (Oxford, 1971) 8, 11, 79, 86, cited by Brunt 1980, 92 (n.60), who claims *c.* 6% of the Roman population in 1586 working on public buildings and perhaps 33% of Paris wage-earners in 1791 engaged in the building trade.
13. Nature of distributions: R. Rowland, *ZPE* 21 (1976) 69-73. 41: Sen., *De Brev. Vit.* 18, 5; Aur. Vict., *De Caes.* 4, 3. Insurance: SC 18, 2, putting the offer after the incident with the stale bread; but see Rickman 1980, 76; Pavis d'Escurac 1976, 219f., with insurance as a once-for-all offer of 51. Coins: *Docs.* 312a, cf. *RIC* I², 126 nos. 84, 86-8, 90, with Rickman 1980, 74f.
14. Problems: SC 18, 1f. '*assiduas sterilitates*'); DC 60, 11, 1, with Mottershead *ad* SC 18, 2, for Egyptian difficulties in 42; famines listed in E.Schürer, *The History of the Jewish people in the age of Jesus Christ (175 BC-AD 135)*, ed. G. Vermes *et al.* 1 (Edinburgh, 1973) 457 n.8: of 41 (below); 42?: DC 60, 11, 1-4; Oros. 7, 6,

12; *c.* 44-8 in Judaea (*JA* 3, 320?; 20, 51; 101; *Acts* 11, 27-30 ('great dearth throughout all the world'); 48-9 in Greece: Eus.-Jer. 181 Helm; for both areas cf. Georg. Sync., *Chronogr.* (Dindorf, Bonn) 332C-335D (under 40); in Armenia: *TA* 12, 50, 3; 51 and/or 49-50 in Rome: *TA* 12, 43, 1; *SC* 18; Eus.-Jer. *loc. cit.*; Oros. 7, 6, 17; see Gapp 1935, stressing price rises.

15. (Pompeius) Paulinus of Arelate: Sen., *De Brev. Vit.* 18, 3. Measures in general: Scramuzza 1940, 118 with n. 56; 167-9.

16. Permanent stimulus to shippers: *SC* 18, 2-19; *GI* 1, 32c; Ulp., *Frag.* 3, 6; Meiggs 1973, 291; Garnsey 1988, 233f. Rhegium: *JA* 19, 205f., with Meiggs 1973, 57. Ptolemais: Ch. 15.

17. Ostia: *SC* 20, 1 and 3; 24, 2; *DC* 60, 11, 1-5; *PNH* 16, 202; 36, 70; 125. Meiggs 1973, 51-64 (58-62 for Trajan); Van Berchem 1939, 82; Momigliano 1934, 108 n. 23; Scramuzza 1940, 165-7. Channels: *Docs.* 312b, of 46; granaries: Blake 1959, 28; Rickman 1971, index, *s.v.* Ostia, *Grandi horrea*; Meiggs 1973, 63; *vigiles*: *SC* 25, 2; *TH* 1, 80. Claudius at Ostia in 48: *TA* 11, 26, 7; *DC* 60/61, 31, 4; earlier: *SC* 12, 3. Whale-hunt: *PNH* 9, 14f. He also passed through in 43. Nero: *TA* 15, 18, 3 (losses). Trajan: E.M. Smallwood, *Docs. illustrating the Principates of Nerva, Trajan and Hadrian* (Cambridge, 1966) 383. Portus Augusti (Ostiensis): Meiggs 1973, 56 n.2. Pictures: O. Testaguzza, *Portus, illustrazione dei Porti di Claudio e Traiano*, etc. (Rome, 1970).

18. Porticus, and a ?granary under S. Clemente: Blake 1959, 28f. Site and relation to existing facilities are disputed: C. Nicolet, *CRAI* 1976, 29-51; salutary scepticism: G. Rickman in *Città e Architettura nella Roma imperiale*, *Analecta Rom. Inst. Dan.*, Suppl. 10 (Odense, 1983) 105-8. Servius Tullius: *Chron. a. 354*; he distributes grain in *De Vir. illustr.* 7, 7. Claudius and Tullius: *Docs.* 369, col. 1 ll. 16-24.

19. *PNH* 36, 124; *SC* 20, 2; *DC* 60, 11, 5. The project: Thornton 1985, 106; work force: 112f. Commemorative plaques *in situ*: *CIL* IX, 3888-90i. Failure: *TA* 12, 56f. (corruption at 57, 4); cf. *SC* 32; *DC* 60/61, 33, 3-5, and *loc. cit.*; Trajan: Smallwood, *op. cit.* 388. Favourable estimate: Thornton 1983 and 1985.

20. Water: Scobie 1986, 422-4. Aqueducts: E.Van Deman, *The Building of the Roman Aqueducts* (Washington, 1934) 187-330 (plates); for divergent accounts of the length of Claudia, 189; Blake 1959, 26-8; P.Grimal, *Roman Cities*, tr. and ed. G.M. Woloch (Wisconsin, 1983) 74f. Virgo: *Docs.* 308a (44-5) and b (46); *CIL* 6, 1254; 31565b; *ILS* 5747b; *AE* 1939, 54 (44). Claudia and Anio Novus: *SC* 20, 1; cf. Suet. *Cal.* 21; *PNH* 36, 122; *Docs.* 309 on the Porta Maggiore, with Front., *De Aquis* 13, on the 'extremely magnificent' scale of Claudius' work; see also 14f.; 18; 20; 72f.; *TA* 11, 13, 2, in terms suggesting completion (of Claudia only? so Bourne 1946, 47) in 47; [Aur. Vict.,] *De Caes.* 4, 5.

21. Procurator: Front., *De Aquis* 105 and 116; Gallus: 102; Scramuzza 1940, 159f.; Trusty: Birley 1981, 47.

22. Floods: Yavetz 1958, 516; Scobie 1986, 413. Commission: *DC* 57, 14, 9; limits: *Docs.* 307b; *CIL* 6, 31772; canals: *Docs.* 312b. Procurator: *Docs.* 265.

23. Fire: *SC* 18, 1, with Mottershead 1986; cf. *DC* 60/61, 33, 12.

24. Spectacles generally: *SC* 21, with Mottershead 1986; cf. *PNH* 8, 54 (lion-taming); 65 (four tigers); *DC* 60, 6, 8f.; 7, 3; bloody gladiatorial shows: 13. 24 races: 27, 2; naval battle: 33, 3f.; *TA* 12, 56, 2.

25. Britain: *DC* 60, 25, 6 (45). Frequency: *SC* 21, 1; see Van Berchem 1939, 147f., and Ch. XII. Nero: *TA* 12, 41, 3.

26. Yavetz 1969, 120. Edicts: Bardon 1940, 141. Friendliness: *DC* 60, 13, 5.

'Assassination': S*C* 12, 3; crusts: 18, 2; T*A* 12, 43, 2; Oros. 7, 6, 17; Eus.- Jer. 181 Helm (50); cf. DC 60/61, 33, 10 (53). Octavian: App., *Bell. Civ.* 5, 67f.

27. Portents: S*C* 22; Ch. 7. Eclipse: DC 60, 26, 1. Ostians: S*C* 38, 1 (the return from Britain is taken for the occasion by Meiggs 1973, 62, and Mottershead 1986; cf. Ch. 13); 40, 3, implying ingratitude. *Scarus*: P*NH* 9, 62.

28. Stability: Ch. 12. Phaedrus 4, 6. Claudius in the taverns, and restrictions on butchers and wine-merchants: S*C* 40, 1 ('*offula*'). These are to be associated with the tavern closures and ban on clubs of 41 in DC 60, 6, 7. Removal of control from aediles (to City Prefect?): 38, 2, with Scramuzza 1940, 30f., and Mottershead 1986.

29. [Sen.,] *Oct.* 183-185; cf. 786-805.

30. *SC Hosidianum*: *Docs.* 365, with Gallivan 1978, 424 (44), Birley 1981, 225 (47); the '*felicitati saeculi instantis*' of l.6 may be a reference to the era inaugurated by the secular games of 47. Intervention in Italy: EJ² 282; edict: *Docs.* 368; method renounced: T*A* 13, 4, 3.

31. Charters: Tarentum, C.Bruns, *Fontes iuris Romani antiqui* (ed.7, Tübingen, 1909) 27, ll.32-5; Urso, 28, ch.75; Malaca: 30, ch.62; *Lex Irnitana*: *JRS* 76 (1986), 166, ch.62. Exemption: *Docs.* 365, ll. 17-19. Interpretation of *SC*: H. Scullard, *From the Gracchi to Nero*, ed. 5 (London and N.Y., 1982) 294, still thought of a defence of arable land; *contra*, Phillips 1973; Garnsey 1976; '*Cruentissimo genere negotiationis*': l. 8f. Population: J. Paterson, *PBSR* 55 (1987) 127f., citing E.M. Smallwood, *Docs. illustrating the principates of Nerva...and Hadrian* (Cambridge, 1966) 437; *alimenta*: 435f. Lucan 1, 23-29.

32. Cyrenaica: T*A* 14, 18; *Docs.* 386, from Kasr Taurguni: '*fines occu[p]atos a privatis p(opulo) R(omano) res[ti]tuit*'. The Alpine agricultural lands and uplands that the procurator (?) Camurius Statutus informed Claudius were '*mei iuris*' were presumably his private property: *Docs.* 368, ll. 13-15.


## 11 LAW, JUSTICE, AND THE STABLE SOCIETY
(pages 115–16)

T*A* 11. 1-7; S*C* 14-16; 23; DC 60, 3, 5-5, 1; 11, 6; 15, 4-16, 5; 28, 6; 29, 4-6ª; Musurillo 1954. Talbert 1984, 460-87. A.H.M. Jones, *The Criminal courts of the Roman Republic and Principate*, ed. J. Crook (Oxford, 1972) 91-118. Crook 1955, 21- 55. G. May, 'L'Activité juridique de l'Empereur Claude', *RHDFÉ* Sér. 4, Vol. 15 (1936) 55-97; 213-54; 'Notes complémentaires', Sér. 4, Vol. 22 (1943) 101-14. R. Bauman, *The Crimen maiestatis in the Roman Republic and Augustan Principate* (Johannesburg, 1967) 171-292; *Impietas in Principem* (Munich, 1974) 177-87; 194-204; P.Brunt, 'Did Emperors ever suspend the law of "Maiestas"?', in *Sodalitas: Scritti in onore di A.Guarino. Bibl. Labeo* 8 (Naples, 1984) 469-80. Devijver 1970. Daube 1969. P.Garnsey, *Social Status and Legal Privilege in the Roman Empire* (Oxford, 1970) 17-42. G. Poma, 'Proveddimenti legislativi e attività censoria di Claudio verso gli schiavi e i liberti', *Riv. storica di Antichità* 12 (1982) 143-74; J. Crook, 'Gaius, *Institutes*, i, 84-86', *CR* NS 17 (1967) 7f.; 'Women in Roman Succession' and 'Feminine inadequacy and the *Senatusconsultum Velleianum*', in *The Family in Ancient Rome*, ed. B. Rawson (London and Sydney, 1986) 58-92; J. Gardner, *Women in Roman Law and Society* (London and Sydney, 1986); S. Dixon, *The Roman Mother* (London and Sydney, 1988).

1. Assiduity: Suet. *Iul.*, 43; *Aug.* 32, 2f.; 33, 1. Additional decuries: 32, 3; Gaius: *Cal.* 16, 2.

2. Tiberius (and senatorial *cognitio*): TA 1, 75, 1f.; Suet., *Tib.* 33 (addressing the jury); DC 57, 7, 6. Libo and Sejanus: Levick 1976, 186; *Hist.* 28 (1979) 368f.; according to Brunt 1984, 477-9, Libo was charged with *maiestas*.

3. Suet., *Aug.* 33, 2; 51, 2; DC 56, 24, 7. See Mottershead 1986, ad *SC* 14, 1, on the difficulty of distinguishing jurisdiction exercised as consul and *extra honorem*.

4. Non-senators before the jury courts: TA 1, 72, 4, with Furneaux ad loc. Knight executed: DC 60, 18, 4. Prefect: Millar 1977, 123-5. Juries: Sherwin-White *ad* Pliny, *Ep.* 10, 58 (p.639f.). Appeal: Garnsey 1966; Delegation: Suet., *Aug.* 33, 3. Paul: *Acts* 25, 11.

5. Appeals: Suet., *Aug.* 33, 3, with Carter 1982 ad loc.

6. Tiberius: DC 57, 7, 2. Gaius: Suet., *Cal.* 15, 4; DC 59, 18, with Balsdon 1934, 150f.

7. Hard work: SC 14, 1 (on holidays); DC 60, 5, 7 (betrothals); 17, 1 (festivals cut); SA 7, 5. Adviser: SC 12, 2. Absentees: DC 60, 28, 6; *Docs.* 367, col. 2, l.2 – col. 3, l.9, with Talbert 1984, 499f. Cf. SC 15, 2.

8. *Consilium*: Crook 1955; Claudius: DC 60, 4, 3; Musurillo 1954, IV A col.ii, ll.5-8. Sack: Sen. *De Clem.* 1, 23, 1; SC 34, 1,. cf. Suet., *Aug* 33, 1; Arena ('*maiore fraude convictos*'); fresh hearings ('*restituit actiones*'); equity ('*duritiam lenitatemve multarum ex bono et aequo ... moderatus est*'); all in SC 14. Idiosyncrasies: 15 ('*mira varietate*'); DC, 60, 5, 6: κρίσει καὶ 'ονχ 'επιτηδεύσει. Livy: Last and Ogilvie 1958. Irrelevance: DC 60, 3, 7. Jurisconsults: SA 12, 2; *De Clem.* 1, 1, 4: '*ex situ ac tenebris*'; May 1936, 252, found one, Cassius, head of the 'Sabinians'; Frézouls 1981, 250, believes that Claudius used them for the problem of the Anauni.

9. SC 15, 2; John Lyd., *De Mens.* 4, 59, p.113W, surely applies the Suetonius story to Claudius II Gothicus: 'a man so just in his judgments'.

10. Riot: TA 12, 43, 2. Greek: SC 15, 4; 42, 1; cf. SA 5, 2 and 4, with B. Levick, *Hist.* 38 (1989). Immersion: DC 61, 33, 8; Gallicus: *PIR*² I 335; he is identified with a Gallicanus by Boissevain ad loc. (3, p.74): cf. *PIR*² G 37 and 14 (Gallicanus taken to be a Gadullius). Egg: *PNH* 29, 52-4.

11. Hearing one side: SA 12, 3, ll.19-22; 11, 5; cf. 14, 2, with Eden 1984 ad locc.; cf. *Docs.* 370, l.87f. '*Crimine incerto nec defensione ulla data*': SC 29, 1, with Brunt 1984, 476 ('*crimen*' signifying 'guilt'). TA 13, 43, 3, has '*agmina*' of knights condemned through Suillius (see n. 16 for a possible occasion); his activities made Claudius in 47 set a limit to advocates' fees: 10,000 HS (TA 11, 5-7; cf. 13, 42. 1f.). *Intra cubiculum* trials: TA 11, 2, 1: '*neque data senatus copia: intra cubiculum auditur*'; 13, 4, 2: '*clausis unam intra domum accusatoribus et reis*'.

12. A legal development: Jones 1972, 93, unconvincingly.

13. Suillius and Julia: TA 13, 43, 3. Augustus: Suet., *Aug.* 65, 2-4.

14. DC 60, 15, 4-16, 5; Wiseman 1982, 65 n.74, citing JA 19, 266, and TA 13, 5, 2, for the place, with D. Thompson, *AJA* 85 (1981) 335-9. A trial in the senate is referred to at SC 40, 2.

15. *Maiestas*: DC 60, 3, 6, cf. 4, 1; so H.Scullard, *From the Gracchi to Nero*, ed. 5 (London and N.Y., 1982) 290; *contra*, Brunt 1984. In general: see, with caution, Bauman 1967 and 1973; Levick 1976, 180-200. A cognitionibus: SA 15, 2.

16. 'Iura lata quam commodissima': Aur. Vict., *De Caes.* 4, 2. See May 1936, noting (67) the approval of E. Groag, *RE* 3 (1899 ) 2817-9; 2827. Census: TA 11, 13. 1; 25, 8; SC 16; Augustus: RG 8. Theatrical knights: DC 60, 7, 1. 4000

unqualified knights prosecuted: *PNH* 33, 8, 33, with Poma 1982, 153-5. Penalties: *SC* 25,3, with A. Mócsy, *Klio* 52 (1970) 287-94.

17. Religion: Ch. 8. 2 BC: B. Levick, *Lat.* 31 (1972) 791-801; R. Syme, *History in Ovid* (Oxford, 1978) 192-8.

18. Computation of games: TA 11, 11, 1f.; *SC* 21, 2, with Mottershead 1986. Pomerium: May 1943-4, 107, believed Claudius' extension sanctioned by the senate; certainly he informed them of his intention: Syme 1958, 705. Criticism: Griffin 1962.

19. Devijver 1970, 73-5, cf. Suet., *Aug.* 38, 3.

20. 41: DC 60, 6, 6; 49: *SC* 25, 4, with Mottershead 1986, App. 2; Oros. 7, 6, 15; *Acts* 18, 2f. Christians: Scramuzza 1940, 151. 'Decree': *Docs.* 377, with M. Guarducci, *Rend. della Pont. Accad. Rom. d'Arch.* 18 (1941-2) 85-98; a better interpretation (a private individual threatening tomb violators with an abbreviated imperial injunction): L. Wenger, *ZSS* 51 (1931) 369-97, esp. 395f. Bibliography: Garzetti 1974, 604f.

21. *SC* 25, 1; *DC* 60, 13, 2; 28, 1; *Dig.* 37, 14, 5; cf. TA 13, 26f.(56).

22. Flogging: DC 60, 12, 2. SC Claudianum: *Dig.* 29, 5. Silanianum: Talbert 1986, 438. Extension: 13, 32, 1 (57); *Sent. Paul.* 3, 5, 5. Secundus: TA 14, 42-45 (61); fellow-feeling 45, 3; Quadrus: Sen., *Quaest. Nat.* 1, 16; others: *PEp.* 3, 14; 8, 14. Prefect: B. Baldwin, *Anc. Soc.* 3 (1972), 152.

23. Hooliganism: TA 11, 13, 1; respect: cf. *SC* 12, 1. Bans: DC 60, 6, 7; *SC* 38, 2, with Mottershead 1986 for earlier restrictions. See also Ch. 10.

24. Just., *Inst.* 2, 23, 1 (Augustus); *SC* 23, 1; *GI* 2, 278; *Dig.* 1, 2, 2, 32 ('duos praetores adiecit'; one removed by Titus); see Crook 1967, 126f., for limitations.

25. *SC* 23, 1; Ulp., *Rules* 16, 3; Sozomen, *Hist. Eccl.* 1, 9, 1-4. May 1936, 224f., suggested that it was intended to apply to Claudius himself, but Claudius was only 58 when he married Agrippina. Talbert 1984, 440, proposes 'Persicianum' after Paullus Persicus (*cos.* 34), and draws attention to the related *SC Calvisianum* (Ulp., *loc. cit.* 4; 44 or 53?) disallowing exemption for marriages between men younger than sixty and women older than fifty.

26. TA 12, 53 (title and context); *GI* 1, 84-6; cf., for difficult cases, 91; injustice: Just., *Inst.* 3, 12; Hadrian: *GI* 1, 84; denunciation required: 91 and 160; Paul, *Sent.* 2, 21a, 17 (three required; post-classical). See Crook (*CR*) 1967, 7f.; Crook 1967, 62; Weaver 1972, 162-9, on the imperial household, and in Rawson 1986, 152-66; Poma 1982, 166-72; references: Talbert 1984, 441. Social background, noting the larger numbers of male slaves in a household: Gardner 1986, 141f.

27. Dates: Talbert 1984, 440; Poma 1982, 164-6, dates the first (by consuls) to 46. The first measure: *Dig.* 38, 4; cf. 23, 2, 48, 2; Just., *Inst.* 3, 8, 3. The second: *GI* 3, 56-7 (rights of masters over different classes of ex-slaves' property); 63-5 (disputes arising); Just., *Inst.* 3, 7, 4; *Cod.* 7, 6, 1, 1a; 12a (abolition).

28. *Dig.* 16, 1 ('*subventum est*'; '*cum eas virilibus officiis fungi...non sit aequum*' in the *SC*: 1, 2, 1; the senate '*opem tulit mulieribus propter sexus imbecillitatem multis...casibus suppositis*'. Edicts: 16, 1, 2 pr. May 1936, 228f., denies Claudian authorship: dominated by women, he would see no need to generalize his edict! References: Talbert 1984, 442 (Claudius or Nero); one M. Silanus was *cos.* 46, another shortly before 56 (*PIR*[2] I 833f.). Elucidation: Crook 1986; Gardner 1986, 75f.

29. TA 11, 13, 2: '*saevitiam creditorum coercuit*'; cf. Suet., *Vesp.* 11 (against *luxuria*), with May 1936, 231f., arguing that Claudius issued an edict as censor

which Vespasian widened. *SC Macedonianium: Dig.* 14, 6, 1 pr.; Just., *Cod.* 4, 28; *Inst.* 4, 7, 7 ('an enactment in favour of children in power'... 'persons in power, when dragged down by...loans which they had squandered in profligacy, often plotted against the lives of their parents'). Further references: Talbert 1984, 443f. D. Daube, *ZSS* 65 (1947) 308-10, cf. 1969, 87-91, advocates cutting the knot: the measure was Vespasian's, as consul in 51.

30. SC 25, 2; DC 60, 29, 7²; *Dig.* 40, 8, 1, 2 (edict); Just., *Cod.* 7, 6, 3 (and right to possessions); Poma 1982, 161 n.76 (bibliography). Changing attitudes: Sen., *Ep.* 47; P*Ep.* 8, 14, 12, with A.N. Sherwin-White 1966.

31. G*I* 1, 145 (Papia Poppaea); 157 and 171 (*lex*; J.Muirhead *ad loc.* prefers an *SC*); 164f. (nearest agnate); 192 (force of statutory *tutela*); Ulp., *Rules* 11, 8. May 1936, 233-6; Crook 1986, 89-91; Gardner 1986, 14; Doubts: Dixon 1988, 89.

32. Just., *Inst.* 3, 3, pr. and 1f. (a consolation for the loss of children); May 1936, 236f.; Crook 1986, 67f.; 79 (spreading property); Gardner 1986, 196f.; Dixon 1988, 44f. (relationship of mother with children); 54.

33. Adoption: *Dig.* 1, 7, 8, with May 1936, 226-8, pointing out that Nero's adoption might be relevant. *Peculium: Dig.* 4, 4, 3, 4. See May 1936, 230.

34. SC Hosidianum: *Docs.* 365, 1.8f.

35. The events: see Ch. 7. Pedantry: Sen., *De Brev. Vit.* 13; see Griffin 1962. *Felicitas: Docs.* 365 l.6.

## 12 FINANCE AND THE ECONOMY (pages 127-136)

SC 20f.; 28. K.Hopkins, 'Taxes and trade in the Roman Empire (200 BC-AD 400', *JRS* 70 (1980) 101-25; A.H.M. Jones, 'The Aerarium and the Fiscus', *JRS* 40 (1950) 22-9 = *Studies in Roman government and law* (Oxford, 1960) 99-114; F. Millar, 'The Fiscus in the first two centuries', *JRS* 53 (1963) 29-42; P. Brunt, 'The "Fiscus" and its development', *JRS* 56 (1966), 75-91; Millar 1977, 133-201; B. Levick '"Caesar omnia habet': Property and Politics under the Principate', *Entretiens Hardt* 33 (Geneva, 1987) 187-218. Van Berchem 1939. Bourne 1946; Blake 1959. Scramuzza 1940, 118-24; 157-9; M. Corbier, 'Claude et les finances publiques: la création du fisc impérial', *Actes du VII Congrès intern. de l'épigr. gr. et lat. 1977* (Bucharest and Paris, 1979) 346f; Thornton 1983; W.M. Green, 'Appropriations for the Games at Rome in 51 A.D.', *AJP* 51 (1930) 249f.

1. Turnover and costs: Hopkins 1980, 119 and 124f.; R.MacMullen, *Lat.* 43 (1984) 580, finds 315m. HS in army costs. B. Campbell, *The Emperor and the Roman Army* (Oxford, 1984) 164, with n. 11, gives the cost of the army as 'at least 40%'. All figures are hypothetical: criticism of M. Crawford's correlation of estimated coinage output with army expenditure, *Roman Republican Coinage* (Cambridge, 1974) 2, 633-95: B. Frier, *Phoen.* 30 (1976) 375-81; T.V.Buttrey, *CP* 84 (1989) 73-5 (alluding to Hopkins' use of it). (I am indebted to Dr C.J. Howgego for these references.) Sheep: Suet., *Tib.* 32, 2; DC 57, 10, 5. System: D.M. Nash, 'Imperial expansion under the Republic', in *Centre and Periphery in the ancient World*, edd. M. Rowlands *et al.* (Cambridge, 1987) 87-103; senatorial wealth: I. Shatzman, *Senatorial Wealth and Roman Politics, Coll. Lat.* 142 (Brussels, 1975); acquisition: W. Harris, *War and Imperialism in Republican Rome 327-70 BC* (Oxford, 1979).

2. Romanization: T*Agr.* 21. Augustus' wealth: Shatzman, *op. cit.* 371).

3. Pliny, *Pan.* 38f.; see C. Nicolet in E. Segal and F. Millar, edd., *Caesar Augustus: Seven Aspects* (Oxford, 1984), 89-128.

4. Tiberius' economy: Suet., *Tib.* 34, 1; 47; 49, 1; see Levick 1976, 122f. Gifts: *RG* 17, 1; *TA* 15, 18, 4. Manpower needs: Thornton 1983, 376, and 1985, 119.
5. Pliny, *Pan.* 36, 3.
6. *TA* 11, 23, 6.
7. Bullion: *TA* 3, 53, 5. Liquidity: 6, 15-17; see C. Rodewald, *Money in the Age of Tiberius* (Manchester, 1976) 1-17; E. Lo Cascio, *JRS* 71 (1981) 76-86. Accusations: Sen., *De Ben.* 3, 26, 1; *TA* 2, 34, 1; Asia: 3, 32, 2f.; 58f.; 71, 3f.; 6, 40, 3.
8. Senate and finance: Talbert 1984, 375-9; commissions: *TA* 15, 18, 4 (62); *TH* 4, 9 (70); Pliny, *Ep.* 2, 1, 9; *Pan.* 62, 2; DC 68, 2, 3 (97). Imperial wealth: Millar 1977, 133-201. Distinction between funds: Jones 1950 and Brunt 1966, against Millar 1963. Confiscations: *TA* 4, 20, 1 (24); 6, 2, 1 (32); 19, 1 (33), with Brunt 1966, 81-3. Alimony: *TA* 14, 60, 5.
9. See Levick 1987, and for Tiberian hoarding, *Scripta Nummaria romana, Essays presented to Humphrey Sutherland*, edd. R. Carson and C.M. Kraay (London, 1978) 225f.
10. Suet., *Cal.* 17-21; 37, 3 (2,700m.); *JA* 19, 201; 205-7; DC 59, 2, 6, gives 2,300 or 3,300m. HS. Shows: R.F. Newbold, *Ath.* NS 52 (1974) 140-3. Auction: Suet., *Cal.* 39; taxes: Jos., *AJ* 19, 25; 28; Suet. *Cal.* 40f.; DC 59, 28, 11; fines: 15, 4; legacies: Suet., *Cal.* 38, 2f.
11. Claudius' solvency: Balsdon 1934, 188; Bourne 1946, 12f., stressing the modesty of Gaius' building operations; cf. 42; A.N. Sherwin-White, *Lat.* 31 (1972) 823 n.6, points out that it was only in 40 that fiscal measures are taken (DC 59, 28, 11.). Underlings' gains: *TA* 11, 4, 6 (reward to Sosibius); 12, 53, 5 (Pallas); 57, 4 (Narcissus' peculation); *SC* 28; Suet. *Vesp.* 4, 1 (bribe to Narcissus?); DC 60, 17, 5f. (Messallina and freedmen selling citizenship; cf. *Acts* 22, 28.)
12. Lo Cascio *art. cit.* 85.
13. Previous donatives: Suet., *Aug.* 101, 2; *Tib.* 76; DC 56, 32, 2 (Augustus); 59, 2, 1f. (Tiberius, doubled by Gaius). Senate's offer: *JA* 19, 160. Other troops received a 'similar' grant, 19, 247, putting the Praetorians at 20,000 each; for the proportions, see Campbell, *op. cit.*, 167f. Sabinus: *TH* 1, 5.
14. *RIC* I², 126 nos. 85, 89, 91, with D.MacDowall, *Schweiz. Münzbl.* 18(1968) 80-6, followed by C. King, *NC* Ser. 7, Vol. 15 (1975) 62f. MacDowall stresses the restoration of gold; the figures for silver alone hardly justify such a claim: D.R. Walker, *The metrology of the Roman silver coinage.* 1, *B.A.R. Suppl. Ser.* 5 (Oxford, 1976) 25. H. Willers, *Gesch, der Röm. Küpferprägung vom Bundesgenossenkrieg bis auf auf Kaiser Claudius* (Leipzig and Berlin, 1909) 203f., cf. A. Wallace-Hadrill, *NC* 141 (1981) 30, citing *CIL* 10, 8067, 1f., *ILS* 8631, and 8633-5, advocates '*Ponderum norma restituta*': 'the standard of weights restored'. '*Norma*' is impossible: it refers to angles, not weights.
15. *Congiaria*: *SC* 21, 1, with Mottershead 1986. In 41 Dio's attention is on the ruling class, Suetonius' on largesse to the Praetorians; *TA* 12, 41, 3 (51). Distributions: Van Berchem 1939, 144-9.
16. Spectacles: *SC* 21; Ch. 10, with references. Criticism: *SC* 20, 1, with Mottershead 1986 for the uncertain text; Bourne 1946, 38f. (Gaius); 42-8.
17. Cost of aqueducts: *PNH* 36, 122; *Docs.* 309. Ostia: DC 60, 11, 3; *PNH* 36, 70. Fucine Lake: 124; *SC* 20, 1f.; DC 60, 11, 5; 33, 3-5. Deployment of labour: and numbers (only up to 3,000): Thornton 1985, 112f. Consequent costs: B. Levick, *Government of the Roman Empire* (London and Sydney, 1985) xvii. Failure: *TA* 12, 56f.; DC *locc. citt.*; (and feasting): *SC* 32; freedmen's share: 28; Subscribers: *SC*

20, 2, with Mottershead 1986.

18. Freedmen partners: *SC* 28. Asiaticus' Campanian interests: Camodeca 1982, 20f. *Horrea Lolliana*: *ILS* 1629, with G. Rickman, *Roman granaries and store buildings* (Cambridge, 1971) 164. Wealthy freedmen: Ch. 6.

19. Gifts and legacies: DC 60, 6, 3 (41); taxes abolished: 4, 1. Treasure: Calp. Sic., *Ecl.* 4, 117-21.

20. Shows: DC 60, 6; 17, 1; 23, 5f. Gaius' presents recovered: 17, 2 . Galba: *TH* 1, 20; monopolies: DC 60, 17, 8. Economies: 17, 1f.

21. Britain: Ch. 13, n.7.

22. *PNH* 33, 54, with C. Haselgrove, *Centre and Periphery in the Ancient World*, ed. M. Rowlands *et al.* (Cambridge, 1987), 123 n. 29; gift from the guild of travelling athletes, *Docs.* 374 (hardly unique).

23. Annexations: *SC* 25, 3; DC 60, 17, 3f.; 24, 4.

24. Magistrates: DC 60, 4, 4; praetors: 10, 3f. Transfer of 44: Ch. 8.

25. Front., *De Aquis* 116, 118.

26. Games: DC 60, 6, 4f.; 5, 6. Speech on Gauls: *TA* 11, 24, 10 (not in the mutilated original, *Docs.* 369, but an obvious idea). Trajan: *PEp.* 6, 19, 4.

27. Census figures: *TA* 11, 25, 8 (later writers have higher figures for 48), discussed by Momigliano 1934, 104 n.8).

28. C.H.V. Sutherland, *JRS* 31 (1941) 70-2; *The Emperor and the Coinage* (London, 1976) 71f. (bibl. n.53) and 93; *RIC* I², 114f.; cf. Kaenel 1986, 223f. Closure of Lugdunum in 37-8: H. Mattingly, *CREBM* 1, cxlii; cf. Sutherland 1976, 64-7; *contra*, J.-B. Giard, *RN* Sr. 6 Vol. 18 (1976), 69-81.

29. Severance: Corbier 1979; cf. Rickman 1980, 73-9. Procurators: H. Scullard, *From the Gracchi to Nero*, ed. 5 (London and N.Y., 1982) 293. Messallina: Ch. 11.

# 13 THE ARMY AND THE INVASION OF BRITAIN
(pages 137–48)

*TAgr.* 10-15; *TA* 12, 31-40; *SC* 17; DC 59, 21; 25; 60, 19-23; 60/61, 30; Oros. 7, 6, 9-12. S. Dušanić, 'The Issue of military diplomata under Claudius and Nero', *ZPE* 47 (1982) 149-171. C.E. Stevens, 'Britain between the invasions (54BC-AD 43): a study in ancient diplomacy', in *Aspects of Archaeology: Essays presented to O.Crawford*, ed. W. Grimes (London, 1951), 332-44. M.Todd, *Roman Britain 55 BC – AD 400* (Glasgow, 1981); S. Frere, *Britannia* (ed. 3, London 1987) 16-80; G. Webster and D. Dudley, *The Roman Conquest of Britain* (ed. 2, London, 1973); G. Webster, 'The military situations in Britain between A.D. 43 and 71', *Brit.* 1 (1970) 179-197; *Rome against Caratacus: the Roman campaigns in Britain, AD 48-58* (London, 1981). Birley 1981; A. Barrett, 'The career of Tiberius Claudius Cogidubnus', *Brit.* 10 (1979) 227-42; P. Crummy, 'Colchester: the Roman fortress and the development of the Colonia', *Brit.* 8 (1977) 65-105; D. Fishwick, 'Templum divo Claudio constitutum', *Brit.* 3 (1972) 164-81. W. Hanson and D. Campbell, 'The Brigantes: from clientage to conquest', *Brit.* 17 (1986) 73-89.

1. DC 60, 24, 3, with B. Campbell, *JRS* 68 (1978), esp. 158.

2. Transfer: *JA* 19, 365f. Diplomata: Dušanić 1982, citing (166) sailors who had taken part in the invasion.

3. *Ornamenta*: *SC* 17, 1; DC 60, 8, 6. *Imp.* II in 41 (the first on accession): *Docs.* 335a.

4. Revolt: Ch. VI. Titles: J. Wilkes, *Dalmatia* (London, 1969) 451. Crown: L. Keppie *Brit.* 2 (1971) 149-59. Mutiny: Suet., *Otho* 1, 2f.

5. 54 BC: Caes., *Bell.Gall.* 5, 22; Cic., *Ad Att.* 4, 18, 5; Augustus' option: DC 49, 38, 2; 53, 22, 5; 25, 2 (34, 27, and 26 BC); scepticism: R. Syme, *History in Ovid* (Oxford, 1978), 50f. Estimates: Strabo 2, 114f.; 4, 200f.

6. Hor., *Odes* 1, 21, 13-16; 35, 29f.; 3, 5, 2-4; cf. 4, 14, 47f. '*Consilium coercendi ... imperii*': TA 1, 11, 7; T*Agr.* 13, 3. The basic work on Britain between 54 BC and 43 remains Stevens 1951, influencing Todd 1981 and Frere 1987. Contacts: Strabo 4, 200f. Threat to Gaul: TH 4, 73. Augustus and Atrebatic kings: *RG* 32, 1. Frere 1987, 30, sees Augustus maintaining a balance of power.

7. Frere 1987, 275-8; agriculture and cohesion: Webster and Dudley 1973, 25; trade: C. Haselgrove in *Centre and Periphery in the Ancient World*, ed. M. Rowlands *et al.* (Cambridge, 1987) 120. Peaceful absorption of Trinobantes, suggested by their harsh treatment by Rome: Todd 1981, 52. Fission: T*Agr* 12, 1.

8. Adminius: Suet., *Cal.* 44, 2. Caratacus: Barrett 1979, 228f. Verica: DC 60, 19, 1. Pretext: 17, 1; perhaps Roman merchants were being attacked or held hostage in an effort to secure the surrender of Adminius and Verica: Frere 1987, 45.

9. T*Agr.* 13, 4 ('*agitasse*'); cf.DC 59, 25, 2. Dangers: A. Barrett, *CQ* NS 33 (1938) 243-5. Gaius on the shore: Ch. 14.

10. Halfmann 1986, 33; 37.

11. J. Mann, *ANRW* 2, 1 (1974), 529, rightly thinks of the whole island 'in the long run', Webster and Dudley 1973, 36f. of the Belgic empire. Frere 1987, 59, like Webster and Dudley, 70, with map at 106, regards the Fosse Way (Exeter-Lincoln) as the basis of a *limes*, 'the intended limits of the first Claudian province' (in 47). But there was no pause in the conquest. The Fosse facilitated communications between legions fanning out as they advanced. Britain an island: DC 66, 20, 1f. '*Aperiat*', Sen., *Cons. ad Pol.* 13, 2.

12. *Docs.* 197, with J. Bogaers, *Brit*, 10 (1979) 243-54; Barrett 1979; Birley 1981, 208-10, with the reading that unacceptably makes the non-senator Cogidubnus 'legate' of Claudius or Vespasian; C.E.Stevens drew the logical conclusion from the reading, that Cogidubnus was given senatorial rank. Early establishment: Todd 1981, 73; Barrett 1979, 230, with 234 for the extent of the kingdom, Webster and Dudley 1973, 42, moot the idea that one division landed amongst the friendly Regni in Chichester harbour. Later: Webster 1981, 25. Control: T*Agr* 14, 1.

13. 54 BC: Caes., *Bell. Gall.* 5, 8, 1. Date of XV and XXII: L.Keppie, *The Making of the Roman Army* (London, 1984) 213. Guard: *Docs.* 282f. Batavians: DC 60, 20, 2, with M. Hassall, *Brit.* 1 (1970) 131-6; Britons: Webster and Dudley 1973, 34f. Eutrop. 7, 13, makes Cn. Sentius Saturninus, *cos.* 41, joint commander, but he won *ornamenta triumphalia*, not an ovation, and may have been deputy, or commander of a division: Barrett 1979, 234; cf. Webster and Dudley 1973, 41-5; scouting the suggestion that he was ambassador to friendly kings; Birley 1981, 361. Certainly the consul of January 41 could not be left in Rome. Sabinus: DC 60, 20, 3, with Birley 1981, 224. Birley, 222f., distinguishes Cn. (Mauretania) from C. (Britain) Hosidius Geta.

14. Laco: Birley 1981, 287. Refusal: DC 60, 19, 2. Britain unknown: SA 12, 3, l.13f.; [Sen.,] *Oct.* 30; *Anth. Lat.* 419-26 (Riese). Fleet's role: Dušanić 1982, 166; early use of a fleet in the Channel: N.Reed, *Hist.* 24 (1975), 315-23.

15. Narcissus sent from Rome, and departure perhaps past the end of April: Frere

1987, 48; 'well into July' after two months' delay: Webster and Dudley 1973, 5.

16. Richborough: Webster and Dudley 1973, 39f.; single landing place: Frere 1987, 49. Medway: Webster and Dudley 49-52, following A.Burn, *History* NS 39 (1953) 107-15. Their suggestion (53f.) that the Thames bridge was captured by Atrebates, supported by Roman cavalry, is not convincing.

17. Delay : DC 60, 19, 3; nothing suggests that Claudius' own victory was won in 44. Halfmann 1986, 172f., tentatively puts Claudius' departure for the north towards September, his return in March. Frere 1987, 51 (Claudius in Britain by mid-August), is more acceptable. Caesar's two-month campaign of 54 opened at the beginning of July. Difficulties in Dio's account: A. Barrett, *Brit.* 11 (1980) 31-5. Augustus' preference: Suet., *Aug.* 82, 1; *Itin. Marit.* 497, 9-508, 1, cited by A. Rivet, *Gallia Narbonensis* (London, 1988) 95 n.27. Luna: Scrib. Larg., *Comp.* 163. Danger and '*pedestri itinere*' : SC 17, 2. Road repair: *Docs.* 336; CIL 12, 5546. Agrippa's network: Strabo, 4, 188f.; 208. Webster and Dudley 1973, 59-61, propose a Rhine-North Sea route, with Claudius arriving in Britain mid-September.

18. Entourage: Halfmann 1986, 247; 252f. nos. 26-32. Vitellius: DC 60, 21, 2. Rufrius Pollio in Britain: Halfmann 1986, 104, following DC 60, 23, 2; *ad hoc* joint appointment: TA 1, 24, 3 (14).

19. Claudius' progress: DC 60, 21, 2-5; cf. SC 17, 2. Galba in Britain: Suet., *Galba* 7, 1, '*in cohortem amicorum*'; questioned by Barrett 1983 (Claudius was aware of the need for quiet in Gaul: *Docs.* 369, col. 2, ll. 35-8); the suggestion (245 n.14) that the soldiers would not board without Galba defending the rear is unsupported, and the claim that he still commanded the Upper Rhine army has been challenged by C. Murison, *Hist.* 34 (1985) 254-6. Elephants: Ch. 8. Participants in Durbar: D.Dudley, *Univ. of Birmingham Hist. Jrnal.* 7 (1959) 13; Webster and Dudley 1973, 165-7; Frere 1987, 53-5. Brigantes: TAgr. 17, 1, with I.A. Richmond, *JRS* 44 (1954) 43-52; Hanson and Campbell 1986, 73, for 47 and the extent of the Brigantes. Subsidies: TH 3, 45. J.Hind, *G and R* 21 (1974) 68-70 claims Caesaromagus (Chelmsford) for the Durbar.

20. Hasty return: DC 60, 21, 5 (to contrast with Plautius' prolonged labour). Adriatic: Pliny, *NH* 3, 119, cited by A. Barrett, *Brit.* 11 (1980) 33.

21. SC I,3. Moguntiacum arch: Eus.-Jer., *Chron.* 179 Helm; others: González 1984, 59f.

22. *Docs.* 368, l.16; Planta in Britain: Birley 1981, 355; equestrian *comites*: Halfmann 1986, 96. Claudius acknowledges 'ἑταῖροι of lower rank in *Docs.* 370, ll, 105, 108.

23. Absence: SC 17, 2; DC 60, 23, 1. IMP. III: *Docs.* 336; V: *CIL* 12, 5476 (both with TRIB.POT. III); VIII: *Docs.* 407a (TRIB.POT.IV). Triumph: DC 60, 22, 1; 23, 1. Dudley, *art. cit.* (n. 19) 6-17 (arch at 10f.); see F.Castagnoli, *Bull. della Comm, Arch. del Gov. di Roma* 70 (1942) 57-73. Pageant: SC 21, 6.

24. End of triumphs: Levick 1976, 34f.; *ornamenta*: Gordon 1952, 305-30 ; on this occasion they went to Vespasian, Geta, Frugi (who was allowed to ride), and ?M. Vinicius; Rufrius Pollio and P. Graecinius Laco (see Gordon 1952, 318f.); junior officers: *Docs.* 261a, 262, 281; freedman: SC 28. Auxiliary *diplomata*: above n. 2.

25. Offerings: ZPE 39 (1980) no. 24 (Rusellae (Roselle)); *Anth. Lat.* 419 and 423 Riese. Athletes: *Docs.* 374; Cyzicus: 45; Aphrodisias: Erim 1982; Smith 1987, 115-7.

26. Scapula: TAgr. 14, 1; CIL 6, 23601, with R. Syme, *Hist.* 17 (1968) 79: marriage tie with a Sallustia Calvina. In Britain: *JRS* 60 (1970) 28. Careers of Plautius and Scapula: Birley 1981, 37-44. Vespasian: Suet., *Vesp.* 4, 1f., with D. Eichholz, *Brit.*

3 (1972) 149-63, 46 or 47; Webster and Dudley 1973, 70-88, for 44. Camulodunum occupied: *Docs.* 284b. Advance towards Lincoln and Midlands: Webster and Dudley 1973, 95-100. Later positions of legions: Birley 1981, 219.

27. Scapula's arrival: *TA* 12, 31, 1. His precautions: the MS of *TA* 12, 31, 2, reads '*cunctaque castris Antonam et Sabrinam fluvios cohibere parat*', but the 'Antona' is unknown. For attempts to emend, see Furneaux *ad loc.* Todd 1981, 83, like Koestermann *ad loc.*, has Scapula preparing to hold down everything south of Trent and Severn by means of fortresses: '*castris cis Trisantonam*'. The Trent is plausible, but the jingle is ugly and '*castris*' could go. Birley 1981, 43 n.17, takes up Mommsen's suggestion, *Röm. Gesch.* (ed. 5, Berlin, 1904) 5, 162, n.1, that the Tern is meant: Tacitus is referring to the establishment of the base at Wroxeter. Welsh campaigning: Webster and Dudley 1973, 105-53. 'Midland triangle': 112.

28. Camulodunum not fortified: Crummy 1977, 87-90. Brigantian offerings on Anglesey: I. Richmond, *JRS* 44 (1954) 48. Rising: *TA* 12, 32. 3f.; cf. n. 34 below.

29. Colony: Frere 1987, 63, who believes on the basis of *TA* 13, 33, 4, that Claudius made Verulamium a *municipium* (cf. *Ant. Jrnl.* 42 (1962) 148-59). Temple: Fishwick 1972.

30. Caersws: Frere 1987, 64, but cf. Webster and Dudley 1973, 133f., advocating the plateau by Dolforwyn Castle, and Webster 1981, 29. Bristol Channel posts: A. Fox and W. Ravenhill, *Antiquity* 39 (1965) 253-7. Caratacus surrendered: *TA* 12, 36; *TH* 3, 45; cf. *TA* 12, 20f. Syme 1958, 391 n. 3, suggests 52 as possible. Scapula's threat: *TA* 12, 39, 4.

31. Arch: *Docs.* 43, cf. 45, with n. 23 above. Orkneys: Eutrop. 7, 13, 2f., cf. Tac., *Agr.* 10, 4, for their conquest under Agricola; C.E. Stevens, *CR* NS 1 (1951) 7-9, accepted the claim; cf. S.Ireland, *Roman Britain: a source book* (London and Sydney, 1986) 24, n.5. Internecine strife: Frere 1987, 43. Vespasian: Sil. Ital., *Pun.* 3, 597f.; Val. Flacc., *Arg.* 1, 7-9.

32. Didius Gallus: *TA* 12, 40, 7; career: Birley 1981, 44-49; in Britain: J.H. Oliver, *Hesp.* 10 (1941) 239-41; *contra*, L. Petersen and L. Vidman, *Actes de la XIIe Conf. internat. d'Études class. 'Eirene', Clúj-Napoca 1972* (Bucharest-Amsterdam, 1975) 667. Legionary fortresses: Frere 1987, 66f. Wales and the Brigantes: T*Agr.* 14, 2f. Chesterfield: Hanson and Campbell 1986, 82.

33. Veranius: *Docs.* 231c with Ch. 14; will: *TA* 14, 29, 1, with E. Birley, *Roman Britain and the Roman Army* (ed. 2, Kendal, 1961) 5f.; Todd 1981, 88f.; Birley 1981, 50-54; Paullinus: *TH* 2, 32 and Ch. 14; Birley 1981, 54-7.

34. Wales conquered: T*Agr.* 17. Boudicca's revolt: for the date, M.T. Griffin, *Scr. Class. Israel.* 3, (1976/7) 140 n.11. Cartimandua's fall: *TA* 12, 40, 3; *TH* 3, 45, with S. Mitchell, *LCM* 3 (1978) 215-9 (a single coup against her, that of 69); so Hanson and Campbell 1986, 77-80; *contra* D. Braund, *Brit.* 15 (1984) 1-6; Frere 1987, 67, makes the struggle follow the surrender of Caratacus.

35. Britain unprofitable: App., *Rom. Hist.*, Pr. 5. Metals: *Docs.* 317 (49-50); Tac., *Agr.* 12, 6, with Ogilvie and Richmond 1967 *ad loc.* and Appendix 4. Grain: 19, 4, with Ogilvie and Richmond. Legionaries: G. Forni, *Il Reclutamento delle legioni da Augusto a Diocleziano* (Milan and Rome, 1953) 192, and *ANRW* 2, 1 (1974) 388.

36. Suet., *Nero* 18, with Syme 1958, 490, n.6 (sceptical of the Hadrianic biographer's claim); C.E. Stevens *CQ* (1951) 4-7 (Nero's mind changed by Veranius' will); Griffin, *art cit.* 148 n.48 (60); Webster 1970, 192 n.98 (several years of indecision between 52 and 57). Eulogy: *TA* 13, 3, 1.

## 14 WARFARE ON THREE CONTINENTS (pages 149–62)

TA 11, 8-10; 16-21; 12, 10-21; 27-30; 44-51; DC 60, 8, 6-9; 60/61, 30, 4-6. J. Mann, 'The Frontiers of the Principate', *ANRW* 2, 1 (1974) 508-33. E. Luttwak, *The grand strategy of the Roman Empire from the first century AD to the third* (Baltimore and London, 1976). M. Rachet, *Rome et les Berbères, un problème militaire d'Auguste à Dioclétien*, Coll. Lat. 110 (Brussels, 1970); D. Fishwick, 'The Annexation of Mauretania', *Hist.* 20 (1971) 467-87; Gascou 1974; H. Devijver, 'L'Armée romaine en Maurétanie césarienne', *Lat.*43 (1984) 584-95. H. Schönberger, 'The Roman frontier in Germany: an archaeological survey', *JRS* 59 (1969) 144-97; Kneissl 1979. H. Nesselhauf, 'Die Legionen in Mösien unter Claudius und Nero', *Laureae Aquincenses* 2 (Budapest, 1941) 40-6; A. Mócsy, *Pannonia and upper Moesia* (Tr. ed. S. Frere, London and Boston, 1974); J. Wilkes, *Dalmatia* (London, 1969). D. Magie, *Roman Rule in Asia Minor* (Princeton, 1950) 540-65; K.-H. Ziegler, *Die Beziehungen zwischen Rom und dem Partherreich* (Wiesbaden, 1964) 64-6; reviewed by E. Gray, *JRS* 55 (1965) 269-71.

1. Ptolemy: TA 4, 26; PNH 5, 11; Suet., *Cal.* 56, 1; DC 59, 25, 1, not implausibly treats wealth as Gaius' motive. Chronology: Fishwick 1971, dating the death of Ptolemy to the beginning of 40 (472); so Gascou 1974, 304 n.4. Volubilis: *Docs.* 407; Fishwick 479f.

2. Frugi: SC 17, 2; DC 60, 8, 6 (*insignia* not won); PNH 5, 2 (the military in Mauretania for the first time under Claudius): events seen from divergent points of view: Pliny preferred anything to allowing Gaius credit. Gascou 1974, 305 n.1, considers *insignia* normal for Principes). Paullinus and Geta: DC 60, 9, 1-5; see B. Thomasson, *Die Statthalter der röm. Prov. Nordafrikas von Augustus bis Diocletian*, Skr. utg. av Svenska Inst. i Rom 9, 1 (Lund, 1960), 241-3, doubting Frugi's presence. Paullinus' career: Birley 1981, 54-7. Numidia: DC 60, 9, 6. Silio: 24, 5, with G. Alföldy, *Fasti Hispanienses* (Wiesbaden, 1969) 153f., dating the end of the war to 44.

3. *Docs.* 407. Date: Rachet 1970, 138f. (end of 43-44); Gascou 1974, 54. Trouble: Gascou 1974, 234: murder of six soldiers on garrison duty; Suet., *Galba* 7; Calp. Sic., *Ecl.* 4, 41f., with Townend, *JRS* 70 (1980) 166.

4. TH 2, 58 (68); M. McCrum and G. Woodhead, *Select Docs. of the principates of the Flavian Emperors including the year of Revolution AD 68-9* (Cambridge, 1961) 277 (75). Controversy: Devijver 1984.

5. Veranius: *Docs.* 231bc,, cf. 408, with Gordon 1952. The tempting restoration '[*Cietarum Tr]acheotarum*', 231c l.3, imports an anomalous phrase; '[*Cilicum*]' seems preferable; '[*restit*]*utionem*' of walls in Cibyra is a possibility in l.5; but close to '*pacavit*' '[*dirut*]*ionem*' is more appropriate.

6. Sen., *Cons. ad Pol.* 13, 2. Turning point: B. Gallotta, *Germanico* (Rome, 1987) 131.

7. Augustus' testament: TA 1, 11, 7, unconvincingly questioned by J.Ober, *Hist.* 31 (1982) 306-28. Long task: TG 37, 2; cf. SHA *M.Aur.* 17, 10. Germany in the first century: E.Thompson, *The early Germans* (Oxford, 1965) 17-28; M.Todd, *The northern barbarians 100 BC – AD 300* (ed.2, Oxford, 1985) 1-38; L.Hedeager, in *Centre and periphery in the ancient world* edd. M.Rowlands et al. (Cambridge, 1987) 125-40.

8. Maroboduus: J.Dobiaš, *Klio* 38 (1960) 155-66; Tiberius' speech: TA 2, 63, 3f.

9. Rhine legions: TA 4, 5, 2; Schönberger 1969, 153.

10. Gaetulicus: DC 59, 22, 5; tribesmen and Galba: Suet., *Galba* 6; Canninefates: TH 4, 15; Suet., *Cal.* 45, 1f.; DC 59, 22, 2 (seven salutations!); *Docs.* 34, celebrating a victory (cf. Suet., *Vesp.* 2, 3). Gaius on the shore: R. Davies, *Hist.* 15 (1966) 124-8; P. Bicknell, *Hist.* 17 (1968) 496-505. For Germanicus in 14 see TA 1, 31-45; 48-51 (dated by Levick 1976, 74, *c.* Oct. 20; cf. M.Sage, *Anc. Soc.* 13/14 (1983) 306); in 15: 55-71; in 16: 2, 5-26.

11. Chaucicus: SC 24, 3; DC 60, 8, 7. Eagles still lost: Florus 2, 30, 38: see H. Küthmann, *JNG* 10 (1959-60) 47-50 (two years' campaigns, the eagles recovered from the Marsi). Claudius was Imp. III by 24 Jan., 43 (*ILS* 201).

12. TA 11, 16f.

13. Schönberger 1969, 152. Corbulo: TA 11, 20, 1; DC 60/61, 30, 4-6.

14. Frisii: TA 4, 72 (28); 11, 18-20, 2; cf. 13, 53.

15. TA 12, 20, 4f.; SC 24, 3. Claudius passed from Imp. XII in 46 to XV in 47 (*Docs.* 312b and 99a).

16. TA 12, 27, 3-28, 2.

17. Cologne: TA 12, 27, 1f., TG 28, 5, with H.Schmitz, *Colonia Claudia Ara Agrippinensium, Veröff. des Köln. Geschichtsver.* 18 (Köln 1956). Settlement: G.E.M.De Ste. Croix, *The Class Struggle in the Ancient Greek World* (London, 1982) 509-18 (33 items; critical).

18. Quiet control: TA 12, 28f. Nero: TA 13, 53.

19. 'Strategy': Luttwak 1976, 51-126. *Limes: Vell. Pat.* 2, 120, 2 (written in 30 of events in 10) and TAgr. 41, 9, etc.

20. Risstissen: G.Mildenberger, *Germ.* 39 (1961) 69-87; Lech-Danube: P. Filtzinger, *BJ* 157 (1957) 181-98.

21. Arrabona: E. Szönyi, *Alba Regia* 19 (1982) 135f. Vannius: TA 2, 63, 7; 12, 29f.; PNH 4, 81.

22. Noricum: Kneissl 1979, 263, citing *CIL* 3, 5709 as the oldest milestone in the province. Plautius in Pannonia: *Docs.* 332. Moesia: TA 1, 80, 1; DC 58, 25, 4f.; Suet., *Cal.* 25, 2. Memmius: PIR² M 268 (p.251f.).

23. Garrisons in 23: TA 4, 5, 5; Mócsy 1974, 43; Wilkes 1969, 96f.; H. Nesselhauf 1941, 42. Revolt in Thrace: TA 2, 64, 3-67, 5 (18); 3, 38, 2-39, 3 (21); 4, 46-51 (26).

24. Wilkes 1969, 96 n.1. Thrace: A. Stein, *Röm. Reichsbeamte der Provinz Thracia* (Sarajevo, 1920) 3, dating the death of Rhoemetalces to 44 and the beginning of the fighting to 45. For V, VIII and other forces, see *ILS* 2713 and *Docs.* 285, with E. Ritterling, *RE* 12 (1925) 1250f.; Nesselhauf 1941, 42 (VII Claudia in Thrace); J. Szilágyi, *Acta Ant. Acad. Scient. Hung.* 2 (1953) 152f. Garrison: JB 2, 368.

25. Mithridates: DC 60, 8, 2 (confused with Mithridates the Iberian, ruler of Armenia); 28, 7. Fleet: JB 2, 367. Grain: PNH 18, 66; revenues: IGR 1, 860 (late second century); Didius' success: *Docs.* 226a and *ILS* 9197. Claudius passed from Imp. VIII in 44 to Imp. XI in 45 (*Docs.* 407a; *CIL* 8, 8877).

26. TA 12, 15-21; 63, 3; J.B.Campbell, *The Emperor and the Roman Army 31 BC-AD 235* (Oxford, 1984) 134.

27. IV Scythica and VIII Augusta: Nesselhauf 1941, 44f. For Silvanus, his opponents, and the date of his governorship, see *Docs.* 228 with Griffin 1976, 244 and 456f., and P. Conole and R. Milns, *Hist.* 32 (1983) 183-200 (60-7).

28. Parthians: '*Romani imperii aemuli*', TA 15, 13, 2; cf. Just. 41, 1. Routes: Mann 1974, 522. Troops: TA 4, 5, 4 ('*quantum ingenti terrarum sinu ambitur*'); 2, 57, 2;

79, 3. Legio III: L. Keppie, *The Making of the Roman Army*, (London 1984) 193, suggests that it shared a base; move: T*H* 2, 74; Suet., *Vesp.* 6, 3.

29. T*A* 12, 55. *CIL* 16, 3, with S. Dušanić, *ZPE* 47 (1982) 163f.

30. Augustus: *RG* 27, 2; Tiberius: T*A* 2, 56; 6, 31-7, with R. Seager, *Tiberius* (London, 1972) 240-3.

31. Mithridates: T*A* 6, 32, 5; 11, 8-10, 1 (suggesting 47 for the restoration); DC 60, 8, 1; see D. Magie, *Roman Rule in Asia Minor* (Princeton, 1950) 1439 n. 33; Garzetti 1974, 124-6. Conference: J*A* 19, 338-42. Judaea: J*B* 2, 219f.; J*A* 19, 360-3. Ituraea: T*A* 12, 23, 2; cf. DC 59, 12, 2.

32. Meherdates: T*A* 11, 10, 8; 12, 10, 1-14, 6; Mithridates: 44-47.

33. T*A* 12, 48-51. '*Illyricum*': *Docs.* 229; cf. R. Syme, *ZPE* 41 (1981) 143f. Paelignus' intervention: I quote Magie, *op. cit.* 551f.; if he is to be identified with the 'Laelianus' said to have replaced Pollio (DC 61, 6, 6, with *PIR*[2] L 41), he had previously been Praefectus Vigilum at Rome. Ala I Bosporanorum at Europus: E. Dabrowa in *The Defence of the Roman and Byzantine East* ed. P. Freeman and D. Kennedy, *B.A.R. Intern. Ser.* 297(i), (Oxford, 1986) 97. Vilification of Claudius' appointees: Casperius the meritorious centurion at Gorneae is later found serving with Corbulo: T*A* 15, 5, 2; if he is connected with Casperius Aelianus (*PIR*[2] C 462) he belonged to a rising military family.

34. Scramuzza 1940, 197, is more favourable to Claudius. Nero: T*A* 13, 6-9; 35-41; 14, 23-6; 15, 1-17; 24-31; 16, 23, 3. Griffin 1984, 226f.

35. Claudius on the east: P*NH* 12, 78 (Parthian drinks); 5, 63 (Egyptian geography); 6, 27; 31; 128 (Armenian geography, the second an underestimate of nearly 400%). (I am particularly indebted to Mrs B.M. Mitchell for suggestions on Claudius's and his subordinates' dealings with east and west.)

## 15 CLAUDIUS AND THE PROVINCIALS (pages 163–86)

Sherwin-White 1973, 221-50. Frézouls 1981. D. Braund, *Rome and the friendly king: the character of client kingship* (London, etc., 1984). Gascou 1981 (Mauretania). B. Galsterer-Kröll, 'Zum ius Latii in den keltischen Provinzen des Imperium Romanum', *Chiron* 3 (1973) 277-306. De Laet 1966 (Gaul). E. Wightman, *Gallia Belgica* (London 1985). Nony 1968 (Spain). G. Alföldy, *Noricum* (tr. A.Birley, London and Boston, 1974); P. Kneissl, 'Zur Entstehung der Provinz Noricum', *Chiron* 9 (1979) 261-73. A.H.M. Jones, *Cities of the Eastern Roman Provinces* (ed. 2, Oxford, 1971); Dörner 1935; D. Magie, 'A Reform in the exaction of grain at Cibyra under Claudius', in *Studies in Roman economic and social history in honour of A.C. Johnson*, edd. P. Coleman-Norton *et al.* (Princeton, 1951; repr. N.Y., 1969) 152-4. J*A* 19, 274-20, 147; J*B* 2, 204-49; E. Schürer, *The history of the Jewish People in the age of Jesus Christ* edd. G.Vermes *et al.* (3 vols., Edinburgh, 1973-87). H.S. Jones, 'Claudius and the Jewish question at Alexandria', *JRS* 16 (1926) 17-35; Scramuzza 1940, 64-79; V. Tcherikover, *CPJ* 1 (1957) 33-81; A. Kasher, 'The Jewish attitude to the Alexandrian gymnasium in the first century AD', *Amer. Jrnl. Anc. Hist.* 1 (1976) 148-61. M. Charlesworth, 'Deus noster Caesar', *CR* 39 (1925) 113-5; V.Scramuzza, 'Claudius Soter Euergetes', *HSCP* 51 (1940) 264-6. See also Ch. 13f., bibliography.

1. Atlas: Sen., *Cons. ad Pol.* 7, 1; *CIL* 2, 1302. Ephesus: *Docs.* 380. Anauni: *Docs.* 368, ll. 7-20, with Frézouls 1981, 241.

2. Thessaly: Ch. II n.22, and see P*NH* 7, 35, for Claudius' information about it.

Baiae: *Docs.* 368, 1.2; B. Andreae, *Odysseus* (Frankfurt, 1982) 199-220; cf. M. Gigante, *PP* 215 (1984) 235-9; G. Tocca Sciarelli, *Baia, il Ninfeo imperiale sommerso di Punto Epitaffio* (Banca Sannitica, 1983) 67-72. Care: J. Béranger, *Recherches sur L'aspect idéologique du Principat, Schweiz. Beiträge zur Altertumswiss.* 6 (Basel, 1953) 186-217. Mendips: *Docs.* 317; porphyry: *PNH* 36, 57.

3. Conscientiousness: DC 60, 11, 7. Gallio: *Docs.* 376; *Acts* 18, 12-17. Starting dates: DC 60, 11, 6 (42: 1 April); 17, 3 (43: mid-April). Interval: DC 60, 25, 4-6. Trials: Talbert 1984, 508; Brunt 1961, 224-7, citing *TA* 12, 22, 4, and *TH* 1, 77, for Cadius Rufus (Bithynia, 49), *TA* 12, 59, for Taurus (Africa, 53), and 13, 59, cf. Suet., *Otho* 2, 2, for Lurius Varus (Asia or Africa, before *TA* resumes in 47), all for extortion; *JA* 20, 134-6 for Cumanus. Philagrus: *Docs.* 408, with Magie 1951. Tegea: *Docs.* 375, with S. Mitchell, *JRS* 66 (1976) 106-131. Collusion: DC 60/61, 33, 5 (52-3), cf. *PIR2* I 744: Iunius Chilo, procurator of Bithynia, saved from protesters in the Emperor's court by a trick of Narcissus; the story was probably devised to explain the retention in office (at least 49-54) of a man hated in senatorial circles.

4. *Docs.* 379, rev. G. Burton, *ZPE* 21 (1976) 63-8.

5. DC 60, 17, 7 (43, just after the section on Lycia; cf. *Docs.* 408); see G. Alföldy, *Lat.* 25 (1966) 37-57. esp. 42, and citing *Docs.* 369 for retention of names previously used.

6. Principle: Sherwin-White 1973, 291; Siculi: *PNH* 3, 41; *CIL* 3, 9712. Cologne: Ch. XIV. Latinity: Galsterer-Kröll 1973; areas listed: 279 n.9. Belgica: Wightman 1985, 57, noting a scattering of men in Claudius' tribe, Quirina. Alps: P. Grimal, *Roman Cities*, tr. and ed. M. Woloch (Wisconsin, 1983) 101. Spain: *PNH* 3, 30.

7. Citizenship: above, Ch. 7. Excess: *SA* 3, 3; with Sen., *De Ben.* 6, 19, 2-5. Claudius' views: *SC* 16, 2; corruption: DC 60, 17, 3-7; *Acts* 22, 28.

8. Method of control: *TAgr.* 14, 1; Suet., *Aug.* 48. Tiberius: *TA* 2, 42, 2-7; DC 57, 17, 7. Gaius : *Docs.* 401 , restoring his συντρόφους καί 'εταίρους, Rhoemetalces III, Polemo II, and Cotys, to Thrace, Pontus, and Armenia Minor; DC 59, 12, 2. Claudius: DC 60, 8, 1f. But for Pontus and Cilicia, where the Cilician M. Antonius Polemo is probably distinct from Julius Polemo of Pontus, see Magie 1950, 1407; Braund 1984, 42. Commagene: *Docs.* 374, with C. Julius Antiochus and Julius Polemo τειμίοις χαί φίλοις. Agrippa I: Jos., *AJ* 18, 165; his brother Herod and nephew Aristobulus: 20, 13.

9. Kingdom of Agrippa I: *JB* 2, 215-7; DC 60, 8, 2f. (with Herod's accession to Chalcis); cf. *JA* 18, 237; 19, 274-7. Annexation: 363; *JB* 2, 247; Agrippa II: *JB* 2, 247 ; *JA* 20, 138; Th. Frankfort, *Hommages à A. Grenier, Coll. Lat.* 58, ed. M. Renard (Brussels, 1962) 2, 659-72; Schürer 1973, 442-54; 565-73. Marriage connexions: *JA* 20, 139-47.

10. Cottius DC 60, 24, 4; Suet., *Nero* 18; roads: Amm. Marc. 15, 10, 2; Galsterer-Kröll 1973, 284-7. Noricum: Alföldy 1974, 78-105; Kneissl 1979; *Docs.* 258.

11. Achaea-Macedonia, Thrace, and Lycia: Ch. XIV. DC 60, 24, 4. Tax demands: *IG* 5, 1, 1432f., with A. Giovannini, *Rome et la circulation monétaire en Grèceau II$^{me}$ S, av. J.-C., Schweiz. Beitr. zur Altertumswiss.* 15 (Basel, 1978) 115-22, dating 35-44.

12. Noricum: *PNH* 3, 146. Aguntum: W. Alzinger, *Ant. Welt* 3, 2 (1972) 2-16; Galsterer-Kröll 1973, 302-5 (no *municipia*). 'Romanization': '*humanitas*' in *TAgr.* 21, 2. Mauretanias: *PNH* 5, 20f.; Gascou 1981. Volubilis not necessarily made a *municipium* by Claudius: Millar 1977, 404.

13. The Valais: D. Van Berchem's dynamic account, *MH* 13 (1956) 199-208; Galsterer-Kröll 1873, 287-9; H.-J. Kellner, *Centro Stud. e Doc. sull' Ital. rom.* 7 (1975-6) 377-89, stressing Claudius' decisive role. Maritime Alps: N. Lamboglia, *Riv. di Stud. Liguri* 24 (1958) 350-4: legionary from Glanate (Glandèves).

14. De Laet 1966. Bavai: M. Amand, *Lat.* 18 (1959) 297-9; 305f.; Wightman 1985, 78. Belgica transformed: 80; stone: 135; cautious on Claudius' activity: 65f., unlike Le Glay and Audin 1976, 17f.

15. Milestone numbers: Walser 1980, 400f. Floods: 445f. Massilia-Lugdunum: *Docs.* 337, from Valbonne, which Scramuzza 1940, 163, regards as part of a Lugdunum-Rhine improvement, is in the dative case and for Walser (440f.) a local dedication. Lugdunum-Andematunnum, with a staging post at Asa Paulini (Anse): Walser 460; P. Wuilleumier, *RÉA* 41 (1939) 246f. Trier: Wightman 1985, 58; 77.

16. Scramuzza, *loc. cit.* Limonum Pictonum-Mediolanum: *CIL* 13, 8934, 8900. Scramuzza (294 n. 41) cites 8877, if genuine, for the link Burdigala-Tolosa (Toulouse). Augustonemetum-Avaricum: 8920 (Enval), is cited by Scramuzza (n.42); Walser 1980, 461, does not indicate the destination. Brittany and Normandy: 9016 (Kerscao); 8976 (Bayeux). Scramuzza (n.43) suggests on the basis of 8976 that the Augustonemetum-Avaricum route was to connect at Autricum (Chartres) with the road terminating on the Channel at Coriollum. He cites (163 with n. 44) the view of C. Jullian, *Histoire de la Gaule* 5 (Paris, 1920) 91 n.1, that Claudius was responsible for the stretch down the right bank of the Loire from Roanne to Nantes. Nantes-Brest: 9016, with Jullian, *loc. cit.* n. 5. Britain: J. Sedgley, *The Roman Milestones of Britain*, *B.A.R.* 18 (Oxford, 1975) 2, though 'much of the main road system... had its foundations in the early years of the invasion'. Scramuzza 1940, 163f., infers Claudian roads from the permanency of the occupation, noting early exploitation of the Mendips (*Docs.* 317).

17. Scramuzza 1940, 161f. Claudius' Alpine roads: *Docs.* 328; Italy: 330. Earlier roads: $EJ^2$ 289-94.

18. Lugdunum festival: Suet., *Cal.* 20, with references in B. Levick, *The Government of the Roman Empire* (London and Sydney, 1986) 205f. Druids: *PNH* 30, 13; *SC* 25, 5. Egg: *PNH* 29, 52-4; Romanized gods: De Laet 1966, 961; cf. Wightman 1985, 186. Change: Pomp. Mela, *Chorographia* 3, 2, 18; see C.E. Stevens, *France, Government and Society*, edd. J. Wallace-Hadrill and J. McManners (ed. 2, London, 1970) 19-34.

19. Scramuzza 1940, 162 with n. 32, cites *CIL* 2, 4916 (fragmentary) for a roadway linking the nearby Caesaraugusta (Saragossa) with the south. Dated stones: Walser 1980, 460f.

20. *CIL* 2, 4750, 4770f. (4th, 20th, 35th from Bracara); Scramuzza 1940, 162; Nony 1968, 62; for the wars see Syme, *RP* 2, 825-54. Tuy: *CIL* 2, 4875.

21. Nony 1968, 58f., counted 82 Claudii, about 100 each of Flavii and Aelii, and more than 400 Valerii; criticism of Scramuzza: 62; Baelo: 56f.; Britain and Mauretania: 67. Ireland: T*Agr.* 24, 1. Ammaia: *Docs.* 406. Claudionerium: Ptol. 2, 6, 21.

22. Coins: Ch.11. West given most attention: Nony 1968, 66. Mauretanians meant: 69f. *Hispanus/Hispaniensis*: Vell. Pat. 2, 51, 3; Martial 12, pr.

23. Eastern route: *CIL* 5, 8002, 8003 (= *Docs.* 328), with Scramuzza 1940, 161, with n. 25 for earlier literature and dating the Altinum branch to 47; Walser 1980, 453f. Western route: *CIL* 12, 5528; Walser 454f., with the inscription from Versvey published there. The lost 12, 5524, also cited by Scramuzza 1940, 293 n.39, is a

dedication in the dative case. Scramuzza (163, with n. 40) has the Gt. St. Bernard route continued to Adematunnum: 13, 9044 (*Docs.* 338, 22 m.p. from Andematunnum), and 9046 (12 m.p.), of 43; Walser (460) assigns these to Dibio (Dijon)-Adematunnum; for the Jura route see L. Berger, *Provincialia: Festschr. R. Laur-Belart*, edd. E. Schmid *et al.* (Basel and Stuttgart, 1968) 15-24. G. Radke, reviewing G. Walser, *Die römischen Strasse in der Schweiz* I (Bern, 1967) in *Gnomon* 1970, 209-11, suggests that the 'FCA' on *CIL* 12, 5528 (47), cf. 5525, refers to the creation of Forum Claudii Augusti (Octodurus). Aventicum from wood to stone: H. Bögli, *BJ* 172 (1972) 180. Noricum: Scramuzza 1940, 164 with n. 49, citing *CIL* 3, 5709. Tergeste (Trieste) – Fiume: *Docs.* 332, with Claudius rectifying an attempt to divert the road from the Rundictes to the property of a local property-owner. La Turbie: P*NH* 3, 136f.

24. *CIL* 3, 13329-31, 13335. Basic: P. Ballif, *Röm. Strassen in Bosnien u. der Hercegovina* I (Vienna, 1893) 12-16 (map). Early building:: Wilkes 1969, 452-5. Trebinje road: *CIL* 3, 10175; cf. Walser 1980, 456 (cautious). Urbanization of Liburnia: G. Alföldy, *Epigraphica* 23 (1961), 53-65 (list).

25. Sardinia: Turris to Carales (Porto Torres, Cagliari): *Docs.* 343, facilitating police-work against bandits (Varro, *De Re Rust.* 1, 16, 2; T*A* 2, 85, 5 (of 19)); Thrace: Scramuzza (164, with n. 50) claims roads on the basis of Th. Mommsen's *The Provinces of the Roman Empire* (tr. W. Dickson, London, 1909) 1, 212, and Daremberg – Saglio *s.v. Via*, 811. He 'restored the whole road system of Pamphylia; probably that also of Lycia': 164f. with n.51, citing *Docs.* 347! Roads in Cyrene: *Docs.* 345 (Cyrene (Shahat)-Barca (El Merj)); Crete: *IGR* 1, 980; 1013 (*Docs.* 346); 1014. Myos Hormos (Abu Shar, Egypt): M. Charlesworth, *Trade Routes and commerce of the Roman Empire* (Cambridge, 1924) 21, arguing that Claudius improved the road from Mons Claudianus (Gebel-Fatire) to the Red Sea. Prisoners used: Wilkes 1969, 452. British slaves: Cic., *Ad Att.* 4, 16, 7.

26. High claims: Scramuzza 1940, 161f., and see previous n. Claudius' inspiration: Walser 1980, 459-62. Italian roads: Scramuzza 161 with n. 23; cf. Walser 455. Via Claudia Nova: paved to confluence of Aternus and Tirinus over 47 m.p., 192 paces: *Docs.* 329 (Foruli); R. Gardner, *JRS* 3 (1913) 205-32; R. Paribeni, *Epigr.* 1 (1939) 13-16 (Reate (Rieti) bridge, ?42). Via Salaria: *Docs.* 330 (Teate (Chieti)).

27. Asia: *CIL* 3, 476 (Ephesus-Smyrna); 7206 (Ephesus-Tralles); Scramuzza 1940, 164, extends it; Aquila: *Docs.* 348. Procurators' duties: S. Mitchell, *JRS* 66 (1976) 124. Touring proconsuls: G. Burton, *JRS* 65 (1975) 92-106.

28. Patronage: E. Albertini, *MÉFRA* 24 (1904) 247-76; E. Rawson, *Hist.* 22 (1973) 218-39. Cities named after Claudius: Magie 1950, 1405-8. Claudiopolis and Claudiconium: H.v.Aulock, *Münzen u. Städte Lykaoniens: Ist. Mitt. Beiheft* 16 (Tübingen, 1976); S. Mitchell, *Hist.* 28 (1979) 409-38. Archelais: P*NH* 6, 8; Tyre: *IGR* I, 132.

29. Delphi: A.Plassart, *RÉG* 80 (1967) 372-8 (chronology); J. Oliver, *Hesp.* 40 (1971) 239f. (text). Title: *IG* 2² 5173-7; 5179. Propylaea: T.L. Shear, *Hesp.* 50 (1981) 367 n.52.

30. 23: T*A* 4, 13, 1f.; EJ² 50. Tiberius' parsimony: S. Mitchell, *HSCP* 91 (1987) 365. Works: *Docs.* 231b. Cibyra in Asia: *JRS* 65 (1975) 70; citizens: *Docs.* 408; *Sebasta erga* constructed under Veranius: *Docs.* 231b. Claudius, Samos, and the earthquake of 47: P. Herrmann, *Ath. Mitt* 75 (1960) 95 and 120; M. Şaçel Kos, *Inscr. lat. in Graecia repert.* (Faenza, 1979) 19f. no.11: Dionysus' temple restored; Claudius become 'New Founder' (*IGR* 4, 1711); H.Freis, *ZPE* 58 (1985) 189-93.

Restoration at Miletus, Ephesus, Smyrna: Malalas, *Chron.* 246D; Laodicea and Hierapolis, Antioch: Georg. Sync., *Chron.* 632D. Miletus: Chr. Habicht, *GGA* 213 (1960) 162f., explaining honours to Vergilius Capito, including games, the Capitoneia. Miletus Caesarea: L. Robert, *Arch. Ephemer.* 1977, 217f. Sidyma: *IGR* 3, 577. Sardis water supply: *Docs.* 318. Kerynea (42-3): T.B. Mitford, *Opusc. Arch.* 6 (1950) 17 no.9.

31. Apameia and Ilium: *TA* 12, 58. Philagrus: *Docs.* 408. Capito's baths: A.v.Gerkan and F. Krischen, *Miletus* I, 9, *Thermen u. Palaestren* (Berlin, 1928), 23-47. Responsibility: S. Mitchell in *Roman Architecture in the Greek World*, edd. S. Macready and F.H. Thompson (London 1987) 20, and *HSCP* 91 (1987) 350f., on Philagrus (also J. Nollé, *ZPE* 48 (1982) 267-73).

32. Gapp 1935, esp. 258f. and Ch. 10 n. 14. 'Worldwide' *Acts* 11, 27-30: Georg. Sync., *Chron.* 628D (44); 630D for Greece and the price (48 HS; normal prices, Rickman 1980, 148f.); 632f.D on Helen, citing Josephus. Flood: *PNH* 5, 58.

33. Augustan Cyrene: *EJ²* 311. Restitution: *Docs.* 386, from Kasr Taurguni: '*fines occu[p]atos a privatis p(opulo) R(omano) res[ti]tuit*'; *TA* 14, 18, 2-4. Cnossus: *Docs.* 385. Alps: 368, ll. 14f.

34. Agrippa and Herod speaking Greek in senate: DC 60, 8, 3; SC 42, 1, with Claudius on '*utroque sermone nostro*', but what matters is when he used the catchphrase: see M. Crawford in *Imperialism in the Ancient World*, edd. P. Garnsey and C. Whittaker (Cambridge, 1976) 335 n. 47. Naples: DC 60, 6, 2. Tiberius: Levick 1976, 45, 129, 155. Greeks favoured: H.-G. Pflaum, *Les procurateurs équestres* (Paris, 1950) 206f.

35. Hymnodi: *Docs.* 372; Athletic Associations: 374; actors: 373; Balbillus: *Docs.* 261. Arcadia: *TA* 12, 53, 3. Zoilus: J. Reynolds, *Aphrodisias and Rome* (London, 1982) 156-8. Court: G. Mazzoli, *Ath.* NS 46 (1968) 354-63: 'fatuo filellenismo'.

36. *JA* 20, 105-36; *JB* 2, 224-46. See *TA* 12, 54, for a 'confused' (Millar 1977, 378 n.18) account elucidated by E.M. Smallwood, *Lat.* 18 (1959) 560-7; Marriage: *JA* 20, 141-3.

37. *PNH* 5, 75. Ulpian's disparaging claim, *Dig.* 50, 15, 1, 3, that it had nothing but the name should not lead one to believe that Claudius' foundation was only titular: B. Isaac, *Talanta* 12-13 (1980-1) 37f. Winds: G. Rickman, *MAAR* 36 (1980) 266.

38. Philo, *In Flaccum*; *Leg. ad Gaium*; *JA* 18, 257-60; 19, 278-91. Tightening up: P. Parsons *ad P.Oxy.* 3020. Jewish aspirations: Tcherikover 1957; *contra*, Kasher 1976. Council: Musurillo 1954, 1-3; 83-92 (the 'Boule Papyrus', Claudian according to Kasher 1976, 151); *Docs.* 370, l. 66-72; 'war': l.74.

39. Edicts: *JA* 19, 280-91. See D.Hennig, *Chiron* 5 (1975) 326 n. 20 and 332 for suspicious features. Hearings: *Docs.* 370 ll.75 and 88; the interpretation depends on the reading in l.92: 'επισπαίειν. or 'επισπαίρειν. Two Jewish delegations? l.90-3, with Jones 1926, 31, arguing that they were orthodox *vs* modernist, Momigliano 1934, 97, that they were Alexandrian citizens *vs* non-citizens; I.D. Amusin, *Jrnal. Jur. Pap.* 9-10 (1955-6) 169, wealthy political moderates *vs* rebels; see Hennig 1975, 330 n.29. Threat: *Docs.* 370, l. 81f.; encroachment: 92f. Roman disturbances: DC 60, 6, 6. Robes: *JA* 20, 6-14.

40. Musurillo 1954, 18-26; 117-40; I follow Hennig 1975 in taking *P.Oxy.* 3021 and *P.Berl.* 8877 as part of the hearing of the embassies in 41. Kasher 1976, 156, dates the condemnation to 41.

41. *Docs.* 370: 'god', l.9; statues: ll.29-7; temples: 48-52. Tiberius: *EJ²* 102.'Cult':

S.R.F. Price, *Rituals and Power: the Roman imperial cult in Asia Minor* (Cambridge, 1984), stresses religious aspects. 'Formula': M. Charlesworth, *PBSR* NS 2 (1939) 1-10.

42. Alexandrians: *Docs.* 370, l.21-27. Aphrodisias: J. Reynolds, *ZPE* 43 (1981) 317-27; R. Smith, *JRS* 77 (1987) 88-138.

43. Thessaly: H. Kramolisch, *Chiron* 5 (1975) 337-47; S*C* 21, 3. Xanthos: A. Balland, *Fouilles de Xanthos* 7 (Paris, 1981), 25-8 no. 11. Iulia Augusta at Ephesus: *Docs.* 380, col. 8, l.24 – col. 9, l.3; Lusitania: *AÉ* 1966, 177; Tarraconensis: Fishwick *AJP* 91 (1970) 79-82.

44. Camulodunum: S*A* 8, 3; D. Fishwick, *Brit.* 3 (1972) 164-81; 4 (1973) 264f.; *ANRW* 2, 16, 2 (1978) 1210f., 1215-9. List of places offering homage: Scramuzza (*HSCP*) 1940.

45. *Docs.* 47, dated a month and four days after Claudius' death, 21st of the month of New Augustus.

# 16 AFTERMATH: THE REPUTATION OF CLAUDIUS
(pages 187–98)

S*A*, ed. P.T. Eden (Cambridge, 1984), with K. Kraft 1966; Scramuzza 1940,227 nn. 22-24; M. Coffey, 'Seneca, Apocolocyntosis, 1922-1958', *Lustrum* 6 (1961 [1962]) 239-71; Griffin 1976, 129-71; Heller 1985; Sen., *De Clementia*; T*A* 13, 1-5. M. Charlesworth, 'Divus Claudius', *JRS* 27 (1937) 57-60; Scramuzza 1940, 5-34; Momigliano (1932) 1975; 'Literary chronology of the Neronian age', *CQ* 38 (1944) 96-100; W. Huss, 'Die Propaganda Neros', *AC* 47 (1978) 129-48. G.B. Townend, 'Calpurnius Siculus and the *Munus Neronis*', *JRS* 70 (1980) 166-76; Wiseman 1982; P. Grimal, 'Du nouveau sur les *Fables* de Phèdre?', in *Mél. de Litt. et d'Épigr. lat.*, etc., *Hommages à...P.Wuilleumier* (Paris, 1980) 143-9. B. Levick, '*Nero's Quinquennium*', in *Stud. in Lat. Lit. and Rom. Hist.* 3, ed. C. Deroux, *Coll. Lat.* 180 (Brussels, 1983) 211-25. Syme 1958; D. Vessey, 'Thoughts on Tacitus' portrayal of Claudius', *AJP* 92 (1971) 385-400; Seif 1973; Mehl 1974; A. Mehl, 'Kaiser Claudius und der Feldherr Corbulo bei Tacitus und Cassius Dio, Mit einem Anhang: Ist der ältere Plinius die Quelle beider Autoren?', *Herm.* 107 (1979) 220-39.T. Carney, 'The changing picture of Claudius', *Acta Class.* 3 (1960) 99-104.

1. *Providentia*: T*A* 13, 3, 2; J. Béranger, *L'aspect idéologique du principat* (Basel, 1953); 210-14, cf. *Docs.* 134. Coins: *RIC*² (Rome, p. 50 no.6f., of 54-5; Caesarea, p.186 no, 613f., of 56-8; 619-22, of 63-4). Divi Claudi f. off coins: Kraft 1966, 121; Huss 1978, 132. Temple: S*C* 45 and Suet., *Vesp.* 9, 1, with Charlesworth 1937, 57.
2. Arvals: Docs. 20f.; M. McCrum and A.G. Woodhead, *Select Documents of the Principates of the Flavian Emperors* (Cambridge, 1961), 2 (all 3 Jan.); Alexander: *Docs.* 391, e.g. l.26. Asseria: *JÖAI* 11 (1908) Beibl. fig. 47. Thessaly: H. Kramolisch, *Chiron* 5 (1975) 347. Individual: *ILS* 219 (Salona).
3. Asc., *In Scaur.* 27C, with B. Marshall, *A Historical commentary on Asconius* (Columbia, Miss., 1985) 28f. Nero's pun: Suet., *Nero* 33, 1; cf. Pliny, *Pan.* 11, 1; Gallio: DC 60/61, 35, 2-4.; see Griffin 1976, 129-31; 216f.; 219f.
4. Seneca's death: T*A* 15, 60, 3-63, 7; hatred of Claudius: 12, 8, 3; 13, 42, 3, with Grimal 1978, 469-78 (nuances); Crispus: Sen., *De Ben.* 1, 15, 5f.; no change of view: Heller 1985, 116.
5. T*A* 13, 4; [Sen.,] *Oct.* 485-90. Grimal 1980, 146f., brings Phaedrus into line with

Calpurnius, but the bouquet of *libertas* he scents in 3, 1, may be of sex. Another interpretation: Ch. VI.

6. '*Tempora Claudiana*' and their wrongs: TA 14, 11, 2.

7. Themis/Bellona: Calp. Sic. 1, 33-53, with Wiseman 1982 ('The Claudian civil war'). Wiseman, 67, with due caution also refers Curtius, *Hist. of Alex.* 10, 9, to this period, but J.E. Atkinson, *A comm. on Q. Curtius Rufus' Historiae Alexandri Magni ... 3 and 4. London Stud. in Class. Phil.* 4 (Amsterdam, 1980) 25-35,, seems correct in connecting it with Claudius' accession. Golden Age: SA 4, 1, ll.9; 23f.; cf. Sen., *De Clem.* 1, 3, 3.

8. *De Clem.*: Griffin 1976, 141-8; Levick 1982, 219f. Past severity: 1, 23,1; cf. SA 6, 2; SC 15, 4 on *saevitia*; Suet., *Nero* 33, 1; these and other passages: Wiseman 1982, 66 n.85; see Griffin 1976, 150f.

9. Laws restored: Calp. Sic. 1, 71f.; Sen., *De Clem.* 1, 1, 4; SA 12, 2. Enactments: 5, 1f.; 49.

10. Polyclitus: TA 14, 39, 1; Helius: DC 62, 12, 1-3. Vespasian: Phil. VA 5, 36.

11. Mushrooms: Suet., *Nero* 33, 1. Antonia: TA 15, 53, 4f.; Suet., *Nero* 35, 4.

12. Tyrants: TH 4, 42. *Lex*: EJ² 364. Brixia: N. Degrassi, *Atti della Pontif. Accad. Rom. di Arch.*, Ser. 3, *Rend.* 42 (1970) 135-72 (reconstruction 162). Vespasian's problems: TH 4, 11; Suet., *Vesp.* 22.

13. Titus' birth date: PIR² F 399. Education and poisoning: Suet., *Tit.* 2. Coins: CREBM 2, lxxviii and 293 no. 306, of 80.

14. Pompeius Silvanus: TA 13, 52, 2; Aelianus: *Docs.* 228; Strabo: TA 14, 18, 2-4.

15. Mehl 1979, 237f. Aqua Claudia: M. McCrum and A. Woodhead, *Select Docs. of the Principates of the Flavian Emperors...AD 68-96* (Cambridge, 1961), 408. Legislation: Ch. XI; Suet., *Vesp.* 11. New men: TH 2, 82.

16. Temple: Blake 1959, 31-3; R.B. Lloyd, *AJA* 86 (1982) 93-5. Officer: ILS 2697. Pliny (with PNH 26, 3, discounted, see R. Syme, ZPE 41 (1981) 126 n.10) uses 'Divus' three times in 26 references (2, 99 (portent); 3, 141 (veteran colony); 7, 74); 'Claudius': 33, 54, the normal style in TH (1, 52, and 3, 45, where it is used to emphasize grandeur, are the only references to Claudius as 'Caesar' out of 13). But even Tacitus, in religious or legal contexts (see Fishwick, *Brit.* 4 (1973) 164f.), grants the title: TAgr. 13, 3 (something may be due to the source, as in Pliny).

17. [Sen.,] *Oct.* 11f.; 256-69.

18. Nonianus: TA 14, 19; Syme 1958, 274-7; 287f.; 338. Grudges: TA 1, 1, 5.

19. TA 13, 20, 3; 15, 53, 4; cf. 13, 31, 1, with Syme 1958, 179f.; 289-93. Apparition: PEp. 3, 5, 4. See Momigliano 1975, 824; Mehl 1979, 237f.

20. JA 19, 91f. See Syme 1958, 178f.; 287f. (Nonianus); 289f.; 293f. Vindex's speech: DC 63, 22, 2-6.

21. Danger: JB 2, 205; role of Agrippa I: 206-210; JA 19, 236-65; cf. DC 60, 8, 2; see Scramuzza 1940, 14f.; 58f.

22. Rusticus: Syme 1958, 179; 289-94; SA 4, 3: '*omnia certe concacavit*'.

23. Date of Suetonius' work: A. Wallace-Hadrill, *Suetonius* (London, 1983) 1 n.1. Sources: G.B. Townend, *Herm.* 88 (1960) 98-120 (Greek, perhaps from Cluvius Rufus, used in hostile passages: 103f., 119); Momigliano 1975, 816f. Tacitus: Mehl 1974, esp. 185-8 (dramatic qualities); artistry: Seif 1973, 295-8. Sources: Syme 1958, *locc. citt.* and *Historia Augusta Papers* (Oxford, 1983) 134 (minutes of senate). Pliny as his main source: J. Wilkes, CW 65 (1972), 200; Mehl 1979, 236f. (critical); Momigliano, *loc. cit.* Thesis: Vessey 1971 (justified).

24. Dio's sources: Townend (*Herm.*) 1961. Cluvius, giving place to Pliny after 47:

Momigliano 1975, 816f. Claudius' works: DC 60 11, 3-5. Messallina: 8, 4f.; Silanus: 14; carnage: 13, 1 and 3f. Possible contradiction between 8, 6, and Pliny, *NH* 5, 11, on Claudius' achievement in Mauretania: Ch. 15.

25. 124: *ILS* 5285. Arvals: W. Henzen, *Acta Fratrum Arvalium quae supersunt* (Berlin, 1874) 148. Prusa: P*Ep*. 10, 70f. Delphi: T. Drew-Bear, *RÉA* 82 (1981) 167-72. Decius' coins: *NC* 24 (1924) 235f., cited by Charlesworth 1937, 59 n. 33. *The Feriale Duranum*, edd. R. Fink *et al.*, *YCS* 7 (1940) 47, col. 2, l.23. *SHA Aur.* 42, 4; date: R. Syme, *Emperors and Biography* (Oxford, 1971) 287.

26. Phil. *Vit. Ap.* 5, 17; 32 (where Claudius is χρηστόν). George Sync., *Chron.* 631D; Oros. 7, 6, 1-5, with A. Mehl, *RM* NF 121 (1978), 185-94 (he used T*A*). Malalas: Malalas, *Chron.* 246D.

27. Carney 1960, 99: '... seen as a devoted and hardworking administrator, the organizer of a complex, centralized bureaucratic machine'; but 'the new view was constructed on *a priori* grounds'. 'Centralization': Momigliano 1934, 39-71, with Ch. VIII.

28. Norms: B.Dobson, *Chron, d'Égypte* 57 (1982) 330, on the post of *primus pilus iterum*, but noting later 'anomalies' and limiting Claudius' role (334).

29. Art: G. Charles-Picard, *RÉL* 59 (1981) 323. For N. Hannestad, *Roman art and imperial policy*, *Jutland Arch. Soc. Publ.* 19 (Aarhus, 1986) 98, the period 'is characterized by a stylistic development away from the pure classicism which marked Tiberius' reign, towards the baroque and a greater realism in portraiture. This is the precursor of the so-called Flavian Baroque to which the period of Nero also belongs'. Augustus: Suet., *Aug.* 89, 3. Conservatism and novelty: Ch. XI. Carney 1960, 101, already remarked that too much in the development of administrative machinery was assigned to personal intervention. Prefect of grain distribution: Ch. VIII. Gaul: Ch. XV.

30. Parsimony: T*A* 3, 55, 4. Cerialis to the Gauls: T*H* 4, 74.

31. Civil war: Oros. 7, 6, 8. The importance of the invasion of Britain was given due weight by D. Dudley, *Univ. Birmingham Hist. Jrnal.* 7 (1959), 6-17.

# CONCORDANCE TO E.M. SMALLWOOD, *DOCUMENTS ILLUSTRATING THE PRINCIPATES OF GAIUS, CLAUDIUS AND NERO*

(For translations of many of these documents, see D.C. Braund, *Augustus to Nero. A sourcebook of Roman History, 31 BC-AD 68* (London and Sydney, 1985)

| | |
|---|---|
| 12 | *Acta Fratrum Arvalium*, ed. G. Henzen (Berlin, 1874) LIIf. (43) |
| 13 | LIVf. (43-8) |
| 14 | LVIIf. (50-4) |
| 20 | LXVIf. (58) |
| 21f. | LXIX-LXXVII (58-60) |
| 34 | *IGR* 4, 1379 |
| 43b | *ILS* 216 |
| 44 | *ILS* 213 |
| 45 | *ILS* 217 |
| 47 | *POxy.* 1021 = A. Hunt and C. Edgar, *Select Papyri* 2 (Cambridge, Mass., and London, 1977) 235 |
| 84a | *ILS* 180 |
| 85a | *ILS* 183 |
| 99a | *ILS* 210 |
| 132b | *ILS* 5025 |
| 134 | *IGR* 4, 584 |
| 172 | *ILS* 1546 |
| 173 | *ILS* 1533 |
| 174 | *ILS* 6071 |
| 197 | R. Collingwood and R. Wright, *The Roman Inscriptions of Britain* I: *The inscriptions on stone* (Oxford, 1965) 91 |
| 226a | *ILS* 970 |
| 226b | *Hesp.* 10 (1941) 239-41 |
| 228 | *ILS* 986 |
| 231b | *IGR* 4, 902 |
| 231c | Gordon 1952, 234 |
| 233 | *ILS* 966 |
| 237 | *Notizie degli Scavi* 1924, 346-8 |
| 256 | *ILS* 1348 |
| 258 | *ILS* 1349 |
| 259 | *ILS* 1321 |
| 261a | E. Reisch, *Forschungen in Ephesos* 3 (1923) 128, no. 42 |
| 261b | *Id. ib.* 41 |
| 262 | *IGR* 4, 1086 |
| 265 | *ILS* 8848 |
| 280 | *ILS* 2681 |
| 281 | *ILS* 2696 |
| 282 | *ILS* 2701 |
| 284b | R. Collingwood and R. Wright, *The Roman Inscriptions of Britain* I: *The inscriptions on stone* (Oxford, 1965) 200 |
| 285 | *CIL* 2, 3272 |
| 307b | *ILS* 5926 |

| | |
|---|---|
| 308a | *CIL* 6, 31565d |
| 308b | *ILS* 205 |
| 309 | *ILS* 218 |
| 312a | *CREBM* 183, no.136 |
| 312b | *ILS* 207 |
| 317 | *CIL* 7, 1201 |
| 318 | *IGR* 4, 1505. |
| 328 | *CIL* 5, 8003 |
| 329 | *ILS* 209 |
| 330 | *CIL* 9, 5973 |
| 332 | *ILS* 5889 |
| 335a | *ILS* 200 |
| 336 | *CIL* 12, 5542 |
| 337 | *CIL* 13, 9055 |
| 338 | *ILS* 8900 |
| 343 | *Notizie degli Scavi* 1892, 289 |
| 345 | *PBSR* 18 (1950) 84f. |
| 347 | *ILS* 215 |
| 348 | *ILS* 5883 |
| 365 | *ILS* 6043 |
| 367 | *Ägyptische Urkunden aus den Museen zu Berlin, Griechische Urkunden* 611 |
| 368 | *ILS* 206 |
| 369 | *ILS* 212 |
| 370 | *Greek papyri in the British Museum,* 1912 = A. Hunt and C. Edgar, *Select Papyri* 2 (Cambridge, Mass., and London, 1977) 212 |
| 373 | *Ägyptische Urkunden aus den Museen zu Berlin, Griechische Urkunden* 1074, 1-3; *POxy.* 2476; T.Wiegand, *Milet* 3 (1914) 381-3 no. 156 |
| 374 | *Greek papyri in the British Museum,* 1178, 8-31 |
| 375 | *ILS* 214 |
| 376 | *SIG*³ 801D |
| 377 | *SEG* 20, 452 |
| 379 | *IGR* 4, 1044 |
| 380 | F. Dörner, *Der Erlass des Statthalters von Asia, Paullus Fabius Persicus* (Greifswald, 1935) 37-40 |
| 385 | *ILS* 8901 |
| 386 | *SEG* 9, 352 |
| 391 | *IGR* 1, 1263 = *SEG* 16, 861 |
| 392 | *ILS* 5947 |
| 401 | *IGR* 4, 145 |
| 406 | *Ethnos* 1 (1935) 5-9 |
| 407 | *CRAI* 1924, 77f.; 1915, 394-7 |
| 408 | *IGR* 4, 914; see J.Nollé, *ZPE* 48 (1982) 267-73. |

# BIBLIOGRAPHY

Works dealing in large part specifically with Claudius, or alluded to several times, are entered below unless they are included in the List of Abbreviations. At the head of each set of chapter notes, relevant items from this bibliography are mentioned in abbreviated form, along with other articles and sections of books relevant to that chapter. Additional references may be found in the individual notes.

Baldwin, B., 'Executions under Claudius: Seneca's *Ludus de morte Claudii*', *Phoenix* 16 (1964) 39-48

Balsdon, J.P.V.D., *The Emperor Gaius (Caligula)* (Oxford, 1934)

Bardon, H., *Les Empereurs et les lettres latines d'Auguste à Hadrien* (Paris, 1940)

Benner, M., *The Emperor says: Studies in the rhetorical style in edicts of the early Empire. Stud. Gr. et Lat. Goth.* 33 (Gothenburg, 1975)

Bergener, A., *Die führende Senatorenschicht im frühen Prinzipat* (Diss. Bonn, 1965)

Birley, A., *The Fasti of Roman Britain* (Oxford, 1981)

Blake, M.E.R., *Construction in Italy from Tiberius through the Flavians. Carnegie Inst. Publ.* 616 (Washington, D.C., 1959)

Boulvert, G., *Esclaves et affranchis impériaux sous le Haut-Empire romain: rôle politique et administratif* (Naples, 1970)

Boulvert, G., *Domestique et fonctionnaire sous le Haut-Empire romain: la condition de l'affranchi et de l'esclave du prince* (Paris, 1974)

Bourne, F.C., *The Public works of the Julio-Claudians and Flavians* (Diss. Princeton, 1946)

Brunt, P.A., 'Procuratorial jurisdiction', *Lat.* 25 (1966) 461-89

Burton, G.P., Review of Boulvert 1970 and 1974, *JRS* 67 (1977) 162-6

Camodeca, G., 'Per una riedizione dell'Archivio puteolano dei Sulpicii' *Puteoli* 6 (1982) 3-53; 7/8 (1983-4) 3-69; 9/10 (1985-6) 3-40

Carcopino, J., 'La Table claudienne de Lyon', in *Points de vue sur l'impérialisme romain* (Paris, 1934) 159-99

Carney, T.F., 'The changing picture of Claudius', *Acta Class.* 3 (1960) 99-104

Chandler, D.C., 'Quaestor Ostiensis', *Hist.* 27 (1978) 328-35

Chastagnol, A., 'Les modes d'accès au Sénat romain au début de L'Empire: remarques à propos de la table claudienne de Lyon', *Bull. Soc. Nat. des*

*Ant. de France* 1971, 282-310

Chilver, G.E.F., '*Princeps* and *Frumentationes*', *AJP* 70 (1949) 7-21

Collart, P., 'Une Dédicace à Britannicus trouvée à Avenches', *Zeitschr. f. schweiz. Arch. u. Kunstgesch.* 2 (1940) 157-9

Crook, J., *Consilium Principis: Imperial Councils and counsellors from Augustus to Diocletian* (Cambridge, 1955)

Daube, C., *Roman Law, Linguistic, Social, and Philosophical aspects* (Edinburgh, 1969)

De Laet, S.J., *De Samenstelling van den romeinschen Senaat gedurende de eerste eeuw van het Principaat (28 vóór Chr. - 68 na Chr.) Rijksuniversiteit te Gent, Werken uitgeven door de Faculteit van de Wijsbegeerte en Letteren* 92ᵉ Afl. (Antwerp, etc., 1941)

De Laet, S.J., 'Claude et la romanisation de la Gaule septentrionale', *Mél. d'arch. et d'hist. offerts à Piganiol*, ed. R. Chevallier (Paris, 1966) 951-61

Devijver, H., 'Suétone, Claude, 25, et les milices équestres', *Anc. Soc.* 1 (1970) 70-81

Devijver, H., 'The Career of M. Porcius Narbonensis (CIL II 4339): New evidence for the reorganization of the militiae equestres by the Emperor Claudius?', *Anc. Soc.* 3 (1972) 165-91

De Vivo, A., *Tacito e Claudio: storia e codificazione letteraria. Forme mat. e ideologie del mondo antico* 7 (Naples, 1980)

Dorey, T.A., 'Claudius und seine Ratgeber', *Das Altertum* 12 (1966) 144-55

Dörner, K.F., *Der Erlass des Statthalters von Asia, Paullus Fabius Persicus* (Diss. Greifswald, 1935)

Eden, P.T., ed., Seneca: *Apocolocyntosis* (Cambridge, 1984)

Ehrhardt, C., 'Messalina and the succession to Claudius', *Antichthon* 12 (1978) 51-77

Erim, K.T., 'A Relief showing Claudius and Britannia from Aphrodisias', *Brit.* 13 (1982) 277-85

Fabia, P., *La Table claudienne de Lyon* (Lyon, 1929)

Frézouls, Ed.,'A propos de la *tabula Clesiana*', *Ktèma* VI (1981), 239-252

Gallivan, P.A., 'Some comments on the *Fasti* for the reign of Nero', *CQ* NS 24 (1974) 290-311

Gallivan, P.A., 'The *Fasti* for the reign of Claudius', *CQ* NS 28 (1978), 407-26

Gallivan, P.A., 'The number of consuls per annum during the reign of Claudius', *List. Fil.* 102 (1979) 1-3

Gapp, K., 'The Universal famine under Claudius', *Harv. Theol. Rev.* 28 (1935), 258-265

Garzetti, A., *From Tiberius to the Antonines* (tr. J.R. Foster, London, 1974)

Gascou, J., 'M.Licinnius Crassus Frugi, légat de Claude en Mauretanie', *Mélanges de phil., de litt. et d'hist. anc. offerts à P. Boyancé, Coll. de l'École fr. de Rome* 22 (Rome, 1974) 299-310

Gascou, J. 'Tendances de la politique municipale de Claude en Maurétanie', *Ktèma* 6 (1981) 227-38

González, J., 'Tabula Siarensis, Fortunales Siarenses et municipia civium romanorum', *ZPE* 55 (1984) 55-100

Gordon, A.E., *Quintus Veranius, Consul A.D. 49* (Berkeley and Los Angeles, 1952)

Griffin. M.T., '*De Brevitate Vitae*', *JRS* 52 (1962) 104-13

Griffin, M.T., *Seneca, a Philosopher in Politics* (Oxford, 1976)

Griffin, M.T., 'The Lyons Tablet and Tacitean hindsight', *CQ* 32 (1982) 404-18

Griffin, M.T., *Nero, the End of a dynasty* (London, 1984)

Grimal, P., 'Les Rapports de Sénèque et l'empereur Claude', *CRAI* 1978, 469-78


Halfmann, D., *Itinera Principum, Gesch. u. Typologie der Kaiserreisen im röm. Reich, Heidelb. Althist. Beitr., epigr. Stud.* 2 (Stuttgart, 1986)

Hennig, D., *L.Aelius Seianus, Untersuchungen zur Regierung des Tiberius. Vestigia* 21 (Munich, 1975)

Heller, J., 'Notes of the meaning of χολοχύντη', *Illinois Class. Stud.* 10 (1985) 67-117

Heurgon, J., 'La vocation étruscologique de l'Empereur Claude', *CRAI* (1953), 92-9


Jung, H., 'Die Thronerhebung des Claudius', *Chiron* 2 (1972) 367-86


Kaenel, H.-M. v., *Münzprägung und Münzbildnis des Claudius. Ant. Münzen u. geschn. Steine* 9 (Berlin, 1986)

Kraft, K., 'Der politische Hintergrund von Senecas Apocolocyntosis', *Hist.* 15 (1966) 91-122 = *Gesammelte Aufsätze*, edd. H. Castritius and D. Kienast (Darmstadt, 1975) 51-77


Last, D.M., and Ogilvie, R.M., 'Claudius and Livy', *Lat.* 17 (1958) 476-87

Le Glay, M., and Audin, A., *Notes d'épigraphie et d'archéologie lyonnaises* (Lyon, 1976)

Leon, E.F., 'The *Imbecillitas* of the Emperor Claudius', *TAPA* 79 (1948) 79-86

Levick, B., *Tiberius the Politician* (London, 1976)

Levick, B., 'Claudius: Antiquarian or Revolutionary?', *AJP* 99 (1978), 79-105


McAlindon, D., 'Senatorial opposition to Claudius and Nero', *AJP* 77 (1956) 113-32

McAlindon, D., 'Senatorial advancement in the age of Claudius', *Lat.* 16 (1957) 252-62

McAlindon, D. 'Claudius and the senators', *AJP* 78 (1957) 279-86

May, G., 'L'Activité juristique de l'Empereur Claude', *Rev. Hist. de Droit Fr. et Ét*, Sér.4, Vol. 15 (1936), 312-54. 'Note complémentaries sur les actes de l'Empereur Claude', Vol. 22 (1943) 101-14

Mehl, A., *Tacitus über Kaiser Claudius: Die Ereignisse am Hof. Stud. et Testimonia antiqua* 16 (Munich, 1974)

Meiggs, R., *Roman Ostia* (ed. 2, Oxford, 1973)

Meise, E., *Untersuchungen zur Geschichte der Julisch-Claudischen Dynastie, Vestigia* 10 (Munich, 1969)

Melmoux, J., 'L'Action politique de l'affranchi impérial Narcisse; un exemple de la place des affranchis dans les entourages impériaux au milieu du 1er siécle', *Stud. Clas.* 17 (1975) 61-9

Millar, F.G.B., *The Emperor in the Roman World* (London, 1977)

Miller, N.P., 'The Claudian Tablet and Tacitus: a reconsideration', *RM* NF 99 (1956), 304-315

Momigliano, A., 'Osservazioni sulle fonte per la storia di Caligola, Claudio, Nerone', *Rend. d. Acc. della naz. dei Lincei, Cl. sc. mor. stor. fil.* Ser. 6 Vol. 8 (1932), 293-38 = *Quinto Contributo alla stor. degli stud. class. e de mondo ant.* (Rome, 1975) 2, 799-836

Momigliano, A.D., *Claudius, the Emperor and his Achievement* (Eng. tr. [by G.W.D. Hogarth], Oxford, 1934; repr. with new prefaces, bibl., and minor corr. Cambridge 1961).

Mommsen, Th., 'Edict des Kaisers Claudius über das röm. Bürgerrecht der Anauner vom J. 46 n.Chr.', *Herm.* 4 (1870) 99-131 = *Ges. Schr.* IV, *Hist. Schr* 1 (Berlin, 1906), 291-322

Mottershead, J., ed., *Suetonius, Claudius* (Bristol, 1986)

Musurillo, H.A., ed., *The Acts of the Pagan Martyrs (Acta Alexandrinorum)* (Oxford, 1954)


Nicols, J., 'Antonia and Sejanus', *Hist.* 24 (1975), 48-58

Nony, D., 'Claude et les Espagnols, sur un passage de l'Apocoloquintose', *Mél. de la Casa de Velazquez* 4 (1968) 51-71


Oost, S.I., 'The Career of M.Antonius Pallas', *AJP* 79 (1958) 113-39


Pflaum, H.-G., *Les Procurateurs équestres sous le Haut-Empire romain* (Paris, 1950)


Rawson, E., *Intellectual Life in the Late Roman Republic* (London, 1984)

Rickman, G., *The Corn Supply of Ancient Rome* (Oxford, 1980)

Rogers, R.S., 'Quinti Veranii, pater et filius', *CP* 26 (1931) 172-7


Saller, R.P., *Personal patronage in the early Empire* (Cambridge, 1982)

Schillinger-Häfele, U., 'Das Edikt des Claudius CIL V 5050 ("Edictum de civitate Anaunorum")', *Herm.* 95 (1967) 353-65

Scramuzza, V., *The Emperor Claudius* (Cambridge, Mass., 1940)

Scramuzza, V., 'Claudius Soter Euergetes', *HSCP* 51 (1940) 261-6

Seif, K.P., Die Claudiusbücher in den Annalen des Tacitus (Inaug. Diss., Mainz, 1973)

Smith, R.R.R., 'The Imperial reliefs from the Sebasteion at Aphrodisias', *JRS* 77 (1987), 88-138

Sherwin-White, A.N., *The Roman Citizenship* (ed. 2, Oxford, 1973)

Stewart, Z., 'Sejanus, Gaetulicus, and Seneca', *AJP* 74 (1953) 70-85

Sumner, G.V., 'The Career of Titus Vinius', *Ath.* NS 44 (1976) 430-6

Sutherland, C.H.V., *Coinage in Roman imperial policy 31 BC - AD 68* (London, 1951)

Swan, M., 'Josephus, *A.J.*, XIX, 251-252: Opposition to Gaius and Claudius', *AJP* 91 (1970), 149-64

Syme, R. 'Seianus on the Aventine', *Herm* 84 (1956) 257-66 = *RP* I (1979), 305-14

Syme, R., 'The origin of the Veranii', *CQ* NS 7 (1957) 123-5 = *RP* I (1979) 333-5

Syme, R., *Tacitus* (2 vols., Oxford, 1958)

Syme, R., 'Domitius Corbulo', *JRS* 60 (1970), 27-39 = *RP* II (1979) 805-24

Syme, R., *The Augustan Aristocracy* (Oxford, 1986)


Talbert, R.J.A., *The Senate of imperial Rome* (Princeton, 1984)

Taylor, L.R., 'Trebula Suffenas and the Plautii Silvani', *MAAR* 24 (1956) 7-30

Thornton, M.K. and R.L., 'Manpower needs for the public works programs of the Julio-Claudian Emperors', *Jrnal. of Econ. Hist.* 43 (1983) 273-8

Thornton, M.K. and R.L., 'The draining of the Fucine Lake, a quantitative analysis', *Anc. World* 11 (1985) 105-20

Timpe, D., 'Römische Geschichte bei Flavius Josephus', *Hist.* 9 (1960), 474-502

Timpe, D., *Untersuchungen zur Kontinuität des frühen Prinzipats* (Wiesbaden, 1962)

Townend, G.B., 'The Sources of the Greek in Suetonius', *Herm.* 88 (1960) 98-120

Townend, G.B., 'Traces in Dio Cassius of Cluvius, Aufidius and Pliny', *Herm.* 89 (1961) 227-48

Townend, G.B., 'Claudius and the Digressions in Tacitus', *RM*, NF 105 (1962) 358-68

Trillmich, W., 'Familienpropaganda der Kaiser Caligula und Claudius: Agrippina Maior und Antonia Augusta auf Münzen', *Ant. Münz. u. Geschn. Steine* 8 (Berlin, 1978) 49-79

Van Berchem, D., *Les Distributions de blé et d'argent à la plèbe romaine sous l'Empire* (Geneva, 1939)

Walser, G., 'Die Strassenbautätigkeit von Kaiser Claudius', *Hist.* 29 (1980), 438-62

Weaver, P.R.C., *Familia Caesaris, a social study of the Emperor's freedmen and slaves* (Cambridge, 1972)

Weaver, P.R.C., 'Social Mobility in the Early Roman Empire: the evidence of the imperial freedmen and slaves', *Past and Present* 37 (1967) 3-20 = *Studies in ancient society*, ed. M.I.Finley (London, 1974) 121-40

Wiseman, T.P., 'Calpurnius Siculus and the Claudian Civil War', *JRS* 72 (1982) 57-67

Yavetz, Z., *Plebs and Princeps* (Oxford, 1969)

# INDEX

Most classical sites indexed may be found on the maps (rivers are indexed by their modern names). T1 and T2 signalize persons in the two Tables. Celebrated figures (Emperors and their households, literary figures) are indexed by their familiar English styles; other Roman citizens by their *gentilicia*. Reference is made to the notes only when material is not available through the text. Additional abbreviations: Cl. = Claudius, -a, -an; h., w., s., d., f., m., b., sis., n. = husband, wife, son, daughter, father, mother, brother, sister, nephew/neice; Emp. = Emperor; K., Q. = King, Queen; Tr. Pl. = Tribune of the Plebs; M. = Militum; Pr. Pr. = Praefectus Praetorio; Aeg. = Aegypti; Proc. = Procurator; c. = centurion; sl., fr. = slave, freed(wo)man; prov. = province.

Augustus) T1, 11, 22, 28, 74, 185; honours 45, 71, 112, 187; Cl. 16, 19
Livia Medullina (Cl.'s fiancée) 16, 23, 60
Livilla, Claudia (d. of Nero Drusus) T1, 22; and Cl. 24
Livilla, Julia (d. of Germanicus) T1, xvii, 11, 28, 34, 45, 51, 56, 61, 116, 118f.
Livy (T. Livius) and Cl. 18
Lixus 149
Lollia Paullina (w. of Gaius) T1, 32, 62, 70f.
Lollia Saturnina (w. of D.Valerius Asiaticus) 62
Lollii 134
London 142
Lousonna 173
Lucus Augusti 172
Lugdunum 11, 27, 41, 101, 135, 142, 145, 167f., 170, 173, 177
Lugii 155
Luna 142
Lusius Geta, L. (Pr. Pr.) 57, 65
luxury 99, 108, 129
Lycia xvii, 17, 133, 147, 150, 164f., 167, 178, 186
Lysanias (tetrarch) 166

Macedon, see Achaea
Macro, Naevius Cordus Sutorius, Q. (Pr. Pr.) 9, 25
C.Maecenas 7
Magdalensberg 156, 166
Magnesia ad Maeandrum 175
maiestas 75, 115, 119f.
Malalas, John, 195
mandata 164
manumission 124f.
Marcomanni 155f.
Marcus Aurelius (Emp.) 97
Marius, C. (cos. VII 86 BC) 1, 6, 9, 26, 93
Maroboduus 151
Massilia 142, 168, 177
C.Matius 7
Mattiaci 154
Mauretania 48f., 58, 88, 133, 137, 147, 149f., 165; Caesariensis 150; Tingitana 150, 172
medicine 20, 112
Mediolanum Santonum 168
Medway, R. 141f.

Meherdates 90, 159f.
Memmius Regulus, P. (suff. 31) 156f.
Mendips 133
Messallina, Valeria (w. of Cl.) T1, T2, xviii, 38, 55–69, 89, 110, 118f., 136, 192, 194
Miletus 178, 179, 185
Milonia Caesonia (w. of Gaius) 26, 29–31, 35f., 96
mining 96, 153f., 172, 175
Misenum 84
Mithridates VIII (K. of Bosporus) 47, 157f., 165f.
Mithridates the Iberian (K. of Armenia) 159f.
Mnester 62, 64, 89
Moesia 32, 49, 111, 156–8, 167, 177
Moguntiacum 143, 168, 177
Momigliano, A. 195
Mommsen, Th. 195
Mona 147
monopolies 133
Morava, R. 151
mortality, ancient 125
murders of Romans 167, 179
Musicus Scurranus (s.) 83
Mussolini, B. 114, 195
Mytilene 101

Naples 182
Napoleon I 8
Napoleon III 43
Narcissus (fr.) 47, 57, 59–61, 65, 70, 75, 141, 190
Nazareth decree 121f.
Nedinum 175
Nemetes 154
Neoclaudiopolis, cities called 178
Nero (Emp.) T1, T2; descent 44, 74; advancement xviii, 37f., 66, 69–75, 112, 126, 181.; accession xviii, 46, 185–90; principate xviii, 47, 50, 67, 99, 102, 113f., 120, 129f., 131, 133, 190f. 192; abroad 114, 147f., 155, 158, 160; fall xviii, 63
Nero Drusus Germanicus (f. of Cl.) T1, T2, xviii, 11, 22, 37, 43, 61, 70, 72f., 156, 177, 192; hero 9, 11f., 17, 33; honoured 22, 45, 112, 143f.

Nerva (Emp.) 36, 84
Nile, R. 110
Ninica Claudiopolis 178
nobility 94f.
nomenclature of Cl. 199 n.1
Nonii 36, 64
Nonius, Cn. 64
Nonius Asprenas, L. (suff. 6) 22, 36
Nonius Asprenas, P. (cos. 38) 29, 34f., 36, 39
Norbanus Balbus, L. (cos. 19) 29, 34f.
Noricum 49, 133, 156, 165–7, 173
Novi (Dalmatia) 173
Novae (Moesia) 158
Noviodunum (Colonia Iulia Equestris) 173
Noviomagus (Chichester) 140, 144
Numidia 150
Nymphidius Sabinus, C. (Pr. Pr.) 131

Octavia (w. of Antony) T1, T2, 11, 55
Octavia, Cl. (d. of Cl.) T1, xviii, 55, 58, 61, 71, 74f., 113, 116, 190, 192
Octavia 188, 192
Octodurus (Forum Cl. Augusti) 167, 173
Oescus 156
Olba 116
Olisipo 172
Oppius, C. 7
oratory 17f., 107, 170, 172, 179
Ordovices 146
Orkneys 146
ornamenta, consularia 21, 24, 47, 158, 166; praetoria 47, 75, 158, 166; quaestoria 47, 69; triumphalia 58, 96, 137, 141, 144, 147f., 154f., 157, 190
Orosius 195
Osca 172
Ostia, Ostians 84, 90, 110, 131, 142, 163; rebuked by Cl. 15, 113
Ostorius Scapula, P. (suff. 39–46) xviii, 144f.
Otho (Emp.) 132
ovation, of Drusus Caesar 4; of A. Plautius xviii, 144